A CULTURAL HISTORY
OF GARDENS

VOLUME 5

A Cultural History of Gardens
General Editors: Michael Leslie and John Dixon Hunt

Volume 1
A Cultural History of Gardens in Antiquity
Edited by Kathryn Gleason

Volume 2
A Cultural History of Gardens in the Medieval Age
Edited by Michael Leslie

Volume 3
A Cultural History of Gardens in the Renaissance
Edited by Elizabeth Hyde

Volume 4
A Cultural History of Gardens in the Age of Enlightenment
Edited by Stephen Bending

Volume 5
A Cultural History of Gardens in the Age of Empire
Edited by Sonja Dümpelmann

Volume 6
A Cultural History of Gardens in the Modern Age
Edited by John Dixon Hunt

A CULTURAL HISTORY

OF GARDENS

IN THE
AGE
OF EMPIRE

Edited by Sonja Dümpelmann

BLOOMSBURY

LONDON · NEW DELHI · NEW YORK · SYDNEY

Bloomsbury Academic
An imprint of Bloomsbury Publishing Plc

50 Bedford Square   175 Fifth Avenue
London   New York
WC1B 3DP   NY 10010
UK   USA

www.bloomsbury.com

First published 2013

British Library Cataloguing-in-Publication Data
A catalogue record for this book is available from the British Library.

ISBN: 978 0 85785 033 1 (volume 5)
978 1 84788 265 3 (set)

Library of Congress Cataloging-in-Publication Data
A catalog record for this book is available from the Library of Congress.

Typeset by Apex CoVantage, LLC
Printed and bound in Great Britain

CONTENTS

LIST OF ILLUSTRATIONS

INTRODUCTION

CHAPTER 1

CHAPTER 4

CHAPTER 5

CHAPTER 6

GENERAL EDITORS' PREFACE

The volumes of this series explore the cultural world of the garden from antiquity to the present day in six particular periods. Each volume addresses the same eight topics, determined by the general editors for their relevance to garden history across different times and cultures. Thus a reader interested more, say, in planting or in types of gardens could read through the chapters devoted to those issues in successive volumes. Contrariwise, either of those interests might be contextualized by a volume's discussion of other aspects of the garden in a given period. There is therefore both a horizontal and a vertical way of using these volumes. Further, each volume includes both its editor's introduction, which rather than abstracting or summarizing the other contributions, surveys the period from a fresh vantage point, and a bibliography, which encompasses references from all the eight chapters augmented with that editor's additional readings.

HISTORY

These volumes are a historical enquiry and not an encyclopedia. They do not pretend to be comprehensive, either geographically or chronologically. The authors of the individual chapters have been encouraged to foreground what seem to be the most significant episodes and examples of their particular topic, leaving it to the reader to envisage how other sites that he or she knows better might further illustrate, challenge, or qualify the given analyses. But in every instance, we intend there to be some narrative of one particular theme as it exists, unfolds, or develops during a particular historical period. The definitions of these historical eras must be taken with some caution and elasticity, since a chronology of garden making does not always fit the divisions of time devised for and endorsed by other histories: André Le Notre did his work after 1650 but is arguably more usefully considered in a volume focused on the Renaissance than on the Enlightenment; similarly, Gertrude Jekyll and William Robinson were designing before 1920, but we understand their work better within the cultural content of the modern age.

CULTURAL HISTORY

There are of course many modes of history that have developed over the centuries. A relatively new one addresses the cultural context of human activity. "Culture" derives from the Latin *colere,* which has as some of its meanings "to inhabit," "to respect," "to pay attention to"; it emerges also in our words "colony" and "cultivation." Gardens, then, must be considered as driven by and evidence of a whole congeries of human concerns; they are not, above all, to be examined in terms of their merely visual appearance, materials, or stylistic histories. The diversity and density of human involvements with those sites we call gardens mean that the discipline of garden history draws upon adjacent disciplines such as anthropology, sociology, economic, and political history, along with histories of the arts with which the garden has been involved. So three large questions are posed: why were gardens created? How were they used or visited (there being no handy term for the "consumption" of gardens)? And how does their representation in different arts express the position and value of the garden within its culture in diverse periods? Regretfully, we were unable to extend the range of these volumes to include the garden making of China and Japan among other Eastern cultures, although inevitably the rich examples of such gardens have been invoked on occasion.

GARDENS

The range of places that can be envisaged within this category is enormous and various, and it changes from place to place, and from time to time. Yet this diversity does not wholly inhibit us from knowing what it is we want to discuss when we speak of the garden. Yet the garden is typically a place of paradox, being the work of men and women, yet created from the elements of nature; just as it is often acknowledged to be a "total environment," a place may be physically separated from other zones but answering and displaying connections with larger environments and concerns. Gardens, too, are often created, and subsequently experienced, as commentary and response: a focus of speculations, propositions, and negotiations concerning what it is to live in the world. Both the physical gardens and the ideas that drive them are cultural constructions, and their history is the topic of these six volumes.

John Dixon Hunt, University of Pennsylvania

Michael Leslie, Rhodes College

Introduction

SONJA DÜMPELMANN

GARDEN EMPIRES

In 1809, at a time when the English landscape gardener Humphry Repton was thinking that his "profession was becoming extinct" due to the effects of the Napoleonic Wars,[1] the wool manufacturer Benjamin Gott commissioned Repton to design his estate on the outskirts of Leeds. Contrary to other businesses at the time, Gott's was thriving as a result of the army effort. Repton's landscape at Gott's Armley House presented the viewer with the entire production process of the nation's most valuable industry. From the terrace, the view was directed toward sheep grazing in the foreground, before it was led to his client's mill in the middle distance, and was finally arrested by the panorama of the manufacturing town of Leeds in the far distance where the wool would be turned into cloth and its various products, then sold.[2] Whereas Repton tended to hide tilled fields and crops, preferring gentlemanly pastures in his designs, on occasion he made careful and subtle use of smoke stacks, furnaces, and other features typical of the city panoramas current at the time that could testify to the nation's progress and well-being.[3] Repton's design for the Armley House estate, illustrated and advertised in one of his characteristic Red Books, presents us with some of the developments central to garden culture in the Age of Empire: the growth of capitalist society based on industry that led to urbanization and facilitated the expansion of empires, most notably the British and French; and the rise of patriotic sentiment and nationalism that would lead to the founding of nation states in the second half of the nineteenth century, and ultimately to the outbreak of World War I.

As much as gardens and their design, such as Repton's, were a product and representation of industrialization and urbanization, they were also a "motor of change."[4] In the Age of Empire, gardens became an industry in and of themselves. Numerous horticultural societies and the first professional organizations in the field of garden and landscape architecture were founded. Repton's fear of extinction in 1809, therefore, while understandable in its context, proved wrong. New public and private institutions, the creation of independent city and municipal governments including departments for the direction of parks and gardens, and the development of a middle class that could afford their own gardens led to a diversification of garden types and designs, and to the expansion of work for landscape gardeners and architects throughout the nineteenth and into the twentieth century. By 1879, the French landscape architect Édouard André could use the divisions "private" and "public" to differentiate further the main two classifications, *jardins* and *parcs,* that he employed to describe contemporary gardens in his treatise *L'Art des jardins* ("Garden Art").[5] Despite the diversification of garden types and designs, many developments, such as the laying-out of carpet beds, historicism, the creation of private suburban villa gardens, public urban parks, garden cities, and national parks, became universal phenomena. Thus, as entire cities and regions were turned into gardens, and the types and styles of gardens diversified, the Western world also became increasingly uniform. Designs and ideas were transmitted through a thriving horticultural press and other specialist journals, and gardeners and landscape architects traveled more, further and faster than ever before.

The gardens developed between 1800 and 1920 were both the last resting places of the dead and cultivated plots for survival. They were therapeutic environments, regarded as civilizing, socializing, and assimilating institutions, as well as social settings and community playgrounds. Gardens in the Age of Empire were the basis of utopian visions, and could be both domestic sanctuaries and prisons. Gardens were considered works of art, and were the subject of and frame for art. In built form, and in literature and fine art, gardens could be symbolic landscapes. As a primary theme, and a frame for this volume, however, gardens in this essay will be highlighted as a means and marker of territorial conquest and expansion, and as a means to foster individual national, regional, and local identities. In this age of empire-, nation-, and city-building, the garden in its diverse forms became a signifier of imperial and colonial cultures; a means of imperial and colonial appropriation and conquest; a safe haven for the collection of new plants and the cultivation of essential, and luxury, food crops; an experiment station for the advancement of science; and a means for colonists and immigrants to make a home and settle in foreign lands.

On the European continent, Napoleon I, feared by many of Repton's contemporaries, used "nature" in the form of tree-lined roads, avenues, boulevards, liberty trees, gardens, and parks to expand and consolidate his empire at the beginning of the nineteenth century. In order to shade his troops from the sun and the enemy's view, Napoleon commissioned the planting of poplars along the French roads. Once he had occupied the Low Countries, parts of the western German states, portions of the northern and central Italian states, as well as his client states in Spain and other parts of the German and Italian states, and incorporated them into his French Empire, Napoleon not only enforced his legal codes and political system upon the conquered states, but also commissioned the laying-out of liberty gardens, parks, and plazas in many cities.[6] Influenced by enlightenment philosophy but striving to establish and lead a French Empire, Napoleon, an avid reader of *Julie ou La Nouvelle Héloïse* in his youth, embraced the revolutionary ideals of life, liberty, and property laid out by Jean-Jacques Rousseau and others. To Napoleon, Enlightenment philosophy with its stress on natural law and rights proved a useful basis for his political ideology of an enlightened despotism. Therefore, nature—attributed in Enlightenment thought with the ability to provide moral and scientific education, influence mind and character, and foster an environment conducive to peaceful individual life and social improvement—was one of the means Napoleon used to consolidate his power.

His conquests in the northern and some of the central parts of Italy between 1797 and 1813 led to the construction of public parks and gardens in cities such as Milan, Mantova, Venice, Padova, Turin, Lucca, and Florence. These parks and gardens were often connected by tree-lined avenues and included parade grounds and botanical gardens.[7] Napoleon's projects in Italy reached an apex with two gardens in Rome, commissioned by the French prefect Comte Camille de Tournon in 1809. The Roman architect Giuseppe Valadier, and the French architects Louis-Martin Berthault and Alexandre-Jean-Baptiste-Guy de Gisors designed the plan for the "Giardino del Grande Cesare," the area enclosing the Pincio and the Piazza del Popolo leading up to the Ponte Milvio. To the south of the city, Tournon proposed the "Giardino del Campidoglio," a public garden that incorporated the campidoglio, the Via Appia, the Colosseum, the Palatine, and the Forum.[8] Like the green open spaces Napoleon had initiated in other Italian cities, these gardens were to provide the setting for ostentatious public rituals and celebrations of liberty that he claimed to grant his subalterns. In Rome, however, he could use the building of public gardens to make an additional claim. As implied in the name "Giardino del Grande Cesare," gardens became Napoleon's stage set for establishing himself as the legitimate heir of Augustus and imperial Rome. Public gardens for the populace could reconcile if not disguise the contradictions inherent in Napoleon's political career spanning a republic and an empire.[9] The incorporation in the public gardens of existing monuments, and the construction of new monuments such as triumphal arches modeled on the ancient Roman examples, and obelisks commemorating the soldiers who fell for the liberation of their land, was to further enhance the citizens' moral education and foster patriotic sentiment. Monuments surrounded by nature were thought to connect to ancient moral philosophy, and reflect Enlightenment thought at the same time. While Napoleon's garden projects had, of course, precedents in post-revolutionary Paris, the Italians Ercole Silva, Luigi Mabil, and Vincenzo Marulli provided a theoretical framework. Largely based on Christian Cay Laurenz Hirschfeld's five-volume *Theorie der Gartenkunst* (*Theory of Garden Art,* 1779–85) their writings supported the use of new and ancient monuments in public gardens for the moral uplift and education of the citizens, the integration of public educational facilities such as libraries and museums in gardens, and the use of public gardens for exercise and festivals.[10] Due to their symbolic importance, the Pincio—demarcating one of the entry points into the city, and offering splendid views across the Eternal City—and the area foreseen as the site for the "Giardino del Campidoglio" remained a focus of attention during the *Risorgimento*, and after Rome had become the capital of a united Italy in 1870, when these garden projects were taken up again—albeit in different forms—for the purpose of nation-building, as we shall see below. After the French had declared Rome a "free, imperial city" in 1809, they also laid out new plant and tree nurseries, and looked for suitable grounds for the introduction of exotic species and a new botanical garden. Seeds and foreign plant species were sent to Rome for acclimatization and cultivation.[11] Botanists at the Jardin des Plantes in Paris, such as Pierre Bernard, and Antoine-Laurent de Jussieu, Ippolito Nectoux, and André Thouin had long been in contact with colleagues of botanical gardens across Europe, including Italy. In the nineteenth century, this network was extended significantly.

COLONIAL GARDENS

Botanical gardens played an important role in the building of empires, both at home and in the colonies. They tamed wilderness, ordered and classified nature, and contributed to the development of a new world order based on the imperialist and capitalist powers of the modern Western world. From the eighteenth century onward, the French, Spanish, Dutch, and British empires had established gardens in their colonies in the Americas, the Caribbean, Africa, Australia, Southeast Asia, and on the Indian subcontinent. Many colonial botanical gardens originated as spice gardens, or company gardens, created by the East India companies to supply their ships with fresh fruit and vegetables.[12] The extensive network of botanical gardens was to serve imperial economic development and expansion through the scientific study and acclimatization of plants. Botanists, plant hunters, explorers, and gardeners contributed to the imperial project, regardless of their varying individual motivations and degrees of political awareness. However, leading botanists such as André and Gabriel Thouin in France, and William and Joseph Hooker in Britain were explicit about their duty to contribute to the betterment of society through economic and scientific botany. They believed that scientific progress, as shown in the work and networks of the Jardin des Plantes in Paris, and the Royal Botanical Gardens at Kew, respectively, could improve the human condition, on both a material and political level. André Thouin, in particular, saw his work and the work of his fellow botanists as the foundation of a peaceful world order based on international exchange. This idea guided him and his brother in the conception of an ideal agricultural experiment station in the tropics. With their written and graphic representations of an ideal *ferme expérimentale de la zone torride* (experimental farm in the tropical zone), the brothers answered a governmental request to make suggestions for the enhancement of the rural economy in the French colonies in India and the Antilles.[13] Gabriel Thouin's 1819 visualization, shown in Figure 0.1, provided a utopian design reminiscent of the ideal, centrifugal city plan for the Royal Saltworks at Arc-et-Senans by his compatriot, the architect Claude-Nicolas Ledoux. The experiment station was laid out around an elliptical town center that was formed by a church—testifying to the pre-Darwinian Christian belief in creation—surrounded by a double ring of buildings including a rectory, and the houses for the director and vice director of the station, and for an architect, custodian, physician, surgeon, pharmacist, and a veterinarian. With a hospital, kitchen garden, public fruit orchards, several mills along the rivers and creeks flowing down the mountainsides into the valley and surrounding the town like a moat, and with a lake for fishing and pastures for cattle, the experiment station was to be self-sufficient. On its central plaza, the station also included enough space for the pioneers to practice armed defense, an ability considered vital in what were largely considered "wild" lands. A spider web of roads radiating outward structured the surrounding agricultural lands that could variously be used for the cultivation of rice, corn, wheat, manioc, indigo, and sugar cane in the lower parts, and for the cultivation of cotton, cocoa, coffee, vines, pepper, vanilla, nutmeg, and other spices on the surrounding hills. Due to the experiment

FIGURE 0.1: Gabriel Thouin, plan for the "ferme expérimental de la zone torride" (1819). Dumbarton Oaks Research Library and Collection, Washington, DC.

station's location in a valley surrounded by mountains, the agricultural and forest belts stretching into higher altitudes provided the different climatic conditions needed for the cultivation and acclimatization of diverse field and forest crops.[14] Gabriel's plan was based on the latest scientific knowledge in plant geography, as laid out most famously in the nineteenth century by Alexander von Humboldt, resident in Paris at the time. In the *Tableau physique des Andes et pays voisins* published in his 1807 *Essai sur la géographie des plantes*, Humboldt had presented a section profile crossing the Andes from the Atlantic to the Pacific, and showing altitudinal zones of vegetation, forms of agricultural production, the distribution of various animal species, the underlying geology, and all other measurable physical characteristics.[15] Humboldt's holistic vision of nature presented in the *Tableau* resulted from the synthetic natural inquiry undertaken during his five-year voyage to South America, and was an early expression of his romantic belief in scholarship that combined scientific with aesthetic enquiry.[16] André and Gabriel Thouin's utopian experiment station embodied a similar holistic vision, symbolized in the station's oval layout and vertical containment. Their garden art provided an Arcadian setting for scientific progress in a fictitious picturesque location in the tropics. Here, as Michel Conan has argued, garden art and gardens were central to agricultural progress and were, therefore, regarded as being at the heart of the progress of the human condition.[17]

Like France, Britain sent botanists and plant hunters abroad. Already at the end of the eighteenth century, Sir Joseph Banks had promoted a network of colonial botanical gardens to be centered on the Royal Botanical Gardens of Kew. His idea was largely realized under Kew's new directors, Sir William Jackson Hooker and his son Sir Joseph Hooker, during the Victorian Empire, when Kew became an imperial and national institution, and the number of botanical gardens in the empire increased from around 10 to 100.[18] The acclimatization and hybridizing work pursued in the colonial botanical gardens secured the empire's supply of luxury goods, such as tea and coffee. Thus, when China lost its monopoly in tea production and trade in the wake of the Opium Wars, botanical gardens provided the British with the grounds for experimentation and transfer of the Chinese tea plants to India. The tea transfer, and the improvement of indigenous tea plants in Assam, enabled the British to turn the Assam forests into a "tea garden." What had in the 1830s still been derogatively referred to as a "vast, fever-infested jungle area"[19] became a productive paradisiacal "garden of silk and cotton, of tea, coffee, and sugar."[20]

Besides collecting and distributing seeds and plants, and enhancing the production of agricultural crops for the colonies and the mother country, gardens for the colonists also functioned as "a familiar reminder of 'home' and a symbol of the norms of their civilization."[21] In the

FIGURE 0.2: Rose Tunnel in Lucknow Botanical Gardens. From *Gardeners' Chronicle*, April 18, 1885. Royal Horticultural Society, Lindley Library.

British colonies, botanical gardens fulfilled the role of Victorian public urban parks. In Australia, in particular, many botanical gardens, as in Melbourne, were looked upon more as public pleasure grounds than as scientific institutions.[22] In contrast to Kew Gardens, where the directors adamantly held up the institution's scientific utilitarian purpose—opposing ornamental plantings, and pre-noon public opening times—[23] in many colonial botanical gardens wholehearted attempts were made to emulate the typical forms, landscape features, and facilities of British parks.[24] Under William Guilfoyle's directorship in the last decades of the nineteenth century, thirty-five acres of lawn were laid out in the Melbourne botanical garden. Many colonial botanical gardens included tea kiosks, bandstands, and, from the 1870s onwards, boasted English rose gardens. As a reference to genteel English landscape gardens and parks, some gardens admitted cattle.[25] While the colonial botanical gardens first and foremost catered to the colonists—the natives maintaining the gardens often lived in shantytowns nearby—[26] they were also regarded as having a "civilizing effect" on the indigenous population.[27] New life styles reflecting Englishness, including the walk in the park, were imposed on the natives. Colonists not only used the gardens to help acclimatize plants and expand local and foreign floras, but also to "civilize" and subordinate the native population, depending on the racial discourses variously chosen in British colonial politics.

Due to the available land and the advances of the latest hygienic knowledge, many colonial towns boasted more extensive gardens and open green space than did towns in the home countries.[28] In Australia, the towns of Adelaide and Melbourne, in particular, developed on the basis of plans that incorporated parkland. Here, homemaking included a system of parks laid out according to picturesque and gardenesque principles. Adelaide's parklands, consisting of a green belt and a number of inner city parks in the original plan credited to William Light and George Kingston, have long been considered an outstanding example of the use of parks and parkland in colonial town planning. While the parklands were credited with providing a healthy and pleasurable environment, in many cases they also formed a physical boundary against the native population.[29] In Melbourne in the 1850s, after its Lieutenant-Governor Charles Joseph La Trobe had retained parcels of land from sale for public use, his cousin Edward La Trobe Bateman was commissioned to design four public gardens.[30] Not all designs had clear design precedents in English parks. Anne Neale suspects that knowledge of Gabriel Thouin's *Plans raisonnés de toutes les espèces de jardins* could have inspired Bateman's avant garde plans[31] but the incorporation of squares and parks into the city plan had precedents in early British colonial towns on the North American continent and was supported by the increasing awareness of beneficial *rus in urbe* (country in the city) in eighteenth-century England.

Like the botanical gardens that provided the colonists with a piece of home, many of the private gardens laid out in the colonies sought to create a home in a foreign land. In British India, colonial residential gardens included familiar design features adopted from Britain, such as central lawns and flower gardens. The gardens were a contrast to the harsh environmental conditions and the life of lower-status Indian society outside their boundaries, and were perceived by the colonists as retreats and safe havens in an otherwise threatening foreign world.[32] Because of the extant imperial garden legacy in India, colonial garden-making on the governmental level became an even stronger political and symbolical gesture. In his years as Viceroy of India (1899–1905), Lord Curzon directed the restoration of the gardens of the Taj Mahal, turning what originally had been fragrant flower gardens lined with fruit trees into flat open lawns. In order to open the views onto the Mughal imperial monuments and prevent any type of informal activities like the "squalid bazaar[s]" in their vicinity, Curzon also ordered the laying-out of greensward in the Taj forecourt. The viceroy adopted and redefined Indian monuments like the Taj gardens as

FIGURE 0.3: View across the central part of the recently executed garden at Government House, New Delhi, ca. 1920. © British Library Board. All Rights Reserved 66/3(5).

his (country's) own, by restoring and isolating them from their original context.[33] With the move of its capital from Calcutta to New Delhi in 1911, the British Empire symbolically occupied the seat of the last Mughal emperor who had ruled over all of India, and in this way hoped to consolidate its power and unify India under its colonial rule.[34] To win acceptance, the new viceroy's Government House and its extensive gardens were designed to combine elements of Indian and Western building traditions.[35] In her pioneering study on *Gardens of the Great Mughals* (1913), Constance Mary Villiers-Stuart prepared the ground for Edward Lutyens's 1918 garden design.[36] In support of the imperial project, Villiers-Stuart praised much of Curzon's work, but criticized "the exposed private garden, a contradiction in its very terms; the public parks with their bare acres of unhappy-looking grass, their ugly bandstands, hideous iron railings, and forlorn European statues; their wide, objectless roads, scattered flower-beds, and solitary trees, and, worst of all in a hot country, their lack of fountains and running water," and suggested designers "turn to some modern Indian garden, and attempt, perhaps, to reconcile these two opposing styles."[37] Lutyens, though at first hard pressed to adopt features found in Indian architecture, followed Villiers-Stuart's proposition, and laid out the viceroy's garden as an extension to the house, on the basis of the symbolic quadripartite plan common in Mughal gardens, as seen in Figure 0.3. He combined features typical of Mughal garden art, such as walled terraces, water jets, lotus-leaf-shaped fountains, and intersecting water canals enclosing a large central platform, with terraces of English flowers, lawns, a pergola, and tennis courts, found in every English manor house garden at the time.[38] The garden was considered by Villiers-Stuart, as by Viceroy Lord Hardinge, a means to reconcile the British and Indian cultures. Villiers-Stuart believed that "a love of nature generally, especially of flowers, is as much a national characteristic of the English as of the Indians."[39] By identifying and using national traits, the colonial rulers hoped to establish a common ground as the basis for a peaceful future rule on the subcontinent. Together with Government House, the viceroy's garden formed the center of the plan for New Delhi. Inspired by Domenico Fontana's seventeenth-century Rome plan for Pope Sixtus V, the chief city planners Lutyens, George S. C. Swinton, and John A. Brodie laid out axes that radiated from the government district outward and opened vistas onto the ancient monuments that were to become focal points in an archeological park.[40] As in Rome, a comparison often evoked to emphasize the imperial status of architecture and city planning at the time, Delhi's ancient monuments were considered symbolic links between the present and the past, and, as in Rome, they were, therefore, deliberately set in public parkland and used as the focal points in visual axes.[41]

IMAGINARY EMPIRES

In turn, gardens and parks in the mother countries were influenced by the plants discovered, and the landscapes experienced, in the colonies. Botanical gardens linked the newly discovered "wild" lands with gardens at home. Acclimatized and hybridized plants enabled these distant landscapes to be drawn into gardens and parks, glasshouses and conservatories, and finally into the house. In Britain, the fast-growing web of agricultural, horticultural, and botanical societies, and the growth of the gardening and horticultural press, further led horticulture to become a fashionable pursuit of the new middle class. As Harriet Ritvo has observed, "it became possible for the middle-class hobbyist to construct a miniature empire in the back garden [, and …] the domestic empire could easily expand to include a slice of the tropics as well."[42] Brent Elliott and Mark Laird in their chapters in this volume elaborate on how the introduction of plants in the early nineteenth century began to determine the design of gardens and instigated new planting fashions. The more plants from the colonies appeared in the botanical gardens, the less fearsome and threatening were these faraway lands and their apparent "wilderness." Through the acclimatization, and hybridization of subtropical and tropical vegetation and its exhibition and use in various exterior and interior environments exotic wilderness was domesticated,

cultivated, civilized, and ordered.[43] Exotic and native plants were used to simulate foreign and exotic landscapes, as well as local and regional ones on different scales and in various interior and exterior environments.

At Biddulph Grange in Staffordshire, James Bateman's religiously inspired
garden created in the 1850s evoked landscapes found in Egypt, the Himalayas,
Italy, and China, leading visitors on a tour in space and time. This outdoor
"cabinet of curiosities" was an example for the exuberant display of an exotic
"other" where miniaturized replicas of buildings like the Great Wall of China
and the appropriate acclimatized plants sought to transport the visitor into the
far reaches of the empire.[44] The novelty of faraway lands also led to extrava-
gant displays of tropical and subtropical vegetation in the newly developed and
intricately designed cast iron and glass conservatories. John Claudius Loudon's
1817 proposal to provide greenhouses not only with "appropriate birds, fishes,
and harmless animals, but with examples of the human species from the different countries imitated, habited in their particular costumes, and who may
serve as gardeners or curators of the different productions"[45] came to fruition
in a different form when "representatives of most nations of the British empire
were constantly in attendance" at the 1851 World Exhibition's Crystal Palace,
and were at exhibitions thereafter unashamedly exploited as casts in tableaux-
vivants.[46]

Following the example of London's Crystal Palace, the construction of public
winter gardens and palm houses reached an apex in the second half of the nineteenth century. In contrast to the late eighteenth- and early nineteenth-century
panoramas that often showed scenes from the colonies,[47] these gardens provided their middle-class visitors with a vivid truly three-dimensional scenery of
distant lands in which they could converse, read, walk, and socialize. Ludwig II
of Bavaria, later declared mad and deposed, seemingly had the means to go to
an extreme and combined a panorama painting of the Himalayan Mountains
with a one-and-a-half-acre glass-covered roof garden. This 1867 addition to
his Munich Residenz (it was demolished in 1897) with its tropical vegetation
arranged by court gardener Karl von Effner, included trees, a pond big enough
to row on, brook, grotto, waterfall, fountain, reed hut, and an oriental pavilion. Swans, peacocks, and hummingbirds enlivened Ludwig's romantic oriental
paradise, along with a special lighting system that could simulate moonlight
and sunsets.[48] While Ludwig's garden is an example of a setting for a frivolous,
eccentric, decadent, and pretentious social life that often also characterized public winter gardens, Émile Zola in his novel *La curée* (1872) lent conservatories
an even-less-inhibited, lascivious, erotically charged, and immoral aura. In one
of the key scenes of his novel, Renée, the wife of a rich building speculator,

meets her lover in a villa conservatory. Zola used the conservatory and "the unrestrained growth of the tropical plants with their heavy, intoxicating scent" as metaphors "for the uninhibited sexuality of the actors, moral constraint surrendered before the backdrop of an artificial paradise."[49]

As John MacKenzie has observed with regard to architecture and design, by the end of the nineteenth century "Orientalism had ... become the language of pleasure and relaxation ... leisure and recreation, 'escapism' and personal fantasies were invariably expressed in Orientalist forms."[50] In an attempt to induce virtual travel abroad and offer paths into foreign lands that did not require leaving the home garden, or city, and to symbolize colonial conquest, wealth and status, around the turn of the century orientalist forms also characterized many buildings of zoological gardens, like the elephant house disguised as an Egyptian temple in Antwerp, and the "antelope mosque," "pachyderm Indian temple," and the Moorish-style bird house in the 1844 Berlin zoological garden designed by Peter Joseph Lenné.[51] Beginning with the 1793 Jardin des Plantes in Paris, the first public zoological gardens emerged in the European capitals during the early nineteenth century. The picturesque walks in gardens and parks, as in London's Regent's Park where a zoo was established in 1828, and Lenné's park designs were thought to provide a suitable setting for caged animals that were initially exhibited for purely scientific purposes. Zoological gardens presenting the richness of the animal world and the exotic "fruits" of empire, however, soon turned into places for public entertainment and amusement, showcasing "the optimism, power, and ambitions of the new bourgeois elite."[52] After models of prehistoric animals had been distributed freely throughout the picturesque part of Crystal Palace Park in Sydenham, England, in the 1850s,[53] by 1890 it also had become more common in zoos to keep live animals in enclosures resembling the respective animal's native environment.

In the United States, where the first zoo had been established in Philadelphia's Fairmount Park in 1874, zoos were also considered a means to encourage wildlife preservation and conservation, and it was this idea that prompted the opening of the National Zoo in Washington, D.C., in 1891. It seems only logical that the conservationist initiative led by the Smithsonian taxidermist William Temple Hornaday would cause the design of naturalistic habitats for the exhibition of indigenous species, and would prompt a series of master plans designed by Frederick Law Olmsted Sr. and his sons that integrated the National Zoo into the capital's Rock Creek Park.[54]

In Germany, a new zoo concept developed, influenced by the animal panoramas of animal dealer and circus impresario Carl Hagenbeck. It exhibited animals moving freely in front of artistically rendered landscape scenes. This

soon turned into his "animal paradise," a zoo that used unbarred enclosures
and dry and water-filled moats. It was realized for the first time in Hagenbeck's
animal park in Stellingen. As Hyson and others have shown, Hagenbeck turned
"zoological gardens" into "zoological parks" by means of more "naturalistic," unbarred animal enclosures. Finally, visitors could feel secure and imagine
themselves in the wild, gazing at various landscape types with their different
inhabitants from only one viewpoint.[55] Adopted throughout the Western world,
many zoos subsequently constructed landscape panoramas and miniaturized
landscapes from faraway lands, such as the Mappin Terraces for mountain-
dwelling animals in Regent's Park Zoo, concrete models of the Atlas Mountains
of Morocco that were made shortly before World War I. These public landscapes had private precedents; for example, in England at Friar Park in Henley-
on-Thames, where a thirty-foot scale model of the Matterhorn was built, and
at Fanhams Hall, Ware, where a miniature replica of Mount Fuji adorned the
Japanese garden.[56]

Despite the criticism caused among some of the garden architects at this time
by these playful private indulgences realized between 1840 and 1870, the miniature reconstruction of larger landscapes in gardens eventually led to the inclusion
of imaginary figures with human traits that inhabited wilderness and nature only
in the human imagination. While elves, pixies, imps, and sprites only peopled the
numerous nineteenth-century children's fairy tales, as Linda Parshall shows in her
chapter in this volume, gnomes were also admitted into adult gardens. The indus-
trious garden gnomes who were considered earth-loving creatures, epitomized the
imaginary empires of spiritualists and garden owners with a weakness for fairytales.
Although scholars have followed the history of gnomes and dwarfs in gardens back
to antiquity, today's garden gnomes were "born" in the ceramic works of two firms
in the town of Gräfenroda in Thuringia, Germany, around 1850. Ceramic gnomes
began to appear in gardens throughout Germany, and from the 1880s onward in
France and England. Besides their adoption by spiritualists, another explanation for
the late nineteenth-century fashion of garden gnomes points toward the eighteenth-
century revivalism that might have caused gnomes to be modeled on the dwarf
statues in German rococo gardens.[57] Commonly associated with mountains and
mining activities, gnomes were often placed to "inhabit" rock gardens. Indeed, the
construction of rockeries, bluffs, and massive rock formations, and the use of outcrops and boulders, was another favorite method of bringing larger landscapes
and tamed "wilderness" into gardens and parks. By providing adequate settings
and sites for acclimatized plants from mountainous regions and other parts of the
world, rock gardens further facilitated the collection of distant landscapes and territories, a popular pursuit of the wealthy middle and upper classes who aspired to

FIGURE 0.4: E. Stuart Hardy, *A Council of Gnomes*. From Frederick E. Weatherly, *The Book of Gnomes*, 1907. Courtesy of Smithsonian Institution Libraries, Washington, DC.

turn science into pleasure. Pointing toward Roman ruins, New World mountains and prairies, "the great mountains of Europe," Greece, Italy, and Spain, "the hills of Asia Minor," and "the alpine regions of the great continents," William Robinson suggested that "from almost every interesting region the traveler may bring seeds or plants, and establish near his home living souvenirs of the various countries he has visited."[58] As much as the scientific curiosity about phenomena above ground increased in the nineteenth century, the urge to understand what lay below ground led to a scientific breakthrough in 1815, when the canal surveyor William Smith published his geological map of England and Wales. Smith's discovery of the interrelation between geological periods, strata, and the fossils within them, and his cartographic representation thereof, sparked public interest in geology and furthered the integration of rocks and rockeries in gardens and parks. Paradoxically, the interest in adhering to geological laws and providing "authentic" stratification led to the development and use of artificial stone made out of cement. Artificial rockwork was employed in private gardens and public parks alike.[59]

Perhaps one of its most impressive uses in a public landscape was made in the Parisian Parc des Buttes Chaumont, one of the five prestigious new park projects commissioned during the Second Empire by Napoleon III and his prefect George Eugène Haussmann, and designed by Adolphe Alphand and his team of landscape gardeners and horticultural engineers. Opened on occasion of the Paris World's Fair in 1867 on the site of a former quarry and dump in the peripheral nineteenth arrondissement, Parc des Buttes Chaumont showcased the exhibition's theme of art and industry. Manufactured materials and innovative building practices including stucco cement and iron-reinforced concrete were used to turn what had formerly been perceived as a dangerous, vicious, and stinking "desert" outside the city into a secure, healthy green oasis for pleasure driving and walking.[60] Stucco cement was used to combine natural and artificial rockwork for the construction of cascades, grottos, and rock faces that provided the playful romantic scenery that has been described as "engineered picturesque."[61] In Parc des Buttes Chaumont, scientific and industrial progress were meant to be visible without diminishing the illusion of naturalness and wilderness. Thus, the lake displayed a concrete edge, and steps and railings throughout the park were made from reinforced concrete imitating branches and logs.[62] As the nineteenth-century bird's-eye view illustrates in Figure 0.5, the park also integrated industrialization's most potent symbol, the railroad. For visitors looking out from the imitation of the temple of Sibyl on top of the island, the park's artfully contrived "nature" framed industrial manufacturing zones, and wastelands on the urban periphery, thereby showcasing the modernity and progress of the Second Empire, and its different, albeit connected resources and products. Nature had become a commodity for conspicuous consumption. Parc des Buttes Chaumont was, as Heath Massey (Schenker) has shown for Central Park in New York City, a "melodramatic landscape."[63] Once the wild wasteland of the dump had been turned into a park featuring subtropical vegetation imported from the colonies, the artificially enhanced awe-provoking steep, rugged rock formation in the lake could safely provide thrills and spectacle. Emotions were especially aroused by a walk across the suspension bridge that led onto the island at a height of thirty meters above the water.[64] Parc des Buttes Chaumont clearly was an attempt to bridge the dichotomy between city and country, as Massey (Schenker) further elaborates in this volume. The Parisian park exhibited industry and progress, and clothed them in an artificial natural paradise. It represented the ambivalence and fickleness inherent in society of the age. Considered an antidote to the city's morally suspect cabarets and guinguettes,[65] the park itself provided thrilling scenery for entertainment, amusement, and even for (romantically inspired) suicides, as the suspension bridge—aptly nicknamed "suicide bridge"—attests.

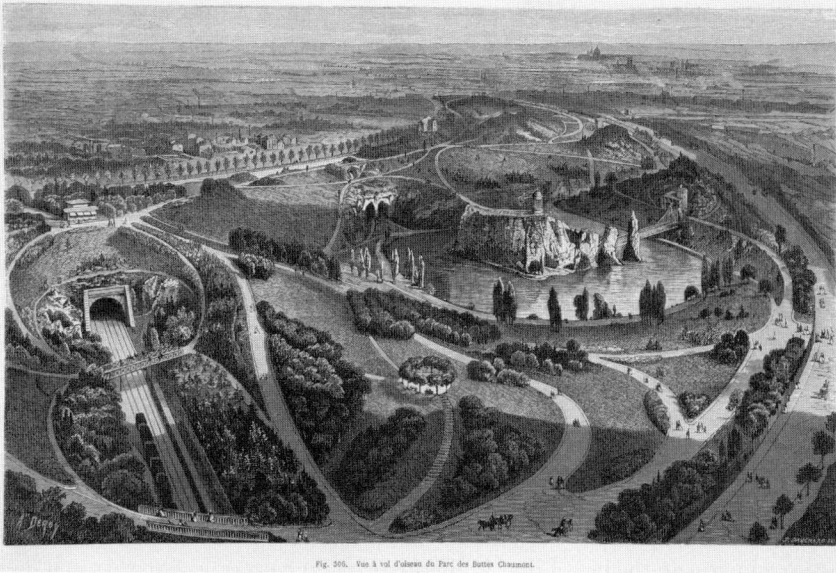

FIGURE 0.5: Bird's-eye view of Parc des Buttes Chaumont. From Adolphe Alphand, *Les Promenades de Paris*, vol. 1 (1867–73), 199. Dumbarton Oaks Research Library and Collection, Washington, DC.

Voluntary death had at the time acquired symbolic status for moralists, physicians, social reformers, and romantics alike. While the latter considered suicide the result of melancholic sensibilities and viewed it simultaneously with "fascination and aversion, compassion, disdain, respect, and condemnation,"[66] the former viewed self-destruction as insanity caused by the effects of urbanization.

GARDENS AND PARKS AS SANATORIUM

In the nineteenth century, when the dirty and overcrowded living conditions in industrial cities were increasingly accused of causing nervous breakdowns, intemperance, idleness, epidemics, disease, and death, gardens were attributed with the capacity to soothe and heal. This belief was not new, but the development of medical science provided an increasing body of research that attempted to prove the theory that the qualities of the environment influenced character, wellbeing, and health. Morals and mental and physical health were considered directly dependent on environmental conditions and aesthetics. In addition to mental illness that was thought to be facilitated by stressful urban life, another part of this theory was the proposition that miasma—gases emanating from disintegrating organic substance prevalent in burial grounds, sewers and swamps—were the primary causes of disease. The miasma theory, supported by the eminent British health reformer Edwin Chadwick, had already in the first half of the nineteenth century influenced burial customs. On account of this theory, in Britain and in the United States, many cities had relocated or established new cemeteries and burial grounds on peripheral sites. This led to cemeteries such as Mount Auburn in Cambridge, Massachusetts (1831), and Highgate and Nunhead in London (1839; 1840) being laid out as gardens with rural or garden scenery.[67] Their rolling hills, curvilinear walks, meandering lakeshores, and monumental grave stones combined character traits of eighteenth-century landscape gardens. Indeed, as much as these new spacious and green cemeteries outside the overcrowded inner cities responded to the health theories at the time, their design was also a result of the romantic, melancholic yearnings and contemplative reveries initiated by the Enlightenment philosophy of Jean-Jacques Rousseau, and of Transcendentalist thought prevalent in the American northeast.[68] In those parts of the American continent, Unitarianism, and Arminianism, the belief that individuals could gain salvation through good deeds, caused graves to become the sites of celebration rather than fathomless sorrow, and death to be attributed with sentimental, melancholic associations rather than terror and anxiety. In contrast to these religious and spiritual attitudes, John Claudius Loudon, an avid promoter of the garden-cemetery movement in Britain, concentrated in his writings on the scientific and utilitarian aspects of cemetery design. Criticizing many of the romanticized features of early nineteenth-century cemeteries in Britain he proposed clear, ordered, and logical layouts that dispensed with clumps of trees, and, for health reasons, preferred the planting of evergreens and well-drained open lawns.[69] Along with John Strang, Loudon argued for the educational value of cemeteries. Similar to the concerns discussed on occasion of the construction of the first rural cemetery in the United States,[70] Loudon believed that the cemetery could become a "school of instruction in architecture, sculpture, landscape gardening, arboriculture, botany and the important points of general gardening: neatness, order, and high keeping."[71] Loudon shared his concerns for the salubrious disposal of dead corpses and for the improvement of the urban living environment with other utilitarians and reformers, such as Edwin Chadwick. It comes as no surprise, then, that Chadwick added extracts from Loudon's innovative plan for the Derby Arboretum, England's first park designed for public use, to his 1842 report on *The Sanitary Conditions of the Laboring Population of Great Britain*.

Chadwick's report repeated the decade-old demands of the Select Committee on Public Walks for public urban parks, and set in motion a process that led to the birth of the public health movement in Britain and the United States. The subsequent founding of public health institutions and the decrees of public health acts finally facilitated the development of landscapes that responded to the beliefs put forth by doctors, sanitarians, and reformers regarding mental and physical human health. In Britain, the first public lunatic asylums had already been constituted in the second half of the eighteenth century, but only between the 1808 County Asylum Act and the 1845 Lunatics Act, when movements to liberalize and reform asylums gained strength, and the provision of publicly funded asylums finally became mandatory, did the siting and setting of public asylums attract increasing attention.[72] The location of asylums shifted from the center to the periphery of towns. While the parks and gardens designed for asylums in some cases resembled country house estates, including rural scenery and ha-has (dry ditches that were not apparent from the dwelling but prevented livestock from entering the grounds immediately surrounding it) so that the patients could enjoy distant views, the boundaries were also designed to prevent patients from escaping, and to shield them from the public. In these controlled compounds the work on farms and in kitchen gardens was considered therapeutic, while at the same time contributing to many asylums' aim of self-sufficiency. Both the physical work in the open air and the exposure to picturesque rural scenery were thought to have a beneficial impact on the patients' mind and body. Beautiful and picturesque landscapes were believed to reorder thoughts, associations, and emotions that, according to John Locke's idea of madness, had become deranged in the patients' minds.[73] In the United States, Andrew Jackson Downing noted in 1848 that "no county-seats, no parks or pleasure grounds, [...] are laid out with more care, adorned with more taste, filled with more lovely flowers, shrubs and trees, than some of our principal cemeteries and asylums."[74] In fact, even before America's first rural cemetery opened in 1831, the grounds of asylums in Philadelphia, New York City, and Boston had been laid out as landscape parks, following the early example of the York Retreat in England, an asylum founded in 1796 by the Society of Friends for moral treatment based on humanitarian values and opposed to the inhumane authoritarian treatment in other institutions at the time.[75] The physician Dr. James MacDonald described the southern entrance to New York City's Bloomingdale Asylum, the exemplary parent institution of all North American asylums, in 1839 as "highly pleasing." He considered it "one of the most successful and useful instances of landscape gardening" due to "various avenues gracefully winding through so large a lawn; ... ornamental trees, tastefully distributed or grouped, the variety of shrubbery and flowers" and "the assemblage of so many objects to please the eye, and relieve the melancholy mind from its sad musings." MacDonald concluded that "no private residence, or public establishment in the vicinity of the city, which for beauty of situation, or exercise of taste in the distribution of grounds, can compare with it."[76] The involvement of landscape architects in designing asylum landscapes was less conspicuous in Britain than in the United States, where Andrew Jackson Downing, Calvert Vaux, Frederick Law Olmsted (who during the Civil War served on the U.S. Sanitary Commission), and Jacob Weidenmann prepared and executed designs for the state asylums in Utica (NY), Buffalo (NY), Trenton (NJ), the Hartford Asylum (CT), the McLean Asylum in Belmont (MA), and the Hudson River State Hospital (NY).[77] Like the early rural and garden cemeteries some asylum grounds, as in the case of Hartford, were open to the public for pleasure driving.[78] They, therefore, also fulfilled some of the functions that public parks provided once North American cities began to establish such amenities in greater numbers after the Civil War.

The creation of public parks was promoted due to public health concerns based on then-current medical theories, and in the light of the growing civic boosterism toward the end of the nineteenth century. The establishment of public parks was also encouraged by economic deliberations based on the increase of land value and productivity; a working class with easy access to open green space was thought to be healthier and, consequently, more productive. With the establishment of public urban parks—Central and Prospect Parks in New York City and Brooklyn were the most prominent examples of American park planning immediately before and after the Civil War—American landscape architects followed initiatives of their European colleagues, which they had in many cases experienced firsthand. Physicians such as John Henry Rauch and park planners such as Olmsted followed the same goal: the abatement of disease through the improvement of air quality and ventilation. Sanitarians and landscape architects agreed that the means to achieve this goal was to plant street trees, establish parks, and drain or landscape marshland. It was believed that vegetation not only purified the air but could also provide a physical buffer against the diffusion of bad air—*mal aria*. Additionally, according to the environmentally determinist position of landscape architects at the time, landscape beauty was thought to heighten the spirits, induce moral behavior, and improve the mental condition. As has been shown by Schuyler, and by Szczygiel and Hewitt, medical theory, including faculty psychology, and the theoretical constructs underlying the design of green open spaces in cities in the second half of the nineteenth century were closely connected.[79] Thus, when Olmsted addressed the American Social Science Association in Boston in 1870, he did not fail to mention that New York physicians recommended nervous patients to visit Central Park twice daily to facilitate recovery.[80] Not only could early asylum landscapes function as public parks, but as the reformer, economist, and professor E.R.L. Gould pointed out in 1888, urban parks were public "sanitariums."[81] They became therapeutic landscapes,

providing workers with the healing landscape that the European and American
middle and upper classes sought in the fashionable spa and mountain resorts
developed in the eighteenth and early nineteenth centuries, such as Bath and
Royal Tunbridge Wells in England; Vichy and Aix-les-Bains in France; Bad Ischl,
Gastein, Marienbad, Karlsbad in Austria; Saratoga Springs in New York state;
and the White Mountains in New Hampshire.

As early as the 1840s, Americans referred to parks as the "lungs of the city,"
a metaphor originally attributed to William Pitt the Younger when describing
the royal parks in London, and influenced by a popular analogy between the
city and the human body.[82] Nineteenth-century sanitarians and social scientists
regarded both as complex natural systems.[83] The production and flow of clean,
fresh air and its distribution throughout the entire city played an important
role in the early park systems developed by landscape architects Olmsted, Horace William Shaler Cleveland, and George Kessler for Buffalo, Minneapolis,
and Kansas City, respectively, and in Benjamin Ward Richardson's 1876 model
for Hygeia, an ideal "City of Health" in Victorian Britain. Both the utopian
sanitarian city and the more realistic idea of transforming tree-lined boulevards connecting publicly accessible royal parks into a system of parkways and
parks of different size and kind were ideas for turning the city into a garden.

CITIES AS GARDENS AND GARDENS AS CITIES

Utopian ideas to reconnect cities and nature preceded and followed the model of
Hygeia. Concern about the deteriorating living conditions in cities led Loudon
to devise his farsighted greenbelt plan for metropolitan London entitled "Hints
for Breathing Places" as early as 1829. In his diagram, concentric greenbelts that
allowed for picturesque landscapes, rural scenery, and geometrical gardens alternated with concentric zones of town. Their number could be increased indefi-
nitely as the city grew.[84] Loudon's greenbelt diagram reverberated in Ebenezer
Howard's garden city concept first published in 1898. After several paternalistic
and philanthropic factory owners, such as Sir Titus Salt, the Cadbury brothers,
and William Hasketh Lever in England, and George Pullman in the United States
had built their own factory towns with ample parks and gardens to sustain a
healthy and productive workforce, and improve its living conditions, Howard's
garden city concept provided a general model for a balanced relationship between city and countryside in an increasingly urbanized world. His garden cities
with their self-sustaining communities based on a cooperative economy brought
together the economic and cultural advantages of the city and the country. Like
Loudon's diagram, Howard's plan was based on the idea that greenbelts would

preserve green space and provide the structural framework for city building and
expansion; and like the city fathers of Chicago, the city where Howard had lived
for four years in the 1870s, and which since its foundation had been working
to comply with its motto *urbs in horto* (City in a Garden), Howard promoted
a green city surrounded by green open land. His garden city combined "town
and country, freedom and order, individualism and socialism."[85] It remained,
however, an ideal abstraction and a modern utopia. Despite its firm grounding in
the nineteenth-century social reform movement many of Howard's initial ideas
did not come to fruition in the garden cities and suburbs that were subsequently
realized throughout Europe and in the United States.

Instead of new self-sufficient towns most of these garden cities and suburbs
were residential expansions of existing cities. As in the case of the 1909 New
York garden suburb Forest Hills Gardens, landscape architects collaborated on
their design. Already by the end of the nineteenth century, landscape architects
in the United States, in particular, had become involved in city planning and
were contributing to the vision of the city as a garden. Besides laying out the
open space surrounding public buildings and institutions they were planning
parks, squares, and tree-lined avenues and parkways. On the European continent, the city planners and urbanists Hermann Josef Stübben and Camillo
Sitte published seminal works on urban design that included a chapter and
a consecutive addendum, respectively, on urban green spaces and plantings.
Stübben's and Sitte's handbooks distinguished between "ornamental" and
"sanitary green," and they set the path for Martin Wagner's ground-breaking
dissertation on "The Sanitary Green in Cities."[86] While their approaches were
based on different functionalist, romantic, and positivist sensibilities, these
studies together marked a turning point in the perception and conception of
the city. Like their progressive colleagues across the Atlantic, European urban
planners, architects, and landscape architects began to perceive the city as a
comprehensive organism that could be managed and turned into a *Gesamt-
kunstwerk*, a cultivated garden. Impressed by the parks and park systems in
American cities, the French landscape architect Jean Claude Nicolas Forestier
published *Grandes Villes et Systèmes de Parcs* in 1906. As an exponent of the
increasingly cosmopolitan professional urban elite, Forestier propagated park
system planning on a regional scale and argued that it could also become a
nationwide, or even international, program crossing political borders. Among
the American examples he discussed was the park system in Chicago.[87]

Chicago's citywide park system plans went back to the 1840s, and many
big pastoral urban parks had been built by 1893 when the city hosted the
World's Columbian Exhibition. The increasing number of immigrants and

deteriorating living conditions around the turn of the century led the city to pioneer a network of small neighborhood parks and playgrounds, providing recreational facilities on a neighborhood-scale (see Chapter 4 and Figure 4.7, this volume). At the time Forestier's book was published, a group of business-men and city officials had decided that the city needed further improvement in the form of a comprehensive city plan. The Plan of Chicago, inspired by the European capitals and the turn-of-the-century plans for Washington, D.C., was published in 1909, and included plans for a metropolitan park system. "Nature" winding its way through the urban fabric in the form of connected parks and gardens, it was believed, could provide order, and the playgrounds embedded in this system would assimilate and integrate immigrant children and their families into American society. The park system was considered to correspond to the City Beautiful movement's aim to combine utility and beauty in city development. For the German architect Hugo Koch, the Plan of Chicago exemplified the "excellent extent to which garden art contributes to the con-struction of the modern metropolis."[88] Landscape architects, planners, and ar-chitects such as Koch literally transformed the city into a garden by attributing to cities the age-old trope of utility and beauty, variously used to characterize garden art.

While Howard and other progressive social reformers, such as Olmsted in the United States, attempted to reconcile the city and the country, many social-ist reformers promoted the movement "back-to-nature." Utopian socialists like Charles Fourier, and writers such as Tolstoy and Kropotkin—all keen garden-ers themselves—promoted the return to the land. William Morris, one of the founders of the Arts and Crafts movement, wanted to "shake off … all foreign and colonial entanglements" and turn England "from the grimy backyard of a workshop into a garden."[89] In the German states in the last decades of the nineteenth century, authors such as Wilhelm Heinrich Riehl and Theodor Frit-sch propagated a "back-to-the-soil" movement that was based on antiurban ideology often paired with anti-Semitism, and that led to the establishment of cooperative settlements outside of the cities. These rural garden settlements, in which utilitarian gardens and fields tied the settlers to the land, were consid-ered the ideal grounds for the rearing of "racially pure" offspring.[90]

In contrast, garden colonies and allotment gardens that were laid out on the periphery of cities, alleviated, and in some instances, even enabled people to live in the cities in the first place. In his conceptual diagram, Howard had included allotment gardens along the periphery of his garden cities, so that citizens could grow their own produce. In 1913, the German landscape architect Leb-erecht Migge even claimed that the metropolis was "the mother of gardens."[91]

The allotment gardens that developed in Berlin in the last decades of the nineteenth century originated in two different movements. Due to overcrowding in the city's tenement districts, many workers settled on parcels of undeveloped land on the periphery, which they rented from the developers' leaseholders. The small temporary huts and the gardens that working class families constructed on the allotted parcels of land were essential for their survival. This working class movement was complemented by so-called workers' gardens implemented by the Red Cross, and the *Schrebergarten* movement, named after the physician Dr. Daniel Gottlob Moritz Schreber and initiated by social reformers of the urban elite. Originally begun in Leipzig by Dr. Ernst Innozenz Hauschild as children's playgrounds following Schreber's ideas, the playground supervisor Karl Gesell soon included planting beds for the children to experience nature. In contrast to Friedrich Fröbel's kindergarten, an educational institution for small children founded in 1840 in Blankenburg, where gardening was firmly integrated into the pedagogy and the children's planting beds were surrounded by communal plots cultivated by adults, children in Leipzig, however, showed little interest. This resulted in their parents seizing the opportunity to turn the plots into the first "Schreber" gardens.[92] Although cities and local authorities feared that allotment gardens could literally provide the working class with the ground for political opposition, they were also aware that the allotment of gardens could function as pacifiers and appeasement, preventing social upheaval. At the beginning of the twentieth century, many cities began systematically to plan allotment gardens, and employed landscape architects like Migge and Erwin Barth in Berlin to layout large stretches of land as garden colonies. These were often located on land that was "left over" and could not be used for other purposes, for example along railway embankments. In 1913, Migge commented on the "green ribbon of peace" that allotment gardens formed around "the raucous city," and that was the first thing one perceived when riding into a city by train.[93] Thus, the railroad, preeminent symbol of industrialization, not only provided the land for the garden, but was also perceived as furthering the reconnection of city and country, as envisioned by Howard.

Railroads gave rise to the development of station gardens, and they inspired landscape architects in the United States to consider how train passengers and observers perceived landscape. When discussions about modernization in the art world led to Etienne Baudry's 1868 satirical proposal to turn train stations into art galleries because these were the only places that could attract and educate a mass audience,[94] landscape architects were taking a more realistic pragmatic approach. In the United States, the experience of European station gardens, and the fascination with the new means of transportation and its velocity induced the railroad garden advocate Donald G. Mitchell to argue in 1867 for openings in screen plantings on embankments so that the train's movement and speed seemed enhanced, thereby heightening the onlooker's sensation. At the same time, these windows would enable train passengers to view the scenery they were passing through.[95] It is also possible that the new mode of transportation and increased speed of passenger travel influenced the design of public urban parks. Anette Freytag has argued that contrary to eighteenth-century landscape gardens where scenes unfolded slowly to the walking or carriage-driven visitor, public parks offered a range of scenes that abruptly alternated between sublime, picturesque, and beautiful effects.[96] Along the railroads, suburban growth led to the laying-out of station gardens that acted as an advertisement for the respective town or suburban development. The gardens exhibited the latest horticultural fads, and provided fresh flowers for dining cars and for purchase by passengers.[97] In 1902, the American City Beautiful advocate Charles Mulford Robinson promoted "the railroad beautiful," a network of station gardens and plantings along railroads that could "have an even national importance, changing the face of the country 'as seen from the car window,' and carrying its influence very far."[98]

PARKS AND GARDENS FOR THE NATION

As the railroad pushed the frontier on the American continent forward, and as it advanced in the colonies and across the European continent, it diminished distances, tied together countries, and facilitated international trade and exchange. True wilderness was becoming scarce. The urban masses conquered the countryside on daytrips and weekend outings, and when the railroad and tourism began to threaten natural beauty and landscapes, conservationists and preservationists across Europe raised their voices for the protection of wilderness, natural scenery, and beauty. In many cases they invoked John Ruskin. Ruskin's ardent opposition to the railway, its commercial profit, speed, air and noise pollution, and its destruction of historic sites and landscape scenery—though at times ambivalent—inspired the founding of the Commons Preservation Society (1865) and the National Trust in Britain (1895), and played an important role in the German, French, and Italian conservation movements.[99] Developing throughout the Western world from the last quarter of the nineteenth century onwards, nature preservation and conservation went hand in hand with growing nationalism, and the evolution of nation-states. As important as it was for the European states and the United States to display their colonial accomplishments at World's Fairs, the exhibition of national characteristics became increasingly relevant and assumed different expressions. Parks and gardens played an important role in fostering local, regional, and national identities, not only as settings for the big national and international exhibitions, and national monuments, but also as repositories and re-creations of "nature" that was on the brink of being lost. In this volume, Gert Gröning and Joachim Wolschke-Bulmahn examine this phenomenon on the basis of "wild," "nature," and "prairie-style" gardens.

Despite Italy's relatively slow industrial and urban development, its unification process provides a conspicuous example of the use of public parks and gardens for nation-building and civic boosterism in the second half of the nineteenth century. In 1855, when Turin was preparing to become the capital of the new Italian state, a competition for a public urban park along the River Po was organized. Accordingly, and not dissimilar from the plan recorded in 1869 by John Rauch to turn the Washington Mall into a "living map" of the United States,[100] Napoleone Tettamanzi's unrealized Italian design was based on the map of the Italian peninsula. Lawns formed the Mediterranean, and tree-lined walks surrounded the landforms, and cut through them. The location of big cities was to be marked by pedestals carrying the respective city's arms and inscribed with its name and number of citizens.[101] In 1864, when the Italian capital was moved from Turin to Florence, the Tuscan city's plans to adapt to its new function included a park-like public walk. The architect Giuseppe Poggi's wide, almost four-mile-long tree-lined *viale dei Colli* on the hillside along the south bank of the Arno river was to provide access to areas for the development of villas for government officials and foreign diplomats.[102] When the capital was finally moved to Rome in 1870, attention was again directed toward the two park projects that had been initiated by Napoleon I. The Pincio had already been the focus of improvement in 1849, when, after the proclamation of the Roman Republic on the piazza del Popolo, nationalist sentiment had led to the proposal to arrange busts of literati and fighters for Italian independence along the Pincio's public walks. Busts of illustrious Italians erected in a public park, it was thought, would create a national consciousness and a shared culture, uniting all citizens in their quest for independence and unification. The construction of patriotic monuments in public gardens and parks was common throughout Europe and the United States at the time, and was copied on the Gianicolo in 1870.[103]

Napoleon's idea for the *Giardino del campidoglio* was taken up in the master plans drawn up for Rome after Italian unification in which it was turned into the *passeggiata archeologica*, envisioned as allées and landscaped grounds surrounding the monuments.[104] As in the two centuries before, the ensemble of nature and ancient Roman ruins attracted nineteenth-century landscape painters, and sparked discussions among British landscape architects, who revived the use of real and sham ruins in gardens.[105] Enthused by the beauty and quantity of flowers on the Roman Colosseum, the French painter François-Marius Granet exclaimed in 1802, that "you could put together a guide to the plants from them."[106] Having compiled a flora of the British isles in 1837, the British physician Richard Deakin did exactly that. In contrast to the work of his Italian colleagues, the physicians Domenico Panaroli and Antonio Sebastiani, who had compiled plant lists for medical purposes in the seventeenth and the early nineteenth centuries, Deakin pursued a romantically inspired educational goal with his *Flora of the Colosseum of Rome* (1855).[107] Flowers associated with ruins, he believed, "form a link in the memory, and teach us hopeful and soothing lessons, amid the sadness of bygone ages." Deakin was skeptical of the restorations that destroyed "the wild and solemn grandeur" and "the impression and solitary lesson which so magnificent a ruin is calculated to make upon the mind."[108] Besides the plant catalogue based on the Linnean system that placed his volume among the numerous nineteenth-century regional and national floras compiled for different parts of the world,[109] Deakin's book also comprised information related to the cultural history of individual species. The physician from Sheffield was guided by the same romantic sensibility that made the Italian archeologist and Ruskin-disciple Giacomo Boni share Deakin's apprehension about the treatment of the Roman ruins and devise a planting scheme for the conservation and beautification of the Roman monuments. Boni experimented with the *flora dei monumenti*, a selection of plant species that he had identified in ancient Roman literature and paintings, to turn the archeological remains of the Roman Empire into a garden that would connect the present to the past.[110]

Patriotic parks and national gardens appeared in other countries and continents, as well. Andrew Jackson Downing's 1851 design for a public "national park" on the Washington Mall, including an area exclusively planted with American tree species between the White House and Capitol,[111] was not realized. However, in New York City's Central Park, Olmsted and Vaux simulated characteristic landscape features of the North American continent. Schist outcrops and rock formations were intended to emulate the Catskills and Adirondacks, and Franziska Kirchner has suggested that the Ramble Arch was inspired by the Natural Bridge in Virginia.[112] Incorporating natural monuments that variously created sublime and picturesque effects into their sweeping gesture of pastoral scenery, Olmsted and Vaux created a national monument and established "Park-making as a National Art."[113] In the early twentieth century, Central Park provided the fledgling film industry with verisimilar sets for film scenes in France, Japan, and England despite its arguably "American" landscapes.[114] This paradox, however, only demonstrated the importance the park had assumed in forging the identity of what had by now developed into an international metropolis. After Andrew Jackson Downing had in the first half of the century prepared the ground for future calls for an American "national taste in gardening,"[115] Mariana Schuyler Van Rensselaer in 1893 demanded "American gardens, American landscapes, American parks and pleasure-grounds." Her request was, to dispense with "the features ... of a dozen different countries huddled together into a scene which has no simplicity, harmony, or unity, and therefore no character—no likeness to Nature, and therefore no artistic worth."[116] In her book *Art Out-of-Doors*, Van Rensselaer echoed some of the ideas that landscape architects in the Midwest were attempting to realize in practice.

In 1888, three decades after Olmsted and Vaux's design for Central Park, the Danish-born landscape architect Jens Jensen displayed native trees, shrubs, and wildflowers in what he called the "American Garden" in Chicago's Union Park. Despite its name, the "American Garden" was a first attempt to establish a specifically regional style, later defined as "prairie style" by Wilhelm Miller, and employed in private estate gardens and public parks. Similarly capturing the larger regional landscape and distilling its essential features was the rationale behind park designs in turn-of-the-century Cologne and Berlin, two of the industrial centers that played an important role in the development of the German nature protection movement during the Kaiserreich.[117] In Cologne's Klettenbergpark (1905–07), Fritz Encke presented the entire range of landscape types in the Rhine Valley. Thus, a lake, meadow and stream, heath landscape, and forested areas, including a rocky creek, waterfall, and quarries, were interwoven so that they created "small individual pictures, that, like paintings in a well ordered gallery, produced a good overall impression."[118] In Berlin, after Friedrich Bauer's Schillerpark, praised for its design based on the regional landscape type and thought to enhance the citizens' appreciation of their home landscape,[119] Erwin Barth's 1912 design for Berlin's Sachsenplatz (today Brixplatz) also followed didactic purposes. Inspired by Klettenbergpark in Cologne, Berlin's garden director designed Sachsenplatz as a nature reserve composed of landscape types and plant communities typical of the region.[120] While many German landscape architects and planners were influenced by the garden and playground reform movements that led them to look toward the United States for suitable examples, preservationists such as Gustav Heick also argued that "the garden, the park, can and should participate in the nature protection movement."[121] Not only were wilderness areas to be conserved in public parks, they were also to be newly created.

As with public urban parks that were either intended to simulate foreign landscapes (taken to the extreme in zoos), and could exhibit subtropical plants, or were created as signifiers of national, regional, and local landscapes, the degree to which exotic landscapes and plants were embraced as an extension of the *private* home, or were regarded as a suspicious "other," varied. When British architect Josiah Conder published his seminal work *Landscape Gardening in Japan* in 1893, which was to further promote the construction of "Japanese" gardens in Europe and the United States some thirty years after Japan had ended its isolationist policies, he was clear-sighted enough to anticipate that "Some may … hold that landscape gardening should be typical of the scenery of the soil, and regard the servile imitation of a foreign style as unnatural and purposeless," but also daring enough to propose that "the abstract principles of the [Japanese] Art may prove not totally unworthy of attention."[122]

In Britain, artists, writers, architects, and designers used the garden in its various forms as a metaphor and symbol for the nation and empire and its wellbeing. The garden was considered to express a culture shared by the English, Irish, Scottish, and Welsh populations, who at the time were seeking to establish their own respective identities through different languages, religion, sport, and culture.[123] John Ruskin saw "all England as a garden," attributing it with "the true nature of home … the place of Peace; the shelter, not only from all injury, but from all terror, doubt, and division."[124] Gardens and plants were used to contrast the "true" home with the adopted one in the colonies. In Frances Hodgson Burnett's children's novel *The Secret Garden*, a Yorkshire garden represents the "true" home of the ten-year-old Mary Lennox who was born in India.[125] Burnett uses the English garden and its plants—roses, lilies, crocuses, daffodils, snapdragons, poppies, mignonette, and larkspur—as symbols and metaphors for homecoming and homemaking. Mary's secret walled garden, comprising the typical characteristics of a cottage garden, and located in the vigorous healthy Yorkshire climate, is juxtaposed with India, portrayed as a "'breeding ground' of lethargy and idleness," and epidemic disease.[126] As Anne Helmreich has observed, the cottage ideal in British gardening "unlike the wild garden, … erased any trace of its relationship with Empire,"[127] and so Indian-born Mary Lennox in her Yorkshire secret garden is "re-born" as an English girl.

The cottage garden ideal, promoted in the later garden cities and disseminated in paintings by Myles Birket Foster and Helen Allingham, among others, was thought to connect England with its romanticized pre-industrial, pre-urban past, and provide a safe haven in the industrial present and uncertain future. For this purpose, many designers and writers such as John Ruskin promoted the use of "old-fashioned" flowers, and referred to the flowers Shakespeare used in his texts.[128] The cottage garden, its flowers, and its connection to domestic rural life functioned as an "invented tradition," as did other garden forms in Britain,

and gardens in other countries at the time.[129] Perhaps not surprising in this age
of the stratification of social classes, the specialization, and diversification of
professions, capitalism, conspicuous consumption, and increasing democratiza-
tion, more than one garden form was considered to exemplify the quintessence
of British culture. Toward the end of the nineteenth century, architects such as
Reginald Blomfield and other members of the Art Workers Guild took pains to
establish the English origins of the formal garden despite its apparent similarity
with Italian Renaissance gardens and the concurrent revival of garden design
based on geometric and symmetric forms in Germany, France, and the United
States. Like the twists and turns undertaken by Italian philosophers and writers to prove the Italian origin of the English landscape garden a century earlier,
English architects did not spare efforts to invent their own tradition. By down-
playing the Italian influence, and referring to the Elizabethan era as the origin
of the English formal garden Blomfield established England's garden culture as
a cosmopolitan and elitist one.[130] In the heated debate between sympathizers of
the wild and the formal garden, the architect John Dando Sedding tellingly rel-
egated the wild garden to the colonies, "which he believed lacked a long history
of cultivation, whereas England—'an old land' with a history of building and
designing landscapes—required an old-fashioned formal garden."[131] Adopting
features from both the cottage garden and the formal garden, Gertrude Jekyll
and Edward Lutyens designed numerous country house gardens that ultimately
came to define what still today is often referred to as "the English garden."[132]
It comes as no surprise, then, that Lutyens, commissioned by the Imperial War
Graves Commission to design numerous World War I cemeteries in Belgium
and the north of France, turned to Jekyll for many of the planting designs. The
cemeteries were to become "English gardens," enclosed by holly or yew hedges,
and displaying colorful borders of familiar "English" flowers, such as roses,
foxgloves, columbines, London pride, bergenias, and nepeta.[133]

GARDENS AS CONTESTED SPACE

As much as gardens were considered to transcend political borders and boundaries, as in the case of the network of colonial botanical gardens; as much
as they were used as a means to overcome the dichotomy between city and
country in the case of garden cities and public urban parks; as much as they
were designed to mediate between the inside and the outside, as in the cases
of the formal and wild garden; and as much as they were meant to transcend
class distinctions and realize the utilitarian belief in happiness for the greatest
numbers, gardens in the Age of Empire also created boundaries. For instance,

parkland created in the colonies could separate the indigenous population from the colonists; early nineteenth-century squares in London were closed by iron railings and locked gates, only accessible to the immediate residents for whom they provided a private park; in the United States, many public urban parks created in the South after the Civil War were segregated, and provided a separation between black and white residential areas. Gardens and parks acted as safe havens, and spaces for respite and recreation, but they could also be controlled and confined spaces that deprived users in their pursuit of life, liberty, and happiness, or denied certain groups access entirely.

As Robert Rotenberg has observed of Vienna, during the time of the Biedermeier, political oppression and state-ordered police surveillance led to private gardens and courtyards becoming the only possible venue for political discussions among family and close friends.[134]

This new importance of the domestic sphere led to the garden not only becoming a domestic sanctuary and an extension of the house, but to the house becoming an extension of the garden. Middle-class women decorated house interiors with plants that also provided the floral and vegetative patterns for textiles, wallpaper, and decorative objects. Domestic gardens revived the seclusion, compactness, and ordered ornamental planting beds of the medieval *hortus conclusus* (enclosed garden), and, as Iris Lauterbach shows in her essay in this volume, were represented accordingly in paintings that used medieval iconography. After the revolutions of 1848, public life revived, but in Europe, as in the United States, middle-class women often remained confined to the (suburban) garden, while their breadwinning husbands conducted business in the city. In the United States, Andrew Jackson Downing's concern that the American people needed to settle and counteract the frontier "spirit of unrest" promoted gardens and suburban living, invariably assigning women the role of housekeepers and homemakers.[135] Even in the early American public urban parks, conservative park designers and reformers strove to retain women and children in a quasi-domestic realm. As Massey (Schenker) has shown, parks included gendered public space. A case in point is the Dairy, opened in Central Park in 1871, and designed "as a secluded, home-like refuge for women and children within the public landscape of the park," that offered healthy milk and provided sheltered areas for child play. Constructed at a time when women were indeed moving much more freely, and when demand for women's suffrage was becoming stronger every day,[136] the Dairy revealed the general disconnection between many designers' wishful thinking and intent, and the actual use and reception of public landscapes.

Like other parks in Europe and the United States at the time, Central Park was designed to serve all classes. However, its pastoral and picturesque scenery

FIGURE 0.6: Charlie Chaplin with Edna Purviance and a policeman in a scene of *In the Park*, produced by Essanay Film Manufacturing Co. *In the Park* © Roy Export Company Establishment.

catered to the interests of the middle classes, rather than to the interest in active recreation that was increasingly voiced by the working classes as the century came to an end. As Daniel Nadenicek illustrates for the United States in this volume, park creators tried to impose middle-class mores and values on the working classes, with varying success. In order to achieve the desired behavior, and prevent rallies and public gatherings that might threaten the social hierarchy, the authorities in charge established regulations for proper use, and employed park keepers to supervise and patrol the parks. In Central Park, Olmsted's regimen demanded that park keepers concluded three seven-mile rounds of the park, taking two hours and forty minutes each, with ten-minute breaks in between. Not surprisingly, then, in 1873 the *New York Daily Times* criticized the fact that Olmsted had "turned the keepers into 'human velocipedes' who could hardly stop to suppress crime because they were pre-occupied with completing their rounds."[137] Some of the first short silent film comedies produced in the second decade of the twentieth century show how ingrained park rules and park keepers were in the public perception, and how much they provoked ritual transgression, and symbolic inversion—"expressive behaviour, which inverts, contradicts, abrogates … cultural codes, values and norms."[138] In the 1915 Mack Sennett film "Caught in the Park," a public park provides the setting for a number of slapstick scenes with Sydney Chaplin, whose character—a bored "sporty husband" sitting on a park bench with his "plain wife" sleeping—steals a drink at a nearby bar, flirts with the lady of a young couple occupying another bench, and finally gets knocked out by his wife after she has overpowered the park keeper who appeared on the scene to reinstall order. In the same year, Syd's famed younger half-brother Charlie produced his comedy "In the Park." Charlie had made his debut as film director with "Twenty Minutes of Love," a short film that like his later "In the Park" was set entirely in Westlake Park (today MacArthur Park) in Los Angeles, and that involved Charlie the tramp performing his typical slapstick comedy amid a number of loving couples sitting on park benches. Chaplin frequently used park scenes in his short films, claiming that all he needed "to make a comedy is a park, a policeman and a pretty girl."[139] Policemen and park keepers in Chaplin's films, and in early short films like "Caught in the Park," "The Child Needs a Mother," (1915) and "The Magic of Spring" (1917) appear as unsuccessful upholders of moral standards.[140]

GARDENS FOR SURVIVAL AND PEACE

These early films provided lighthearted diversion shortly before many gardens and parks in the cities would be turned into plots for the cultivation of vegetables and fruit in support of the war effort. Gardens during the Age of Empire were not only a means of nation-building; they finally also became a means to defend the nations, and to defy their splitting-up and defeat. Early in the war, Britain passed a law that allowed untaxed land to be allotted to raise food. Following this and other examples in Europe, the United States founded the National War Garden Commission in 1917. Advertising war gardens with slogans like "Every Garden a Munition Plant," and "Can the Kaiser," the commission appealed to "Sow the Seeds of Victory," and provided the necessary instruction in pamphlets, books, cartoons, and show gardens, targeting women and children in particular.[141] In the United States and Germany, as in other warfaring countries, war gardening emerged out of, or merged with, earlier movements like the allotment and Schrebergarten movement in the German states, and the school gardening movement and vacant-lot cultivation in the United States. The school gardening movement, based on experiences in Europe, and initiated by social reformers and educators to produce "a better crop of boys

FIGURE 0.7: Poster by Maginel Wright Barney advertising the United States School Garden Army, 1919?. Library of Congress, Prints and Photographs Division, Washington, DC, LC-USZC4–3691.

and girls"[142] through teaching nature studies, nature appreciation, the natural sciences, and practical agricultural training on the local level, gained increasing support through pamphlets and reports from the Bureau of Education and the Department of Agriculture on state level, as soon as the United States began mobilizing for war.[143] In 1918, both departments constituted the United School Garden Army that was to spark and further encourage the children's enthusiasm with militaristic rhetoric, and turn what had initially been an educational movement for social, aesthetic, and moral uplift into a pragmatic movement fostering patriotism and food production. In support, President Woodrow Wilson claimed that, "to have children establish and maintain gardens 'is just as real and patriotic an effort as the building of ships or the firing of cannon.' "[144] Gardening, however, not only occupied those on the home fronts, but as Kenneth Helphand has shown, soldiers on the battlefields used their shovels both to dig trenches and to create gardens. Gardens were planted in and behind the trenches to provide sustenance and beauty in an otherwise depleted and devastated environment. While pictures of gardens at the front were used in the British press to trivialize and romanticize the war, in many cases the gardens facilitated the soldiers' survival. They offered hope, and "stood for peace, and home; resistance, [and] respite."[145] The importance attributed to nature, gardens, and gardening for the psychological health of soldiers led the German plant breeder Karl Foerster, as soon as he himself had returned from his military service in 1917, to publish a book on "flowers, earth, and sky" with the programmatic title *Vom Blütengarten der Zukunft* (*Of the Future Flower Garden*). Commissioned by the German Student Union, the book, in which he announced a new era of the German flower garden, was dedicated to and distributed among soldiers at the front and in military hospitals. Combining practical advice, lists of perennial plants for various garden locations with color and black-and-white photographs and emphatic plant descriptions, it was designed to give its readers hope for a peaceful future in their home country.[146]

Towards the end of the Age of Empire, in the life-threatening environment of World War I, gardens displayed the Horatian ideal—the essence of all gardens—in its purest form: their beauty and utility provided the soldiers at the front with a means and hope for survival. Despite the similar devastating experiences undergone by the people of the war-faring nations, however, the popular nineteenth-century belief voiced by Villiers-Stuart and others that, "Gardening, and its interwoven architecture, go to the very root of national life,"[147] lived on after the war. Like many of his compatriots, American landscape architect Fletcher Steele, known for the eclectic private gardens he designed for wealthy patrons on the Northeast coast, attempted to discern national characteristics in the design of the land. For Steele, "the little gardens of the world are very different from each other, just as the nations differ."[148] Corresponding to this belief, the war-faring countries chose distinctly different designs for their war cemetery grounds, although their soldiers were buried in uniform graves. While red roses functioned as symbols of French war cemeteries, and mixed borders were typical of the English grounds for mourning, German war cemeteries were designed to blend into the surrounding countryside, using what were considered "natural" and "German" materials, like wood and manually hewn Weser-sandstone. Influenced by the ideas and concepts developed for "heroes" groves during World War I, the German sites often resembled woodland cemeteries and were to represent a people that saw itself connected to nature and rooted in the soil. This way, the lost war was trivialized, and "naturalized," rendered as a natural, rather than as a human, disaster.[149]

Throughout the Age of Empire, the garden was used to mark territory, and to construct empires. It imbued places with identity, and made new places home. Gardens came in various forms and sizes; entire cities, whole regions, and nations were considered gardens, or were represented and symbolized in gardens. Gardens came to be understood as essential for the wellbeing of all people. They were made to live, to remember, and to console, but they were also used to confine, impose, and to subordinate.

CHAPTER ONE

Design

BRENT ELLIOTT

In the nineteenth century, the accepted styles of garden design changed with greater frequency than in any previous period. During the course of the century, stylistic change came to be accepted as a cultural norm. Whereas previous generations of architects, gardeners, and critics had tended to assume the existence of a correct style, in the nineteenth century the idea of a multiplicity of possible styles was increasingly accepted. The nineteenth century also witnessed the rise of a profession, which was variously called landscape gardening, landscape architecture, or simply garden design.

THE CONCEPTS OF STYLISTIC CHANGE AND DIVERSITY

Before the nineteenth century, the garden designer could hardly be said to have had a choice of styles available to work with. Stylistic variation, of course, existed within the framework of a general range of assumptions—the landscape garden allowed a significant range of differing approaches even within a single country; and it was always possible to incorporate features from a vanished, superseded, or exotic style—witness chinoiserie, or the discussions of whether classical or gothic was more appropriate for a garden ruin.[1] However, the idea that different styles were incommensurable but of equal importance only began to emerge in the closing decades of the eighteenth century.

On a theoretical level, this could be seen in the incipient cultural relativism of Johann Gottfried Herder, who maintained that each culture or period produced its own specific art forms, and should not be judged by the standards of other cultures or periods.[2] The early adumbrations of this principle generally took as their examples past (and previously despised) periods in European cultural history. It is therefore not surprising that on a more practical level, the new approach took shape in an antiquarianism that addressed the question of stylistic change. Sometimes the comparison went no further than the assertion that early gardens were formal and geometric to contrast with the untamed wilderness, and that once the countryside had been subdued and turned to agriculture, gardens, again by contrast, developed into informal landscapes. This argument was put forward by John Claudius Loudon in 1840,[3] and was repeated by garden designers such as Robert Marnock in England and Andrew Jackson Downing in America. By that time, however, more sophisticated accounts of stylistic variation had already been put forward.

Humphry Repton published an essay on the changes of style in garden history, and by Loudon's time the styles of the past, hitherto regarded as superseded, were being revived.[4] At the same time that the first chronological analysis of gothic architecture was being undertaken, garden history took its first steps toward becoming a discipline. Loudon's *Encyclopaedia of Gardening* (1822 and later editions) contains the best history of gardening before the mid-twentieth century. Serious-minded antiquarians such as Thomas Hudson Turner busied themselves tracking down the available documentation on mediaeval gardens. By mid-century, the editorial team of the weekly magazine *The Cottage Gardener* was praising the gardening literature of the seventeenth century as superior to that of the eighteenth, so that on a practical as well as a stylistic level the relevance of the more distant over the immediate past was being asserted.

The landscape garden was repudiated in varying degrees by the new generation of gardeners after the Napoleonic wars. Already before the end of the eighteenth century, writers such as Uvedale Price regretted the destruction of older formal gardens to make way for landscape gardens. By the 1830s, Loudon was arguing that surviving formal gardens should be preserved as national monuments, and at various estates the formal terraces destroyed by Capability Brown and his coevals were being replaced.[5]

This effort was initially confined to Great Britain. While, in the other arts, forms of cultural relativism began to appear from the 1790s onward, the arrival of the landscape garden in Europe was too recent a phenomenon to be overthrown quickly. In France, the obliteration of seventeenth- and early eighteenth-century parterres gathered momentum after the Revolution, and was still continuing when the first experiments at restoration were made in the 1830s.It has been estimated that ninety percent of parterres allegedly designed by Le Nôtre and still visible today are nineteenth- or twentieth-century restorations.[6] Since the *jardin anglais* had never completely excluded the use of formal elements in the immediate vicinity of the house, it was able to gradually accommodate the return of some degree of formality without overt conflict. For example, the layouts of Adolphe Alphand, the chief designer of the mid-century Paris parks, owed much to the tradition of the *jardin anglais*, but in his book on the Paris parks he made a case for Le Nôtre's gardens as a step in the development of naturalism in the garden, a compromise between the geometric rigor of his predecessors and the liberation of nature that followed.[7] Similarly, in Germany, the *Landschaftsgarten* was able to absorb a number of experiments in formal bedding, as shown in Pückler-Muskau's *Andeutungen über Landschaftsgärtnerei* (1834), before the arrival of more geometric layouts from England in the 1860s.[8] Italy had been one of the last European countries to adopt the landscape garden. The first important book was Ercole Silva's *Dell' arte dei giardini inglesi,* published in 1801, only a few years before the first Italianate-revival terrace was designed at Wilton House. In Italy, the surviving Renaissance garden at Pratolino, near Florence, was anglicized as late as 1822.[9]

HISTORICAL REVIVALISM AND GARDEN STYLES

The restoration of superseded garden styles passed through three distinct, if overlapping, stages in Britain. Repton had declared that before the arrival of the landscape garden, English gardens had been predominantly Italian in inspiration, so it is not surprising that the first revivalist style to become widely established was the Italianate. It had a long and leisurely development from the first decade of the century to the 1840s, when the series of country house gardens designed by Charles Barry attracted attention at Trentham, Staffordshire (as well as at Harewood, Yorkshire, and Shrubland Park, Suffolk). In the 1850s, Prince Albert gave the style the royal seal of approval by having an Italianate house and garden built at Osborne on the Isle of Wight. Thereafter, and until the last quarter of the century, the majority of new gardens designed in Britain was Italianate in style.[10]

Repton had also declared that the French style of Louis XIV and the Dutch style of William III were merely variants of the Italian, so that, consequently, both styles were being experimented with by the 1840s. The French style was

FIGURE 1.1: Trentham, Staffordshire. Garden by [Sir] Charles Barry. Retouched chromolithograph. From E. Adveno Brooke, *Gardens of England*, 1856–57. Royal Horticultural Society, Lindley Library.

primarily associated with a single designer, William Andrews Nesfield, and it peaked and declined more sharply. It was only after Nesfield's landscaping of the Royal Botanic Gardens, Kew, that his country house work attracted the attention of an initially skeptical press. By 1860 he was being acclaimed as the leading garden designer in the country, but by 1870 the enthusiasm for his style was already fading. He lived to see some of his high-profile gardens being replaced. Nesfield's work was primarily identified with the box-and-gravel parterre, which after his death was derogatively described in the press as a French style.[11]

The "Dutch" style was primarily identified in the English imagination with topiary. The first experiment in reviving topiary was made by Repton in the gate lodge garden at Woburn Abbey. By the time topiary had become widely popular, its Dutch associations had been largely replaced by medieval and Tudor ones. At Elvaston Castle, Derbyshire, a garden had been created using hedged enclosures for the segregation of different architectural or horticultural themes, as shown in Figure 1.2. After it had been opened to the public in the early 1850s, architectural topiary quickly spread across the country. The open prospect had been

Topiary work at Elvaston Castle. The Yew Garden.

FIGURE 1.2: Topiary at Elvaston Castle. Wood engraving. From James Veitch and Sons, *Manual of Coniferae*, 1883. Royal Horticultural Society, Lindley Library.

a characteristic of both the Italian and French styles, and the idea of a garden without extended views was greeted with horror in certain circles. In 1848, for example, John Lindley of the Horticultural Society published a paper denouncing the Elizabethan revival in architecture, and arguing that the garden ought to reflect the surrounding landscape rather than the style of the house. But by the 1870s, enclosed garden spaces, whether achieved by hedges or walls, had been widely accepted. Hidcote, begun in 1908, and sometimes claimed to be the most influential English garden of the twentieth century, was very much a garden in the Elvaston mode.[12]

As historical revivalism became more established in Britain, it developed a nationalistic emphasis. The styles which in the first half of the century had been seen in terms of different national traditions (Italian, French, Dutch) were reinterpreted in the last quarter of the century in terms of the chronology of styles in England: medieval, Elizabethan, and "English Renaissance."[13]

Elsewhere in Europe, the development of historical revivalism followed a similar trajectory, but with a generation's delay. In France, the restoration of Le Nôtre's parterres began on a small scale in the 1830s, and only in the last quarter of the century, Le Nôtre's reputation once again began to rise. The

FIGURE 1.3: Parterre at the Jardin du Carrousel, Paris. Photograph from *Le Jardin*, 1909. Royal Horticultural Society, Lindley Library.

introduction of English-style patterned bedding in the 1870s led some horticulturists to a renewed appreciation of the *parterre de broderie*.[14] Garden designers such as Édouard André, who had been initially identified with the modified landscape approach of Alphand and the Paris parks, increasingly turned to seventeenth-century precedents in their designs.[15] Two major restoration projects in the 1890s highlighted the return to favor of Le Nôtre and French classical design: Vaux-le-Vicomte and Versailles, both largely the work of the father and son, Henri and Achille Duchêne.[16] But perhaps the most rigorous restoration was the Le Nôtre-style parterre at the Jardin du Carrousel, seen in Figure 1.3, laid out in 1909 by Dubois, the head gardener of the Tuileries.[17] By the time of Le Nôtre's tercentennial in 1913, he was once again being claimed as the greatest French gardener.[18]

Historical revivalism, and the resulting increased range of stylistic choices, followed a similar course elsewhere on the continent. The 1860s and 1870s formed a transitional period in which the English landscape garden began to be widely perceived as out of fashion. Italy was one of the last countries to become actively involved in the revival of its own national garden style. Ironically, it was in large part English expatriates creating villa gardens on the Italian peninsula who helped to promote the revival of the Italian Renaissance garden.[19]

THE RISE OF THE PROFESSIONAL GARDEN DESIGNER

At the beginning of the nineteenth century, there were no formal professional qualifications and no recognized program of training for garden designers. In all European countries, garden designers had, until the eighteenth century, emerged from one of three categories. First, there were architects, who treated the design of a garden as an additional element of the house. Until the arrival of the English landscape garden, this was a normal extension of the architect's remit, and the geometric layout and architectural details of the garden were often made to match those of the house. Examples during the seventeenth and eighteenth centuries ranged from Nicodemus Tessin in Sweden to Luigi Vanvitelli at Caserta, but even the pioneers of the landscape garden, such as William Kent, were commissioned as architects before they undertook landscape designs. A second group consisted of nurserymen. While most nurserymen in the seventeenth and eighteenth centuries simply supplied plants or engaged in planting, a few, such as George London and Henry Wise of the Brompton Park Nursery, also designed gardens.[20] A third group comprised estate owners, like the Hoare family of Stourhead, or their gardeners, whose work was generally confined to the garden they owned or were employed on. However, there were cases of gardeners who achieved such recognition that they were asked to undertake multiple commissions: royal gardeners such as André Mollet in the mid-seventeenth century, who transferred from the Tuileries to St James's Palace, and Le Nôtre, whose services were shared among the French nobility. The most famous of English garden designers of the eighteenth century, Capability Brown began his career as a gardener at various estates in Northumberland. Brown was the first garden designer to operate a garden design consultancy that did not depend on a nursery or an architectural practice. Eventually, he himself became involved in architectural designs, without having an architect's training.[21]

In the 1780s, a figure emerged outside of any of these traditional groupings. Humphry Repton, a failed businessman, announced in 1788 that he intended to become Capability Brown's successor. His training consisted, first, of reading the growing literature on garden making, and second, of some practical experience as a land agent.[22] With this background, it is not surprising that Repton became famous above all for his marketing strategy, as seen in his Red Books.[23] Repton made a practice of presenting his design proposals in a manuscript volume for the estate owner, with before-and-after views of his proposed improvements illustrated by the use of "slides," flaps of paper that could be folded down to reveal the detail underneath. He produced more than 400 of these Red Books, which he insisted should never be printed, so that they would always remain unique specimens in the possession of the respective client and landowner. He did, however, use the same principle in his printed works, large portions of which were extracted from the Red Books, and so the device of the slide became known to a wider audience.[24] Other garden designers, such as Loudon, Lewis Kennedy, and Nesfield, copied the idea, and produced imitation Red Books during the 1820s and 1830s.[25]

Brown had called himself an "improver"; Repton called himself a landscape gardener. Most British designers during the nineteenth century adopted the latter title. The term *architecte-paysagiste* had been introduced by Jean-Marie Morel in 1804, but was not adopted by others, and it is uncertain whether Morel's usage was remembered when Édouard André described himself as an *architecte-paysagiste* in 1879.[26] The phrase "landscape architecture" appeared in the title of Loudon's edition of Repton's collected writings: *The Landscape Gardening and Landscape Architecture of Humphry Repton* (1840), but was not defined in the text. A few years later in America, Downing used the phrase in his *Treatise on the Theory and Practice of Landscape Gardening* (1850), but only to refer to architecture within a landscape setting—in other words, the country house and its appurtenances. But the term was adopted by his self-proclaimed successors, Calvert Vaux and Frederick Law Olmsted, who in applying for the commission for Central Park, New York, described themselves as landscape architects. The phrase was still not widely adopted, and references in American publications of the late nineteenth century emphasize its French origins. However, by the time the American Society of Landscape Architects was founded in 1899, French usage was no longer being pointed to as a justification. From America, the term gradually spread back to England. Patrick Geddes and Thomas Mawson adopted "landscape architect" as their title around the turn of the century, but as late as 1913 the prestigious gardening writer W. J. Bean still used the term "landscape gardener" to describe Olmsted and André, while naming William Goldring as their professional equivalent in Britain.[27]

As the new discipline grew, its practitioners were recruited from a wider range of backgrounds than in previous centuries, and sometimes found their commissions in new ways. Architects continued to produce plans for gardens, Charles Barry being the most notable example in Britain in the first half of the century; but architects' work was increasingly confined to gardens attached to the house, and they did not figure significantly as creators of the new municipal parks and other public landscapes. By the end of the century, the "architect's garden" was perceived, at least by its critics, as a stylistic type, associated with Reginald Blomfield's demand for archaeological accuracy in the recreation of seventeenth- and early eighteenth-century designs.[28] The trend for nurserymen to become actively involved in design grew slowly throughout the century. With the rising number of small suburban villa gardens, the nurseries that provided their plants were increasingly called on to carry out the design work as well. By the end of the century, probably most large nurseries also had landscape contractors; most of these have left little published record behind, though an occasional designer such as Simeon Marshall, who designed gardens for the Backhouse nursery in York, attracted notice in the press.[29] On the continent, and in America, the rising profession of forestry provided a training system that yielded some important designers; but in Britain, despite calls for professional training for foresters, the forestry industry remained in private hands. There, the country estate managers and important foresters were likely to emerge from the garden staff.[30] The majority of garden designers and landscape architects continued to emerge from the ranks of professional gardeners.

THE TRAINING OF GARDENERS

The phrase "professional gardeners" could be misleading, however; there was no professional body for gardeners, no organized or regulated training scheme, and above all, little that could be regarded as public recognition of professional status. While some gardeners had enjoyed fame, wealth, and reputation in the past, the only ones whose fame long survived them were royal gardeners, superintendents of botanic gardens, and gardeners whose books kept their names alive. In the 1760s, one of the most famous gardeners was Thomas Mawe, head gardener to the Duke of Leeds. When the young John Abercrombie sought a publishing partner for a gardening manual, he ingratiated himself with Mawe in order that his fame might be a good marketing ploy. And he succeeded: *Every Man His Own Gardener*, officially by Mawe and Abercrombie, went through at least thirty editions over the course of a century. Mawe's status is indicated by an anecdote told about their meeting: "When introduced to Mawe, whom he had never before seen, poor Abercrombie (as he used facetiously to narrate) encountered a gentleman so bepowdered, and so bedaubed with gold lace, that he thought he could be in the presence of no less a personage than the Duke himself."[31] Nothing survives today of Mawe's gardening, and his contemporary fame has faded so that we even lack reliable dates for him. Mawe's glory certainly did nothing for his profession—or trade, as most at the time would have called it. When, in the 1840s, the young D. T. Fish—later a famous head gardener at Hardwicke Hall, Suffolk—was offered a salary of thirty pounds for his first position as a gardener, he exploded: "Why couple the knowledge and culture of professional men with the rewards of a livery servant?" But being described as "professional" at that time was only an ambition for gardeners, not a fact.[32]

This changed, at least for a while, around the middle of the nineteenth century. The rise of periodical literature written by and for gardeners drew publicity to their accomplishments. In the hands of its pioneer, John Claudius Loudon, the gardening press became an instrument to campaign for improved wages, education, lodging, and professional recognition for gardeners. Gardening journalism eventually became a means of entry into the world of garden designers. William Goldring worked on William Robinson's magazine *The Garden* for three years, visiting and reporting on important gardens around the country, before launching his career as a landscape gardener. The gardening fraternity had a figurehead in the person of Joseph Paxton, pictured in Figure 1.4, who began his career as an under-gardener at the Horticultural Society's garden at Chiswick, was appointed head gardener at Chatsworth at the age of twenty-three, began designing glasshouses and gardens for people other than his employer in the 1830s, and for public corporations in the 1840s, was knighted for creating the Crystal Palace, and ended his days as a Member of Parliament and a railway millionaire.[33] His rise in social status met with some resentment in conservative circles. An aristocratic commentator on the Crystal Palace sneered, "A break down was all but certain, when a gardener dropped in and suggested a big conservatory ... Of course toadies and wonder-mongers were not wanting to make the lucky hit of a clever man ridiculous by fulsome praise."[34] Even if only few gardeners could hope to reach the heights of wealth and power that Paxton did, all could hope to be pulled a certain distance in his wake. By the 1880s, the *Journal of Horticulture* could say of Heckfield Place, Hampshire, that it boasted two national figures: the Speaker of the House of Commons and his gardener William Wildsmith, who was famous as an innovative horticulturist and a writer.[35] The non-horticultural press might not have seconded such a claim, but it is evidence of the claim to professional status being made within the gardening world.

Genuine professional status involved a recognized training program, however, and until the late nineteenth century, the training of gardeners was largely a matter of apprenticeship. Some gardens, like the Edinburgh Botanic Gardens under James M'Nab, Chatsworth under Paxton, and Heckfield Place under Wildsmith, were known as good "teaching gardens." An apprenticeship at such an establishment was an impressive addition to a gardener's curriculum vitae. The first official training scheme was established in 1822 by the Horticultural

FIGURE 1.4: Sir Joseph Paxton (1803–
1865). Carte-de-visite photograph,
1860s. Royal Horticultural Society,
Lindley Library.

Society of London at its new garden at Chiswick. Apprentice gardeners would
be trained in every department of the garden. When their training had been
completed, they would be recommended to positions in important gardens. Due
to Chiswick's international fame, the great German landscape gardener Friedrich Ludwig Sckell sent his son Carl August there to train.[36] After less than a
decade, however, financial problems caused the discontinuation of the formal
training scheme. Meanwhile, in the German states in 1824, Peter Joseph Lenné
had founded the longer-running Landesbaumschule und Gärtnerlehranstalt, the
major center for the training of German gardeners, at Potsdam.[37] In England,
although the park designer Alexander McKenzie expressed his hope of setting
up a school of garden design associated with Alexandra Palace in north London,
it was left to Paxton's protégé Edward Milner to establish the Crystal Palace
School of Gardening in 1880. Milner and his son Henry Ernest Milner succes-
sively administered the school until the early years of the twentieth century.[38]
The Royal Horticultural Society had meanwhile become involved in organizing

national examinations for gardeners. Eventually, after moving to a new garden at Wisley, it was able to repeat its Chiswick experiment. By establishing the Wisley School of Horticulture in 1907, it began a century of practical training.[39]

Part of the claim for professional status was based on the increasing range of skills that the country house gardener was expected to demonstrate. The revolution in glasshouse technology that Loudon began in the 1810s meant that by mid-century, gardeners were expected not only to manage plants growing under glass, but also to supervise, build, and sometimes design the structures and technology of the glasshouse. Accordingly, D. T. Fish, in 1872, asserted that, "To build new or repair or rebuild old houses is a sure and certain part of the duties of the modern gardener."[40] A long-term consequence of this state of affairs was that twentieth-century historians, at a time when the reputation of Victorian gardening had sunk to its nadir, transferred the figures they respected into other disciplines. Paxton was long referred to as an engineer by architectural historians, and Jean-Pierre Barillet-Deschamps can still be found on internet sites today described as an architect, though his training and posts were resolutely horticultural.[41]

CHANGING STYLES AND THE ROLE
OF THE HEAD GARDENER

The claim by gardeners for professional status was closely tied to the role that head gardeners on country estates played in the development of gardening styles in the nineteenth century. Despite the rise of garden design as a profession, for the last three-quarters of the century it was the head gardener who received the greatest publicity and prestige for determining the style of the garden.

In the 1830s, Loudon declared that there were two ways of making a garden into a work of art: by formal or geometric design, or by the use of exotic planting, that, as anyone familiar with the local flora would realize, owed its position in the garden to the hand of man.[42] This statement in itself represents a decisive rejection of the English landscape style, the rhetoric of which always emphasized its dependence on the imitation of nature. While the rise of garden design as a profession may be regarded as based on Loudon's first strategy, formal design, the rise of the head gardener was based on exotic planting.

Bedding—the temporary arrangement of flowering plants in beds for ornamental effect—had a long history before the nineteenth century. The parterres of French chateaux during the reign of Louis XIV relied heavily on seasonal changes of flowers in the beds.[43] During the heyday of the landscape garden, when the flower garden was kept in seclusion so as not to interfere with the image of pastoral countryside, the composition of bedding schemes was seldom the topic of

FIGURE 1.5: Title page of the first volume of Loudon's *Gardener's Magazine*, 1826. Royal Horticultural Society, Lindley Library.

essays. Only unpublished manuscript sources, therefore, provide us with information about William Mason's proposal in the 1780s, for what would later be called ribbon borders in red, white, and blue.[44] But beginning with Repton, and his later motto that "Gardens are works of art, not of nature," the return of flower gardens to the main view from the house meant that bedding schemes began to attract more attention. The years after the Napoleonic wars saw a great increase in the number of foreign species of plants being introduced into Europe, a large proportion of which were half-hardy, requiring glasshouse protection during the winter, but capable of being planted outdoors for the summer season.[45]

The new importance of bedding schemes might not have assumed the dimensions it did, had it not been for the arrival of the horticultural press. In 1826, Loudon launched his *Gardener's Magazine*, which soon became a monthly publication. For the first time, there was a magazine in which gardeners could engage in correspondence on horticultural matters, and publicize their achievements. Earlier horticultural periodicals such as the *Allgemeines Teutsches*

Garten-Magazin (from 1804) and the *Transactions of the Horticultural Society* (from 1807) only published papers, not correspondence, and they avoided debate. Within a few years of Loudon's venture, there were rival gardening magazines in Britain publishing on a monthly or quarterly basis, and the continent followed quickly: in France the *Revue Horticole* was launched in 1829. In 1837, the first weekly gardening newspaper in Britain, the *Gardeners' Gazette*, was published. This was rivaled and succeeded in 1841 by the *Gardeners' Chronicle*, founded by Paxton and John Lindley. It remained the most important gardening magazine until the 1960s. The *Chronicle* also had significant rivals: the *Cottage Gardener*, later the *Journal of Horticulture*, from 1848; Shirley Hibberd's *Gardeners' Magazine*, from 1865; and William Robinson's *The Garden*, from 1871. By the end of the century, it was common for the owners of major country house gardens to subscribe to two or three of these specialist weeklies for the benefit of their staff.[46] On the continent, the weekly gardening newspaper emerged more slowly. *Koch's Wochenschrift* began in 1858, and *Le Jardin* not until 1887.

The development of horticultural weeklies paralleled the new gardening practices. Bedding schemes made it possible for the head gardener to change the appearance of the garden on an annual, and eventually a seasonal, basis. Summer bedding—planting for the period between June and September—was the original focus of attention, but by the 1860s experiments in spring and autumn bedding were being loudly trumpeted, and, in municipal parks at least, year-round bedding was possible by the end of the century. The question of appropriate planting, especially from the point of view of acceptable color combinations, was heatedly debated: John Caie, head gardener at the Duke of Bedford's London estate, published the first articles on color schemes for the flower garden in Loudon's *Gardener's Magazine* in the late 1830s. Caie's views, which entailed the juxtaposition of large masses of contrasting colors, were broadly accepted by mid-century. In the 1860s, the high contrast was toned down, and foliage planting became popular instead. In 1868, the term "carpet bedding" was coined for patterns created with low-growing foliage plants, and during the 1870s, more gardens were described in the press for their carpet bedding than for their flowers. This fashion was succeeded by a return to a modified version of the bedding system. On the continent, it was not until the 1860s that a similar excitement over the new forms of English bedding (variously called *mosaiculture* and *Teppichgärtnerei*, and mixing together genres of bedding that the English regarded as stylistically distinct) influenced the press. During the mid-nineteenth century, herbaceous borders were of secondary interest, but by the close of the century they came to take the central role that parterre bedding had held in previous decades.[47]

Bedding and its related forms of flower gardening dominated the specialist periodical literature in Britain up to the First World War, and guaranteed head

FIGURE 1.6: Bedding scheme by John Caie. Chromolithograph from the *Florist's Journal*, 1841. Royal Horticultural Society, Lindley Library.

gardeners a limelight that left professional garden designers somewhat in the shade. When head gardeners and park superintendents such as Joseph Paxton (Chatsworth), William Barron (Elvaston Castle), Edward Kemp (Birkenhead Park), and Alexander McKenzie (Alexandra Palace Park) launched their careers as garden designers, whether or not they continued their supervisory roles at their respective gardens, they were guaranteed a more respectful and attentive press than were architects whose practice included garden design. William Robinson used the term "architects' gardens" as a pejorative term for gardens whose main qualities lay in a design on paper rather than in planting, while the nascent profession of garden design did its best to dismiss the claims and status of gardeners.[48]

The twentieth century saw the somewhat dismissive term "plantsmen's gardens" applied to gardens in which, it was alleged, the ad hoc arrangement of the plant collection either ignored or spoiled the clarity of the design. The role of architects in garden design was never downplayed on the continent to the extent it was in Britain, and head gardeners' designs remained a secondary source of material for the French and German gardening press.

While the flower garden remained the primary focus of publicity in the horticultural press, it was not the only aspect of the garden that demonstrated the skills of the head gardener. The rock garden, considered primarily as a decorative structure, increased in importance during the first half of the nineteenth century; as a place for growing exotic alpine plants, it attracted further attention from the 1850s onwards, reaching its peak of popularity in the 1920s and 1930s.[49] As a result of the cultivation of hardy hybrid water-lilies at Latour-Marliac's nursery in France in the 1880s, ornamental water gardens became fashionable.[50] The principles of color combination, first proved in the flower garden, began to be applied to the wider landscape in the 1870s. Trees and shrubs were grouped in masses of single colors. The twentieth-century fashions for autumn color and the flowering shrub garden grew out of this trend.[51]

As a result of the partisanship of William Robinson, whose *English Flower Garden* went through fifteen editions between 1883 and 1933, it became customary to treat gardens as sequences of particular genres of planting. Robinson's views were spread in France by Édouard André, a contributor to his magazine *The Garden*, and in Germany and America by the attention paid to the Arts and Crafts movement. Wilhelm Miller, the founder of the magazine *Country Life in America*, had an immense influence as the founder of the "Prairie school" of landscape gardening. He modeled his book *What England Can Teach Us about Gardening* (1911) on *The English Flower Garden* and cited Robinson enthusiastically. In Germany before the First World War, a group of nurserymen and gardeners, including Karl Foerster, Graf Silva Tarouca, and Willy Lange, brought a similar influence to bear on garden planting, with greater or lesser degrees of acknowledgement. Thus, Robinson's way of categorizing gardens (as flower, rock, and water, etc.) dominated the international literature on the subject at the beginning of the twentieth century.[52] This perceived subdivision of the garden in terms of planting rather than architectural style remained an enduring legacy of the three phases of the gardener's ascendancy in the press.

The twentieth century was to see the status and authority of the garden designer increase, while social and economic changes reduced those of the head gardener. But the notions of stylistic change, of the availability of a range of styles to choose from, and of style seen in terms of planting choice rather than architecture and layout, had all become established by the beginning of the century, and underpinned further developments in the twentieth century.

CHAPTER TWO

Types of Gardens

BRENT ELLIOTT

By the beginning of the nineteenth century, the function and form of many old surviving gardens had changed, and previous typologies of gardens were being eroded. Before the nineteenth century, gardens were classified according to the social status of their owners (royalty versus gentry), and depending on their function for institutions that by the nineteenth century had already vanished or were disappearing (monastic gardens, physic gardens). As the middle class gained influence, the layout, size, and function of gardens became their distinguishing characteristics.

The fate of Kew and Versailles, probably the two most famous royal gardens in Europe in the late eighteenth century, exemplifies these changes. Kew, a royal estate that had been partially superseded in use, had been developed as a botanic garden under the semi-official jurisdiction of Sir Joseph Banks. Kew was the first British botanic garden to send plant collectors overseas. After Banks's death it had declined, and in 1840 proposals were made to discard the botanical collections and turn Kew into a kitchen garden for the royal family. The plants were privately offered to the Horticultural Society, the matter was leaked to Parliament, and the result was a committee of inquiry, which determined that the botanic garden should be handed over to the government and maintained from public funds as a national botanic garden.[1] In contrast, Versailles, as the symbol of discredited royal power, was turned into a national museum, and the gardens became a public park. The royal kitchen garden, the

Potager du Roi, continued to fulfill the purpose of market production, and the establishment of the École Nationale d'Horticulture at Versailles in 1867 helped to ensure its survival as a major training establishment. The parterres were reduced for ease of maintenance, until Henri Duchêne undertook the first attempt at their restoration toward the end of the century.[2]

THE DOMESTIC GARDEN

In 1838, John Claudius Loudon, the most important theorist of gardens in early nineteenth-century Britain, proposed a classification of gardens in his *Suburban Gardener and Villa Companion*. His categories were based not directly on social status but on size, the accompanying variables of distance from house to gates, and on the presence of a separate kitchen garden.[3] A "first-rate" garden—his example was a deliberately chosen suburban garden at Wimbledon House—was bigger than ten acres. A "second-rate" garden (example: the garden of Louisa Lawrence, a famous promoter of horticulture and exhibitor of plants, at Drayton Green, Middlesex) encompassed two to ten acres. A "third-rate" garden (example: Hendon Rectory, in what is now part of north London) was upwards of an acre, and a "fourth-rate" garden was under an acre (example: Loudon's own garden in Bayswater, then a suburb of London). Using this criterion reduced the difference between a royal palace and a semi-detached house in the suburbs to one of scale. While Loudon's hierarchy largely reflected differences in economic status, it did not necessarily reflect social stratification: the owner of a "first-rate" garden in the country might also own a "fourth-rate" garden in central London. This potentially more democratic hierarchy of gardens naturally suited the American commentator Andrew Jackson Downing. Downing confined his list of major gardens to those of judges and senators, whose gardens could be taken as models for smaller plots without any modification of principles.[4]

The qualities of the domestic garden can best be examined by looking at the "first-rate" garden since the "second-" to "fourth-rate" gardens can be understood as reductions of the "first-rate" entailed by economic necessities or characteristics of the site. The country house garden, then, was divided into four parts: pleasure ground, kitchen garden, orchard, and glasshouses. Farms and forests were managed separately. Garden histories usually deal with the pleasure grounds as the part of the garden that exhibited the greatest stylistic diversity. However, pleasure grounds were optional and an estate could exist without them. The kitchen garden and its related divisions were the principal focus of the country house garden, for families needed to eat before they could devote their attention to leisure, and the country house, by definition

FIGURE 2.1: Hendon Rectory. Woodcut from Loudon's *Gardener's Magazine*, vol. 14, 1838. Royal Horticultural Society, Lindley Library.

distant from the market towns, had to be self-sufficient. Glasshouses, ranging from forcing-houses in the kitchen garden to ornamental conservatories, were still few at the beginning of the nineteenth century; kitchen gardens contained frames for tender crops or for forcing crops out of season. Glass buildings in gardens multiplied only after the characteristic nineteenth-century iron-framed glasshouse had been developed. Then, a distinct staffing team became necessary for their maintenance and upkeep. A typical late-nineteenth-century country house garden included an ornamental conservatory and possibly specialist houses for particular categories of plants, as well as glasshouses for forcing and growing the plants used in bedding. Additional houses enabled the cultivation of peaches and apricots, pineapples, and other non-hardy fruits.[5]

The smaller domestic gardens differed primarily in their functional subdivisions. Loudon's "first-rate" garden had a park or farm accompanying it. The "second-rate" garden had no park or farm, but a separate walled kitchen garden. The "third-rate" garden encompassed an unenclosed kitchen garden. In the "fourth-rate" garden, Loudon did not differentiate between functions.

Plans for middle-class suburban villas in the 1830s and 1840s show small kitchen gardens, sometimes with glass copings for fruit, at the end of the garden furthest from the main views.[6] Gardening manuals for the suburban villa began to appear in the second quarter of the nineteenth century. In the third quarter, gardening magazines directed at villa owners rather than professional gardeners began to be published. A consistent piece of advice they offered was that it was impractical to try to copy with limited means the expensive and labor-intensive effects achieved in country house gardening. Nonetheless, each horticultural fashion made popular in the "first-rate" gardens was adopted in turn in the "second-" and "third-rate" gardens. In the 1870s, William Robinson, the most prominent gardening journalist of the late nineteenth century, attempted to change the course of suburban gardening by recommending planting schemes that mimicked the effects of fashionable horticulture with hardy plants. However, not even Robinson succeeded in turning householders' minds from the pursuit of the prevailing fashions.[7]

Loudon's "fourth-rate" gardens can be divided into two separate types: the town garden and the cottage garden. Although both were under an acre in size, they were characterized by different environmental conditions, purposes, and economic circumstances. House owners in urban centers had few opportunities for gardening in the fashionable modes. Because of smaller lot sizes, urban gardens tended to remain geometric in design even during the heyday of the landscape garden. Some mansions and large rectories were exceptions from this development, but as towns expanded, an increasing proportion of what had been villa gardens was absorbed into the inner city. In urban centers, the communal gardens of housing developments, and garden squares—Edwardes Square in west London (1819) is an early example—provided the principal opportunities for informal gardening and horticultural display.[8] Easy access to markets in town centers meant that there was little need for kitchen gardening. Air pollution, the perennial concomitant of urban life, limited the possibilities for plant selection.[9] The town garden, thus, became a distinct garden type, for which a separate literature was developed in the last decades of the century.

SCIENTIFIC AND EXPERIMENTAL GARDENS

The physic or botanic garden requires special attention in this taxonomy. The distinction between the two emerged only in the eighteenth century, when plant collections began to be maintained for purely taxonomic purposes, instead of for the training of physicians and apothecaries. During the nineteenth century, the physic garden gradually lost its importance. Physicians relied less on medicinal plant knowledge and became more dependent on the developing pharmaceutical industry. Although medical schools and large teaching hospitals continued to appoint professors of botany into the twentieth century, physic gardens played a lesser role in medicinal research.[10]

The same trend held true in America. The first botanic garden in the United States, the Elgin Botanic Garden in New York, was founded in 1802 by a professor of medicine, David Hosack. By 1872, when the Arnold Arboretum was founded as the botanic garden for Harvard University, the medicinal purposes of plants had been forgotten. The taxonomic arrangement of plants was the guiding principle in Frederick Law Olmsted's design for the arboretum that was also to form a stylistic continuity with the "emerald necklace" of municipal parks he laid out for the Boston Parks Department.[11]

The earliest botanic gardens had geometric layouts, because the ability to group plants in compartments of limited size was a good teaching aid. The development of the landscape garden throughout the eighteenth century affected the design of botanic gardens. At Kew, it led to the grouping of trees on a larger scale than before. In botanic gardens established in the nineteenth century, the proportions of formal and landscaped areas varied according to the prevailing design fashions established in the larger domestic gardens. The Royal Botanic Gardens, Kew, may stand as an example. On the one hand, they fulfilled a scientific and imperial role: collecting information on plants of economic value growing throughout the British Empire. On the other hand, Kew mirrored the trends in garden design displayed in country house gardens of the time.[12] Botanic gardens had ceased to be stylistically different from other gardens.

The only significant visual element that continued to distinguish the botanic from the domestic garden was the grouping of plants. In some scientific gardens, however, even this was constrained by aesthetic considerations. In the 1820s, Loudon, for example, criticized the arboretum design at the Horticultural Society's experimental garden at Chiswick and emphasized the necessity of keeping taxonomic groups together for purposes of comparison, and placing them in close proximity to walks so that they could be easily studied and observed.[13] "Order beds" remained the botanic garden's version of the domestic flower garden. This principle characterized many plant collections even in the private sector, and some important botanic gardens began as country house estates whose owners had developed an enthusiasm for botany. Examples are Westonbirt (later the Forestry Commission's arboretum), Wakehurst Place (taken over by Kew as an arboricultural outstation), and the Villa Thuret at Antibes (which began as Gustave Thuret's private cactus collection before being taken over by the state after his death). In a parallel development,

Rothamsted, the estate of Sir John Bennet Lawes, who conducted experiments on plant growth and fertilizer trials, eventually became a research center for the Ministry of Agriculture.[14]

GARDENS FOR THE PEOPLE: COTTAGES AND ALLOTMENTS

Loudon's "fourth-rate" gardens covered an area from one perch (272.5 square feet) to one acre. The smallest gardens, most often belonging to the laboring classes, frequently did not even meet that space requirement. These gardens were divided into two categories: the cottage garden, forming the curtilage of a dwelling house; and the allotment at a distance from the house. The allotment was the subject of controversy, and is, therefore, better documented than is the cottage garden.

The private cottage garden's function was ambiguous. A number of manuals on the management of cottage gardens were published during the nineteenth century, and they were based on the assumption that the primary purpose of the garden was food production.[15] At the same time, however, many estate owners considered their estate villages showcases of their artistic taste, and had their head gardeners draw up ornamental planting schemes for them. Therefore, manuals such as Robert Adamson's *The Cottage Garden* of 1850 reveal that many cottagers were growing ornamental plants, whether the writers approved of this or not. By the end of the century, writers such as William Robinson and Gertrude Jekyll were promoting cottage gardens as flower gardens, in which the flowers were indiscriminately mixed rather than arranged in color schemes. Robinson, however, also used the term "cottage garden" to describe the gardens of small manor houses. This ambiguity allowed garden writers to assert that the cottage garden had survived from times before the Victorian period when gardens had become garish and architectural. The term "cottage garden" suggested an air of old times, although the style of floral gardening associated with it was largely a creation of the second quarter of the nineteenth century.[16]

Partly as a response to the enclosure movement and the resulting loss of open space, a few writers in the 1770s had begun to recommend that wasteland be made available for cultivation by the poor. During the Napoleonic Wars, landowners gradually took the advice and created allotments for the inhabitants of their parishes. Sir Thomas Bernard published a pamphlet, shown in Figure 2.2, describing how he had allotted a cottage and small garden to a laborer, who was thereafter able to grow his own food and never again had to apply for poor relief.[17] Throughout the nineteenth century, municipal authorities randomly experimented with the provision of allotments, which only became the norm in

AN
ACCOUNT
OF A
COTTAGE AND GARDEN,
NEAR TADCASTER.

WITH

OBSERVATIONS

UPON LABOURERS HAVING FREEHOLD COTTAGES
AND GARDENS,

AND UPON A PLAN FOR SUPPLYING COTTAGERS
WITH COWS.

PRINTED AT THE DESIRE OF THE SOCIETY
FOR BETTERING THE CONDITION, AND
INCREASING THE COMFORTS OF THE POOR.

LONDON:
PRINTED FOR T. BECKET, BOOKSELLER, PALL-MALL.
1797.
PRICE ONE SHILLING A DOZEN.

FIGURE 2.2: Sir Thomas Bernard, *An Account of a Cottage and Garden near Tadcaster*, 1797, title page. Royal Horticultural Society, Lindley Library.

the twentieth century. Most allotments were provided on private estates. Paternalistic Tories such as Benjamin Disraeli and his "Young England" movement considered the provision of allotments a revival of mediaeval practice and good cement for the social order. In contrast, Chartists such as Feargus O'Connor established a land company in order to lease allotments to applicants. While the Chartists' efforts failed, the Co-operative movement continued its work and became one of the major proponents of allotments into the twentieth century.[18]

The idea of the allotment was exported from England onto the continent in the last decades of the century. In France, Albert Maumené and others spearheaded a campaign for workingmen's gardens (*jardins ouvriers*) in the 1890s, and the Société National d'Horticulture de France began to address the matter at its meetings. The best publicized philanthropic gesture was undertaken by a wealthy notary in Sceaux in 1900, who provided twenty-four garden plots, each measuring 150 to 200 square meters (1600 to 2000 square foot), for local families. Soon a charitable organization, L'Oeuvre Marguerite Renaud, and a horticultural school to improve the gardeners' skills were established. An international conference on *jardins ouvriers* was held in Paris in 1903, and an exhibition was staged at the Grand Palais in 1906.[19] Similar initiatives were undertaken in Germany and Scandinavia. In Leipzig, *Kleingärten* developed out of children's play areas that had been set up by Dr. Ernst Innozenz Hauschild in the 1860s, and in Sweden, the first allotment gardens were established in Malmö in 1895, and in Stockholm in 1904.[20]

GARDENS FOR THE PEOPLE: PUBLIC PARKS

The provision of allotments and cottage gardens for the poor to use for growing food was one thing. Greater and more immediate attention was devoted to the provision of ornamental gardens as areas for public leisure. "Till lately," wrote Loudon in 1822, "Hyde Park, at London, and a spot called The Meadows, near Edinburgh were the only equestrian gardens in Britain, and neither were well arranged."[21] Late-eighteenth-century public gardens in France and the German states, like Ange-Jacques Gabriel's public garden created in Bordeaux in the 1750s, and the Englischer Garten laid out in Munich thirty years later, had no significant municipal counterparts in England. The Royal Parks of London had always been accessible to the public under certain conditions, but Regent's Park, the first royal park created in the nineteenth century, was not opened to the public until 1841. Instead, commercially operated pleasure gardens like Vauxhall, Ranelagh, and Cremorne in London, provided public open space in a tradition going back to the 1660s. These pleasure gardens relied on music and entertainment rather than on horticulture to attract visitors, and all closed down during the course of the nineteenth century.[22]

Before most towns in the United Kingdom and elsewhere had municipal parks, they had cemeteries, and these served the purpose of public walks. The campaign to discontinue burials within urban centers and replace existing churchyards with extramural burial grounds began on the continent. Vienna may have been the pioneering city. In 1732, the city decreed the termination of the use of cathedral precincts for burial and authorized the creation of new cemeteries. As soon as there was no more space left, these early cemeteries were succeeded by extramural cemeteries under a new decree of 1784. The Cimetière de Père-Lachaise in Paris, which opened in 1804, achieved greater publicity than had any previous cemetery, and became the administrative, if not stylistic, model for many cemeteries that followed. Whether established by local authorities or by private companies, municipal cemeteries allowed the funeral rites of all denominations, and thus became a focus in the demand for religious liberty and anti-clericalism. In his manual on cemetery planning, Loudon advocated a grid layout and the restriction of tree planting to avenues and geometric layouts. Following the Burials Acts of 1850 and 1852, which ended churchyard burial in British cities and demanded the establishment of extramural cemeteries by the local authorities, cemeteries across the country were being laid out according to Loudon's guidelines. The stylistic evolution of the cemetery ran parallel to that of the public park.[23]

The years after the Napoleonic Wars saw a revival of trade, and a building boom that affected most European countries. In Britain, a Select Committee on Public Walks was convened in 1833 to discuss the disappearance of public open space as a result of the previous decade's building projects. One of the recommendations was the establishment of new royal parks in London to provide open space in the more congested districts. Two of these parks were constructed as planned: Battersea and Victoria Parks, both of which were quickly devolved onto the management of local authorities. Work on the third park, the proposed Albert Park in north London, stagnated, but the park was finally developed by the local authority and opened as Finsbury Park in 1869. A distinct mode of public park creation developed in the industrial cities of northern and midland England. There, a number of wealthy philanthropists financed the creation of publicly accessible open spaces, sometimes with educational aspirations. Joseph Strutt financed the creation of the Derby Arboretum, which opened in 1841 and was designed by John Claudius Loudon. Richard Vaughn Yates had Joseph Paxton lay out Prince's Park, Liverpool. Both parks levied entrance fees in their early years, but in the 1840s, the first parks

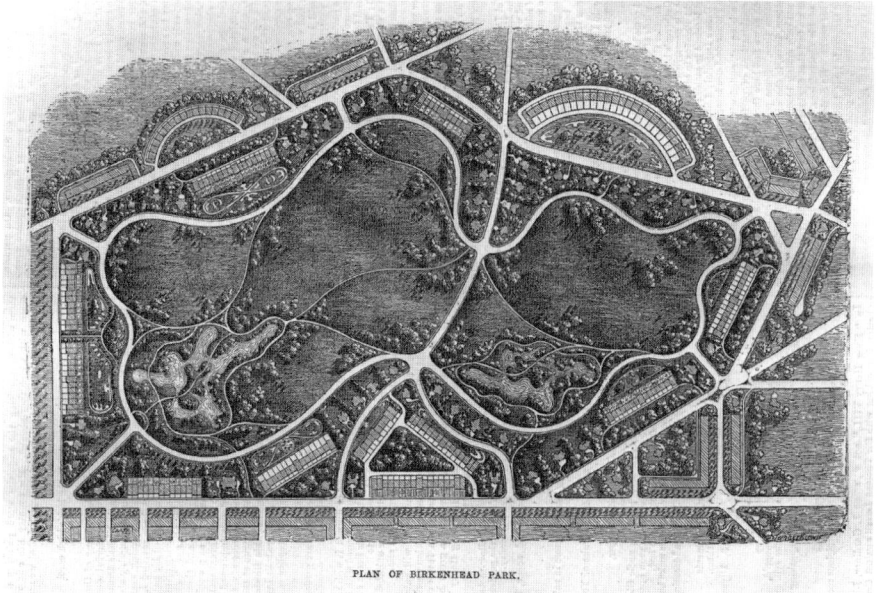

PLAN OF BIRKENHEAD PARK.

FIGURE 2.3: Plan of Birkenhead Park. From *The Garden*, vol. 10, 1876. Royal Horticultural Society, Lindley Library.

created by local authorities did not charge for admission. The corporation of Birkenhead commissioned Paxton to design Birkenhead Park in 1842; by the time the park was opened in 1847, three parks designed by Joshua Major had already been opened in Manchester and Salford. In the wake of these, the days of paid admission were numbered. In 1855, a court judgment finally ruled that Nottingham Corporation could not charge admission for its recently opened Nottingham Arboretum. Thereafter, the only parks to charge admission fees were those run by private companies—most notably, Crystal Palace Park. The design of the early parks continued in the landscape garden tradition, but soon a geometric and axial organization emerged that is best exemplified by Crystal Palace Park. This formal park provoked a backlash and a partial return to the informal landscape in some significant parks of the 1860s and 1870s.[24]

On the continent, the existing movement for the establishment of public walks grew stronger during the nineteenth century. The reduced threat of war after the Napoleonic era saw many walled towns either demolish their fortifications or turn them into public walks. When Lucca returned to its former status as an independent duchy after the Congress of Vienna, its enclosing walls were planted with trees. The unification of the German and Italian states later in the century helped to promote this trend, though a proposed peripheral park for Paris was never carried out.[25] The model of English parks also encouraged

FIGURE 2.4: Parc de la Tête d'Or, Lyon, a celebrated municipal park in France. Wood-engraving after Auguste Anastasi. From Arthur Mangin, *Les jardins*, 1867. Royal Horticultural Society, Lindley Library.

cities on the continent to develop urban parks. Many former royal and noble estates that had been swallowed by the suburbs, such as Parc Monceau in Paris, were turned into public urban parks. The parks that Adolphe Alphand and his colleagues created during the Second Empire in Paris were based on the tradition of the landscape park, but also incorporated formal design elements. The largest work created in this tradition was the Parc de la Tête d'Or in Lyon (1857–62), designed by the brothers Denis and Eugène Bühler. Both the English and the French park models were copied across Europe.[26] By the beginning of the twentieth century, the prevailing wisdom was summarized by the Commission d'Extension de Paris: "large areas planted with trees and shrubs in the middle of urban agglomerations are as indispensable to public hygiene as water and light."[27]

In the United States, the example of Birkenhead Park was used as a model by Frederick Law Olmsted, the most important and prolific American park designer. The free and open access for all citizens he experienced in Birkenhead provided a model for the social role of the park in the city. His first major commission, Central Park, New York, on which he collaborated with Calvert Vaux, provided a standard in both function and design for two generations of American parks from the 1860s to the early twentieth century. Olmsted worked all over the continent, from New York and Boston to San Francisco and Seattle, designing not only individual parks but, where possible, entire park systems that structured city development.[28]

The late nineteenth century saw a diversification of park types. Local authorities that lacked convenient open space for park development began to lay out small parks on limited sites. They bought up properties with large gardens and converted them into public parks (like Brockwell Park in south London, the first property acquired by the London County Council for park purposes), and rescued areas of natural beauty and turned them into parks run under governmental auspices (e.g. Hampstead Heath in London, Jesmond Dene, and part of the Sunderland coastline as an extension of Roker Park in Newcastle). The 1880s also saw the beginnings of the functional specialization of parks. In 1880, Stamford Park, Altrincham, and West Park, Wolverhampton, became the first parks laid out as sports parks, with subdivisions devoted to particular sports, and by the end of the century smaller-scale recreation grounds were being commissioned.[29]

COMMERCIAL GARDENS

What the kitchen garden was to the country house, market gardens were to the town: the most important form of horticulture. Market gardens had for generations fringed the perimeters of every large town, in Britain and elsewhere. The political stability of Britain ensured that market gardening became an organized industry. In contrast, in the walled towns of continental Europe, the threat of war and the retreat of the populace within the walls at times of conflict prevented a similar development until the nineteenth century. The Napoleonic Wars led to the destruction of much market gardening in the German states, including the celebrated fruit collections of the pomologist Johann Volkmar Sickler, that were wrecked by plundering troops.[30]

In London at the beginning of the nineteenth century, the principal market gardening areas were arranged in a ring around the urban centre in Hoxton, Pimlico, Battersea, and Camberwell. By the end of the century, the market gardens had virtually disappeared from all these areas, forced out by suburban expansion. They had moved outward to Barking, Romford, Bedfont, Isleworth, Mitcham, Carshalton, Dartford, and Swanley, since rail had taken over from cart as the principal means of transportation. In the twentieth century, most of these areas were taken over by suburban expansion, and the arrival of motor vehicles made it possible for the market gardening industry to relocate to the outer fringes of the home counties.[31]

Cloches with one cos and four cabbage lettuce under each. (10,000 cloches in all.)

FIGURE 2.5: *Culture maraichère* in operation, or "French gardening" as it was called in England: 10,000 cloches, each covering five cabbages. Photograph from C. D. McKay, *The French Garden in England*, 1909. Royal Horticultural Society, Lindley Library.

In France, the experience of market gardening was very different. Since Le Normand and his successors at the Potager du Roi at Versailles, cloches and frames had been used to force vegetables. In the wake of the French Revolution, and of the local famines induced by poor harvests, the idea was vigorously promoted that waste ground anywhere in an urban area could be made productive by the use of cloches. *Culture maraichère*, as the practice became known, spread steadily through Paris and other cities during the mid-nineteenth century.[32] Vinyard cultivation around Paris ended during the 1850s. Cereal-growing ceased soon after, and both were replaced by intensive vegetable production. Where open-strip farms were sufficiently close to the suburbs, they were converted to *culture maraichère*. While the former farmers had tended to live in clustered settlements, surrounded by the strips of land, the market gardeners preferred to build detached houses near their holdings, rather than in villages.[33]

One of the major transformations within the city fabric during the nineteenth century, first in England and later on the continent, was the reorganization of urban markets. Market halls had been common in northern Europe, where the weather was less conducive to open-air market typically held in the squares of the Mediterranean. The introduction of iron and glass technology resulted in major reconstruction projects throughout Europe, from Covent

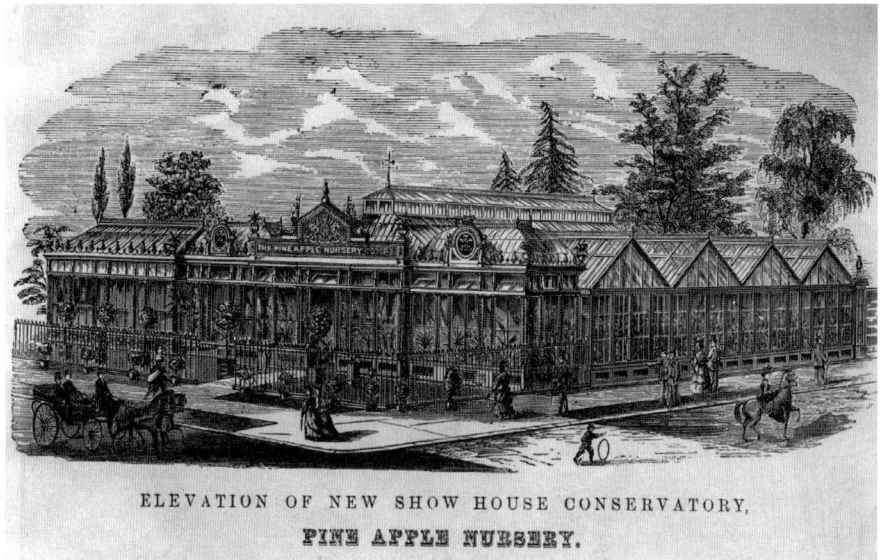

ELEVATION OF NEW SHOW HOUSE CONSERVATORY,
PINE APPLE NURSERY.

FIGURE 2.6: E. G. Henderson, Pineapple Nursery, Maida Vale, London. Wood engraving of new show house from 1878 seed catalogue. Royal Horticultural Society, Lindley Library.

Garden Market (Charles Fowler) in London in the 1820s, Les Halles in Paris (Victor Baltard) in the 1850s, to the complex of market halls built by Hermann Blankenstein in Berlin in the 1880s and 1890s. The progressive centralization of wholesale produce markets in this manner led to the creation of an official bureaucracy for the regulation of market gardening, and the formation of workers' co-operatives to deal in a more organized fashion with the authorities. By the end of the century, market gardening in nearly every European country was changing, and losing its former character.[34]

Distinct both in design and social function from market gardens were nurseries—the grounds that provided plants for sale rather than market produce. As with market gardens, nurseries tended to spring up on the perimeters of towns, where both space and lower rents were available. Beginning with William Rollisson's nursery at Tooting at the end of the eighteenth century, some nurseries began to experiment with programs of plant breeding. The larger firms began to distinguish between display gardens, where customers did their shopping, and propagating grounds, often located at a considerable distance. The development of glasshouse technology in the nineteenth century made it possible for some nurseries, such as the prominent London examples Loddiges in Hackney, Veitch and William Bull in Chelsea, and E. G. Henderson in Maida

Vale, to maintain establishments in the urban centers with glazed display houses. Already in the eighteenth century, nurseries had established an international trade: the first important American nurseryman, John Bartram, had provided American plants to prominent British collectors. But his contacts tended to be wealthy amateurs who raised the new plants in their own gardens before eventually passing them on to the nursery trade in Britain.[35] During the nineteenth century, this phase was succeeded by the direct trade between nurseries, such as Loddiges and Veitch, in different countries. By mid-century, the wealthiest nurseries could also afford to send their own collectors abroad to bring back new samples from overseas.

Nurseries eventually showed the same pattern as market gardens and were relocated to the urban periphery, due to the rise in property prices and pollution as a result of continuing urbanization. In London, the nurseries that had been operating in Kensington, Chelsea, Hammersmith, and Hackney had closed down or moved further out by the 1860s. Like market gardens, nurseries were forced further and further outside the urban area with each succeeding generation.[36]

CHAPTER THREE

Plantings

MARK LAIRD

During the nineteenth century, plantings in Western gardens moved in tandem with sweeping social, technological, and geo-political changes. They reflected diverse intellectual and ideological movements. Among the myriad shifts affecting planting design, the following are considered in this chapter: the introduction of Indian and Chinese styles as part of eclecticism and historicism; the tension between "natural" and "artificial" systems of gardening; the disposition of plants in large blocks or "drifts" as a departure from prior picturesque practice;[1] the planting of specimens for art and science, as the public park emerged from its horticultural beginnings; the rise of middle-class gardening and its organizations and publications; the application of rigorous color theory to planting—adapted from textile manufacturing just prior to the discovery of industrial dyes (and concomitant chemical insecticides); the developments in "bedding" (i.e., the massing of annuals) that came with an influx of tender plants from the southern hemisphere and with glasshouse technology; the upsurge of the East as a source of horticultural treasures, facilitated by transportation of living materials, and buoyed by the expansion of empire from its mercantile roots; and the emergence of women as garden writers and preeminent horticultural designers. Within these shifts, continuity with past practices—planting lore—proved equally important. Britain, as the dominant imperial power and the leader in horticulture and garden design, provides the focus of the chapter. However, developments in British planting were often linked to change elsewhere, for example in France or Germany. China serves here to illustrate shifts in Western attitudes to nature, culture, horticulture, and planting design. India, and to a lesser extent Canada, are referred to in passing as representative of "plantings in Empire" to East and West. Appropriating the plants of the entire globe, British gardeners were able after 1900 to realize Humphry Repton's dream of a perpetual garden of every climate. By 1920, however, with landscape architecture in North America ascendant, and with the push to modernism, West and East had become potent forces in their own right in the new art and science of planting.

The planting of gardens in the Age of Empire has its symbolic roots in two proposals just after 1800 for the gardens at The Royal Pavilion at Brighton. While one reflects British India, the other has an indigenous character.[2] These two rival visions—Humphry Repton's Red Book (1806) and John Nash's realized scheme (1817–21)—also represent strands in the enormously complex fabric of nineteenth-century gardening.[3] Repton's approach looked forward to the artifice of high-Victorian styles associated with "artificial climate."[4] By contrast, Nash looked back to the "forest lawns" of picturesque taste.[5] Yet Nash gave the shrub beds a massed roughness that anticipated the late-nineteenth-century "wild garden." With John Claudius Loudon's first essay of 1803, these polar visions entered the public sphere. For the twenty-one-year-old Loudon, the issue was clear enough: "natural Forests" (rather than Repton's "formal" structures) were the ideal for planting a London square in "honour of the British nation."[6] Paradoxically, though, it was Loudon who came to make the effects of the "artificial" possible through glasshouse technology.

At Brighton, Repton was first consulted from 1797 to 1802, thus overlapping with Henry Holland's work on a Chinese suite, 1801–3. In 1805, William Porden proposed enlarging the pavilion in a style that recalled scenes from Lord Macartney's embassy at the Chinese court. In autumn 1805, however, Repton persuaded the Prince of Wales of the merits of the Indian style.[7] Repton's interest in Indian architecture had been aroused ca. 1803 when Sir Charles Cockerell consulted him at Sezincote, Gloucestershire. A former East India Company officer, Cockerell employed his brother, the architect Samuel Pepys Cockerell, to design his seat, using drawings in Thomas Daniell's *Oriental Scenery*.[8] Repton's contribution was minimal. However, in his *Enquiry* of 1806, he declared that the scenery and buildings of India amounted to "some great future change" in the arts of architecture and landscape.[9] This coincided with Francis Blagdon's *History of Ancient and Modern India* of 1805. The latter saw the British ascendancy unchallenged. Repton thus anticipated projects in Britain that glorified the nation's ascent in historical or cultural terms: from the world under glass

THE GENERAL VIEW FROM THE PAVILION

FIGURE 3.1: Humphry Repton, *General View from the Royal Pavilion*. From the Red Book for the Royal Pavilion, Brighton, 1806. The Royal Collection © 2007, Her Majesty Queen Elizabeth II.

at Crystal Palace to the evocation of civilizations in James Bateman's millennial Biddulph Grange.[10]

Repton's Red Book of 1806 took its architectural detailing from Daniell's first volume of *Oriental Scenery* (1795–97). Yet, despite his proposition that Indian architectural motifs corresponded to flower forms, Repton found nothing horticultural in Daniell's scenes. Rather, they show sparse vegetation or vegetation in picturesque abandon. Hence, Repton summoned up Francis Bacon's idea of a garden for every month: "a perpetual garden, enriched with the production of every climate." As he realized that "cast iron ... is peculiarly adapted to some light parts of the Indian style,"[11] he gave the pheasantry and aviary the respective features of Mughal palace and Hindu temple. Glass and iron structures were central to his concept, as they had been in his 1805 proposal for Woburn's "Forcing Garden." The stained glass of the pavilion could further enhance the artifices of horticulture:

There is a curious effect from purple glass, of which little advantage has yet been taken; viz. All green objects seen through purple glass appear white and thus a beautified landscape illuminated by the midday sun of Summer will appear a perfect Winter scene covered with snow.[12]

In his pavilion views, Repton disposed beds in a manner akin to the celebrated flower garden at Nuneham Courtenay. Yet his basket-edged profiles in the "Chinese" style were far from the pinnacles of flowerbeds in eighteenth-century gardens before and after Nuneham.[13] Perhaps Repton had the containers of courtyard gardens in Canton in mind, as opposed to the park of Jehol that inspired Sir George Staunton's Leigh Park, Hampshire.[14] This basketwork—whether inspired by Chinese containers, French corbeilles, Dutch still-life paintings, or the effects of interior décor—meant in effect abandoning the Nuneham model. It was a first step toward the flat effects of "bedding," which only came later with color theory and glasshouse technology.[15]

Repton's designs of 1805–15 thus mark a radical departure from the "theatrical" and "mixed" style that had emerged in the picturesque from baroque antecedents.[16] Repton's decision to keep planting low instead of graduated "like seats in a theatre," and "massed" instead of intermixed like a bunch of flowers, was detailed as mounds of red or pink roses. The Ashridge Red Book of 1813 exemplifies this change.[17] The return to parterre—for example, the children's garden at Endsleigh of 1814—perhaps induced him to think in flat blocks of uniform color.

John Nash took a different approach than Repton—one that defined "massing" in shrubbery. Drawing on principles in William Gilpin's *Remarks on Forest Scenery* (1791), Nash gave his plantings an indigenous, windswept look. Prince Pückler-Muskau later described the new Nash manner at Brighton and in London: it brought the irregular profile of park plantations down to the scale of the pleasure ground.[18] Yet, in aiming for a bolder effect by "massing" in blocks (akin to Loudon's "select or grouped manner"), Nash shared one element with Repton: a shift from the dainty rhythms of "mixing," that is, intermixtures of flowers. The repercussions of that shift became apparent in William Robinson's "wild garden" and in the "drifts" of Gertrude Jekyll's herbaceous border.

Nash understood little of practical horticulture, less even than did Repton, who confessed in 1800 to "ignorance in Botany."[19] Hence, for the realization of planting at Brighton and in St. James's Park, Nash relied on W. T. Aiton, the royal gardener. Aiton is said to have sent the Chinese *Nandina domestica* (introduced 1804) and the Australian *Kennedia rubicunda* (introduced 1788) from Kew to Nash's own garden.[20] At Brighton, the extensive records for 1816 to 1830 reveal new Oriental species (e.g., *Aucuba japonica* (1783) or *Chaenomeles speciosa* (1796)) amid the still popular European shrubs. Eclipsing the American woody plants, so fashionable in the eighteenth century, Chinese species would become predominant by 1900. When Repton proposed in his Woburn Red Book of 1805 that *Aucuba japonica* and *Hydrangea macrophylla*

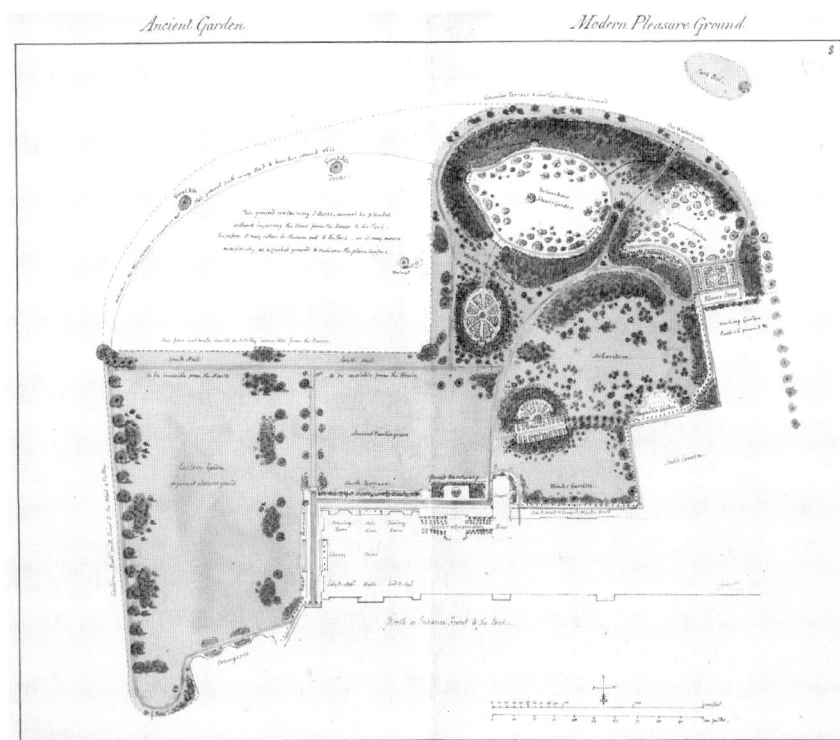

FIGURE 3.2: Humphry Repton, *Plan of the Ancient Gardens at Ashridge*. From the
Red Book for Ashridge, Hertfordshire, 1813. Research Library, The Getty Research
Institute, Los Angeles, California (850834).

ornament the Chinese Dairy, he showed an acute awareness of horticultural
trends that included the first marginal and aquatic plantings. His pictorial
visions are at once luminary and fantastical. That *Cobaea scandens*—the cup-
and-saucer vine of Mexico—shows up in the Brighton accounts and in his
Red Book for Montreal, Kent (1812), implies how quickly novel plants found
a place in plantings and professional consciousness. A strong nursery trade, the
royal gardens at Kew (invigorated under Joseph Banks's imperial leadership),
the expansion of botanical gardens within empire (e.g., Robert Kyd's appeal
for the Royal Botanical Gardens in Calcutta, 1786–93), and the newly founded
Horticultural Society of London (1804) contributed to the global supremacy
of British gardening.[21]

Brighton differs from Woburn (or Ashridge and Endsleigh) in its unified aesthetic—picturesque dressed in Oriental garb. However, with Bulstrode as one
early example, Repton also appears as the first to emphasize zoning. Zoning
created "specialized gardens" (e.g., up to fifteen discrete zones at Ashridge, as

shown in Figure 3.2). In a similar vein, he brought back "formal" elements to structure zones for utility and comfort. Yet, at Bulstrode, "formal" elements had in fact survived de-formalization. Moreover, the second Duchess of Portland developed special garden zones herself: an American grove, a flower garden, a menagerie, and a botanic garden of native and exotic plants. Hence, Repton's plan for Bulstrode, published in *Observations* in 1803, might be more precisely defined as working within the baroque-picturesque continuum.[22]

J. C. Loudon was as influential as Repton in attaching the specific cultural needs of plants to special garden zones and, thereby, following pioneers in botanic gardens from John Bartram in Philadelphia to William Curtis in London.[23] In his *Observations* of 1804, Loudon listed among the discrete categories gardens for winter, spring, and autumn. He itemized the modern British, Chinese, Grecian, Roman, Italian, Dutch, and French gardens.[24] By 1824, his *Encyclopaedia* was revised to include "flowers for particular purposes": wall climbers, shade-tolerant species, "aquatic" and "marsh" plants, rock plants and peat-loving plants. Rock gardens had a long and complex ancestry, upon which Loudon built.[25] But there was little precedence for water-loving plants. Hence, he detailed how to construct a pond and cultivate "showy" flowers (e.g., water-lilies). This provided the basis for the construction of all later water gardens up to and including Claude Monet's Giverny (from 1893). Baron Dumont de Courset (from 1784) likewise contributed the notion of constructing habitats for water plants or bog plants or alpines.[26] At his estate of Courset, the baron had thirty-six specialized gardens, including genera collections, spaces categorized by seasonality, and enclosures for "Rhododendron," potted plants and climbing plants.

The Reptonian parterre, with its treillage and corbeilles, certainly drew on earlier styles: English Tudor, and French baroque or rococo. This self-conscious borrowing of motifs foreshadowed historicism: rococo revival from Maria Jackson, 1822; topiary from Alexander Forbes at Levens Hall, 1810; and the "Italian garden" from Richard Westmacott at Wilton, 1820–21.[27] For example, the cottage garden of the keeper's house at Apsley Wood, Woburn (1810), revealed Repton's antiquarian interest in knot and maze. The division of the Ashridge pleasure ground into ancient and modern, and the evocation of the medieval past by a Monk's Garden with false headstones, all point to the new sensibility of emergent historicism.

What Repton developed at Woburn was the idea of a series of gardens as "apartments" interconnected to the architecture by passageways and glass. If "summer" was turned into "winter" through glass at Brighton, winter was made comfortable inside glass at Woburn. Repton also had an instinct for envisaging new forms of planting within the framework of the old. For example, he used an established radial motif for the Ashridge "Rosary," but gave it a novel horticultural dressing. This coincides with the mania for roses that resulted from the introduction of the repeat-flowering China rose. The Empress Josephine's rose collection at Malmaison, begun in 1804, was not apparently concentrated in a special garden; nor did Baron Dumont possess a rose garden at Courset.[28] Thus, it was Repton's promotion in *Fragments* (1816) of the Ashridge "Rosarium" as round (i.e., not the elliptical zone of the Red Book) that inspired Muskau (ca. 1830) and Babelsberg (ca. 1845) and countless other iterations thereafter.

In his memoir, Repton confessed that he had "of late viewed with a jealous eye the irruption recently made by the new China Rose, which however valuable in winter from its dark glossy foliage and hardy flower is but like a rouged beauty—and must not attempt to vie with the genuine English scented Rose."[29] To offset such meretriciousness at Woburn, he made the "English garden" a "shrubbery walk, connecting the whole." Yet, in his *Fragments* of 1816, he still found positives in China. He wrote that, just as the compression of women's feet was equivalent to nurturing exquisite diminutive forms, so, too, the English obsession with size could result in fruit without taste and flowers without scent.[30] China would later take on a different meaning in the theory of J. C. Loudon and A. J. Downing. With imperial trade wars, China became associated with despotic governance rather than the delights of Cathay.[31]

The ratio of size to scent or other attributes proved key in hybridization. The English horticulturist Shirley Hibberd marveled in 1883 at the "hybridist" who had mastered the art "with almost mathematical exactitude."[32] The large-faced pansy came from crossing petite *Viola* species in 1813. By 1816, Repton had already picked up on the "gigantic Viola tricolor."[33] France would play an equally important role in early hybridization, from roses to lilacs to magnolias. Étienne Soulange-Bodin, for example, first general secretary of the horticultural society of Paris (founded 1827), developed *Magnolia* x *soulangiana*.

In effect then, global outreach, hybridization, and specialization within gardening advanced the departure from the universalizing art and science of eighteenth-century planting. For example, one special type, the American garden, evolved elusively from the wilderness on the one hand, and the "theatrical" compendium of shrubbery on the other. It was related to any number of classificatory collections, both geographical and cultural.[34] Thus, whereas hardy ericaceous plants might belong in an American Border at Croome in 1801, by the 1820s and 1830s, distinct gardens for *Rhododendron* and *Erica* were being established.[35] While the former tended toward naturalization (Fonthill, Bagshot, Kenwood, Dropmore, Craigside, etc.), the latter (a "heathery") could be artificially structured like a radial parterre or rosary. Loudon illustrated one such "Ericetum" in his *Arboretum et Fruticetum Britannicum* of 1838.

Loudon's account of the heath garden at Woburn Abbey points to how Repton's specialized gardens—the American garden, the arboretum and taxonomic botanical garden—had been further differentiated through the Duke of Bedford's botanical zeal: first with George Sinclair's collection of grasses, second with James Forbes's additions of the *Hortus woburnensis* of 1833. To the heathery was added a pinery, holly garden, willow garden (salicetum) and camellia house.[36] Repton anticipated such genus collections with his "thornery,"[37] while in 1806, Loudon, in his first use of the term "arboretum," was only too willing to recognize the "different families of vegetables, as an *arboretum, fruticetum, harbarium* [sic]."[38] By 1796, the Hortus Linnaeus of the Glasnevin Botanic Gardens, Dublin, was already divided into three such parts—herbarium (herbaceous), fruticetum (shrub) and arboretum (tree) sections.[39] Yet, what Repton meant by "Arboretum" at Bulstrode, Woburn and Ashridge is far from clear; and for Montreal, he listed "Arboretum" with "American Garden" as fashionable accessories. Likewise, how the "pinetum" emerged from the "arboretum" is complex; and the development of the arboretum into the early twentieth-century "woodland garden" is a case of further complexity.[40] Put simply, two broad tendencies were codified around 1826–27. By the 1820s, the term "arboretum" was increasingly attached to collections of trees, notably at Loddiges Hackney nursery and at the Horticultural Society's Chiswick arboretum—so designated on a plan of 1826.[41] Loudon's 1838 publication—*Arboretum et Fruticetum Britannicum*—thus merely encouraged a more formal adoption of the term, for example in the German-speaking world and in the United States.[42] Collections of conifers existed in English Georgian gardens such as Painshill. Yet it was the collection at Dropmore (beginning with seeds from New York in 1795–6) that first subsumed the conifers of West and East under a common collectivity. Lambert's *Genus Pinus* of 1805–7 played a key role in elevating the ideal beyond Painshill (with associated "winter gardens" first adumbrated in Addison and Whately). Loudon would describe the Dropmore pinetum in his *Gardener's Magazine* of 1827.

The arboretum and pinetum emphasized the individual tree over trees in assemblage. Hence, individualism—the specimen on the lawn or the detached flower in its bed—stands alongside pluralism in garden design characterized by historicism and eclecticism.[43] It also stands in counterpoint to "massing" in shrubbery and flower garden. Perhaps the founding of horticultural societies after the model of London (for example, Berlin in 1822) encouraged the tendency to individualize.[44] Whether this meant the identification of plants with human individuality in an age of greater political emancipation is less certain.[45] Repton recognized how proprietors love individual plantings, in the way that parents are "most fond of their own progeny."[46] Yet collectors had always loved individual specimens. A difference was that Loudon's elevation of individual specimens through the gardenesque coincided with the development of urban parks as outdoor "living museums." The tree became, through cultivation, an object of art as well as of science. For example, types of weeping and fastigiate tree (e.g., the Camperdown elm) increased over the century. Peter Joseph Lenné already demonstrated in his 1824 design for the Magdeburger Volksgarten, an early public park, how weeping and fastigiate forms might be displayed to effect.[47]

Pückler-Muskau, visiting England in 1826, noted the practice of isolating specimens on lawn, or of detaching shrubs in a bed "so that you see more of black earth than of green foliage."[48] Hence, this scattered aesthetic goes back before the formal definition of the gardenesque (1832), perhaps as far back as some late-eighteenth-century flower gardens. However, Loudon saw a need in theory to elevate the cultivation of the specimen. By bringing the tree or shrub to perfection, the gardener embedded the principle of "recognition of art" demanded by Quatremère de Quincy within the garden,[49] while otherwise handling the raw materials of "nature." Even the junction of the main surface roots with the trunk should be visible, argued Loudon. Hence, in his most celebrated gardenesque layout—a first urban park, the Derby Arboretum—he brought trees up on the pedestal of low ridges. Loudon's ally, Robert Errington, wrote of the gardenesque scatter of flowers: that bare earth offered a "sort of relief that suits the human eye."[50] While "massing" took over conclusively in the 1830s in "bedding" (and had a place in Loudon's "select" manner), scattering would survive beyond early-Victorian times in botanic gardens and arboreta as a pleasing and instructive aesthetic.

J. C. Loudon, and Jane Loudon from 1840, saw gardens and garden literature as a means to increase knowledge. The gardenesque has, thus, been associated with empowering middle-class owners and with encouraging women and children to learn horticulture.[51] Yet, as early as 1821, Loudon's attention was drawn as much to gardeners' training and living conditions. He drew on his experience of the German territories, where apprenticeship led to travel as a journeyman en route to becoming a master gardener.[52] Following the success of his *Encyclopaedia of Gardening* in 1822, Loudon ventured into journalism as a way to further cultivate an audience: the working man as much as the bourgeois owner. The *Gardener's Magazine* (1826–1843), for example, provided a forum for the gardener to discuss his work or political questions, such as the cooperative or allotment, and to campaign for better wages.[53] The fact that simple engravings—the Dropmore flower garden or the new lawnmower—accompanied the text made the journal accessible and affordable. The *Gardener's Magazine* set the standard for rival and successor journals, including the *Gardeners' Chronicle* (founded by John Lindley and Joseph Paxton in 1841).

Jane Loudon was not the first to publish books expressly for women. An unpublished manuscript by Sylvia Streatfield (*Sylvia's Flower Garden* of 1735) is one early example;[54] Maria Elizabeth Jackson was a more immediate forerunner.[55] Botanical learning and flower painting were already two areas of female competence.[56] Patronage was a prerogative of ordinary as well as extraordinary women.[57] In his 1803 essay on London squares in the *Literary Journal*, Loudon mentioned botany in connection with ladies. Pückler-Muskau later invoked female taste in the flower garden.[58] Jane Loudon's *Lady's Magazine of Gardening* of 1840 thus expanded the scope of gardening articles in eighteenth-century women's magazines. Like her husband, she extended the audience within middle-class circles.[59] Women gardeners, of course, had no forum equivalent to those for men. There was no career path to head gardener.

Joseph Paxton, whose career epitomized all the brilliance of a self-improved head gardener, is a key figure in the "artifice" of planting: from "bedding" to the "flowering" of *Victoria amazonica*. By 1838, he could write: "In modern flower-gardens, the old practice of having a variety of plants in one large bed, and arranging them according to their height and color, has been entirely superseded, and the system of grouping plants of one sort in small beds substituted for it."[60] Within the new system, contemporary advances in glasshouse technology, of which he was a leading exponent, helped promote tender exotic annuals over hardy perennials. The idea of "artificial climate" had already appeared in the late eighteenth century. Yet, Loudon seized upon the implications of the phrase, in writing that the greenhouse "is entirely a work of art: the plants inclosed are in the most artificial situation."[61] Loudon's invention of a curved glazing bar in wrought iron made possible glass-and-metal construction dreamt of by Repton at Brighton and visualized in detail by Sir George Mackenzie in 1815.[62] Mackenzie's was curvilinear; other types were based on a ridge-and-furrow system. Advances in heating, roof design, and prefabrication also led to the most splendid models of glasshouse construction, including the Crystal Palace.[63] It would allow Joseph Paxton to engineer a brilliant coup in getting the *Victoria amazonica* to bloom for the first time in November 1849 under artificial conditions.[64] To Loudon's dismay, the ability to control the environment for the production of masses of annual "bedding" plants would transfer the artificiality outside.

Advances in color theory were central to the "artifice" of planting. Erasmus Darwin's new application of complementary colors in gardening was later interpreted through J. W. Goethe's *Farbenlehre* of 1810 and Michel-Eugène Chevreul's influential work of the 1830s.[65] This helped promote the cause of bold contrasts (whether complementary or not) over the easy gradations of the picturesque. Thus, in 1850, a correspondent could write in the *Cottage Gardener*: "There is no doubt that arranging flowers according to their contrast is more pleasing to the eye than placing them according to their harmonies. Consequently, a blue flower should be placed next to an orange flower, a yellow near a violet.[66] This represented, it is true, just one phase and one strand of thinking in Victorian planting, with Donald Beaton leading the move against Chevreul.[67] Moreover, the mixed border never disappeared entirely and was revitalized as Gertrude Jekyll's "herbaceous border" of the 1880s.[68] Nevertheless, the popularity of massing, whether in the shrubbery or flower garden, and the preference for bold color contrasts in general, marks a break in a continuous tradition of planting in the "mixed" style that spans baroque and picturesque.

Dropmore, Buckinghamshire, celebrated for its exotic collections, demonstrated that, "Nature must acknowledge the supremacy of Art."[69] This principle was extended from the specimens in the pinetum to the introduction of exotic *Rhododendron ponticum* in the woods,[70] to the massed splendor of the flower garden. When Loudon visited in 1827, he found Lady Grenville's flower garden was newly laid out as a French parterre. Each bed contained a single color of flower, massed for effect, and planted in seasonal succession with much resort to "plunging." Thus, Philip Frost as head gardener proved "the advantage of placing beauty in masses."[71] By the late 1830s, John Caie took over from Frost as the main proponent of the bedding system. It was said to have derived its first impulse from "nature," for example, the masses of *Eschscholtzia* in California,[72] yet it was later controlled by the "art" of color theory and glasshouse cultivation. Of course, the effective distinction between "massing" and "mixing" was not always immediately apparent. When Lord Braybrooke's "Jacobean" revivalist parterre was planted at Audley End in the 1830s, the gardeners made some beds "mixed" and others "massed."[73] Given the height reached by the plantings, the overall impact was quite textured, as close to a prairie as a flat carpet. Hence, it was the development of carpet bedding that first helped to assert the advantage of keeping "massed" plantings low.

In his *Andeutungen über Landschaftsgärtnerei* of 1834, Prince Pückler-Muskau illustrated the novel concept of *Blumenteppiche*. The term *Teppichgärten*—"carpet gardens"—was first used by Rudolf Wörmann in 1864, and *Teppichbeet* in 1867.[74] Whether in the form of abstractions or emblems,

FIGURE 3.3: The flower gardens seen from the castle on Hermann Fürst von Pückler-Muskau's estate at Muskau. From Hermann Fürst von Pückler-Muskau, *Atlas zu den Andeutungen über Landschaftsgärtnerei*, 1834, plate 12. Dumbarton Oaks Research Library and Collection, Washington, DC.

Pückler delighted in the artifice of decorating the garden as an outdoor apartment. He looked back to mannerist expression in knots yet forged a new aesthetic that anticipated carpet bedding. Like the baroque masters of "decoration,"[75] he still relied on a seasonal repertoire of bulbs (e.g., hyacinths) and annuals (e.g., globe amaranth).[76] In contrast, the proponents of carpet bedding proper took advantage of a range of dwarf foliage plants available by the 1860s. These included species of *Iresine* and *Alternanthera* from South America that remained fresh all summer long. John Fleming of Cliveden was one innovator. He laid out a bed in 1868 that featured the monogram of Harriet, Duchess of Sutherland—"HS"—in *Arabis*, *Echeveria* and *Sempervivum* against sedum of various colors. This provoked a leader in the *Gardeners' Chronicle* to label it "carpet bedding." George Eyles gave an account of "carpet bedding" in the *Gardeners' Chronicle* in 1877. William Robinson in *Alpine Flowers for English Gardens* (1870) substituted "mosaic beds."[77] His usage was perhaps related to French *mosaiculture,* as invented by Jules Chrétien in Lyon and publicized by Édouard André in Paris, though the meaning of such interconnected terms defies easy categorization.[78]

Carpet-bedding was not invariably flat. Indeed, the first illustration of a carpet-bed in the *Chronicle* showed the 1870 mound at Kew.[79] However, flat effects were akin to the "garden of embroidery" that William Andrews Nesfield perfected during the 1850s in revivalist French parterres.[80] Foliage chromatics in mosaiculture also had links to a counter trend: tall foliage of the 1840s. In part, this was a reaction against "primary colour with symmetrical flatness," which came with color theory and "bedding."[81] Tropical foliage planting, in turn, shaped the development of William Robinson's "wild garden."

After the 1840s, with the fern craze including the *fernery* as a Wardian case,[82] the great fern enthusiast, Thomas Moore of Chelsea Physic Garden, began to promote foliage bedding. He favored rhubarb, maize, and kale.[83] Yet true tropical foliage planting seems to have arisen first in Germany. G. A. Fintelmann's report of 1833 referred to *Blattzierpflanzen* on the Pfaueninsel outside Berlin.[84] By the early 1850s, word of bedding *Canna* and *Marantha* reached England from Germany.[85] As late as the 1880s, such assemblages of foliage could still be called "German beds." The term "phyllomania" was coined in 1864, yet "picturesque bedding" took over as the fashionable label. Only after plantings at Battersea Park were called "tropical looking" did "subtropical bedding" become standard. This coincided with reports from Paris that Jean-Pierre Barillet-Deschamps was using the broad-leaved *Caladium*, *Dieffenbachia*, *Philodendron*, along with shrubby types of *Solanum*, and the flashy foliage of bananas, illustrated in Figure 3.4.

The color of foliage rather than of flowers had other repercussions in the landscape of shrubbery and woodland. In the 1850s, for example, autumn color emerged as a theme in debates over Hampstead Heath. American woody species, long known in the landscape garden, were now seen for the first time as producing an "Indian summer" of "autumnal drapery."[86] By the 1870s, with the rejection of conifers (associated with the pinetum), an interest developed in the purples of the newly introduced Japanese maples.[87] Variegated foliage assumed obsessive status among late Victorian plantsmen. In 1880, William Paul's proposal for Epping Forest emphasized "every shade of colour, from grass green and silvery grey to inky black."[88] Yet, for all this, by the end of the century, following counter movements, including William Robinson's shift to northern-hemisphere exotics, the cult of green returned.

If planting taste was generated by horticultural trends and plant introductions, it was also influenced by color in interior décor and the textile industry. In these domains, color had psychological and cultural dimensions—bright colors being associated, for example, with "savages."[89] The chemist Michel-Eugène Chevreul, commissioned to improve dyes in the Gobelin tapestry works,

FIGURE 3.4: Wigandia Vigierii. From Adolphe Alphand, *Les promenades de Paris*, 1867–73. Dumbarton Oaks Research Library and Collection, Washington, DC.

published *De la loi du contraste simultané des couleurs* in 1839. Textiles thereafter exerted a contested influence over color theory in planting. Fabrics were also affected by the development of "industrial color." Synthetic dyestuffs originated with William Henry Perkins and his accidental discovery of "mauve" in 1856.[90] "Magenta" followed in 1859. These less-expensive textiles influenced popular consumption in Europe and North America, such that Hippolyte Taine complained of the "glare" of ladies in Hyde Park.[91] The reaction against aniline dyes in the work of John Ruskin and William Morris had implications for planting, especially in the gardens of Gertrude Jekyll.

John Ruskin looked at both color aesthetics and industrial conditions. When he wrote about the loss of pure scarlet sunsets—at the onset of a "dry black veil" in 1871 due to industrial pollution—he proposed that the sacred in art and nature was profaned.[92] He was unaware of the possible links between natural atmospheric pollution—volcanic dust—and the art of J. M. W. Turner.[93] He passed on to William Morris and Gertrude Jekyll a keen apprehension of color and industrial process. Morris's use of madder and kermes as dyes meant a return to pre-industrial practices, abjuring all the ills associated with low wages and poor conditions. Gertrude Jekyll's artful marrying of textile construction, notably quilts, with color composition, derived in part from Turner, was thereafter a key step toward the herbaceous border at Munstead Wood in the 1890s.[94]

One by-product of the industrial process was an arsenic-based compound called "London purple," used as an insecticide. "Paris green" was an alternative spray.[95] Spraying-engines and pumps emerged along with the technology of watering pipes that changed garden maintenance in London and Parisian parks.[96] While a concern arose over the health of those who wore dresses colored by aniline dyes or who consumed fruit sprayed with industrial insecticides, the advantage of high yields prevailed. The masses of plants, raised under glass, had a similar brightness to the new dresses—those crinolines that mirrored glasshouse structures. Thus, Gertrude Jekyll, in using the term "malignant magenta," perhaps had in mind fabrics made with industrial dyes as much as the flower-color itself.[97] Yet, she was not averse to using "bedding" pelargoniums of a strong scarlet or intense salmon.

Gertrude Jekyll's herbaceous plantings recall the "theatricality" of borders in the picturesque: a graduation of plantings up to tall hollyhocks, as Helen Allingham's paintings of the great border at Munstead Wood indicate.[98] To that tradition, she brought knowledge of drifts, which had entered public gardens with John Nash; familiarity with "massing," which came in as "bedding"; and a deft use of wall-climbers.[99] Plants were to be grouped in masses, "large enough to have a certain dignity."[100] This meant resort to the materials and

FIGURE 3.5: Red section of the south border at Gertrude Jekyll's Munstead Wood. Autochrome ca. 1912. Courtesy Country Life Picture Library.

methods of "bedding," which she praised in *Garden Ornament*.[101] An autochrome view of her long border at Munstead Wood, ca. 1912, reveals how she composed the red-hot center of the border not just with red hollyhocks, *Lychnis chalcedonica*, *Kniphofia*, *Phlox*, and other perennials, but with border dahlias and gaudy annuals: *Salvia*, *Celosia* or *Pelargonium*, *Canna*, and *Tropaeolum*. In terms of color schemes, however, a key innovation was replacing a uniform progression of hue by an interrupted sequence.[102] Thus, bold relief to the central mass of scarlet came not just from the gray and whites at either end, but from the subtle ebb-and-flow of cool and warm colors in between, and from the foamy white *Gypsophila* within the hot center.

Meanwhile, furnishing "garden rooms" with seasonal plantings (e.g., Spring garden, June garden, October aster border) or with chromatic plantings (e.g., white and gray) was entirely new. Furthermore, in her sensitivity to color, she inspired other plants-women—Beatrix Jones Farrand and Ellen Biddle Shipman—who came to professional practice through horticulture. She also consolidated a literary genre—horticultural writings by plantswomen—that extends through Vita Sackville-West to Penelope Hobhouse.[103]

The largest part of Munstead was taken up with woodland gardening. Once again, her color effects with rhododendron and azalea and other "flowery incidents" were magisterial.[104] However, given the soil type—acidic, sandy, and peaty—and the associated tree types—birch, holly, Scots pine, oak, beech, and sweet chestnut—Jekyll was working within the old medium of Surrey picturesque. Woodland embellishment at Kenwood or Dropmore,[105] as well as in the High Weald aesthetic of William Robinson,[106] were other precedents in a lineage extending back to the picturesque. Likewise, the early nineteenth-century Scottish practice of naturalizing bulbs (which, with John Fleming's 1860s Cliveden, influenced William Robinson's "wild garden" and thereby Jekyll) surely sprang in part from "enameling" in picturesque planting.[107] The "wild" in Rousseau's *La nouvelle Héloïse* played its part in this lineage.[108]

In the German-speaking world, Christian Cay Lorenz Hirschfeld was the first to make a cultural-nationalistic linkage among native plants, patriotic statuary, and the public park.[109] The science, as opposed to the art, of planting drew upon the work of Alexander von Humboldt.[110] In 1822, Loudon would summarize Humboldt's *Ideen zu einer Geographie der Pflanzen* (1807). He referred to "Botanical geography, or the knowledge of the places where the plants grow (*habitationes plantarum*) and the causes which influence their distribution over the globe."[111] Berlin, he noted, already had a botanic garden arranged by "native *habitations*." Yet, Loudon himself, like Paxton, moved only tentatively from systematic collections toward botanical geography (the defining criterion of K. L. Wildenow's Berlin botanic garden). Gustav Meyer and Eduard Petzold responded explicitly to geographical groupings within landscape design itself.

Botanical geography still meant for most appropriating exotic floras and denigrating the cultures from which they came. Loudon's 1834 edition of the *Encyclopaedia*, compiled on the eve of British imperialist-mercantile attacks on China, intensified the denigration of the Chinese garden.[112] William Robinson in *The English Flower Garden* of 1883 made a figurative link between the "cramming of Chinese feet"[113] and clipped yews. He inverted the logic of Repton's celebration of horticultural ingenuity.

The revival of "old-fashioned" English flowers was part of a revivalist cult fostered by William Morris and Alfred Tennyson. The cottage garden, for example, as nostalgic construct, epitomized "authentic" folk culture rooted in the past and a "romantic nationalism."[114] At a time of flagging confidence, these associations helped bolster English identity at home and abroad, from Canada to India.[115] In this sense, "old-fashioned flowers" featured in an imperialist rhetoric that used the inferiority of tropical plants from "uncivilized" regions (e.g., Africa) to flaunt the supremacy of the civilized world.[116] William Robinson's fusion of naturalized exotics with old English flowers was based on the premise that they came from places of civilization such as America, the Mediterranean, and the Alps. His favorite plants, previously considered weeds or scrub, gained authority from the theorist of evolution Alfred Russel Wallace. After having spent twelve years in the tropics, Wallace stated that he had seen nothing to equal English gorse or broom.

Yet, there is no obvious ideological source for William Robinson's "wild garden." It is, indeed, a story of pragmatic shifts: drawing on existing traditions of planting such as woodland embellishment, naturalized bulbs, and absorbing new styles such as subtropical foliage plantings.[117] Robinson, born in Ireland in 1838, moved to England in 1861. He took up work for the Royal Botanic Society in Regent's Park, where he was responsible for the herbaceous collection until 1867. During his tenure, he had the opportunity to survey the work then taking place under Markham Nesfield.[118] Around 1863, the famous Broad Walk, which had been planted by 1827 for John Nash's picturesque landscaping, was being turned into the new Avenue Gardens. Between August that year and September 1865, when Robinson's name was attached to the editorial, the *Gardeners' Chronicle* shifted tone. It changed from fulminating against the "evil genius of alteration,"[119] to praising "the clever and beautiful CLASSICAL GARDEN,"[120] to claiming the bedding was "the most original and beautiful examples of colouring seen for a long time."[121] Just a few years later, however, William Robinson began a volte-face—his dogmatic opposition to bedding. First announcing his preference for a garden of botanical rarities, he migrated to the opposition camp. By 1872, he had formalized his attack on C. P. Peach, a defender of the bedding system.[122] The trip to Paris in 1867 as correspondent for *The Times* was a key step. He ended up devoting portions of three books to the merits of subtropical gardening, which meant, in effect, the replacement of color by form, the substitution of foliage for flowers.[123]

Adolphe Alphand featured "bedding" and "subtropical foliage" exotics in his magnificent volume *Les promenades de Paris*. Robinson responded enthusiastically to the "subtropicals," highlighting things with gigantic leaves—"Caladium, Colocasia, Canna, Ficus, Monstera, Solanum Warscewiczii, Wigandia, Dracenas, and Musa Ensete." He had seen the banana in Baron Haussmann's garden in September 1868, flourishing after a winter protected by a thatched shed and dry leaves. The experience of the Bois de Boulogne in Paris led to the formulation of *The Wild Garden*; for, in addition to sub-tropical foliage beds, he had seen hardy plants naturalized. Yet, looking back in 1932, he turned the seeds of this experience into a throwaway remark. It was calculated to root the "wild garden" in his locality. He wrote:

As to the origin of my ideas of the Wild Garden, I think they first occurred to me along the banks of the Southern Railway between East Grinstead and West Hoathly. Sometimes when I went through the station I had a pocketful of seeds of some bush or plant which I used to scatter about, usually forgetting all about them afterwards, but most certainly they all came up again.[124]

The new ideal (already established in 1870) was "naturalizing or making wild innumerable beautiful natives of many regions of the earth in our woods, wild and semi-wild places, rougher parts of pleasure grounds, etc., and in unoccupied places in almost every kind of garden."[125] The advantages were reduced costs, the greater range of plants that could be employed, and a closer connection to nature.

The intention was not to eliminate bedding-out. Instead, by shifting attention to under-utilized areas, marginal places such as hedgerows and bogs could become wilder shrubberies. In the agricultural depression of the late nineteenth century, when poor land was left fallow, it proved fitting to use such areas. In the county of Surrey, for example, the farming population experienced an agricultural failure of sixteen to twenty percent from 1871–73.[126] Hence, the wild garden turned the depression into an aesthetic statement to counteract the unsettling effects of the financial collapse of English farming. Similarly, architectonic historicism, which led to the "formal garden" associated with Reginald Blomfield's 1892 publication and the Blomfield/Robinson feud that followed, may be viewed as a revivalist attempt to bolster identity.[127] Nevertheless, as with Charles Adams Platt's *Italian Garden*, it also involved a battle over whether architects or horticulturists controlled the emerging profession of landscape architecture. Significantly, Jekyll wrote in 1896: "Both are right and both are wrong. The formal army are architects to a man … they exhibit the weakness of an army that is campaigning at too great a distance from its 'base' and certainly do expose themselves to the assaults of the enemy."[128]

In practice, Robinson and Jekyll both worked within an architectural armature. The Arts and Crafts synthesis of art and nature resulted in the perfectly resolved plantings of Hestercombe (among other Lutyens/Jekyll collaborations). Yet, "natural" garden design had persistent ideological leanings, for example in the work of Willy Lange. Lange followed Robinson's mix of nonnatives and natives. He departed from Robinson in his allegiance to Humboldt's phytogeography as one proto-ecological approach,[129] which he subsequently manipulated for racist reasons under the National Socialists.[130] By contrast, Erwin Barth's 1912 proposal for Sachsenplatz in Charlottenburg, Berlin, simply

FIGURE 3.6: Beatrice Parsons (1870–1955), *The Paved Garden*, Gravetye Manor. Signed watercolor, 9 × 11 1/2 inches. Private Collection. Photograph courtesy Christopher Wood Gallery, London.

represented the "natural vegetation types and geological formations" of the Brandenburg area. Hence, he applied "ecological principles" to design so as to edify the public.[131]

By 1920, a "natural" approach to planting thus meant a tentative application of ecology. The "artificial" approach took many forms, including evocations of parterre, but without reference to bright baroque *plate-bandes* or Victorian bedding (e.g., Achille Duchêne's flowerless work at Nordkirchen in Germany, 1906–14, or at Blenheim in England, 1925–30). This aversion to flowers in historicism developed into the anathema of flower color in early modernist thought. In Canada, the governor general's grounds at Rideau Hall kept up a conservative blend of formal and pastoral plantings, displaying more innovation in winter landscaping than in its summer cricket pitch.[132] In India, Viceroy Curzon oversaw replanting of the Taj Mahal grounds as grass plats that evoked the Edwardian "golden age," not the aromatic flowers of Mughal-empire gardening.[133] It was in the herbaceous-woody planting of "garden rooms" at Lawrence Johnston's Hidcote[134] or Beatrix Farrand's Dumbarton Oaks that Repton's vision of zoned "apartments" was revitalized for a post–War generation a century after Waterloo. Repton's artful "summer in winter" or "winter in summer" was realized by China's winter-flowering wonders (*Jasminum nudiflorum* or *Viburnum* x *farreri*), which formed a seasonal sequel to the "Indian summer" of Japanese foliage.

That planting was increasingly subject to rhetoric obfuscating continuities of planting lore becomes clear in two examples on the edge of modernism. Gabriel Guevrekian brought a new sensibility from the Middle East, which he exploited in his provocative "Garden of Water and Light" for the Exposition des Arts Décoratifs et Industriels Modernes in Paris (1925). For planting, however, he resorted to traditional "bedding" (and, significantly, he left it to horticulturists to make the choice of flowers). The tilted triangles were in the complimentary chromatics of Chevreul: orange *Pyrethrum* against blue *Ageratum*, green grass against red *Begonia*.[135]

In 1938, Canadian-born Christopher Tunnard published his groundbreaking modernist theory, *Gardens in the Modern Landscape*. Inventing the term "muddled pointillism," he came down heavily on Gertrude Jekyll. He concluded: "As it was, in upsetting the crude Victorian paint pot, she failed to provide an alternative large enough to serve as a source of inspiration for posterity."[136] While Tunnard's plantings moved toward sculptural abstraction, his border design for a house in Leicester fell back on distinctly Jekyll-like drifts. Jekyll's way with forms and color outlived him (in gardening terms, at least), finding a receptive audience among a few professional landscape architects in the late twentieth century.[137]

Nevertheless, cultivating an edgy viewpoint at the center of a declining empire, Tunnard correctly identified the need for an emerging profession to distance itself from planting design with all its baggage. Horticulture was still associated with elite cultures, with colonial acquisitiveness, with amateurish ways (trade workers, women horticulturists, and rich clients), and with tired Western traditions. It required an infusion from the East, from abstraction, and above all, from a universalizing aesthetic based on functionalism, social conscience, and the science of ecology.

CHAPTER FOUR

Use and Reception

DANIEL J. NADENICEK

> But the use of a public park—like Liberty itself—can be made equitable
> only by the fair apportionment of the amount of freedom to be permitted
> to each class of visitors.
>
> —Frederick Law Olmsted

How can liberty be about restricting freedom as the quotation suggests? The
answer to that question is wrapped in a complex understanding held by a nineteenth-century American ruling elite about the influence of carefully designed
naturalistic scenes on the moral development of lower-class citizens. Those
leaders believed that with the proper behavior, visitors to designed landscapes
would acquire life-changing insights over time.

  Prior to the nineteenth century, "impression management" was an intended
social purpose of many of the grand European designed landscapes.[1] In ex-
travagant gardens such as Versailles, the source and extent of power and authority were openly displayed in their grand designs, and the representational
intent of these gardens was, therefore, obvious to the general populace. The
emergence and evolution of public parks during the nineteenth and early twentieth centuries in Europe and the United States led to a more subtle social
agenda, as elite members of society desired to maintain authority in the wake
of massive and rapid change. The practice of persuasion through public works
was particularly pronounced in nineteenth-century America, where leaders in

a democratic society sought to maintain order and control as physical changes inspired accompanying social and cultural changes.

The ruling elite carefully considered the meaning and purpose of parks for the public. Because there was so much focused intent to influence a broad base of society in the period between 1800 and 1920, public parks are more useful than gardens (many of which were private, smaller, and visited by fewer citizens) in describing a gap between intended uses and meanings, and the actual use and reception by the hundreds of thousands who recreated in those spaces. That wide chasm between the creators' intentions and the actual use and meaning for a broader base of society was especially pronounced in America, where no legal or official hierarchy dividing citizens existed.[2] Despite this lack of aristocracy, leaders in the United States held fast to a social hierarchy, which they saw as necessary to instill citizens with the appropriate values in order to eventually bolster society itself. The design and construction of parks were clearly intended to fulfill that social purpose.

Several other essays in this volume address the phenomenon of the nineteenth-century public park in other cultures and also the uses of private gardens, notably Sonja Dümpelmann's Introduction; Chapter 5—Meaning, by Heath Massey (Schenker); and Chapter 8—Gardens and the Larger Landscape, by Gert Gröning and Joachim Wolschke-Bulmahn. This essay will take advantage of those discussions to concentrate on the public park phenomenon in the new world, or New World, of the United States, which during this period began to assume a dominant cultural and economic position.

PARKS AND THE AMERICAN SOCIAL
SCIENCE ASSOCIATION

During the eighteenth century, the preferred design style of grand allées, *rond-points*, and other expressions of geometric order gave way to composed landscape scenery. The new style first appropriated by the English landed gentry and aristocracy was later applied in other parts of Europe and in the United States. This modern style (as opposed to the ancient style comprised of Renaissance and baroque forms) was transferred from the private realm to the public and applied in numerous parks. Some of the earliest public parks were designed and built in Germany during the first half of the nineteenth century. For example, Peter Joseph Lenné was commissioned in 1824 to lay out a park in Magdeburg, which was sanctioned by town authorities and paid for with public funds. In England, Birkenhead Park near Liverpool was established by law in 1843 for the purpose of providing for "the free recreation of the inhabitants," following an evolutionary period in which growing numbers of citizens were privileged to recreate in the Crown Parks of London.[3] After the design of New York's Central Park in 1858, public parks were built throughout the United States. A similar proliferation occurred in various parts of Europe before and after the design and construction of Central Park.

The period 1800–1920 was a time of unprecedented social, economic, and political change. In the wake of considerable tumult created by those changes, leaders sought ways of maintaining order, stability, and authority. In Europe and the United States, the design of parks was intended to provide some means of reform, while still maintaining the basic system of order. Consequently, especially in the United States, social historians have labeled the provision of parks "conservative reform."[4] The nature of that reform, however, differed from one nation to the next. For example, in France, an imperial regime wished to maintain control in the wake of more than half a century of shifting governments and populist engagement originally spurred by the French Revolution.[5] In America, leaders fearing uncontrolled disruptions sought to instill the proper morals and values in communities across the nation. Because of the democratic nature of the United States and the need to accomplish work in the political arena (and through persuasion), the American story is particularly useful in evaluating use and reception in landscape design.

The ideas embodied in reception theory developed in literature, the performing arts, and history when adapted to the study of park usage provide a framework to explain the divide between designers' intentions (as far as they can be ascertained), and the actual use and understanding of places over time.[6] Scholars such as Hans-Robert Jauss and Stuart Hall have written about ways audiences (readers, viewers) interpret texts (written, designed) based on their cultural backgrounds and life experiences.[7] Through an analysis of German reception theory scholarship, Martyn P. Thompson has further identified the contrast between substantialist theory—text as constructed by the author—and pragmatic theory—text as interpreted by audiences.[8] Thompson's work differs from some reception theory scholars in that he suggests a balanced approach to interpretation that considers the ideas of the creators as well as various audiences. Scholars who study "reception history" also seek to understand reception within a particular historical and social context.[9] It is this balanced approach that is applied in reflecting on nineteenth- and early-twentieth-century American Parks.

The social purposes attributed to parks by the ruling elite in the United States was one of the results of massive immigration and the related rapid settlement of the nation. The state of change brought about by immigration was well stated in 1851 by landscape gardening theorist and popular writer Andrew Jackson Downing (1815–52). Downing had written *A Treatise on the Theory and Practice of Landscape Gardening* in 1841 and edited the *Horticulturist* from 1846 until his untimely death in 1852. In one of his *Horticulturist* essays about the need for a public park in New York, he wrote: "Every ship brings a live cargo from over-peopled Europe, to fill up its [New York's] over crowded lodging houses; every steamer brings hundreds of strangers to fill its thronged thoroughfares."[10] According to Downing, the solution to the chaos and tumult was a type of guided refinement for citizens. In the same essay, he wrote: "Open wide, therefore, the doors of your libraries and picture galleries, all ye true republicans! Plant spacious parks in your cities, and unloose their gates as wide as the gates of morning to the whole people."[11] Ultimately, Frederick Law Olmsted (1822–1903), and Calvert Vaux (1824–95) would design New York's Central Park, as though in fulfillment of Downing's mission.

In 1865, a group of leaders interested in guiding social change in mid-nineteenth-century America formed the American Social Science Association (ASSA). The group, which included Olmsted as a member, believed that all people were capable of guided advancement. The designed landscape was seen as one significant means of contributing to the moral and intellectual improvement of citizens. While some writers such as Albert Fein (and to some extent, Laura Wood Roper) have portrayed Olmsted as the ultimate of social reformers and a true believer in social equality, those historians do little to explain the rich layered social perspectives and the views held by Olmsted within the general context of the time.[12] Thomas L. Haskell in the *Emergence of Professional Social Science: The American Social Science Association and the Crisis of Authority* discusses the clash of idealist (romanticist) and positivist social theories during the nineteenth century.[13] The positivists, some strictly following Herbert Spencer's theories of Social Darwinism, believed in immutable social laws that led to a more rigid hierarchy of people, based in race and ethnic origin.[14] The positivist perspective gained greater strength by the end of the nineteenth century as more people accepted the preeminence of science (or in some cases, pseudo-science). In contrast, members of the Social Science Association, including Olmsted, embraced the idealist perspective—a view of human advance that had developed in New England over a period of years at least since the advent of American Unitarianism in the late eighteenth century. The idealist view held that human improvement was not only possible and necessary, but also that the advancement should be guided by gifted individuals in society, those with money, intellect, and artistic ability.[15] Many societal leaders from New England, including captains of industry, elected officials, and intellectual leaders, promoted and sustained this conservative approach to reform, which in their eyes promised a society of morally upright citizens. Immigrants and African Americans needed education, and those benevolent superintendents of society were equipped to supply it. In other words, they believed in a type of surface reform, which would happen without any wholesale disruptions of society or the economy. Ironically, the disruptions they feared were being created by their own actions. For example, industrialists created insatiable thirst for cheap labor, and railroad entrepreneurs sought settlers for their western land grants and developed a program to attract immigrants from abroad. Conservative reform was also very paternalistic. The ASSA charter referred to the responsibilities of the educated and gifted classes to the "weak, witless, and ignorant."[16]

In the following pages, I first explore a substantialist theory base by discussing national policies developed by the Northern Pacific Railroad and found in the work of its president Frederick Billings (1823–90). As a societal leader and renowned entrepreneur, Billings advocated a clear and prevalent plan for landscape and social change, generally adhered to by era landscape architects. An exploration of two urban parks: Central Park, New York, and Minnehaha Park, Minneapolis, Minnesota, designed thirty years apart, provides a more detailed explanation of the persistent strength of conservative reform as it relates to the designers' intentions. A pragmatic perspective is next offered by demonstrating the ways in which many rank-and-file citizens differed from the designers in their use and reception of those parks. By the turn of the twentieth century and in the progressive era, many new functions inconsistent with the earlier ideals were added to parks, in direct relation to the preferred uses of numerous immigrant groups.

MORAL ORDER AND THE NATIONAL GARDEN

In his essay the *Young American,* Ralph Waldo Emerson wrote: "a well laid garden [would make] the face of the country … a beautiful abode worthy of men."[17] The point of that statement is that the entire nation would be reshaped and designed to accommodate and nurture the settlers who were coming to America from numerous nations. Emerson's prediction about nation-building written in the 1840s came true after the Civil War. The railroad industry was the principal industry involved in making the national garden. Thomas Haskell has discussed how the influx of immigrants and the advance of transportation technologies led to the loss of island communities upon which a system of moral behavior and values had been grounded.[18] Despite those rapid changes, industrialists and entrepreneurs attempted to infuse those small-town values, which had evolved over a long period of time, across the entire nation. Following that purpose, new communities were founded, forests were planted, and parks were developed along the rails of the Northern Pacific Railroad (NPR).

Frederick Billings, president of the NPR from 1879 to 1881, attempted to install island community values and forms as he worked to develop a national landscape. In the 1870s, Billings had established a scientific forest and private park landscape that he opened to the general public in his hometown of Woodstock, Vermont. He concurred with the goals of the American Social Science Association and regularly conferred with some of its members. He also formed personal and professional associations with landscape architects. Olmsted, for example, whom Billings had met at least as early as the mid-1860s, when both men sought the preservation of the Yosemite, was later hired by the NPR to provide a master plan for the settlement of Tacoma, Washington. Billings employed Robert Morris Copeland (1830–74) to design his home landscape in Woodstock.[19] He also maintained a home in New York and was familiar with the design intent and physical layout of Central Park, where his doctors sent him to convalesce.[20] In the early 1870s, Billings had also served as chairman of the NPR Land Committee, charged with the sale and development of lands within the railroad's huge land grant. During that period, he corresponded with Horace William Shaler Cleveland (1814–1900), who in 1873 published *Landscape Architecture as Applied to the Wants of the West with an Essay on Forest Planting on the Great Plains*. The book is best understood as a plan for the physical and social development of a nation being built along rails. The larger vision was that of cities built upon a connected park system and tied to an expansive hinterland, its resources would be transported daily to the city by rail. Those urban parks, as he would later write, were to provide something more than "the workshop in which we have wrought."[21] For the larger landscape, Cleveland envisioned rural communities along the rails carefully designed to fit the natural topography connected to the nurturing elements of nature. Beyond that he suggested the strategic planting of millions of trees for the benefit of the railroads and citizens alike.[22]

As chairman of the Land Committee, Billings pursued a development philosophy similar to Cleveland's. He desired for each new town along the rails to include a designed park. In concert with Cleveland's scheme to plant millions of trees in the West, Billings suggested that the trees would enlighten the people

FIGURE 4.1: F. Jay Haynes, photograph of Missoula, Montana, 1884, built along the NPR. Note the tree-lined square slightly left of center. Courtesy of the Montana Historical Society.

and provide a utilitarian benefit (to the railroads). Of tree planting activities, he wrote that the NPR should "set the example and encourage the practice of setting out trees" in new communities and among the settlers. He also suggested that "in disposing of lands ... the Land Department should, as far as possible, by conditions of reservations [of lands and the design of] ... squares, and every practicable method help the organization into a life of moral order, and spare no effort to keep out the vicious elements and disorders, which generally affect new civilizations,"[23] Billings was personally shaken by the significant social and cultural changes that were taking place in communities across the nation. Ironically, he and other members of the ruling elite caused those changes, as they recruited people from across Europe to emigrate to the United States. The Northern Pacific published brochures to encourage immigration to its western lands, and sent recruiting agents to several European countries. However, the ideals and moral fiber that Billings saw in the stalwart people of Woodstock, Vermont, were the same values he wished to inspire in new communities across America. In setting the right example for those settlers, he considered the lay and the look of the land of paramount importance. The profession of landscape architecture developed during the nineteenth century as a means of achieving the social ideals espoused by Billings and other American leaders sympathetic with ASSA ideals. While Olmsted and Cleveland believed that the new profession should intervene in the landscape at all scales, they were particularly sanguine about the power of urban parks to reach the hearts and minds of people.[24]

OLMSTED'S INTENTIONS: CENTRAL PARK

While in California during the mid-1860s, Olmsted set out to write a *History of Civilization*, a work he never completed. In the manuscript, he discussed the similarity between rough-and-ready frontier environments such as those conceived by Billings and built by the NPR, and Eastern cities fast filling with uncultured immigrants.[25] New York's Central Park was designed to quiet the frontier mentality. Olmsted had established his social theories in the years prior to the American Civil War. He witnessed the great throng of immigrants Downing had reported, and studied slavery and social conditions in the South, where he traveled as a columnist for the *New York Daily Times*. He later published those experiences in *Journey in the Seaboard Slave States* (1856) and *Journey through Texas* (1857). Like his associates and future colleagues in the ASSA, he advocated and believed in the possibility of moral advance for all people, including African American slaves. The question was how long those advancements would take. He believed that it would take the longest amount of time for the ex-slave because the slave was "little better than a cunning idiot and a cowed savage" in need of close guardianship.[26] Olmsted maintained a similar perspective on immigrants from various nations, suggesting that the United States were receiving "[c]hiefly those elements of European population which were the most inharmonious and unmanageable."[27]

Olmsted's 1870 paper to the ASSA explained how parks might help elevate New York's lower classes. In the paper, Olmsted discussed the affective consequences of urban life on the masses of people coming from the countryside and abroad. For Olmsted, it was essential to counter "the effect on their minds of street contact" in order to quiet and then educate each citizen. Olmsted went on to explain his theory of recreation adapted for the purpose of moral and physical advance of the people. He stated that there were two major categories: exertive recreation and receptive recreation. The exertive category included games, vigorous movement, and various sports. Receptive recreation was devoid of significant physical exertion or challenging mental activity. Receptive recreation, which always involved slower movement through the landscape, was divided by Olmsted into the categories of gregarious and neighborly forms of receptive recreation. When large groups came together for show or to partake in boisterous activity, they were engaging in gregarious recreation. Olmsted commented that those in polite New England society saw such activities as "childish and savage," because there was "little of what we call intellectual gratification in it."[28] Olmsted, then, preferred the neighborly form of receptive recreation, which would "be highly counteractive to the prevailing bias to degeneration and demoralization" found in the city, instead creating circumstances "favorable [to] pleasurable wakefulness of the mind without stimulating exertion."[29] This type of recreation and movement through the park in small numbers would stimulate greater mental and physical health, inspire "virtue," and bring a facsimile of domestic gathering to all classes of people. In designing parks, the goal was the creation of a "ground to which people may easily go after their days work is done, and where they may stroll for an hour, seeing, hearing, and feeling nothing of the bustle and jar of the streets, where they shall in effect, find the city put away from them." "What we want to gain," said Olmsted, is "tranquility and rest to the mind" in order to fend off "opportunities and temptations to shabbiness, disorder, and indecency."[30]

Olmsted and Vaux's artistic strategies in Central Park directly aligned with those social goals. The design moves were inspired by the English Landscape School and picturesque theory, German romanticism, and especially John Ruskin's writing. Large open spaces were not meant to accommodate large crowds—in fact, political rallies and demonstrations (such as organized labor) were not allowed in the park—rather, they were part of an experience where the individuals or small groups were to move through the landscape along paths within dark glades and then discover warmth, light, and a long view as they came to a sunlit open space. The experience was intended to be much like discovering a natural clearing while walking through a country forest. In a January 1872 letter to H. G. Stebbins, president of the New York Public Parks Department, Olmsted and Vaux likened the aesthetic influences of the open pastoral landscape to the mysterious but wondrous affects found in paintings.[31] During the early phases of the park's construction, Olmsted oversaw numerous site scale plantings with the specific purpose of creating the appropriate picture. In the same letter to Stebbins, Olmsted and Vaux demonstrated the detail to which they envisioned artistic influences to occur:

> A cluster of hornbeams and hemlocks, the trunks of some twisting over crannied rock, the face of the rock brightened by lichens, and half veiled by tresses of vines growing over it from the rear, and its base lost in the tangle of ground pine, mosses, and ferns would be of considerable value, [and the] … intricate disposition of lights and shadows seen in the back parts of it would create a degree of obscurity not absolutely impenetrable, but sufficient to affect the imagination with a sense of mystery.[32]

SCENES IN CENTRAL PARK.

FIGURE 4.2: Central Park Scenes. From W. C. Bryant, ed. *Picturesque America; or the Land We Live in*, 1874, vol. 2, 556.

It is little wonder that Olmsted desired a quiet and contemplative experience for park visitors given the layered complexity of the multiple aesthetic experiences he envisioned for the populace.

CLEVELAND'S SOCIAL INTENTIONS IN MINNEHAHA PARK

Horace Cleveland developed a slightly different design approach, while still grounding it in a similar social agenda focused on guiding and uplifting lower-class citizens. There is no record that Cleveland ever attended ASSA meetings, but he was personally acquainted and maintained correspondence with many of the association's members, such as George Williams Curtis, Charles Eliot Norton, George Barrell Emerson, and Olmsted. In *A Few Words on the Central Park*, 1856, Cleveland and his partner Robert Morris Copeland wrote of the importance of paternal guidance through design. "[The landscape gardener is] to interpret and render legible to the popular mind lessons [held in nature] …, and this is to be done not by any finical display of artificial embellishment but by the tasteful use of such natural additions as are required to develop and carry out the sentiment which to the truly devoutly cultivated mind is evident at a glance even without addition."[33] In the quotation, Cleveland and Copeland reveal their belief that because they were blessed with cultivated minds, they also had a duty to educate and morally advance the mass society. They went on to suggest, "The moral influence resulting from [the designed landscape], is one of the strongest that can be brought to mind [and] … the silent and unseen influence exerted will constitute the most vital feature of [moral advancement]."[34] Cleveland, like Olmsted, had been nurtured in the "mind of New England."[35] In part because of his Unitarian background and associations with ASSA members and others with similar views, he was convinced of the great potential for human advancement guided by those gifted for the purpose. Like Olmsted, Cleveland also believed in maintaining an ordered society and that social change should happen slowly, even as urban and regional landscapes rapidly changed.

While his social goals were similar to Olmsted's, his design approach was somewhat different. In Central Park, Olmsted was very willing to sacrifice indigenous plants for the sake of intended artistic effects. Cleveland generally accepted and built upon the existing conditions.[36] For example, in the master plan that he and Copeland completed for Sleepy Hollow Cemetery in Concord, Massachusetts, in 1855, a natural amphitheater became the center of the design and native plants were used throughout the landscape.[37] Minnehaha

FIGURE 4.3: Minnehaha Falls. From W. C. Bryant, ed. *Picturesque America; or the Land We Live in,* 1874, vol. 2, 350.

Park in Minneapolis is a good example of a design in which Cleveland melded his naturalistic aesthetic and social purpose through design. The landscape was first protected from industrial encroachment and then designed by Cleveland as a park beginning in 1889. Minnehaha Falls, the central feature of the park, had been made famous by Henry Wadsworth Longfellow's classic book-length poem, *The Song of Hiawatha*. For years prior to the preservation of the site, thousands of people journeyed to the falls on pilgrimages to contemplate Longfellow's poetic messages. Although Native Americans were the subject, *The Song of Hiawatha*, in its essence, was intended for white society, to contemplate the inevitability of the progress of America and the movement of civilization across the continent. At the same time, the poem presented a sense of melancholy about fast-fleeting nature, of which the Native American was the essential symbol. The sense of loss and collision with progress was represented in Hiawatha's vision.

I beheld, too, in that vision / All the secrets of the future, / Of the distant days that shall be. / I beheld the westward marches / Of the unknown, crowded nations. / All the land was full of people, / Restless struggling, toiling, striving, / Speaking many tongues, yet feeling / But one heart-beat in their bosoms. / In the woodlands rang their axes, / Smoked their towns in all the valleys, / Over all the lakes and rivers, / Rushed their great canoes of thunder.

   Then a darker, drearier vision / Passed before me, vague and cloudlike: / I beheld our nation scattered, / … Saw the remnants of our people / Sweeping westward, wild and woeful, / Like the cloud-rack of the tempest, / Like the withered leaves of Autumn![38]

In the wake of that massive change, Cleveland offered a basic naturalistic design for the site carefully fitted to the existing conditions. In a sense the landscape stood as a remnant or ruin of the nature that was quickly disappearing because of the inevitable advance of civilization. At the beginning of his poem, Longfellow identified his audience; those with a sense of forlorn contemplation about what had passed.

Ye who sometimes, in your rambles / Through the green lanes of the country, / Where the tangled barberry-bushes / Hang there tufts of crimson berries/ Over stone walls gray with mosses, / Pause by some neglected graveyard, / For a while to muse, and ponder / On a half-effaced inscription, / Written with skill of song-craft, / Homely phrases, but each letter / Full of hope and yet of heart-break, full of all the tender pathos / Of the Here and the Hereafter;— / Stay and read this rude inscription, / Read this song of Hiawatha![39]

Nature and the Native American were seen as romantic ruins in the poem to guide, educate, and provide for the moral advance of the people. The designed landscape at Minnehaha would, likewise, stand as a remnant of fast fleeting nature. The landscape above the falls and the ravine directly below were intended to remain in as natural a state as possible allowing visitors to contemplate both the scenery and Longfellow's poem. Areas that had been worn by use were restored to reflect the original vegetation on the site.

THOSE WHO VIEWED IT DIFFERENTLY

This substantialist reading of Olmsted and Cleveland's design work and written texts suggests that they believed that carefully managed artistic expressions would almost magically (Olmsted used the words "ancient charm") uplift citizens to a higher order. From a pragmatic (reception) theory perspective, the mass of society, particularly lower classes and immigrant groups, were probably

SHOO!

The superintendent of parks has informed the park board that the zoo at Minnehaha is out of place.

FIGURE 4.4: *Minneapolis Tribune* cartoon from February 7, 1906.

unaware of the social purposes and attached artistic meanings. To them, Olmsted's open spaces created opportunities for gathering and community events; they did not share his belief that the landscape would be diminished through use. Evidence of the divide can be found in the many ways groups chose to recreate in Central and Minnehaha Parks. Over time, the politicians dependent on votes from the poor sections of the cities, learned that the addition of active recreation and amusements in opposition to the designers' ideals would placate the masses. At one point, a speeding track (racetrack) was seriously considered for Central Park. In a letter to Paul Dana of the *New York Sun* in 1890, Olmsted vehemently argued that the facility would attract large and unruly crowds and that the specific use had nothing to do with the park's character, "a place of rural recreation."[40] For many years following the Greensward Plan for Central Park, its designers Olmsted and Vaux argued against many more encroachments suggested for the park. Challenges to Cleveland's naturalistic expression in Minnehaha came immediately after the park's completion. In both cases, an array of amusements and concessions were proposed. The small Central Park Zoo (often referred to as the menagerie) was slated for expansion on a number of occasions. In circulars and letters, Olmsted argued against expansion plans for the zoo. He was concerned that the facility would undermine the artistic and expressive nature of the park and the crowds of people would disrupt the tranquility he intended for the landscape. After the turn of the century, the Minneapolis Park Commissioners officially removed an animal collection from Minnehaha Park. That action was met with entrepreneurial resolve, when Robert "Fish" Jones kept animals directly offsite in a landscape named Longfellow Gardens. Longfellow Gardens was similar to an amusement park and included rides, unsympathetic statues of Native Americans, and food and drink. A scaled down replica of Longfellow's Cambridge, Massachusetts home was also built near the park.

In both parks, concessionaires wished to profit from the crowds. Goat-cart rides were common in Central Park and vendors attempted to sell food and drink whenever they could escape the watchful eye of the park keepers. Peanut vendors seemed ubiquitous in both parks. Charles Loring, longtime president of the Minneapolis Park Board, pasted a parody of Longfellow's poem into his scrapbook, which spoke directly to the negative consequences of the peanut:

Where is the lovely Minnehaha—/ Where the peerless Laughing Water? / On the site of papa's wigwam, / Where the arrow maker dwelt once, / Now are stands to foist the peanut / On the Paleface who loves Nature / Those who come to dream of romance / And to lay their souls in quiet, / Find the peanut ever present / Find it haunting every footstep.[41]

A photography structure planned for an area near Minnehaha Falls raised the ardor of Cleveland and his compatriots. The idea for that structure was that visitors would be provided with Native American costumes so that they could have their pictures taken with the falls in the background. The stand would also sell trinkets and Native American paraphernalia. Cleveland could imagine nothing more offensive, and argued against the scheme at a Minneapolis Park Board meeting. "Now this building is one whose only object is the making of money. To erect it at that place would be an intrusion and all together contrary to the spirit of the place and the kind of improvement that should be made."[42]

In both parks statues, plaques, and monument structures were added, often in support of the heritage and culture of immigrant groups residing in the cities.

When a statue to Gunnar Wennerburg, Swedish scholar, poet, and statesman, was set in Minnehaha Park, hundreds of Scandinavian immigrants crowded into the park for the unveiling.[43] Numerous statues were placed in Central Park in support of immigrant cultures, even though Olmsted wished to tightly control the placement of such monuments. One of the earliest examples was the monument to Alexander von Humboldt promoted by German-Americans and placed in the landscape in 1869. While active recreation in the form of sporting events was not originally allowed in either park, groups regularly broke the rules. Baseball was particularly popular. Olmsted was on a constant look out for such infringements and, in one instance, railed against a large group of "rude fellows" playing ball in one of the park's open spaces.[44] As time passed, local politics yielded to numerous pressures from various constituencies, and active recreation facilities were added to both parks.

In his 1870 paper to the ASSA, Olmsted had argued that Central Park was successful and that generally boisterous and rowdy citizens were almost magically respectful in the way they used the park, which ultimately led to their own refinement. In 1880, while clearly worn down from numerous battles to insure that the park was properly used, he presented a paper titled *Justifying the Value of a Public Park* to the same organization. During that decade, Olmsted had become convinced that more control was needed to enforce the proper use of the park. He told the association that the people's preferred use should not determine the design, because the rural expressions were intended for their benefit. He went on to suggest that the many advocates for various incompatible uses were not "naturally, all at once perfectly clear-headed, coherent, [and] perspicuous in [their] demands."[45] What undermined Olmsted's earlier belief that the park would naturally refine citizens without regulation?

In 1870, by Olmsted's own calculation the park was still a great distance for the center of population. While thousands visited the park during that period, a large percentage of the most destitute were unable to recreate there. By 1880, the number of challenges to Olmsted's intended purpose increased as those groups augmented their park usage. Many immigrant groups had long preferred what Olmsted had referred to as gregarious recreation, in part because of the community cohesion it brought. Numerous privately held gardens, including beer gardens in New York, had served that purpose for years. During the early years after the opening of Central Park, German immigrants preferred to visit the private establishment known as Jones' Wood over Central Park, because there they were allowed to gather in groups, engage in games of chance, listen to music, and enjoy each other's company, in keeping with the spirit of the occasion.[46] Eventually representatives from the Irish and German communities served on the Park Commission increasing the pressure for change.

FIGURE 4.5: As this image of Central Park's Bethesda Terrace in the 1870s shows, mostly members of the middle and upper classes visited Central Park in its early years. The only lower class person in the image is there to care for children of the "more fortunate." From W. C. Bryant, ed. *Picturesque America; or the Land We Live in*, 1874, vol. 2, 556.

Over time, even Olmsted and Cleveland acquiesced, to some degree. In Minneapolis, Cleveland created parks fit to the unique characteristics of various neighborhoods. When Olmsted designed Boston's Franklin Park in 1886, he called for an ante-park to include a children's play lot and amusement park, an athletic field, and an amphitheater for musical events. Beyond the ante-park was a large country park meant to allow people to retreat from the city into simulated rural scenery. While the country park was intended for the quiet contemplation of scenery, from the beginning people flocked to the natural open spaces to "play baseball and lawn tennis, attend larger school and charity picnics, and enjoy a Fourth of July Celebration."[47]

Despite those alterations, Cleveland and Olmsted would go to their graves (Cleveland in 1900 and Olmsted in 1903) believing in the integrity of their approaches and the attached social ideals. In an 1889 letter to William Watts Folwell, University of Minnesota president and later president of the Minneapolis Park Board, Cleveland wrote of his distaste for the socialist and utopian thinking of Edward Bellamy, who had recently published *Looking Backward, 2000–1887*.

The author goes to sleep in 1887 and wakes up in 2000 and finds a total social revolution. It is ingenious and well managed and well written. All of the social problems of today have been solved, there is no money and no shops and no buying and selling. Everything is managed by government and all independence is gone ... The whole theory is based on what appears to me to be three monstrous errors, and it is very painful to me to accept such evidence as the popularity of this book affords that they are generally believed—first that labor is a curse instead of a blessing,—second that happiness is the end and object of life, and third that wealth is essential to happiness,—I deny every one of them.[48]

Cleveland detested the utopian mindset and also firmly believed that the general populace was incapable of such advancements without clear guidance from above.

NEW PROGRAMS FOR SMALL URBAN PARKS

By the turn of the twentieth century, many others, not only utopians, contributed to changing social ideas in America. In 1899, Thorstein Veblen published *The Theory of the Leisure Class* in which he criticized the conspicuous leisure

FIGURE 4.6: Jacob Riis, *Street Arabs in Night Quarters*. From J. Riis, *How the Other Half Lives*, [1901] 1971, 208.

that inevitably led to conspicuous consumption and conspicuous waste. The work of the ASSA became more academic and specialized, which spurred the formation of professional organizations such as the American Political Science Association (1903) and the American Sociological Society (1905). In addition to those scholarly explorations and organizations, more and more people became aware of the negative conditions within urban environments from the writing and photography of those directly involved. As a police reporter for the *New York Tribune* and the Associated Press Bureau, Jacob Riis photographed haunting scenes of the deplorable conditions in New York's East Side slum district. In 1890, he published *How the Other Half Lives: Studies Among the Tenements of New York*. Riis's book helped replace abstract and idealistic vantages typical of the ASSA with vivid images, uncomfortable descriptions of reality, a litany of problems, and a cry for action. Jane Addams's social experience at Chicago's Hull House had also received growing attention by the first years of the twentieth century.[49]

Because of that richer and more realistic understanding of urban life, parks would never again be seen as a panacea, but only as one integral part of a larger reform effort. Early-twentieth-century articles in the *Annals of the American Academy of Political and Social Science* explained how urban parks were seen as part of a larger social agenda focused on community building.[50] In 1910, the *Annals* included a revealing description of changes in the Chicago parks. The article described the addition of numerous small parks in the city, most of them with ample provision of recreation centers, ball fields, and playgrounds.[51] Those developments in Chicago reflected similar developments taking place in urban environments across the United States. The Playground Association of America was organized in 1906 with President Theodore Roosevelt's support, expanded its scope, and in 1911 was renamed the Park and Recreation Association of America, and the National Recreation Association in 1926. Engaging urban communities through a multifaceted approach to park design and programming was a central focus of the organization. In a 1923 article in the *Annals*, Helen Sedgwick Jones, a Playground and Recreation Association of America member, suggested that while Olmsted's passive approach to recreation was still important, it was but one of many methods of assisting urban youth and adults. She described:

> The Community idea [as]—that of bringing people together in common interest, in more neighborliness and understanding—the idea which is coming more and more into prominence in recreation programs of today. This is demonstrated by the number of neighborhood organizations and associations which have formed; ... by the amount of community drama

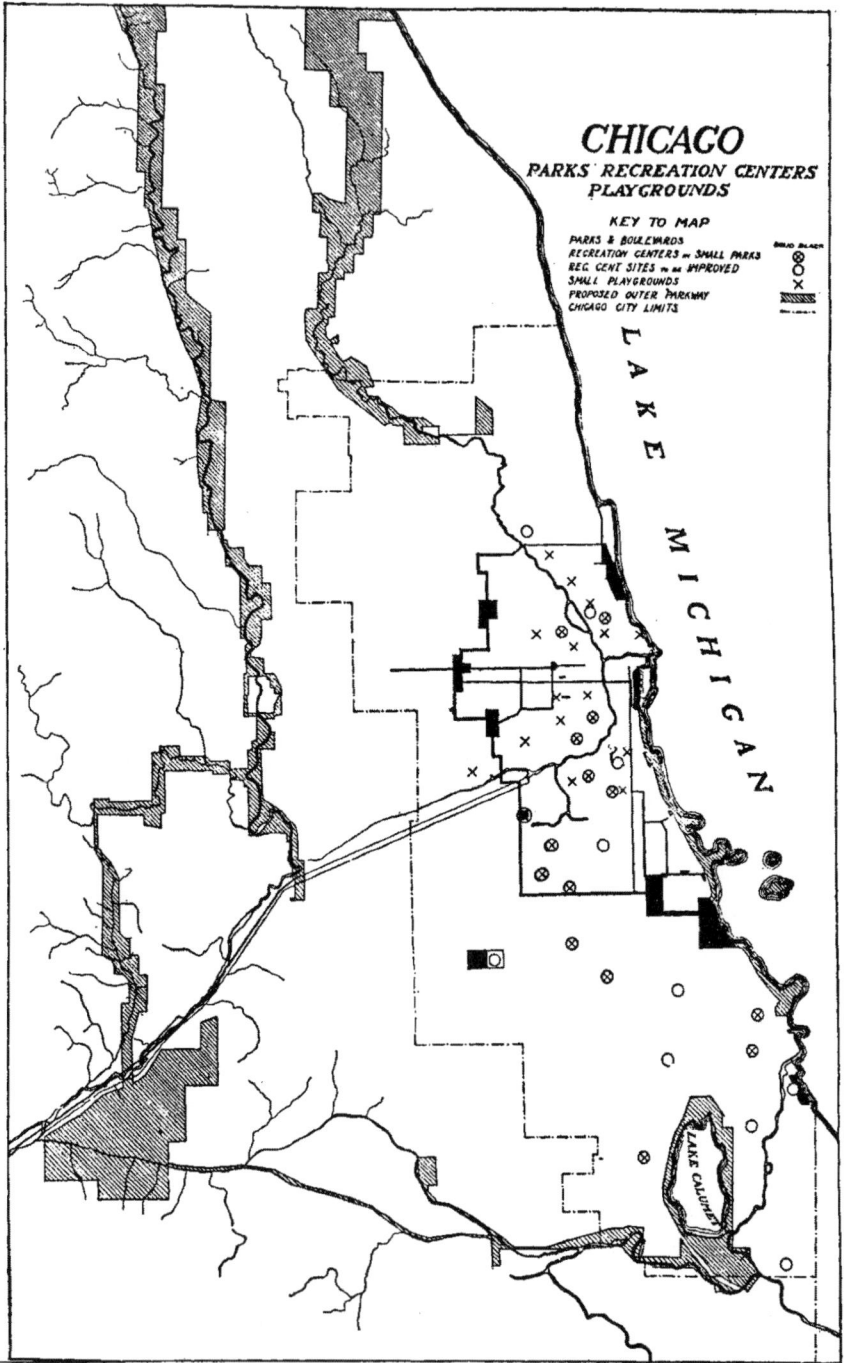

FIGURE 4.7: Map showing the proliferation of small neighborhood parks and recreation centers. From G. R. Taylor, "Recreation Developments in Chicago," 1910.

and community music which has developed; by summer camps which are being conducted; and by city-wide carnivals and festivals and community days. It is further reflected in the group idea which has come into favor during the last few years in athletic and game contests for boys and girls and the tendency to make many recreation activities of children take on the aspect of a group game.[52]

While Olmsted's passive recreation was expanded to embrace empirical exploration and was often called "nature study" during the first years of the twentieth century, it was only one part of an overall system of community building and engagement. At the same time that cities embraced the more utilitarian park forms, the nation pushed forward with the organization and expansion of national parks. Under the auspices of the National Park Service, formed in 1916, passive recreation alternatives amid some of the nation's natural wonders were offered to those with the means to travel.[53]

CONCLUSION

In the 1890s, Cleveland retired to suburban Chicago. When Charles Loring, Minneapolis Park Board president, asked him to deliver a paper at a meeting of the American Park and Outdoor Art Association, Cleveland at first reacted negatively, suggesting that he was out of sync with a quickly changing perspective on parks. The quiet pastoral approach he, Olmsted, and societal superintendents such as Billings advocated could not fulfill the desired result, because the task was too immense and the destiny of dramatic change too disquieting.[54] In implementing their social agendas, Olmsted and Cleveland vastly misjudged the amount of necessary cultural knowledge it would take for poor citizens of multiple nationalities to understand the intricacies of design based in a long heritage and great depth of aesthetic theory. The urban poor would choose to recreate in their own way. By 1920, a greater appropriation of science and progress in the social sciences brought a multifaceted approach to urban social problems.

An understanding of the use and reception of nineteenth- and early-twentieth-century American parks provides deep insights on significant social and cultural changes taking place in the United States during the period under study. The American story also provides a clear distinction between the substantialist (text as constructed by creators) and the pragmatic (text as interpreted by users) perspectives. As the nation entered the progressive era during the first decades of the twentieth century, the leadership base broadened, and new professions and professional organizations reached out to rank and file citizens with greater effectiveness. The design of urban parks, especially, reflected the social agenda resulting from those interactions. However, the fact that new park forms were envisioned, and that the reception of Olmsted and Cleveland's design work was often different from what they had expected, does not diminish the artistic qualities of their parks and the rich design legacy they left for future generations of landscape architects and the general populace. It is also worth remembering that Olmsted and Cleveland, and Billings' idealist vantage, led them to believe that all people were capable of achieving a richer existence.[55] Today, their landscapes are filled with all classes of people enjoying that legacy.

CHAPTER FIVE

Meaning

HEATH MASSEY (SCHENKER)

What is the meaning of gardens in the nineteenth century? This simple question demands a complex answer. Depending on the place or particular historic moment under scrutiny, gardens convey many different meanings. Yet, it is possible to step back and describe the meaning of nineteenth-century gardens broadly, in terms of a sweeping sociocultural change that occurred during this period: the nineteenth century was the century that gave rise to the modern, industrial city. Industrialization and the new capitalist order transformed both the rural and urban experience in the nineteenth century, but cities grew and changed at an extraordinary rate. The century saw a general and widespread shift toward urban experience, both literally and figuratively. It can be characterized as a period in which the Western world tipped to funnel rural populations into towns and cities. Cities represented progress in the public imagination as never before, riding a great wave of scientific and technological advancements. Yet, the social and cultural momentum toward cities in this century engendered considerable cultural ambivalence. Gardens embodied conflicting, often ambivalent reactions to urbanization and the social changes that attended urbanization in this period.

THE COUNTRY-CITY DICHOTOMY
IN THE NINETEENTH CENTURY

In his exhaustive study *The Country and the City*, Raymond Williams noted that the tendency to contrast the country and the city as fundamentally different

MEANING

ways of life can be traced at least as far back to the classical period, if not further. The country-city dichotomy has been a constant theme in Western culture at least since Virgil celebrated the pastoral ideal in the face of threatened "loss and eviction … a contrast already familiar from some earlier literature, in times of war and civil disturbance, when the peace of country life could be contrasted with the disturbance of war and civil war and the political chaos of the cities."[1] In the ensuing centuries, the country-city contrast has changed in nuance responding to social and environmental transformation of both the countryside and cities. This dichotomy is particularly apropos to understanding the cultural meaning of Western gardens in the nineteenth century, as the differences between these two realms of cultural experience gained resonance in this period. Physically, both the rural and urban landscapes changed markedly and rapidly in this period, due to widespread modernization of both agriculture and industry. Traditional ideas about the country and the city evolved more slowly, reflecting not only change but also cultural resistance to change.

Large demographic shifts occurred in the nineteenth century on an international scale. Rural populations decreased in industrializing nations in proportion to the whole and urban populations expanded proportionately. Larger cities such as London, Paris, and New York grew into bustling, international centers of industry and finance, and the growth rate of smaller industrial cities even outpaced them. Britain, as the leading industrial nation in the world in the early nineteenth century, led the way in modeling changes that would soon sweep the rest of the industrializing world. "London between 1821 and 1841 grew by twenty percent; Manchester, Birmingham, Leeds and Sheffield by more than forty percent; Bradford by sixty-five percent."[2] Similar changes occurred in France, as Paris grew exponentially in the 1850s and 1860s, becoming a manufacturing and financial center to rival London, and other cities in France, such as Lille, Rouen, and Rheims, built factories and connected up to an expanding rail network with Paris at the center.[3] In the United States, New York grew from a small seaport into a major manufacturing city, and with the expansion of the railroad across the North American continent, cities such as Chicago, Saint Louis, and San Francisco boomed and became manufacturing centers. Expanding towns and cities encroached on pastures and woodlots. The growing urban centers acted like giant magnets, sucking up workers from farms and villages, or at least this was a common perception. Agriculture, although thriving, accounted for a decreasing proportion of the national economies in the industrializing nations. In England, early in the century, agriculture "provided forty percent of the national product; in mid-century twenty percent; by the end of the century, less than ten percent. At the beginning of the century, a third of all workers were employed in agriculture; in mid-century, a fifth; by the end of the century, less than a tenth."[4]

The critical shift in the balance between the country and the city that occurred in the nineteenth century in England foreshadowed similar shifts in other Western countries. But it is important to keep such statistics in perspective, as Williams has pointed out. For example, although "by the middle of the nineteenth century the urban population of England exceeded the rural population: the first time in human history that this had ever been so, anywhere ... as late as 1871 more than half the population lived in villages or in towns of less then twenty thousand people. Only just over a quarter lived in cities, and the mark for the city, in that computation, is a hundred thousand people."[5] Yet, the significance of urbanization as a social phenomenon and cultural force in the nineteenth century must not be underestimated. The image of the city was even more powerful than its reality; the nineteenth century perceived itself as "an age of great cities" (the title of a book by Robert Vaughan published in 1843).

As industrial growth invaded the countryside, the areas that remained untouched by human presence steadily diminished. These areas were increasingly recognized as threatened, and as they shrank, they gained cultural value. A heightened sense of loss fostered growing appreciation of the wilder parts of the rural landscape that remained untouched by human intervention. This sensibility, that is, an appreciation of wild and uncultivated landscapes, had by the end of the eighteenth century grown into an aesthetic known as the Picturesque. The picturesque sensibility gained popularity internationally, as over the course of the nineteenth century increasing understanding of the complexities of nature and the effects of human culture on the natural world went hand-in-hand with accelerated exploitation of the countryside. Increasingly mechanized agriculture and expanding extraction industries left indelible marks on rural landscapes and these signs of progress intensified the sentiments of loss and anxiety attached to the areas that remained undisturbed by such progress. The picturesque aesthetic codified and heightened appreciation of the vanishing pre-industrial countryside in the face of inevitable and inexorable change. As George Perkins Marsh noted in his book *Man and Nature* (1864), "Man is everywhere a disturbing agent. Wherever he plants his foot, the harmonies of nature are turned to discords. The proportions and accommodation which insured the stability of existing arrangements are overthrown."[6]

The new countryside reflected new social structures and new agricultural practices. As a new capitalist order replaced older social systems, land was redistributed and managed differently. Farms became larger; commons disappeared. These transformations occurred throughout Europe and also in newly

FIGURE 5.1: George Inness, *The Lackawanna Valley*, c. 1856, oil on canvas. Gift of Mrs. Huttleston Rogers, Image © 2007 Board of Trustees, National Gallery of Art, Washington, DC.

settled communities, such as the United States, where massive clearing of forests signaled the relentless march of settlement. Railroads closed the distances between coasts and knitted towns and cities together in a tightening network of rails, noise, and smoke. American painter George Inness, who was influenced by the French Barbizon School during trips to Paris in the 1850s, famously depicted the transformation of the American countryside in a painting entitled *The Lackawanna Valley*, shown in Figure 5.1, commissioned by the Delaware, Lackawanna and Western Railroad in 1855. Following shortly behind the trains came new towns, as Ralph Waldo Emerson noted in his journal in the 1840s:

> I hear the whistle of the locomotive in the woods. Wherever that music comes it has its sequel. It is the voice of the civility of the Nineteenth Century saying, "Here I am." It is interrogative: it is prophetic: and this Cassandra is believed: "Whew! Whew! Whew! How is real estate here in the swamp and wilderness? Ho for Boston! Whew! Whew! ... I will plant a dozen houses on this pasture next moon, and a village anon."[7]

While the countryside became increasingly a locus of nostalgia, the city came to represent progress and opportunity. The landscape of the future was clearly understood to be urban. Rapidly growing urban centers were fed not only by migration from the countryside, but also by waves of immigrants from various "other" places in the world, as people sought a better life in the emerging capitals of industry. Cities were becoming more self-conscious about being centers of culture, as well as of government and commerce, finance and industry. Governments poured resources into cities, transforming the urban landscape, applying new theories of urban design, creating boulevards, parks and squares, new civic institutions and new buildings to house them, new sewers and new fresh-water delivery systems. "Modernity" became the mantra of civic leaders around the world.

Yet the new nineteenth-century cities also generated anxiety along with their promises of progress and modernity. The accelerated and unprecedented expansion of cities often outpaced the authorities' ability to manage the growth. Cities seemed out of control as they became crowded, dense and vertical as never before. As cities around the world harbored numerous epidemics of disease, such as cholera and tuberculosis, city life was increasingly viewed as unhealthy. Large parts of cities lacked proper sanitation. The streets were visibly dirty and coal-fueled industries created a pall of polluted air, that hung over cities like a deep fog. Indeed, the London "fog," a thick, noxious haze resulting from burning coal, became legendary. Poverty in cities was more concentrated and visible than poverty in the country, which was more diffuse. Unlike small towns in the country, where many nineteenth-century city-dwellers had been born and raised, cities were viewed as impersonal, lacking in sense of community and inhospitable. Crime rates rose hand in hand with urban poverty. These negative images of the city contrasted vividly in the public imagination with images of the country, which became an imaginative repository for everything the modern, industrial city was not: safety, cleanliness, fresh air, health, community, morality. These contrasts were enhanced and reinforced by increasingly popular novels and melodramas in the theater.[8]

Perhaps the most significant change in the country-city dichotomy in this period was related to the phenomenal growth of the British Empire. "The Victorian British empire was noteworthy for its size and diversity: in 1837 it was some three million square miles in extent; by the 1890s it had grown to over 11 million square miles, about a fifth of the earth's land surface."[9] As Britain evolved into an industrial and predominantly urban society, the country-city dichotomy took on new meaning at the scale of the empire. Britain became the urban, manufacturing, and commercial center for the extensive colonies, and the colonies acted as the new countryside, supplying food and raw materials. Migrations of people from the outposts of the British Empire to the British Isles mirrored, on a larger scale, migrations from the countryside to cities within Britain. These waves of migration were accompanied by reverse migrations of British citizens leaving to take up new lives in the colonies. "The lands of the Empire were an idyllic retreat, an escape from debt or shame, or an opportunity for making a fortune. An expending middle class found its regular careers abroad, as war and administration in the distant lands became more organized. New rural societies entered the English imagination, under the shadow of political and economic control: the plantation worlds of Kipling and Maugham and early Orwell; the trading worlds of Conrad and Joyce Cary."[10] It is helpful to keep this changing, expanding sense of the country-city dichotomy in mind as one looks for meaning in nineteenth-century gardens, particularly the gardens of the new international bourgeoisie that gained in power and influence in the Age of Empire.

The meanings embodied in nineteenth-century gardens reflect a heightened cultural perception of the country-city dichotomy in this period. In a large sense, nineteenth-century gardens were an antidote to rapidly growing nineteenth-century cities. They offered idealized imagery of the countryside to counterbalance the rampant urbanism of the period and moderate some of the negatives associated with urban growth. Nineteenth-century gardens were fundamentally conceived as refuges from urban life and they provided an outlet for the considerable nostalgia associated with the changing country, recreating the rural landscape of an idealized agrarian past. Romanticized cottage gardens dominated the major garden literature of the nineteenth century.[11] In England, "through the writing of specialists such as William Robinson, cottage gardens were transformed from local practices of the rural working classes to potential source material for middle- and upper-class gardens," as the cottage garden became an icon of English national identity.[12] Wild gardens and rock gardens were also extremely popular, evoking the rapidly disappearing wild areas of the countryside. William Robinson and Gertrude Jekyll, in their "crusade for natural gardening" late in the century, were contemptuous of the artificiality of earlier trends, yet even the proliferation of greenhouses, the practice of "bedding out," and the aesthetic of the "gardenesque" that John Claudius Loudon introduced early in the century, offered an imagery of neat, clean agriculture in contrast to the grimy manufacturing industries that were the life-blood of the modern city.[13] The wealthy acquired large estates and designed them as havens from cities, as places where they could escape from city life and revel in country life. New suburbs created a middle ground between country and city, offering escape to the country for the burgeoning middle class. Large urban parks in cities replicated the experience of the country in the very heart of the

FIGURE 5.2: "A Roadside Cottage Garden." From Gertrude Jekyll, *Wood and Garden*, 1899. Courtesy Dumbarton Oaks Research Library and Collection, Washington, DC.

city. The collective effect of all of these trends and garden types was to sharpen and focus the country-city dichotomy.

THE COUNTRY IN THE CITY: URBAN PARKS

It is not surprising that the so-called "English" prototype for gardens spread around the world and exerted its most extensive and lasting influence at this time. The English style, with its naturalistic imagery, had been codified in England in the eighteenth century, but it did not attain widespread popularity until the nineteenth century, when it inspired gardens and garden designers internationally. While this style of garden design had originally developed in opposition to more formal and geometric French and Italian-style gardens, as a nationalistic interpretation of English natural scenery, the expanded popularity of this style in the nineteenth century had to do, in large part, with the fact that it offered such vivid rural metaphors in maximum contrast to the modern, industrial city. It was a landscape style that interpreted and incorporated into gardens the nostalgic imagery of an older and increasingly idealized country-side, an English landscape of rolling pastures, dense woods, and meandering streams emptying into natural-looking ponds and lakes. By the beginning of the nineteenth century, with the advent of the picturesque sensibility, this style had evolved to encompass wilder, less-manicured country imagery along with the pastoral. It embodied a palpable sense of loss, which, under the sway of the Romantic sensibility, had become poignant and pleasurable.

This naturalistic style of garden design, which had reached a high point in the large country estates of the English landed gentry in the eighteenth century, attained broad-based popular appeal in the nineteenth century through various applications, but the large urban parks that were created in cities around the world in the nineteenth century were the most significant vehicle by which this naturalistic style spread. Urban parks officially introduced the country into the modern city for maximum contrast and lasting effect. As urban parks proliferated around the world in this period, wherever western culture exerted influence, large tracts of land were designed in the naturalistic, English style and thereby dedicated to representing the country in the midst of increasingly dense, modern cities.[14]

The urban public park is an iconic landscape of the nineteenth century. These parks represented an idealized rural landscape of rustic cottages and country lanes in contrast to the new urban context. In the midst of elegant townhouses and dense working-class tenements, the typical park landscape induced a quieter, slower pace, inserting pockets of respite, peace, calm, health, and decorum into the fabric of the frenetic, modern city. Many of the large royal parks in London's West End had been redesigned in a more naturalistic style in the preceding century, and then opened gradually to the public as the city grew and engulfed them. By the 1840s, most of these large, private parks had been designated "royal public parks" and they served as models for brand new parks created in London in the first half of the nineteenth century. Regents Park, opened to the public in 1838, offered the country in the city for the wealthy at the terminus of Regent's Street, a fashionable new shopping street. The goal here was to entice the traditionally landed gentry, as well as the new bourgeoisie, to purchase expensive terraced houses surrounding the new park and take up residence in the city, at least for the social season. The economic and social success of Regent's Park was widely noted and it spawned many imitators. Birkenhead Park, in Liverpool, opened in 1848, offering a similar country-in-the-city contrast for the middle class. Victoria Park (1846) opened in London's East End, in response to political pressure. The goal was to serve the other end of the social spectrum, offering the benefits of the country (fresh air and healthful exercise, socialization, and decorous leisure activities) to the poor and working classes crowded into the new tenements constructed to accommodate the large population growth in London.[15]

FIGURE 5.3: "*Vue du Pont des Iles*," Bois de Boulogne. From Adolphe Alphand, *Les Promenades de Paris*, 1867–73.

The English parks were emulated internationally—throughout Europe, North and South America (see Daniel Nadenicek's essay "Use and Reception" in this volume), Australia and New Zealand, Africa and India. But, as the naturalistic or "English-style" landscape was adapted to parks in other locations, it took on some additional meanings. New, English-style parks around the world signaled the ambitions of growing industrial cities to compete with London, then the leading industrial capital of the world. The new urban parks signified not only the country-city dichotomy, but also a certain level of urban sophistication; they became associated with the new bourgeoisie, the class of industrialists and financiers that had turned London into the leading industrial capital of the world. The parks that Haussmann created in Paris during the Second Empire illustrate this association. In remodeling the Bois de Boulogne, the first park redesigned in Paris in the naturalistic, English style Napoleon III signaled to the world that France was on a mission to become a modern industrial nation, rivaling England. The Bois de Boulogne was on the edge of the newly fashionable west side of the city and the bourgeoisie of Paris soon instituted a daily parade from four to six each afternoon in the new park. This daily display of fashionable finery against the backdrop of the fashionable new English-style park was a sight that all the Paris guidebooks urged visitors not to miss. It became a world-renown spectacle of bourgeois prosperity and an important image as Paris began to rival London as the capital of modernity.

Around the world, as urban public parks were constructed in growing cities they were recognized as a product of a burgeoning international bourgeois culture, becoming a mark of distinction for modernizing cities everywhere.

Besides serving as a sign of bourgeois prosperity, urban parks signaled modernity in another way; they were also part of a strategy to improve public health in nineteenth-century cities (the public park and issues of modernity and public health in the United States are explored in more detail in the Introduction and in Daniel Nadenicek's essay in this volume). Many officials cited public health benefits as general justification for public expenditures on parks. Referring to the parks he designed in Paris, Adolphe Alphand wrote:

> Public gardens [and] wide planted streets where air can circulate freely are absolutely necessary in the interior of large cities in respect to health. The progress of science and of man requires the most hygienic conditions inside and near dwellings. This is, above all, important for the populations of cities.[16]

The mechanisms by which diseases were transmitted remained poorly understood and in dispute for most of the nineteenth century, but the miasmatic theory was most often used to justify public parks. This theory held that epidemics of infectious disease were caused by the state of the atmosphere (miasma). An unhealthy atmosphere was somewhat vaguely understood to be a function of poor sanitary conditions, including dirt, overcrowding, poor sewers, and foul air. The miasma theory supported the creation of naturalistic parks as pockets of healthful fresh air in the city. Parks were thought to be healthy because they afforded clean, green expanses of open space where air could circulate more freely, that is, an atmosphere like the country, which was thought to be healthier than the city in most respects. Tree canopies and shrubs were thought to filter and purify the air, preventing miasmas from spreading.

In the United States, the public health argument for public parks was expanded to include moral, as well as physical, health. Leading park proponents in the United States, such as Frederick Law Olmsted, argued that parks would offer the experience of the country to the poor and working classes who couldn't escape the city otherwise, and that this experience would be both physically and morally beneficial. The physical benefits were fresh air and exercise. The moral benefits accrued from engaging in decorous, calming leisure activities, often envisioned as solitary and contemplative. Olmsted, the designer of Central Park in New York and the leading expert on parks in the United States in the nineteenth century, was influenced by Transcendentalism.

He believed that engaging in quiet contemplation of nature—a sojourn in the countryside—was a potentially transcendent experience that could improve the spirit as well as the body of the city-bound. He and his American colleagues designed urban parks with this benefit very much in mind. Although nineteenth-century park proponents worried about the potential disruption of raucous crowds in the new parks, they also believed there could be moral benefit at a societal level from mixing the new urban social classes in the new naturalistic parks. The idea was that the lower classes would pick up manners and mores from mingling decorously in a naturalistic setting with their betters, in a throw-back to the supposedly more "natural" mixing of the social classes in a nostalgically remembered rural past.[17]

BETWEEN THE COUNTRY AND THE CITY: GARDENS OF THE MIDDLE CLASS

In the nineteenth century, capitalism transformed the social order in growing industrial nations around the world. Social status became less a function of birth, more a matter of wealth and influence. Societies became more stratified and social identities were more fluid. With the increasing emphasis on material wealth came increasing reliance on external markers to indicate social standing, such as fashion and a good address. Social identity was easier to fake, especially in the rapidly growing cities, which afforded more social mobility and more social anonymity. It was an age of social uncertainty and considerable social anxiety. As material wealth rose and fell with the unstable stock market, maintaining appearances could get one through the ups and downs of fortune, sometimes without substantial loss of status. The defining social change of the century was the rise of the middle class. As members of the growing middle class carved out new social identities to distinguish themselves from both the upper classes and the working classes, gardens played an important role in this process.

In his book *The Theory of the Leisure Class* (1899), Thorstein Veblen famously observed of society in the United States at the end of the nineteenth century that not only had conspicuous consumption become the distinguishing characteristic of the nouveaux-riches, but also that leisure was a mark of social distinction at various social levels. Leisure is a sign of the ability to spend time unproductively, that is, it connotes freedom from the necessity of working for a living. As Veblen observed, leisure may "commonly take the form of 'immaterial' goods ... [such as] quasi-scholarly or quasi-artistic accomplishments and a knowledge of processes and incidents which do not conduce directly to the furtherance of human life ... These accomplishments may, in some sense, be classed as branches of learning."[18] In the nineteenth century, more people gained some measure of leisure and sought new outlets for it. Industrialists, real-estate developers, financiers, and investors rose to the top of the social pyramid and the new wealth transformed the landscape of both the country and the city. It produced elegant new urban neighborhoods, with new urban parks as centerpieces offering various leisure pursuits. It also produced lavish, private pleasure gardens and supported new garden institutions, such as botanical gardens, as wealthy amateurs contributed much to the growing fields of botany and horticulture.[19] Pleasure gardens dedicated to leisure had always been a mark of social distinction for the upper classes, but in the nineteenth century the new leisure classes conceived new ways to distinguish their gardens as they competed for distinction in a much bigger pool of gardens and gardeners, all contributing in some measure to new branches of learning in botany, horticulture, and landscape gardening.

The wealthiest segment of society in the nineteenth century, as in previous centuries, spared no expense to transform vast tracts of land out in the country into sumptuous pleasure gardens. But their gardens reflected a growing internationalism, as they relied on an expanding body of international knowledge about plants and horticulture, and depended for this knowledge on a network of institutions that were connected internationally. Gardens in the nineteenth century showcased the spoils of the Age of Empire and reflected the expanding international scope of botany and horticulture. They were bolstered by new internationally available technologies: green houses, irrigation systems, and lawnmowers. When Kew Gardens was restructured in the Victorian period into a world-renowned repository of botanical and horticultural knowledge, it became a resource for botanists, horticulturalists, and garden enthusiasts around the world, dispensing seeds and plants to the far-flung British colonies in an information network that circled the globe.[20] While, in previous centuries, large gardens usually had a connection to the local land, and economic and social roots often going back for centuries, many of the larger gardens in the nineteenth century had little connection to the land they occupied and weren't anchored by local traditions. They were constructed on newly acquired property, financed by new money, and showcased international collections of exotic plant specimens and various garden styles. They were laboratories of the new technology, repositories of new, international botanical and horticultural knowledge. Like the greenhouses that made exotic plant collections possible in the nineteenth century, the most lavish gardens of the period were often imported and assembled onsite and represented the latest scientific and technological advances of Western society in the fields of horticulture and landscape gardening.[21]

While a country house, with its associated country life style, had long been a mark of social distinction for the upper classes, and particularly for the new bourgeoisie aspiring to rise in social standing, in the nineteenth century a country lifestyle fell within reach of increasing numbers of people.[22] As more people acquired the means and the leisure to develop and maintain gardens devoted to pleasure, rather than subsistence, gardens took on new meanings. The less-affluent middle class could not afford to compete with the lavish gardens of the very wealthy in terms of size or extent of plant collections, but they developed distinctive ways of gardening, styles, and information networks that contributed to a new middle-class social identity and helped create social cohesion among middle-class garden enthusiasts, particularly in the growing suburbs within the orbit of urban centers. Horticultural societies became popular and their ranks were swelled by amateur, middle-class horticulturalists. The popular garden magazines and books that emerged in this period, by Andrew Jackson Downing, John Claudius Loudon, Jane Webb Loudon, and others, aimed mainly at a middle-class audience. These publications instructed the middle class in horticulture and gardening as a means to improve not only quality of life, but also social status. Gardens and gardening became part of the new middle-class lifestyle and an important aspect of middle-class social identity in this period.[23]

The middle-class suburb was a product of the nineteenth-century city. In increasing numbers, middle-class businessmen and professionals moved out of cities into new suburbs within commuting distance of city centers, creating a new zone that bridged, both literally and figuratively, the country and the city. Suburbs were a product of industrialization and improved transportation networks. They were a manifestation of the increasingly stratified social structure in nineteenth-century cities. As cities attracted the poor and working classes in increasing numbers, the middle class began to migrate out of cities to new suburban communities where they could enjoy the benefits of both the city and the country. Owning a house and garden in the country became a focus of middle-class aspiration. The gardens created in the new suburbs occupied an expanding middle ground not only between the country and the city, but also between conspicuous consumption (embodied by the sumptuous gardens of the fabulously wealthy at one end of the social spectrum) and subsistence (embodied by the hard-scrabble gardens of working poor at the other).

John Claudius Loudon, the English horticulturalist, was one of the most influential figures guiding the emerging middle class in shaping gardens and gardening to its needs in this period. His many publications fed the demand for horticultural and gardening knowledge internationally. His books, such as *The Suburban Gardener and Villa Companion* (1838), and *The Gardener's*

FIGURE 5.4: Plan of Two Suburban Residences at Albany, NY. From Jacob Weidenmann, *Beautifying Country Homes*, 1870, plate 1.

Magazine (1826 onwards) found an audience wherever English was spoken.
Loudon was part of the vanguard of a new professionalism gaining hold in the
middle class. In the nineteenth century, the professions were developing distinct identities and the new professionals were emerging as a strong segment
of the middle class. As professional societies were founded in the nineteenth

century, universities developed professional curricula to teach specialized professional knowledge in these various fields: medicine, law, architecture, landscape architecture, etc. One of Loudon's major goals was to increase and codify professional knowledge in the fields of botany, horticulture, and landscape gardening, and to make this knowledge widely available to a growing middle-class readership.[24] He recognized an increasing market in the middle-class for professional knowledge in these fields and he foresaw that the middle class would become increasingly important as both producers and consumers of such knowledge.

Loudon instructed the emerging middle class in the finer distinctions in landscape design, explaining the various stylistic choices to his readers, arguing that different garden styles had different merits and that a particular style should be selected because it was suitable to a particular property and the owner's interests, not just because it represented the latest fashion.[25] Professional knowledge was one of the ways Loudon offered his middle-class readers to distinguish themselves. He recounted how garden styles had evolved historically, often as a function of wealth and taste, but he posited professional and practical knowledge as superior to mere taste. Loudon urged his readers to follow rational principles in selecting different styles, to consider the objectives and the utility of various design approaches in various circumstances. In this way, Loudon helped carve out a distinct identity for middle-class gardens and gardeners, grounded in scientific and technological knowledge, education, and pragmatism. A garden designed according to Loudon's advice could evince these qualities and would be a mark of social distinction, no matter how small the property.

In *The Suburban Gardener and Villa Companion* (1838), Loudon grouped garden examples into chapters ranging from fourth-rate ("gardens of houses in a connected row or street") to first-rate gardens defined as properties of 50—100 acres that included "a park and farmery."[26] But Loudon was most interested in the smaller, fourth-rate (and mostly suburban) gardens of attached row houses and/or double or detached villas (this is explored more fully in Brent Elliott's essay, "Types of Gardens," Chapter 2 in this volume). He devoted 225 pages of his book to fourth-rate gardens and only 52 pages to first-rate gardens. In his view, the fourth-rate gardens were more interesting because they presented new challenges. They could be just as valuable as first-rate gardens, because size was not the only measure of a garden's value. The horticultural expertise evinced in a garden actually mattered to Loudon more than did its size. All of the gardens he selected for this book gave evidence of botanical and horticultural expertise, which, for Loudon, was the ultimate mark of distinction. The important point was that garden art could be practiced at every level of society. As Loudon noted: "all the necessaries of life may be obtained in as great perfection by the occupier of a suburban residence in the neighborhood of London, who possesses 200 £ or 300 £ a year, as by the greatest nobleman in England, and at a mere fraction of the expense."[27] This income falls squarely in the ranks of the middle class in England in this period.[28]

Loudon introduced a new style of garden art, which he called the "gardenesque", in *The Gardener's Magazine* in 1832. The gardenesque was a style "more suitable for those persons who are botanists, rather than general admirers of scenery, because it is best calculated for displaying the individual beauty of trees and plants" and for maintaining order among them.[29] This was a style developed to showcase the botanical knowledge and horticultural expertise of the property owner, rather than the extent of the property or the owner's material worth. It could be used on properties of any size. It was a practical style that allowed gardeners to employ more geometric layouts as needed to maintain all or part of a garden in an orderly and efficient manner. It was a style more suitable for smaller properties than was the naturalistic picturesque style, which required more space.

Loudon described the gardenesque as one possibility in a range of garden styles available to his readers.[30] In promoting the gardenesque, he offered the middle class a point of entry into the world of garden design, as it was a style particularly suited to more modest means and modest properties. The gardens he most admired were the ones that made the best use of the property, however modest, where the plants were selected to create variety and interest, showing off the horticultural expertise of the gardener. His favorite examples often combined picturesque and gardenesque effects. If there was room, Loudon advocated giving plants enough space to grow naturally and, thus, more picturesquely. In this way, he showed his readers how to appropriate the cultural authority represented by the more naturalistic styles to smaller properties and limited means.[31]

Horticultural advice and garden design ideas became readily available to the middle class around the world in a flood of new books and periodicals addressing the developing demand for instruction in garden art. In the United States, Andrew Jackson Downing, who was much influenced by Loudon, offered aesthetic guidelines in his *Treatise on the Theory and Practice of Landscape Gardening Adapted to North America* (1841). Downing opened this treatise by noting that wealth and prosperity had "become apparent in the great increase of elegant cottage and villa residences ... wherever nature seems to invite us by her rich and varied charms." The American middle class had begun an exodus from cities into the surrounding countryside. Downing addressed the book to the "hundreds of individuals who wish to ornament their grounds and embellish their places, [but] are at a loss how to proceed, from the

FIGURE 5.5: The Loudons' double-detached villa, Porchester Terrace, Bayswater. From J. C. Loudon, *The Suburban Gardener and Villa Companion*, 1838, fig. 109.

want of some *leading principles*, with the knowledge of which they would find it comparatively easy to produce delightful and satisfactory results."[32] Much like Loudon, Downing offered his readers a range of styles and examples to inspire the design of their more modest gardens. Other aspiring landscape architects followed in Loudon and Downing's footsteps, producing books with examples of gardens and gardening advice.[33] The collective effect was that an aesthetically pleasing garden, especially one shaped according to professional principles, if not actually designed by a professional landscape architect, became a mark of social distinction in the middle class.

By the Victorian era, when pattern books became popular, middle-class aspiration had settled firmly on a house in the country. Victorian pattern books included many examples for garden enthusiasts to choose from, suitable for a range of properties, from very large to very small. Landscape architecture became increasingly professionalized in the second half of the century and there was more focus on aesthetics as the profession's area of particular expertise. Olmsted, for example, argued increasingly that landscape architecture was a form of art dedicated to interpreting nature and/or working with nature's effects. Others, such as Gertrude Jekyll, developed particularly artful ways with flowers. Still others interpreted historical garden styles, adapting Renaissance Italian gardens or other classical precedents to new nineteenth-century contexts. But the fantasy of a country estate became ritualized in gardens in the nineteenth century, with areas, however small, dedicated to flower and kitchen gardens, orchards, park-like lawns, and specimen trees. Even the smallest examples often included rustic gazebos and/or small greenhouses. The miniature rural fantasies that proliferated in the new suburbs became a mark of distinction for the emerging middle class, whose livelihood was earned in the cities, but whose family life played out in the country.

WOMEN, GARDENS AND THE SEPARATION OF SPHERES

Even as they moved into the suburbs, and acquired property, middle-class men and women were sometimes ambivalent about materialistic displays of social status. They developed strong religious and social codes emphasizing work and family values, and pointed to these as part of their middle-class identity. The doctrine of separate spheres emerged as a conceptual structure for middle-class social life, delineating different responsibilities and zones of influence for men and women. According to this conceptual framework, the public sphere was primarily a masculine domain where men were involved in work outside the home, in business and commerce and civic affairs. The private sphere came to be viewed as the domain of women, as women were increasingly concerned with running the household and overseeing the moral and religious life of the family and the education of children. For many middle-class women, the private sphere increasingly encompassed a house and garden in the suburbs.

The doctrine of separate spheres had strong moral overtones. The private sphere became a conceptual repository of virtue and decorum, as opposed to the sometimes-questionable morals and manners tolerated as part of competitive business and commerce in the public sphere. As the middle class moved to the suburbs, their new houses and gardens represented not only an increase in material wealth, but also a moral refuge. A sequestered garden, tucked away behind the house, was an inner bastion of domestic life. Even more than the new house, the garden offered a sanctuary from the evils of the city and the materialistic and moral temptations of the public sphere.

"Love for a garden has a powerful influence in attracting men to their homes, and saves them from many temptations; and on this account, a taste for gardening is an additional security for domestic happiness and comfort. It is also a recreation that adds materially to health, promotes civilization, and softens the manners and tempers of men."[34]

John Ruskin famously used a garden metaphor to describe his ideal of woman, in an address to an audience of middle-class men and women at the Town Hall of Manchester in 1864. This passage paints a vivid picture of the Victorian ideology of separate spheres:

> To see her, with every innocent feeling fresh within her, go out in the morning into her garden to play with the fringes of its guarded flowers, and lift their heads when they are drooping, with her happy smile upon her face, and no cloud upon her brow, because there is a little wall around her place of peace; and yet she knows, in her heart, if she would

FIGURE 5.6: View of Hendon Rectory with women and children in the garden. From J. C. Loudon, *The Suburban Gardener and Villa Companion*, 1838, fig. 177.

only look for its knowledge, that, outside of that little rose-covered wall, the wild grass, to the horizon, is torn up by the agony of men, and beat level by the drift of their life-blood.[35]

As gardens fell within the realm of the private sphere, they became part of a cultural packaging of women and children, domesticity and virtue. One need only think of Victorian greeting cards and valentines, or the many impressionist paintings of women in gardens, their flowery dresses blending into the scenery, to realize the power of these associations.

Yet, middle-class women developed new identities within the conceptual structure of the private sphere, working it to their advantage, and gardens and gardening offered them opportunities for self-expression and helped them fit into and identify with the new suburban communities. Increasing numbers of women discovered gardens as a creative outlet, and became enthusiastic producers and consumers of the growing literature on gardens. Because gardens and gardening were so strongly identified with the private sphere, they offered many women a safe and acceptable conduit into the public sphere. Women became active participants in newly forming horticultural societies, entered prized flowers in society competitions and shared knowledge with other garden enthusiasts. From the point of view of middle-class women in the nineteenth century, gardens were an "arena for the formation and enactment of social identity," within the social structure of separate spheres.[36]

Far from fitting Ruskin's image of merely playing with flowers, many women were actively involved in all aspects of gardens in the nineteenth century, from laying out to heavy labor, and they contributed significantly to the field of garden design, particularly in the early decades of the century. Loudon's *The Suburban Gardener and Villa Companion* included numerous examples of gardens attributed to women and he addressed the book particularly to women, noting, "If we can succeed in rendering every lady her own landscape-gardener, which we are confident we can do, we shall have great hopes of effecting a general reform in the gardening taste, not only of this country, but of every other."[37] He also noted that many women were very well versed in horticulture and took particular care "to render garden scenery botanically as well as pictorially interesting."[38] Through his activities in the Horticultural Society, Loudon knew that women were contributing to the growing body of knowledge in horticulture.

In the early nineteenth century, many amateurs participated actively in the development and dissemination of botanical and horticultural knowledge. A sizeable percentage of these amateurs were women. Between 1790 and 1830, woman writers produced a large number of books on botany and horticulture. Botany was becoming an increasingly male-dominated science, while horticulture remained more open and accessible to amateurs, and many women contributed. As Ann Shteir has noted, women's botanical writing "stayed for the most part within limits on subject matter shaped by the gender ideologies of the day," that is, the doctrine of separate spheres. The majority of women botanical writers wrote for a popular audience, and particularly for other women and for children.[39] Women wielded significant power and authority from their sovereign position in the domestic sphere, and they continued to exert considerable influence on horticulture and garden design throughout the century.

A number of women developed professional stature as horticulturalists and landscape designers in the nineteenth century and enjoyed reputations disproportionate to their numbers. Jane Loudon dominated the early part of the century. As Geoffrey Taylor notes, "apart from whatever share she had in her husband's books—she was his acknowledged amanuensis in most of them, and was doubtless more than an amanuensis in many—[Jane Loudon] produced on her own account more than sixteen separate works on gardening and botany," and although she died at a relatively young age in 1858, "down to the very end of the century her influence and importance were out of proportion to the comparative fewness of her years."[40] Jane Loudon's books were useful to gardeners of both sexes, but they were particularly addressed to women.[41] Her advice helped untold numbers of women, who suddenly found themselves in charge of a house and garden in the country or the suburbs, to rise to the challenge and find fulfillment in the garden.[42]

In the century in which "the woman question" was much discussed in Western societies, when women were actively seeking new identities, entering the work force, agitating for political representation, and beginning to demand the right to vote, gardens meant different things for women. On the one hand, the association of women and gardens in the nineteenth century reinforced the ideology of separate spheres, reiterating the prevailing view that a woman's place was in the home. But at the same time, gardens offered women opportunities to grow and develop professional knowledge and skills beyond the traditional domestic realm.

In many ways, nineteenth-century gardens were progressive, in keeping with the progressive spirit of the age, serving as laboratories for experimentation in botany, horticulture, and landscape architecture and as platforms for new professionalism in these fields. In the hands of the new professionals, gardens showcased new knowledge and new wealth. They reflected new social class distinctions and changing gender identities. But, at the same time, gardens were a locus of widely felt resistance to "progress," an outlet for nostalgia and a means to counter some of the social and cultural momentum of the period. Nineteenth-century gardens celebrated the simplicity of an idealized rural past, and also helped to shape the modern, urban landscape. Occupying this middle ground, they embodied ambivalent, and sometimes conflicting, meanings, reflecting complex reactions to social and environmental change.

CHAPTER SIX

Verbal Representations

LINDA PARSHALL

Wer meinen Park sieht, der sieht in mein Herz. (Whoever sees my park, sees into my heart.)

—Bettina von Arnim

In 1835, Bettina von Arnim published *Goethes Briefwechsel mit einem Kinde*, a volume she presented as her own youthful correspondence with Johann Wolfgang von Goethe and his mother. Arnim was acquainted with leading figures in the German Romantic movement and many of the era's culturati, among them Prince Hermann Ludwig Heinrich von Pückler-Muskau. The prince was well known to German society for his park at Muskau, his writings on travel and gardens, and his social shenanigans. In dedicating her book to Pückler, Arnim espoused the appreciation of gardens and designed landscapes typical of her era:

You once wrote to me: "Whoever sees my park, sees into my heart." It was last year in mid-September that I stepped into that park, early in the morning just as the sun's rays were beginning to spread. All of nature was silent. Clean paths led me between fresh green lawns on which separate groups of flowers seemed still asleep ... At other times on other days I walked even further in every direction, and wherever I went I found the same care being taken and a peaceful charm pervading everything. A lover cares for and nurtures his beloved's spirit and beauty just as here you cultivate the inheritance of nature entrusted to you. I am happy to believe that this is the mirror of your deepest heart, since it implies so much that is beautiful; I am happy to believe that a simple trust in you is no less tended and treasured than every single plant in your park.[1]

That a garden embodied the character of its owner was a well-established conceit. Since the eighteenth century, gardens had enjoyed a particular cultural relevance in the West; like nature itself, they were invested with aesthetic and moral significance; the expression of taste in a garden indicated an understanding not just of the beautiful, but also of the good. This notion appears in relation to a fictional garden in Jane Austen's *Pride and Prejudice* (1813), where Elizabeth's first view of Pemberley Woods, Mr. Darcy's vast estate in the English landscape style, offers her a glimpse into his true essence: "She had never seen a place for which nature had done more, or where natural beauty had been so little counteracted by an awkward taste."[2] Thus, taste exemplifies excellence. Near the end of the novel, Elizabeth reflects on the dawning of her love for Darcy and once more draws the connection: "It has been coming on so gradually, that I hardly know when it began. But I believe I must date it from my first seeing his beautiful grounds at Pemberley."[3]

The human response to gardens and nature is profoundly significant in the literature of Western Europe and America from 1800–1920.[4] Gardens not only indicate moral values and express ideas, they also form character and kindle the memory. They are realms of peace and enchantment, danger and conflict; they represent aspirations as well as fears; lost dreams and the promise of perfection yet to come. These textual gardens function in a diversity of ways: their role may be passive or active, and their depiction may be literal or figurative. Personal experiences of gardens are recounted unvarnished in diaries, journals, letters, or travel descriptions; and the same occurrences were often relived and transformed in memoirs and fiction. We find gardens everywhere in this literature, bridging genres and defying easy categorization.

GARDENS OF RECORD: DIARIES, JOURNALS, TRAVEL ACCOUNTS

One of the major figures who both designed and wrote about gardens was the same Prince Pückler-Muskau whose garden (and person) so affected Bettina von Arnim. He was much admired for transforming his hereditary estate into a park in the English landscape style, a project to which his wife, Lucie von

Pappenheim, was equally devoted. When they ran short of funds, they obtained a divorce of convenience, and Pückler-Muskau set off on a lengthy journey to the British Isles in search of a wealthy bride, although his landscaping aspirations were not forgotten: part of the time he was accompanied by his head gardener for what he termed "parkhunting." Pückler-Muskau wrote regularly to Lucie about his adventures and the more than seventy estates he visited, and in 1830 the first two volumes of these letters appeared anonymously under the title *Briefe eines Verstorbenen*. They caused a sensation.[5] This literary success led him to publish the remaining letters as well as *Andeutungen über Landschaftsgärtnerei* (1834), a book about his Muskau estate.[6] In all of his writings, Pückler-Muskau's deep appreciation for nature and gardens emerges through detailed descriptions and poetic accounts, evocations that reflect the abiding element of romanticism that continued to inform the reception of gardens and landscape throughout the century.[7]

Gardens figure in many journals of this period. Dorothy Wordsworth kept diaries filled with the enjoyments and distractions of working in her garden.[8] Many of Nathaniel Hawthorne's gardening experiences are recorded in "The Old Manse,"[9] including his innumerable daily visits to gaze at his beloved "vegetable progeny" and his aggravation over horticultural pests. For Hawthorne, "every tree, every plant was an individual," a personal bond eerily corrupted in the garden of his story "Rappuccini's Daughter" (see below).

Elizabeth von Arnim's first novel, *Elizabeth and Her German Garden*, which appeared anonymously in 1898, is a fictionalized journal, a kind of hybrid.[10] Born in Australia and raised in England, she met her future husband (a distant cousin of Achim von Arnim) on a trip through Italy. Although their relationship was troubled, she fell in love with his estate in Pomerania and immediately undertook a long-term project of transforming its enormous abandoned garden. Her book is filled with detailed observations about this process and about how, for her, "every flower and weed is a friend and every tree a lover."[11] Far from a practical guide, it records the various mistakes of an amateur gardener (early reviews were critical of this), but its cheerful and amusing narrative made it enormously popular. Lamenting the strictly supervisory role imposed on her as mistress of the estate, Arnim tells of one occasion when she crept out of the house unobserved to indulge in some spading, raking, and digging that she found utterly invigorating, "a blessed sort of work, and if Eve had had a spade in Paradise and known what to do with it, we should not have had all that sad business with the apple."[12]

The list of authors who wrote about their gardens is long: Rainer Maria Rilke, for example, wrote an essay on Worpswede, where he stayed in 1900, and Émile Zola conjured up Paradou (see below) while sitting beneath the trees of his own garden. Henry James was deeply attached to his garden in Sussex, where he lived from 1897 until his death in 1916. Many writers also published inspired accounts of the gardens they saw on their travels, above all in Italy: for example, Edith Wharton's *Italian Villas and Their Gardens* (1903 serially; book 1904), a scholarly work describing more than seventy-five estates; Goethe's *Italienische Reise*, 1816–17; and Henry James's *Italian Hours*, 1909.[13]

GARDENS IN FICTION

Many of the gardens encountered by authors rematerialize in their fictional works. The Medici and Pincian Hill gardens appear in Hawthorne's *The Marble Faun* (1860). Wharton incorporated a number of Italian gardens in *The Valley of Decisions* (1902) and in several short stories; gardens closer to home inspired her portrait of Bellomont, the country estate in *The House of Mirth* (1905).[14] Similar patterns abound. Hermann Hesse had gardens of his own on the Bodensee and later in Bern, and his novels are pervaded by the theme of nature, often of its destruction by urbanization. Of particular importance for Hesse was the jungle-like park surrounding the house he rented on Lake Lugano, which he transformed into the visionary landscapes of *Siddhartha* (1922).[15] There beautiful gardens, flowers, stately groves, and magnificent natural landscapes provide the setting for most of the action, as well as constituting a symbolic world of their own.

The gardens portrayed in fiction of this period may be reflections of an author's personal experiences at home or abroad, but they are also indicative of a general cultural valuation of the garden as the epitome of nature's power, often as a representation of the divine. The medieval topos of the *locus amoenus* persists alongside the wild, threatening settings of the *Sturm und Drang* period and the pastoral idyll. These literary gardens may be temporary or permanent, actual or metaphorical, places of escape or seductive traps. The Garden of Eden recurs in myriad manifestations, as a realm of earthly delights or an otherworldly paradise; as a domain of prelapsarian purity undone by human failing; as a refuge where mankind can be restored. Very often, the garden is contained, a *hortus conclusus* invisible from outside its walls, yet the same garden may, from within, appear infinite. Such walled gardens are often difficult to access and, once left, all but impossible to regain.

Fictional Gardens as "Real" Settings

Goethe's novel *Die Wahlverwandtschaften* (1811) is set on a large estate that encompasses regular parterres and natural landscapes, orchards, forests, ponds, pathways, and panoramic viewpoints. The gardens are backdrops for much of the action and also catalysts in the plot.[16] Clashes between styles of garden design echo conflicts between personalities: abandon or restraint, passion or reason, the enormous parkland with its seeming unboundedness in opposition to the imposed moderation of its formal areas. Being or working in these gardens often transforms the characters, as they themselves transform the landscape. As Walter Benjamin wrote, the garden is the power of nature that drives the entire plot of this novel.[17]

Goethe's characters engage different areas of the estate through planning and executing its design. As the novel opens, we see Eduard in his orchard grafting new shoots onto young trees. He then decides to visit the moss-hut his wife Charlotte has built high on a hill in the new landscape park. Leaving his regular terraces, he chooses a winding path that mounts through overgrown thickets, and once there, he finds himself charmed by the simple, isolated structure and the distant panoramas. Yet the couple's compatibility proves transitory. The underlying discord in their respective attitudes toward nature is portentous. Their emotional bond is gradually eroded by the influence of other characters, while in the gardens certain elements take on a disquieting resonance.

The interweaving of landscape and human relationships is alluded to in Charlotte's discussion with a schoolmaster, where she argues that gardens should resemble "open country; there should be no evidence of art or constraint, we want to breathe the air in absolute freedom." The schoolmaster counters that no situation, restricted or free, is without its difficulties, and furthermore that no generation can be sure the next will share its values: "A young shoot is easily grafted to an old stem, a grown branch cannot be grafted at all," a metaphor that recalls the opening scene in Eduard's orchard.[18] For all the celebration of abandonment to the natural world's beauty and power, the novel seems to caution against too much freedom, both in the garden and in human relationships. The immutable conflicts of nature are also those of individual character that, left uncontrolled, lead to tragedy.

Gardens and gardeners figure importantly in the fiction of the Austrian Adalbert Stifter, who was, like Goethe, on intimate terms with the natural world. Stifter held deep respect for working the land, and nearly all of his writings abound with descriptions of landscape and gardens, although they are not as complexly bound up with the plot as in *Die Wahlverwandschaften*. Gardening is most often a metaphor for the means to salvation; sometimes, as in *Der Nachsommer* (1857), the garden permeates the novel as a realm of moral harmony.[19] In *Brigitta* (1844), the main character, a woman and a gardener, turns a barren landscape into a place of bounty and loveliness.

FIGURE 6.1: Cover of Frances Hodgson Burnett, *The Secret Garden*, 1911.

A private garden hidden behind a high wall is part of the subterfuge underlying the plot of *The Aspern Papers* (1888) by Henry James.[20] James's own experience of Italy is reflected in this story of an American scholar looking back on his failed attempt to gain access to the letters of a well-known author. Believing them to be in the custody of the writer's former mistress and her middle-aged niece, he insinuates himself into their Venetian palazzo by persuading them of his desire to tend their overgrown garden. Although he secretly prefers "its weeds and its wild rich tangle, its sweet characteristic Venetian shabbiness,"[21] he cultivates the garden as promised. Midsummer nights within its walls provide the setting for his repeated attempts to win the niece's favor, but the dying aunt sees through his stratagem, and the niece declares she will release the papers only in exchange for marriage, an option he refuses. His landscaping work was fruitless, yet he credits the hours spent reading and dreaming in the garden as the happiest of his life.

Gardens in nineteenth- and early twentieth-century fiction are often part of large estates and, thus, ready vehicles for critiquing the social order.[22] In Joseph Freiherr von Eichendorff's *Aus dem Leben eines Taugenichts* (1826), the engagingly unambitious hero is a lowly gardener's assistant. Through his unsophisticated eyes, we see various aristocratic gardens, those he likes—well-tended and boasting "temples, arbors, and lovely green pathways,"[23] and those he disdains—overgrown topiaries, unclipped lawns, damaged statues, and uncouth plantings (such as cabbages mingled with flowers). Gardens are settings for several crucial scenes, and social boundaries like garden walls are ultimately breached, to general benefit. The hero's innate goodness carries the day, and his deep affection for the beauty of untouched nature accords with the aesthetics of German Romanticism. Several decades later in Hans Christian Andersen's morality tale, "The Gardener and the Manor" (1872), an aristocratic landowner's lack of appreciation for his own garden, and for his gardener, symbolizes the selfishness of the ruling classes.

Frances Hodgson Burnett's still popular story *The Secret Garden* (1911)[24] bridges distinctions of class and gender. Here an abandoned garden, walled up to hide away painful memories, becomes the source of physical and emotional healing. By learning to care for its many plants, two disagreeable upper-class children restore their innate goodness, a process that also depends on assistance from the lower social orders: an aged gardener and the chambermaid's young brother serve as moral paradigms of respect for the natural world. Further romantic themes abound: the candor of youth breaking down culturally imposed barriers, and the ability of children to commune with animals and plants (the garden's hidden door and its key are found with a robin's assistance).

FIGURE 6.2: John Tenniel, Spades working as gardeners. From
Lewis Carroll, *Alice's Adventures in Wonderland,* 1865.

Nature's moral sway combined with labor returns the garden and the children
to life and vigor. Mary, the intrepid protagonist of the story, has provided a role
model for generations of young girls.

Fictional Gardens as Magical Settings

The Secret Garden shares a number of characteristics with classic fairy tales
of a century earlier, not least the presence of talking plants and animals and a
happy ending. In Novalis's "Die Geschichte von Hyazinth und Rosenblütchen,"
embedded in the unfinished novel *Die Lehrlinge zu Sais* (1802), the young
hero, who lives in complete harmony with nature, turns inexplicably melancholic, abandons his familiar garden along with his young love Rosenblütchen,
and undertakes a quest for an uncertain and indefinable goal. As in many

Romantic adventures, during this trial he must pass through forbidding, unfamiliar territory, along the way losing his ability to converse with nature's creatures until he arrives at his destination, or better, a state of mind: the joyful condition of perpetual longing. At last, his heart still filled with "delicious yearning," he is reunited with Rosenblütchen in the shape of the goddess Isis. Within a constant state of becoming (*das immer Werdende*), Hyazinth has found his home in a garden of love.[25]

No discussion of magical gardens would be complete without *Alice's Adventures in Wonderland* (1865) by Lewis Carroll, which opens with the heroine sitting on a daisy-strewn bank and deciding to follow a rabbit under a hedge and down a hole. After a long fall, she finds a tiny door and a view into "the loveliest garden you ever saw."[26] In the classic manner of the secret garden, Alice loses her way and must undertake detours in her search for perfection, thereby providing Carroll with the opportunity for playful allusions to contemporary debates over the merits of the natural and artificial in garden design.[27]

In the Queen's croquet-ground, she discovers three playing cards—appropriately spades—who have been engaged as gardeners to paint a white rose red.[28] And in the later volume, *Through the Looking Glass* (1871), we find Alice still in search of the garden. She inquires of the Red Queen ruling over her chessboard, and the Queen responds: " ... when you say 'garden'—*I've* seen gardens, compared with which this would be a wilderness."[29] Appropriate to the elusive nature of her quest, Alice is never able to find that original garden.

Edgar Allen Poe wrote two stories centered on gardens as places of transcendence, one a visionary Shangri-la, the other an earthbound paradise. The first of these, "The Domain of Arnheim" (1846),[30] is a frame story in which the narrator tells of his friend Ellison who unexpectedly inherits an enormous fortune, freeing him to create a landscape garden, in his mind the highest form of beauty.[31] After several years in search of an ideal location, he finds Arnheim. The description of this site begins realistically, but we are quickly "imprisoned within an enchanted circle" where nature exhibits "a weird symmetry, a thrilling uniformity, a wizard propriety," and nothing disturbs the perfection, not a single pebble, withered leaf, or dead branch. The impressions catalogued by the narrator mount from the sensual to the magical, suggesting "a new race of fairies, laborious, tasteful, magnificent, and fastidious," until the whole of this "paradise" floods the senses with "a gush of entrancing melody," and we are engulfed by exotic trees, masses of fragrant flowers, lakes and streams, "the phantom handiwork, conjointly, of the Sylphs, of the Fairies, of the Genii, and of the Gnomes."[32]

In Poe's later story, "Landor's Cottage: A Pendant to 'The Domain of Arnheim'" (1850), the narrator describes his walking tour to a nirvana, a charming hidden valley where human artifice unobtrusively complements the beauties of nature. Following mysterious tracks on a velvet-like path, he comes upon an ideal landscape. The lifting fog reveals a cottage draped in blossoming vines and, at its door, a young woman, "the perfection of natural, in contradistinction from artificial grace."[33] The narrator has entered a gentle paradise, an Eden without threat.

GARDENS AS PARADISE LOST

The texts we have reviewed thus far demonstrate the complexity of the fictional garden as a realm of magic, reality, or something in between. Whatever the degree of human involvement in their design, they are celebrations of the beauty of nature and its positive effect on mankind. Yet the literature of this period also abounds with gardens of a more dubious character, gardens of Eden that harbor both perfection and seduction. These gardens may have the potential to heal, but they are also predisposed to punish; readily entered, at least by the innocent, they are a testing ground for human imperfection and, like the biblical Paradise, once lost, they become inaccessible.

"The Door in the Wall" (1906)[34] by H. G. Wells tells of a man's life-long obsession with a garden concealed behind a green door. The narrator skeptically relates the story of his recently deceased friend Lionel Wallace,[35] who was just a boy when he first saw the door in an ivy-covered wall; feeling passionately drawn to it, he, nonetheless, hesitates before entering. When he then passes through, he finds himself utterly at home amid naturally ordered flowerbeds, marble-lined paths, colonnades, fountains, exotic animals, and welcoming playmates. But when he is shown a picture book with animate images from his own life, he becomes impatient to see the future and suddenly finds himself back on a chilly grey street in West Kensington, alone and weeping. The doorway has vanished. Here, unlike most such tales—including the biblical Eden—redemption is possible, for Wallace occasionally happens upon the door in later years. Yet, in each instance, his worldly concerns outweigh the appeal of paradise. Eventually, he mourns his refusal to enter "the door that goes into peace, into delight, into a beauty beyond dreaming, a kindness no man on earth can know."[36] Then, in a final moment of irony, the narrator tells us that Wallace's body was found in a deep excavation site near East Kensington Station, where he apparently fell through a small doorway cut into the protective wall. The border between fantasy and reality collapses; the problem of sin and redemption remains.

Wallace, like Eve, could not be satisfied with paradise alone, and self-absorption barred him from re-entry. In many similar stories of a once-visited paradise, the temptation offered is erotic and the consequence likewise

FIGURE 6.3: Lester Ralph, *Eve in the garden*. From Mark Twain, *Eve's Diary*, 1906.

expulsion. Some are fairy-tale-like, such as "The Garden of Paradise" (1838) by Hans Christian Andersen, where a prince (a book collector) is tormented by curiosity about Eden and convinced of his ability to resist its temptations. He is facilitated by a personified East Wind, who sweeps him across the earth, finally descending to a soft carpet of grass amid figs, pomegranates, and spices. Here he finds "the island of happiness," the perfumed air of Eden, where "the flowers and the leaves sang the sweet songs of his childhood."[37] Like so many others, this garden represents the innocence of youth; but there is also a reminder of the temporal world, a series of brilliantly colored windows, living tableaux depicting all of history from Adam and Eve in their prelapsarian bliss to the pyramids in Egypt and the blue mountains of New Holland. Although remaining in the garden requires him only to resist the temptations of a lovely princess, in a Faustian bargain he concludes that a single kiss "is worth an eternity of darkness and woe." This Adam loses his Eve and, with her, the garden. The Edenic myth is given a humorous twist by Mark Twain in *The Diaries of Adam and Eve,* where Adam's stubborn indifference to nature and to his mate is contrasted with Eve's immediate and tender regard for both.[38] Her love for Adam outweighs her sorrow in leaving the Garden,[39] yet many years must pass before he arrives at the same conclusion: "it is better to live outside the Garden with her than inside it without her," an acknowledgement of the power of love reminiscent of John Milton's conclusion to *Paradise Lost.*[40]

In many a tale, the temptations of paradise are quite sinister, especially so in Hawthorne's "Rappuccini's Daughter" (1844). This, too, is a story within a story. It begins on a playful note as the unnamed narrator attributes his tale to a little-known author "M. de l'Aubepine" ("hawthorn" in French), whose titles are all French translations of Hawthorne's own titles in *Twice-Told Tales* (1837). Hawthorne's narrator thus establishes his ironic distance, preparing us for Aubepine's "inveterate love of allegory" and "fantastic imagery."[41]

The three main characters evoke an inverted Eden: Dr. Giacomo Rappuccini, the mad scientist and creator of the garden; his daughter Beatrice, its loveliest "flower;" and the student Giovanni, the interloper who will eventually destroy the garden's equilibrium. Looking through his window into an apparently inaccessible walled enclave, Giovanni is immediately captivated by eerily beautiful vegetation, including a magnificent but sinister purple shrub. He observes a sickly man (Rappuccini) who seems afraid of the plants and their "oppressive exhalation," but Giovanni's hesitations evaporate as he observes Beatrice moving intimately among the leaves and blooms, inhaling their scents. Although her breath has a lethal effect on flora and fauna from the outside world, he longs to enter, and eventually locates a hidden door to this beguiling yet perverted haven, "the monstrous offspring of man's depraved fancy." Through his intimacy with the garden and with Beatrice, Giovanni, too, absorbs the deadly power. Realizing this, he plans to escape. He urges Beatrice to take an antidote to the poison so she can depart with him. This she willingly accepts, knowing it will mean her death: "Oh, was there not, from the first, more poison in thy nature than in mine?"[42] In this ambivalent paradise, both creator and intruder are demonic, whereas the lethal Beatrice is also a Dantesque vision of perfection.

In Émile Zola's novel *La Faute de l'Abbé Mouret* (1875), a young priest excessively devoted to the Virgin Mary is consumed by his duties to an indifferent congregation. For Serge Mouret, "nature offered only snares and abominations; he gloried in maltreating her, in despising her, in releasing himself from his human slime."[43] His extreme, ascetic single-mindedness begins

to waver when he visits the nearby estate of Paradou ("Paradise" in Proven-
çal), once a magnificent palace surrounded by a splendid park—a "miniature
Versailles." Abandoned more than a century earlier upon the death of the owner's beautiful mistress, the palace burned down and the gates to the overgrown
property were nailed shut. A caretaker still resides in his lodge with Albine, his
niece, who has made the unruly park her haven. When Serge first sets eyes on
her, she is the embodiment of the garden's wild and savage beauty, its female
vitality:

> A door suddenly opened at the end of the vestibule; a dazzling breach
> was made in the black darkness of the wall, and through the breach came
> a vision of a virgin forest, a great depth of woodland, beneath a flood of
> sunbeams … such a tangle of greenery, such riotous luxuriance of vegeta-
> tion, that the whole horizon seemed one great burst of shooting foliage.[44]

Albine quickly closes off the view, yet the garden has entered the room along
with her—in her slender, golden arms, her delicious fragrance, and the flowers
covering her hair, throat, and bodice.

Once granted this vision, Serge's prior obsession with the Virgin Mary merges
with his image of Albine. Then he becomes deathly ill, and when he regains consciousness weeks later he finds himself at Paradou under Albine's care. The vast,
otherworldly park, with every species of plant and a perfect climate, becomes the
setting for his recovery and a growing intimacy. But the garden's effect is ambiguous. When we see Albine partially buried in roses—a flower conventionally understood as a symbol of the Virgin—the image is unsettling: enormous clusters
of blooms shower down on her, and "like a living snowfall these roses already
hid her feet in the grass. And they climbed her knees, covered her skirt, and
smothered her to the waist."[45] Furthermore, in its return to nature, the garden
resists human intervention. Indeed, nature works with "rabid fury" to eradicate
the traces of human improvement: weeds conceal paths, vines strangle statues,
and flowers proliferate "into such numberless families, and scampering in such
mad fashion throughout the whole garden, that the place was now all helter-
skelter riot to its very walls, a very den of debauchery."[46] There is a sense of
foreboding as the two venture further into the park, searching with "tremulous
excitement" for a secret and forbidden place of "perfect happiness," a happiness they recognize may be "perilous."[47] The ground underfoot begins to smell
foul; the plants turn menacing: an araucaria stands "with large regular arms resembling reptiles grafted one on the other, and bristling with imbricated leaves
that suggested the scales of an excited serpent."[48] Once they find the forbidden

FIGURE 6.4: Serge and Albine in the garden. From Émile Zola, *La Faute de l'Abbé Mouret*, illustrations by Bieler, Conconi and Gambard, wood engravings by Ch. Guillaume, Paris: Marpon et Flammarion, 1890.

tree and fully acknowledge their love, the Edenic pattern prevails: they become self-conscious, and paradise is lost. Serge is stricken with remorse and retreats to his church with intensified piety. Much too late, he ventures back to Paradou but is unable to remain. Albine carries all the flowers of the garden into her room and dies there, engulfed by nature's bounty.

The bizarre garden fable in Goethe's "Der neue Paris" appears in the autobiography of his early years, *Dichtung und Wahrheit* (1811–33), a title that alerts the reader to the creative aspect of recollection.[49] Here Goethe recalls telling his schoolmates about a dream in which he is asked to choose among three apples that transform before his eyes into doll-size goddesses (hence the title's allusion to the Judgment of Paris). They escape his grasp, along with a fourth little nymph who vanishes despite his desperate attempts to keep her. True to form, he later comes upon a small door in a wall, hesitates, and then enters into a lush garden, a Dantesque landscape of concentric circles, each hierarchically more important as he moves toward the center. In fairy-tale fashion, the innermost circle is attainable only by submitting to a series of conditions. As he approaches its axis, the garden draws him forward just as much as it gives him warning. Then in a pavilion set amid a great sweep of flowers and cypresses, he finds his nymph, who suggests they play a game of soldiers. It is, of course, a test, and in his enthusiasm for the game the boy becomes aggressive, destroying his opponent's warriors, whereupon the entire garden repels him. He barely escapes, and once he is outside, the door in the wall disappears. Goethe's garden is a dream within a recollection of youth, a memory filtered through the lens of autobiography. In a final gesture obliterating the boundary between fiction and reality, he describes how his schoolmates searched repeatedly for the garden, and a few claimed to have discovered the door, although none could ever open it. The violence in this odd allegory of adolescent sexuality and gender formation adds an unsettling twist to the trope of the lost garden.

GARDENS AS PARADISE REGAINED THROUGH MEMORY

Gardens that figure in memoirs are most often those of childhood and are, as it were, "real," rather than magical. Yet they can assume the power of magic in their ability to conjure up the sights, smells, sensations, and emotions of youth. We find such charged recollections in Pierre Loti's *Le Roman d'un Enfant* (1890), an autobiographical account of his early life.[50] Loti claims a prodigious memory. He relates the experience of a garden when he was not yet three, associating it with his first awareness of the sweetness of reverie.[51] Such moments recur throughout his childhood: an oblique ray of sunlight evokes a tender sorrow, or a small bouquet of violets elicits the fragrance and texture of an open landscape. He recalls his first return to the garden after convalescing from scarlet fever:

> Seated under the bower of jasmine and honeysuckle I felt as if I were experiencing the enchantment of paradise, of another Eden. Everything was budding and blossoming; without my knowledge during the time that I

was confined to my bed, this wonderful drama of the spring had enacted
itself upon the earth ... to which only the very aged seem indifferent; it
ravished me and I allowed my joy to take possession of me almost to the
point of intoxication.[52]

The springtime garden invigorates him—a leitmotif in several of the plots we
have examined. Tender recollections of blossoming trees and flowers in various
gardens (often enclosed and locked) pervade his early memories in re-imagined
dreamlike visions filled with the splashing of water and the fragrance of roses,
honeysuckles, and jasmine. A romantic yearning for the past and the potency
of remembered experiences in these gardens is tinged with melancholy, as the
narrator confesses that these things can only be revisited through language.

    It is easy to understand how the texture and poignancy of Loti's recollec-
tions drew the attention of Marcel Proust, whose *À la recherche du temps
perdu* stands as the preeminent example of the sensory power of memory.[53]
That our existence is given meaning through reliving moments of childhood
is most famously embodied in the madeleine episode of the first volume,
Swann's Way. Gardens bear a comparable power over the narrator; for the
young Marcel, flowers, trees, parks, and morning walks all resonate with
meaning:

> The sight of a single poppy hoisting upon its slender rigging and holding
> against the breeze its scarlet ensign, over the buoy of rich black earth
> from which it sprang, made my heart beat as does a wayfarer's when he
> perceives, upon some low-lying ground, an old and broken boat which
> is being caulked and made seaworthy, and cries out, although he has not
> yet caught sight of it, "The Sea!"[54]

Among the many flowers in Proust's recollected gardens, orchids—not surprisingly—acquire an erotic meaning. A scene often cited in regard to Marcel's ambiguous sexuality entails the pollination of a rare orchid. He attends the event
but misses the crucial moment when he is distracted by the sight of two men
engaged in what he later realizes is a homosexual encounter.[55] Another species
of orchid, the *Cattleya labiata*, is a recurring motif in the sexual relationship
of Swann and Odette, for whom the "indecency" and "fleshy cluster" of its
blooms come to symbolize their passion.[56] The madeleine incident itself calls
up garden memories: "so in that moment all the flowers in our garden and
in M. Swann's park, and the water-lilies on the Vivonne and the good folk
of the village and their little dwellings and the parish church and the whole of

Combray and its surroundings, taking shape and solidity, sprang into being, town and gardens alike, from my cup of tea."[57]

Many flowers prove evocative for the narrator, but lilacs and hawthorns carry particular intensity, especially because—like the madeleine—they engage more than one sense. Lilacs are personified as "pliant forms" he wishes to embrace, drawing down their "starry locks."[58] But hawthorns affect him most profoundly, awakening rushes of sweet memory. The following passage captures the mingling of longing and sensual delight in a recollected moment:

> I found the whole path throbbing with the fragrance of hawthorn-blossom. The hedge resembled a series of chapels, whose walls were no longer visible under the mountains of flowers that were heaped upon their altars ... the scent that swept out over me from them was as rich, and as circumscribed in its range, as though I had been standing before the Lady-altar, and the flowers, themselves adorned also, held out each its little bunch of glittering stamens with an air of inattention, fine, radiating "nerves" ... here spread out into pools of fleshy white, like strawberry-beds in spring. How simple and rustic, in comparison with these, would seem the dog-roses which, in a few weeks' time, would be climbing the same hillside path in the heat of the sun, dressed in the smooth silk of their blushing pink bodices, which would be undone and scattered by the first breath of wind.
>
> But it was in vain that I lingered before the hawthorns, to breathe in, to marshal before my mind (which knew not what to make of it), to lose in order to rediscover their invisible and unchanging odor, to absorb myself in the rhythm which disposed their flowers here and there with the light-heartedness of youth, and at intervals as unexpected as certain intervals of music; they offered me an indefinite continuation of the same charm, in an inexhaustible profusion, but without letting me delve into it any more deeply, like those melodies which one can play over a hundred times in succession without coming any nearer to their secret. I turned away from them for a moment so as to be able to return to them with renewed strength.[59]

The many-faceted richness of the hawthorns invades nearly all the senses and is imbued with a divine spirit. Yet in his awareness of the elusiveness of remembrance itself, the narrator betrays a sense of melancholy, even at this youthful moment. Garden scenes inhabit the recollections of Marcel's early years, from his grandmother's passionate devotion to nature to his first glimpse of

Gilberte, standing with a trowel in her hand in the Swann's beautiful park.[60] Indeed, Gilberte's very name, "uttered across the heads of the stocks and jasmines … unfolding through the arch of the pink hawthorn," merges with the perfumed air around her; she is a mysterious life-force that, like the garden, he will always long for, yet exquisitely never possess.[61]

For Proust, a garden is not so much a representation of character or moral structure, or a place of magic and escape, but a reservoir of memory all the more intense for that, and yet at the same time withered and ineffable:

> … how paradoxical it is to seek in reality for the pictures that are stored in one's memory, which must inevitably lose the charm that comes to them from memory itself and from their not being apprehended by the senses … The places that we have known belong now only to the little world of space on which we map them for our own convenience. None of them was ever more than a thin slice, held between the contiguous impressions that composed our life at that time.[62]

In the words of Henry James, "the charm of looking over a garden-wall into another garden breaks down when successions of walls appear … We are divided of course between liking to feel the past strange and liking to feel it familiar; the difficulty is, for intensity, to catch it at the moment when the scales of the balance hang with the right evenness."[63]

Throughout the post-romantic era, gardens were most often metaphors of interiority. Removed from the secular world, they were repeatedly conceived as frame stories, enclosed spaces, and arenas able to be retrieved only through imagination or memory. The preoccupation with gardens was at the same time an expression of anxiety about actual social uncertainties, for example the inexorably degrading effects of the Industrial Revolution on human relations and the natural world. This larger crisis is mirrored as much in the gardens of retreat as it is in the gardens of evil. In retrospect, the literary realizations of the garden in this period are in essence reactionary, a longing for an arcadia impossible to recover, for a youth impossible to relive. And yet if a garden, like the past, is still alive, we have, as Proust tells us, not aged.

CHAPTER SEVEN

Visual Representations

IRIS LAUTERBACH

In the history of the visual arts, the period from 1800 to 1920 has produced by far the most representations of gardens.[1] There are various reasons for the rapidly growing number of garden subjects in nineteenth-century painting that are to be found in the period's cultural and social history. In the nineteenth century, the emphasis shifted from the representation of princely gardens to the depiction of gardens as living space and as a backdrop to middle-class and bourgeois life, be it small private gardens near the dwelling or public urban parks in the European metropolises. In the second half of the nineteenth century, the gardens of the impressionist and post-impressionist painters became an experimental field for their plein air painting. It was typical for elderly and sick painters to withdraw to their own gardens that offered them the comfort of a manageable domestic space, and the richness of visual impressions.

On the one hand, garden motifs used and developed between 1800 and the early twentieth century continued existing traditions; on the other hand, they introduced new ways of representing and interpreting designed open spaces and landscapes. Since the late eighteenth-century debates about garden art, gardens had increasingly been considered a place that evoked many different sentimental reactions. Gardens were supposed to arouse sensations, and evoke emotions and recollections. At the same time, they were attributed with the ability of transcending spatial and temporal borders. In many landscape gardens of the eighteenth and nineteenth centuries, *fabriques*, buildings designed to evoke different countries and time periods, offered the strolling visitor a journey around the world and into the past. In the fictional accounts of theatrical, literary, and other artistic productions, gardens were interpreted as emotional metaphor and as the mirror image of feelings, as a place of metamorphoses and of wonders, of the innocence and the fall of man, of the origin and the death of all beings.

Around 1800, some representations of gardens in the visual arts followed existing traditions. As can be seen in pattern books and garden *vedute*, these traditions had persisted into the nineteenth century, when new motifs and representations finally appeared. The family portrait in the private garden, a motif used since the seventeenth century as Rubens's famous *Self Portrait with His Wife Isabella Brant in the Honeysuckle Bower* attests,[2] was developed further during the nineteenth century. In that period, the visual development and the rendering of three-dimensional garden space in particular seem to have interested landscape architects, architects, and visual artists. At the turn of the century, and in the first decades of the nineteenth century, many painters and designers studied, and interpreted, the visual connections between architecture and its setting, and between the domestic interior and the garden. Interior decoration including mirrors, paintings, and wallpaper reflected and imitated gardens, arousing multiple associations. Renowned, and fictional, gardens appeared on interior walls. The luxurious, exotic gardens that were depicted on wallpaper and appeared as stage design responded to the collective nostalgia for a remote paradise.

THE "MAGAZINE OF IDEAS": THE GARDEN AS A SUM OF ITS PARTS

The widespread late-eighteenth-century debate on garden art led to the development of new kinds of visual representations of gardens during the nineteenth century. The discussion about the preference for the French or English garden styles soon involved art lovers and an informed public, and this discussion therefore developed on several theoretical and artistic levels. In France, England, and Germany, the theory and practice of gardens was now discussed not only by experts and owners—mostly noblemen—but also by the middle class.

Garden owners, gardeners, artists, and writers who cultivated a passion for gardens not only read and consulted garden literature, but many also expressed their passion in writing. Since the 1770s, several garden books had appeared and had been translated in other languages. These publications by Thomas Whately (1770), William Chambers (1772), Claude-Henri Watelet (1774), Jean-Marie

Morel (1776), and Christian Cay Lorenz Hirschfeld (1779–1785), however, contained only few, if any, images relating to their complex theoretical texts. Hirschfeld's successful treatise, for example, was illustrated with an eclectic selection of small, vignette-like clippings from older pattern books and architectural treatises. The huge compilation of nearly 500 plates published by the German-born Georges-Louis Le Rouge between 1774 and 1791, therefore, bridged a gap in the market.[3] In twenty-one *cahiers*, or issues, the cartographer Le Rouge edited a large collection of maps, plans, perspective views, architectural elevations, and cross sections showing the designs of historic and recent gardens and garden buildings in France, England, Germany, Italy, and the Netherlands. The individual issues, known as *Cahiers des jardins anglo-chinois*, served garden experts throughout Europe as pattern books. In contrast to the theoretical texts, they offered garden lovers pragmatic advice in the form of lavish illustrations of design features that could be selected and variously assembled to create a garden.

Le Rouge combined several editorial and artistic concepts used for the visual representation of gardens. One of these concepts derived from the late-sixteenth-century French celebration of royal castles and gardens in a series of views, which was begun by Jacques Androuet Ducerceau, and continued in the seventeenth and eighteenth centuries by the family Perelle, Jacques Rigaud, Pierre-Jean Mariette, Jacques-François Blondel, and Emmanuel Héré. In comparison with Le Rouge's work, these series were of superior artistic quality, and in contrast with Le Rouge, these artists assumed a franco-centric perspective. This franco-centric perspective can be found almost two decades after Le Rouge's pattern book in Alexandre-Louis-Joseph de Laborde's 1808 *Description des nouveaux jardins de la France et de ses anciens châteaux*, although it included texts in three languages. Besides the French influence on Le Rouge's work, English pattern books that included gothic, Chinese, and Moorish architecture and had been published in the second third of the eighteenth century by William and John Halfpenny, Charles Over, Paul Decker, and William Wrighte, provided models. In turn, Le Rouge's international pattern book influenced Jean-Charles Krafft's *Plans des plus beaux jardins pittoresques de France, de l'Angleterre et de l'Allemagne* (1809–1810), and comparable collections published by Gijsbert Van Laar in the Netherlands, and by Pierre Boitard in France (*Traité de la composition et de l'ornement des jardins*), 3rd edition, 1825). Le Rouge's most influential follower, however, was Johann Gottfried Grohmann whose *Ideenmagazin für Liebhaber von Gärten* (1796–1811) was the most successful garden pattern book in the early nineteenth century. Its success was based on its clever choice of subjects, its relatively low price, and a successful marketing strategy. The merit of the editor Grohmann and the publisher, Friedrich

FIGURE 7.1: Etching showing garden toilets. From Johann Gottfried Grohmann, *Recueil de dessins*. First Italian edition, Venice 1805, plate 31. © Zentralinstitut für Kunstgeschichte, Munich, Germany.

Gotthelf Baumgärtner, was that they successfully selected examples from the rich English garden literature around 1800—for example, publications by the architects John Plaw, John Soane, and James Malton—that suited German circumstances, thus propagating the picturesque garden in Central Europe.

By 1800, garden art had become an international business that transcended national boundaries. The widely distributed pattern books and engravings such as Le Rouge's *Cahiers des Jardins Anglo-Chinois* and Grohmann's *Ideenmaga-zin* offered the European public a versatile collection of garden motifs, suggesting that the creation of a landscape garden and the construction of its fabriques consisted of the mere combination of individual motifs from a catalogue. The pattern books catered to the needs of aristocratic and bourgeois dilettantes, and lovers of architecture and gardens, who aspired to design their own gardens. Le Rouge, Grohmann, and Boitard neither followed a definite style or garden tradition, nor proclaimed a certain style as morally and ethically correct. Their eclectic collections served the heterogeneous taste of a large public.

Two generations later, in his posthumously published last novel, *Bouvard et Pécuchet* (1881), Gustave Flaubert wrote about the problems concerning the medial "crossover" in the rendering, creation, and contemplation of gardens and of the movement through garden spaces.[4] The two main characters, Bouvard and Pécuchet, present a view into their garden, that shows with pathos sentimental scenery, laid out according to Boitard's *Manuel complet de l'Architecte des Jardins, ou l'art de les composer et de les décorer* (1834). In response to a signal given by the hosts, and to their guests' surprise, the curtain is theatrically drawn, opening a view into the garden. The view out of the window reveals "something horrible"—"*quelque chose d'effrayant*"—something that cannot be explained in words, and that is rendered ridiculous once the guests undertake a walk through the garden. For the visitors, the walk in the garden is grotesque, reminding them of a horror cabinet, and it ends in a debacle for the two patrons. Bouvard and Pécuchet's attempt to create a garden following a pattern book fails, and so does their mise-en-scène of the garden. Flaubert treats with irony the failed visual mise-en-scène, the clumsy garden layout and designs imitating examples in a pattern book, and the disillusionment experienced on a walk through the garden itself.

"ALL MAGIC OF OPTICS": THE GARDEN REFLECTED IN INTERIOR DECORATION

While pattern books represented fragments and individual motifs for assembly in gardens, in interior decoration, real and imaginary gardens often appeared in their entirety:

Adjacent to the residence and the utility buildings lay pleasure gardens, orchards, and mowings; thence one wandered unexpectedly into a wood, through which a lane broad enough for driving wound back and forth. At its center, at the highest elevation, had been constructed a hall with adjoining chambers. Entering by the main door, one saw in a great mirror the finest view the entire region had to offer, then quickly turned around to recover with the help of reality from the unexpected tableau. For the approach was artfully designed and everything ingeniously hidden to achieve this surprise effect. No one entered without turning with pleasure back and forth from the mirror to Nature and from Nature to the mirror.[5]

The frame story of Johann Wolfgang von Goethe's novel *Wilhelm Meister's Journeyman Years* contains a short novella. While walking through a garden landscape, the protagonist comes across a pavilion on top of an elevation. Drawn by curiosity, he enters the building, and stops, for on the wall of the main hall, the image of the garden landscape he thought to have left behind suddenly opens up in front of him. A huge mirror ingeniously installed evokes a perfect optical illusion. As soon as the visitor becomes aware of the mirror effect, he tries to trace the artful deception, and, noting the mounting of the mirror, turns back and forth, not knowing what to admire more: the real garden, its two-dimensional reflection, or the optical deception. Apart from its inversion, the reflected image in the mirror appears identical to nature. In this case, the artificial imitation of nature is achieved through its reflection in the mirror. The visitor's glance into the mirror transforms the hall into a variable landscape, and garden. This blending-together of exterior and the interior is a particularly subtle example for an ephemeral interior decoration with garden motifs. It also defines the mirror as the intersection between the garden landscape and the outside world on one hand, and the senses, and the inner, emotional world of the beholder on the other hand. In Goethe's literary work, the "inner" spiritual world of his characters often corresponds, though in different contexts and intensities, to the "outer" world of a living, growing garden landscape.

In the first decades of the nineteenth century, interior decorations with imaginary gardens remained popular. Floral and garden motifs were considered attributes of Venus, the goddess of love and beauty. Mirrors that enlarged and changed the visual appearance of rooms also brought designed nature into the domestic realm. In most cases, however, these intricacies of "the magic of optics" would not have been available.[6] Instead, there were wall frescoes and paintings depicting gardens and landscapes that can be followed back to antiquity, and around 1800, wallpaper printed with floral or landscape motifs became very popular.[7] Printed wallpaper was less expensive than were silk wall coverings, and by the 1870s William Morris was producing his well-known floral prints for the decoration of interiors.

PANORAMA

Besides simple patterns, large representations of gardens were produced. Already in the second half of the eighteenth century, a fashion for expansive wall paintings representing heroic, bucolic, or exotic landscapes had developed, complete with ruins of antique Roman architecture, peasants and shepherds, or with luscious tropical vegetation. Often, framed by pilasters, the wall paintings appeared as framed images, despite their large scale. Shortly before 1800, panoramic wallpaper was invented,[8] again depicting entire landscape scenes, and thus evoking a continuous natural setting. Panoramic wallpaper was produced as grisaille, or through color woodblock printing. Jean Zuber and Joseph Dufour, the most renowned manufacturers, worked in Alsace, and sold their products on the European market.[9] The Alsatian wallpaper revealed the encyclopedic and international interests of a wealthy, culturally astute bourgeoisie. As one of the first "mass media," wallpaper incorporated an educational program geared toward the educated middle classes. The scenes depicted derived from mythology and other literature; realistic and mythical landscapes, city panoramas, and battle scenes predominated. Landscapes and scenes in France and its capital, Paris, appeared particularly often. The wallpaper title *Palais Royal* appeared in the first decade of the nineteenth century, and was followed by titles such as *Les Jardins Français* (1822), *Monuments de Paris* (1812–14), and *Fêtes parisiennes* (1815–20). Historic and exotic gardens also provided motifs for wallpaper and, by adapting exotic landscapes as interior decoration, they became "domesticated" garden settings. Wallpaper patterns and landscapes were promoted at the World's Fairs, beginning in London in 1851. At the Paris Universal Exhibition in 1855, the French company Jules Lefossé showed the wallpaper *Jardins d'Armide*, a particularly beautiful, colored print depicting exotic gardens and plants. Indeed, almost all travel destinations that played a role in the imagination and lives of the educated urban elite were found on wallpaper of the early and mid nineteenth century: Italy, Greece, Spain, Central America, Brazil, the Orient, China, and India. On occasion, these landscapes provided the backdrop for mythological and literary themes, and characters. The illusions produced by this vividly colored wallpaper paralleled the effects achieved by the popular panoramas installed in purpose-built buildings in several European metropolises. Panoramic wallpaper, and expansive wall paintings of gardens and landscapes experienced a renaissance when, in the 1890s, Edouard Vuillard painted nine large canvases showing everyday urban life in Parisian public parks and boulevards for Alexandre Natanson's Parisian Hôtel,[10] and in 1896 the post-impressionist painter Pierre Bonnard depicted his family in a garden on his large-sized screens.[11]

BIEDERMEIER: THE GARDEN AS INTERIOR

Private gardens played an important role during the so called Biedermeier period, the period that designates a style of interior decoration and furniture design in Central Europe from circa 1810 to the middle of the nineteenth century.[12] The numerous representations of interiors reveal a growing interest in the decoration of the house with fragrant flowers. Journals dealing with lady's fashion and housekeeping flourished, and promoted flower arrangements, and gardening as appropriate activities for the lady and the mistress of the house. The florists, and plant breeders—called *Blumisten*—were well organized in associations, and they published their own journals. The indoor representation of gardens ranged from opulent luxurious flower arrangements in wealthy households to the individual pelargonium proudly displayed by its owner. In paintings, the flower decoration usually signaled an iconographic program. Georg Friedrich Kersting's painting *Stickerin am Fenster* ("A Woman Stitching at a Window")[13] shows a girl working on a piece of embroidery. The flowers embellishing her room reveal the girl's hidden feelings: Near the window, a rose seems to look out for a distant lover. His portrait on the wall is clasped by a tendril of Ipomoea tricolor, symbolizing fidelity.

GARDEN VEDUTA AND FRAMED GARDEN VIEW

With the exception of situations that described the threshold between interior and exterior—for example, a view through a window into a garden—painters of the romantic period such as Caspar David Friedrich were less interested in gardens as works of art than they were in nature and landscape as the garden of God. However, gardens continued to be depicted as classical vedute. In fact, when the landscape gardener Friedrich Ludwig von Sckell, the major proponent of the classical landscape garden in Germany, described his design methods, he compared the landscape gardener's work with that of a landscape painter.[14] While the design of landscape gardens followed the compositions of seventeenth-century heroic and idyllic landscape paintings by Claude Lorrain, Nicolas Poussin, or Gaspard Dughet, in the early nineteenth century, landscape painting was in turn inspired by landscape gardens. Johann Georg von Dillis repeatedly painted Sckell's Munich English garden, and Hermann Prince of Pückler-Muskau illustrated his book *Andeutungen über*

FIGURE 7.2: Karl Friedrich Schinkel, *design for Orianda palace in the Crimea*. Fourth edition, 1873. Lithograph. © Zentralinstitut für Kunstgeschichte, Munich, Germany.

Landschaftsgärtnerei (*Hints of Landscape Gardening*, 1834) with Wilhelm Schirmer's vedute of different parts of his garden in Muskau.

The architectural projects carried out by the Prussian architect and painter Karl Friedrich Schinkel after his journey to Italy in 1804 show his strong interest in antique models, especially in Pliny the Younger's villas Laurentinum on the coast near Rome, and Tuscum on a Tuscan hillside. Schinkel's early projects for Charlottenhof palace in Potsdam (1825), planned together with the landscape gardener Peter Joseph Lenné, reveal knowledge of the Latin author's villa descriptions. In 1833, Schinkel made plans for the reconstruction of both of Pliny's villas, and again inspired by these antique buildings, between 1834 and 1838 he planned the Orianda palace in the Crimea. The colored lithographs of the plans, elevations, and views of this unexecuted project published in 1840[15] (Fig 7.2) show directed views into the garden that were characteristic of Schinkel's work—especially of his famous stage designs—and of the drawings of his fellow artists, including Carl Blechen, who painted gardens and greenhouses.[16] In his stage designs, Schinkel used central, or oblique axes, following Galli Bibbiena's *scena per angolo*. Thus, in his drawings, the luxurious oriental gardens enclosed by the Orianda palace appeared like fantastic stage sets leading beyond the picture plane.

Among the many architects, gardeners, theorists, and literati who studied, interpreted, reconstructed, and visualized Pliny's villas in the eighteenth and nineteenth centuries were Hermann Prince of Pückler-Muskau, who quoted Pliny in his *Hints on Landscape Gardening*, and Johann Wolfgang von Goethe, whose garden descriptions in *Elective Affinities* testify to his knowledge of Pliny's villa descriptions. However, not only the layout and the general disposition of the villas and their gardens have been interpreted and copied; the visual relationships described between the interior and exterior spaces, and the landscapes, attracted attention, as well. In Pliny's description, views through windows into the gardens, and into the surrounding countryside were part of the interior decoration. Early nineteenth-century representations of gardens followed these sightlines, and the visual relationships formed by the axial layout, pergolas, and crypto porticos described by Pliny.

DIORAMA: LONGING FOR THE SOUTH

"Know'st thou the land where lemon-trees do bloom, / And oranges like gold in leafy gloom; / A gentle wind from deep blue heaven blows, / The myrtle thick, and high the laurel grows?"[17] Mignon's famous song in Goethe's novel *Wilhelm Meister's Apprenticeship* (1795/96) describes the ideal of the Italian garden as perceived north of the Alps. By 1800, the gardens of the Roman villeggiatura, like Villa d'Este in Tivoli, and Villa Aldobrandini in Frascati, had been overgrown, and appeared as if they had been returned to nature. From the late eighteenth century onward, the picturesque qualities of these neglected but varied and manifold "tableaux" inspired tourists and artists, such as the French painters Jean-Honoré Fragonard and Hubert Robert. Artists from northern Europe rediscovered ruined Roman gardens, and felt that they produced melancholic moods and mournful thoughts about the futility of human existence. They painted a new picture of these gardens, and by doing so arguably created on their canvas a new form of Italian garden.

The classicist architects of the early nineteenth century, however, opposed the romanticized images of Italian villa gardens. With their publication on Roman villas, *Choix des plus célèbres maisons de plaisance de Rome et de ses environs* (1809), the French architects Charles Percier and Pierre-François-Léonard Fontaine tried to replicate an exact and true image of Roman gardens that contrasted with the romanticized vision of the same sites in many artists' paintings. Instead of the "sad image of decay that the painters take pleasure in presenting," Percier and Fontaine conveyed precise data and measurements.[18] Their garden views are monumental architectural representations of Roman villas and their gardens.

A monumental, *and* romantic, view of the Villa d'Este in Tivoli was painted by Carl Blechen, a friend of Karl Friedrich Schinkel, and later a professor at the Berlin academy, who traveled to Italy during the years 1828, and 1829. Like his

French colleagues, he chose the view of the visitor entering the garden from the old main entrance at the foot of the hill. His garden is peopled by figures with gestures and costumes that reference the sixteenth-century origins of the villa. The historic fictional garden scene is confined by the façade of the main building in the distance that is framed by the tall cypress trees along the central pathway. Blechen's garden and landscape differ from the romantic, heroic, or mythic landscapes painted by Caspar David Friedrich, Jakob Philipp Hackert, Joseph Anton Koch, and Carl Rottmann, and the strong and differentiated lights and colors of his paintings precede the plein air painting of the mid nineteenth century.

Since the late eighteenth century, the Moorish culture and art on the Iberian peninsula had increasingly aroused the interest of central and western European travelers, writers, and artists.[19] In the discussion about national architectural styles, Moorish architecture was ascribed an important role in the genesis of gothic architecture. The courtyards of Moorish palaces, like those of the Alhambra in Granada, had been planted and transformed into gardens only recently. The appearance of the Generalife gardens had also changed over time, and their water works were in grave disrepair. Nevertheless, the lithographs, and steel engravings illustrating publications on the Alhambra and the Generalife in the 1830s and 1840s show the overgrown gardens as luxurious paradise. These romanticizing and picturesque views appeared in books by Washington Irving (1832), Thomas Roscoe (1835), Girault de Prangey (1841), Jules Goury and Owen Jones (1842–45), and Théophile Gautier (1843), and confirmed the vision of the Alhambra as "the most voluptuous of all retirements," a magic castle and an earthly paradise.[20] Irving and Gautier described their visual impressions of Granada as "tableaux," and fittingly the title of Irving's book, *Alhambra; or the New Sketch Book*, alluded to word paintings and sketches. In their ekphrastic writings, they employed various types of literary paradise descriptions: the ravishing luxury and the overwhelming fragrance of plants and flowers, the mellow song of birds, the murmuring fountains, the gay splashing of water jets, and the panoramic view into the surrounding landscape were common motifs used to describe the *locus amoenus* in Occidental, and in Arabic poetry. The nineteenth-century authors' fusion of original Arabian texts with Occidental garden traditions produced a poetic and, at the same time, ecstatic vision of the Alhambra. The literary and pictorial mise-en-scène of the architecture and garden of the Alhambra in a moonlit or sunset ambience enabled the leap into a distant and fictional Oriental world. Gautier described this impression by comparing it to the effects produced in the fashionable dioramas, the predecessors of the cinema.[21]

Greenhouses attached, or belonging to, urban dwellings were another location in the cities that attracted visitors due to their exoticism. In literature, as for example in Eugène Sue's *Mystères de Paris* (1843), the humid air of a greenhouse makes emotions thrive, as it does exotic plants and flowers. Édouard Manet used the greenhouse adjacent his studio as background for several portrait paintings. The greenhouse provided the setting for the portraits of his wife, and of his friends Mr. and Mrs. Guillemet (*Dans la serre*, 1878–79).[22]

GARDENS IN PAINTING, 1850–1920

At the time Manet was training and beginning his career as a painter, the painters of the Barbizon school promoted plein air painting, and depicted the Forêt de Fontainebleau in intimate, idyllic landscape paintings. From circa 1860 onward, the garden became an increasingly popular subject. French painting of the second half of the nineteenth century influenced artists across Europe, and in America and Japan, and encompassed a big variety of profane garden representations: Gardens were presented as landscapes and as urban space, as domestic interior and as a background for family portraits, as plein air studio and as a place of rich visual and aesthetic experiences and challenges. This general development can be explained by growing urbanization. With increasing urbanization and industrialization, gardens gained importance as private, domestic retreats, and as public urban space. While he captured the railway, industrial plants, and steel mills in Berlin in many of his paintings, Adolph Menzel also depicted garden courtyards, beer gardens, and the public Tiergarten in the Prussian capital. These paintings offered seemingly random glance, and oblique views into private and public garden landscapes.

THE FLANEUR'S FLEETING GLANCE,
AND THE URBAN PROMENADE

Already in the eighteenth century, the promenades of Paris were known as public walks and meeting places that also attracted foreign tourists, and already at the end of the century, artists such as Gabriel de Saint-Aubin and Louis-Philibert Debucourt had depicted the public life in the Tuileries and in the Palais Royal gardens in large-scale etchings and aquatintas. The grands boulevards realized during the Second Empire, and through the 1870s under the direction of Georges-Eugène Haussmann, embraced the old city on both sides of the Seine, and in some instances, as in the case of Park Monceau, cut through historic gardens. On the whole, however, Haussmann's radical undertakings allowed the French capital to develop and expand further. The existing Tuileries gardens and the Jardin du Luxembourg, the new boulevards and the many pleasure gardens, open-air restaurants, and beer gardens became part of a larger system of public urban spaces. Due to their new role in modern urban life, it is perhaps not surprising that garden subjects played a central role in impressionist work.[23] In his painting *Concert in the Tuileries Gardens*,[24] Édouard Manet, friend of Charles Baudelaire and "painter of modern life," showed the public at leisure. The eye of the beholder parallels that of the single flaneur communicating with the crowd. The children in the foreground are absorbed in their game; several figures, painted as the artist's friends, look toward the beholder. The lights and reflections on the garments, hats, veils, and the men's shimmering top hats, seem to correspond to the vivid concert of voices, sounds, and music. During the 1867 Universal Exhibition, the Parisian public gardens, painted by many French impressionist and foreign artists, turned into tourist attractions. Claude Monet and Pierre-Auguste Renoir painted the Tuileries gardens in different atmospheric lighting from an apartment in Rue de Rivoli that an art collector had put at their disposal. Menzel, Monet, Renoir, Gustave Caillebotte in his pictures of Parisian streets, and later Camille Pissarro mostly worked with oblique perspectives that seemed to reproduce accidental views. Their paintings reflected the spontaneous impressions of a single flaneur in the capital.

ADAM AND EVE IN THE GARDEN: GENDER RECONSIDERED

Representations of gardens in the visual arts offer a rich field for gender studies. The art produced during the Biedermeier period reflects the ideal of a family life whose nucleus is the bourgeois home. Women worked in the house and in the garden, which was considered an intimate open-air room. As in Christian iconography, where the enclosed domestic garden is the symbol of Mary's chastity, gardens in Biedermeier paintings appeared as a *hortus conclusus* for the innocent child, the modest young girl, and the decent housewife. Children, whose education was compared by Jean-Jacques Rousseau to growth in the natural world, were often shown playing in a garden, for example by Philipp Otto Runge in *The Hülsenbeck children*.[25] A painting by the Viennese painter Erasmus von Engert shows a woman in her garden, as seen in Figure 7.3.[26] Doing needlework, she is reading a book, which judging from its size and clasps appears to be the Bible. Tendrils of vine, perennial flowers, and unpretentious flowers like sunflowers and hollyhocks decorate the beds, and, together with the fence, they form a protective shell around the female figure. In the nineteenth century, Biedermeier, impressionist, and symbolist paintings often portray women in enclosed and sheltered spaces, or at a threshold: at the gate, behind the fence, under a bower, on the terrace, at the window, or in the main doorway. In many cases, the spatial

FIGURE 7.3: Erasmus Ritter von Engert, *Viennese House Garden* (Wiener Hausgarten), 1828–1830. Oil on canvas. Nationalgalerie, Staatliche Museen zu Berlin. Bildarchiv Preussischer Kulturbesitz / Art Resource, NY.

arrangement appears predestined for a feminist interpretation. One example is the impressionist painter Eva Gonzalès's depiction of a girl and her young nanny. It is probably not by chance that the nanny shown behind a garden fence looks like a caged animal.[27]

The garden as a theme in the visual arts reached its apogee with the work of the male and female impressionist painters, who between 1874 and 1886 showed their work in their own exhibitions. An abundance of depictions of private gardens characterizes the work of Monet, Renoir, Caillebotte, Pissarro, and that of their female colleagues Berthe Morisot, Eva Gonzalès, Marie Bracquemond, and Mary Cassatt. Private gardens also provided the setting for many female and family portraits.[28] The enclosed and limited space of the private garden did not correspond to the active life led by men, who at the most were shown as active gardeners or as painters. As demonstrated by the impressionists' paintings, the garden was mostly considered female domestic terrain. In the ideal and undisturbed world of the garden, mothers and governesses played with their children, rested under trees and in the shadow, did needlework, and served meals and tea on the terrace. In the paintings, as in Morisot's painting showing her daughter, sister, and brother-in-law Eugène Manet, only family members and friends are portrayed together in the garden that seems to form a protective shield around them. When women were depicted, as in many of Monet's paintings that showed his first wife Camille, they appeared as "flowers" among flowers. Monet also depicted young ladies strolling alone under their umbrellas. When intimate family portraits were painted, the sitters often appeared contemplative, concentrated, or absorbed in other activities in the garden. Thus, Morisot's governess was depicted reading to an attentively listening child. Morisot's young women bend over their needlework. In the shadow of huge orange trees, Caillebotte's brother and cousin are completely absorbed in their reading.

In the work of the Munich painter Carl Spitzweg between 1850 and 1890, the garden is represented as *hortus conclusus*, as a place for retreat and complete self-absorption in old age. Spitzweg's gardens are ironic, and male-gendered. In several of his paintings, the lonely bachelor dedicates his entire affection to the only flower of his cactus. The domestic garden appears as the habitat of the established bachelor, of the widower, and the elderly womanizer. In the garden, he reads his newspaper, smokes his pipe, or unsuccessfully tries to make advances toward the young girls walking past. Reversing Christian, Biedermeier, and impressionist iconography, Spitzweg shows the garden as a male, not as female, *hortus conclusus* and retreat.

NEO-CYTHERA: IMPRESSIONIST FÊTES GALANTES

In 1920, as a condition for receiving the *Nymphéas* for the Tuileries Orangery, Claude Monet required the French state to acquire his monumental painting *Women in the garden at Ville d'Avray,* seen in Figure 7.4.[29] The painting shows

FIGURE 7.4: Claude Monet, *Women in the Garden at Ville d'Avray*, 1867. Oil on canvas. Paris, Musée d'Orsay. Réunion des Musées Nationaux / Art Resource, NY.

four women in a garden. In the foreground, a young woman, the painter's model Camille, lifts a single flower from a bouquet of roses in her lap. Her gesture has repeatedly been interpreted as the painter's comment on his relation to the portrayed woman, his first son's mother and later first wife. In the background, an attractive red-haired woman seen from behind bends down to a rosebush to pick a flower. On the left, two more young women silently stand side by side, one of them hiding her face in a flower bouquet. The shadow of the tree and the bright sunshine produce vivid light effects on the path, leaves, and on the garments. Not unlike hovering butterflies, the clearly outlined figures of the women in their resplendent and bright dresses appear detached from the green background. The schematic, decorative character of the composition was likely influenced by Japanese woodcuts that attracted impressionist and post-impressionist painters into the early twentieth century.

Another influence becomes apparent when studying Antoine Watteau's *Le pèlerinage à l'île de Cythère*. Watteau had presented *Cythera* in 1717 as his entry piece to the Parisian academy. Exhibited in the Louvre ever since with only short interruptions, it was Claude Monet's favorite work of art in the museum.[30] Thus, it might not surprise that Monet's *Femmes* seemingly "floating" side by side, the woman depicted from behind in a loose-cut dress, and the enigmatic mood of the painting recall Watteau's famous masterpiece of the early eighteenth century. Watteau's famous iridescent palette with its wealth of color and "ethereal light" appealed to painters such as Monet, and seem to have inspired them,[31] and perhaps even induced them to move from figurative paintings to pure, and almost abstract, garden and landscape motifs.

Cythera is not a destination or a point of departure but a utopia, an imaginary place where love reigns. Watteau's *Cythera* and his fêtes galantes show couples and single figures in fantasy landscapes, and in overgrown, enchanted gardens. Watteau was rediscovered in the nineteenth century, and eighteenth-century art was rehabilitated climaxing in the so-called Second Rococo.[32] The authors Gérard de Nerval and Paul Verlaine admired the elegance, the charm, and the aesthetic potential of the spontaneity, uncertainty, and the je ne sais quoi of Watteau's paintings. Charles Baudelaire, author of *The Flowers of Evil* (1857), saw in the "gay and elegant princesses" in Watteau's "fantasy landscapes"[33] characters not unrelated to his own, who were familiar with the intensity and the abysses of the modern urban psyche. From 1860 onward, the authors and art critics Edmond and Jules Goncourt published on Watteau, whom they described as "the great poet of the eighteenth century" and "a marvellous utopian."[34] Not until 1870, however, was Watteau's art, and the work of other eighteenth-century French painters, presented to the public in a new light. The previous year, the Parisian doctor Louis La Caze had bequeathed to the Louvre one of the most magnificent collections of eighteenth-century French art, including outstanding works by Watteau, François Boucher, Jean-Honoré Fragonard, and Hubert Robert.[35] With the installation of the La Caze collection in 1870, artists, critics, and the public became familiar with Watteau's *Cythera* and the eighteenth-century dreamy fêtes galantes. Quoting Watteau's entry piece for the academy, the Duc de Trévise in 1927 entitled the records of

his visits to Monet's Giverny house *Le Pèlerinage de Giverny*.[36] Renoir's painting *La balançoire*[37] was described by a critic as "something of the Pèlerinage
to Cythera with a special air of the nineteenth century," revealing "the same
spirit, the same French taste."[38] Morizot appeared as Fragonard's pupil, Gonzalès's works were reminiscent of Greuze and eighteenth-century drawings,
and Bracquemond's portraits of her sister and of female friends in the garden
convey a strong *neo-dixhuitième* appeal.[39] The poetic atmosphere and charm
of fictional eighteenth-century garden scenes lingered in impressionist garden
paintings.

THE ARTIST'S GARDEN AS PLEINAIR STUDIO

For many impressionist painters, their own garden was their plein air studio.
Growing public acceptance brought wealth, which allowed the painters to settle down and live a bourgeois life style. The development of public transportation from the center of Paris to the city's periphery enabled the bourgeoisie
to live a life divided between the city apartment and the house and garden on
the Seine or in the Parisian outskirts.[40] Claude Monet always owned a garden
near his houses, in Argenteuil as well as in Vétheuil and later in Giverny. In
time, he became a passionate gardener and florist. He subscribed to the most
important garden journals, and practiced garden art both as a gardener and
as a painter. Monet, Renoir, and Pissarro worked together in their gardens. In
many paintings, Gustave Caillebotte depicts the park of his family's country
houses in Yerres and in Petit Gennevilliers near Paris. As mentioned above,
when the paintings portrayed his family, its members were usually strolling in
the landscape park, absorbed in reading or needlework, or sitting under huge
orange trees. A critic of the impressionist exhibition in 1877 objected to the
"exhalations of bourgeois perfume" escaping from Caillebotte's paintings, and
accused them of showing the "dull absorption of bored provincials."[41] Caillebotte's paintings of his gardeners at work in the big kitchen garden at Yerres
did not appear more exciting. Outside France, the most prominent German
impressionist painter, Max Liebermann, also addressed scenes of the bourgeois
life style in his paintings. Like his French colleagues, he painted his villa garden
located on the Wannsee near Berlin many times during the 1910s and 1920s.[42]

The garden not only became a popular motif in impressionist painting,
where it often provided the background scenes of bourgeois life and work, but
it was also used in other visual arts, including caricatures, as demonstrated by
the German painter and caricaturist Wilhelm Busch. In 1873–74 he wrote and
illustrated *The Mole*, seen in Figure 7.5: "A gardener by the name of Knoll /
Goes for a joyful garden stroll. / His joyfulness, however, sours: / A mole is

Der Maulwurf.

In seinem Garten freudevoll

Geht hier ein Gärtner Namens Knoll. –

Doch seine Freudigkeit vergeht.

Ein Maulwurf wühlt im Pflanzenbeet.

FIGURE 7.5: Wilhelm Busch, *The Mole / Der Maulwurf*, 1873/74. From H. Guratzsch and H. J. Neyer, *Wilhelm Busch. Die Bildergeschichten. Historisch-kritische Gesamtausgabe in drei Bänden* (2002), 2, column 548. © Zentralinstitut für Kunstgeschichte, Munich, Germany.

FIGURE 7.6: Louis Lumière, *Arroseur et Arrosé*, Lyon, 1895. © Association frères Lumière.

digging up the flowers."[43] A similar caricature appears as a moving image in the earliest movie with a fictional plot: the short film shown in December 1895 in Paris entitled *Arroseur et Arrosé*, a still from which is shown in Figure 7.6. This milestone in the history of film is a short burlesque slapstick played by two men with a hosepipe. Louis Lumière filmed it in his garden at La Ciotat on the Mediterranean coast. The view of the garden is reminiscent of Caillebotte's paintings of his Yerres Potager. Due to its lighting conditions the open space of a garden was certainly even more important for cinematographic experiments than it was for plein air painting.

IRIS: COLORS AND LIGHTS OF THE GARDEN IN THE BEHOLDER'S EYE

In 1883, Claude Monet settled in Giverny, a village in Normandy northwest of Paris, where he lived until his death in 1926. He passionately devoted himself to the layout of his garden that consists of several parts, and was divided by a railway line.[44] The artist called his garden his most beautiful creation. His flower paintings and his famous series *Water Lilies* show exuberant flower beds, irises, water lilies, weeping willows, and a Japanese bridge crossing the pond. These motifs were the features he concentrated on almost exclusively in his work during the last twenty-five years of life. Monet's compositions of the colors, lights, and forms of his gardens were also an artistic reflection on the physiological act of seeing and perceiving occurring in the beholder's eyes. "Mr Monet sometimes makes rainbow orgies. No more no less than a chemist, he would draw from a piece of black coal all the dazzling of Iris's drapery, all the complementary colors and nuances."[45] As Georges Clemenceau has pointed out, looking at Monet's works requires "a new ocular flexibility" to discern "the finest net of luminous sensations."[46] After 1897, Monet thought of creating with his Giverny garden pictures a panorama for interior decoration. He referred to existing traditions and to Japanese art, and built a larger studio adjacent his Giverny garden, where he worked on the *Nymphéas*.[47] After the armistice in 1918, Monet announced his intention of offering the *Nymphéas* to the French state. On Clemenceau's initiative, from 1927 onwards, the paintings have been exhibited in the Tuileries Orangery that had been converted into a museum, and where they can still be seen today. The paintings representing the water lily pond in Giverny show immaterial phenomena that the beholder perceives when gazing at the water surface: blurring shapes, shadows, lights, and reflections. An impression of spatial depth emerges from the surface of the painting. Monet's monumental and almost abstract water lily paintings are, as Clemenceau calls it, an apotheosis of the garden in painting—"the Tuileries apotheosis"—and at the same time they are "the solution to a simple painting problem."[48]

The artistic enhancement of the garden as a subject in painting developed by the impressionists was furthered in early twentieth-century painting. The works of the post-impressionists Edouard Vuillard and Pierre Bonnard, of John Singer Sargent and other contemporary American painters, of the German impressionists Max Slevogt, Lovis Corinth, and Max Liebermann, as well as in the Viennese Art Nouveau, show the garden in all its different variations as a well-established subject for visual artists.

CHAPTER EIGHT

Gardens and the Larger Landscape

GERT GRÖNING AND JOACHIM
WOLSCHKE-BULMAHN

Changing ideas of nature and wilderness have been reflected in garden design and in the relationship between gardens and the larger landscape over the centuries and in different cultures. In medieval times, the garden was an enclosed piece of ground protected against nature and wilderness. During the Renaissance, nature and wilderness found their way into the garden. In the nineteenth and early twentieth centuries, entire cities and states were turned into gardens. This movement had already begun in the eighteenth century, and the idea to design and shape whole territories again became relevant in the early twentieth century. In turn, gardens became small-scale representations of the larger landscape as soon as increasing industrialization and urbanization in the nineteenth century threatened what was considered primordial nature and wilderness. During the last third of the nineteenth century, landscape gardeners and landscape architects developed concepts such as the wild garden and the nature garden that sought to capture the essence of the larger landscape besides expressing particular worldviews common at the time.

By the end of the eighteenth century, most of Central Europe was inhabited and, therefore, influenced by humankind. Nature and wilderness, defined as areas without human influence, hardly existed by the turn of the century. Additionally, territorial gardening and landscape improvement schemes had been developed by enlightened princes, electors, civil servants, and landowners and shaped parts of the European continent into the nineteenth century. In contrast, the United States was at the time still characterized by wide stretches of primordial nature. The far-reaching improvement schemes in Europe found a counterpart in the schemes for the United States National Park system in the late nineteenth and early twentieth century. Whereas European landscape gardeners and their patrons had sought to cultivate and beautify the last remains of the "wild" lands, in the United States half a century later, the threat of losing precisely this wilderness was the cause of wide concern. Many Americans, including writers, painters, and landscape architects, argued and worked for the preservation of wilderness that had since the early Republican times constituted the basis of an American identity. Despite these different starting positions, by the beginning of the twentieth century, not only the preservation of nature and wilderness but also the attempt to reproduce them in the garden had become ideals on both sides of the Atlantic. This essay contrasts selected developments in Europe and in the United States that exemplify the changing relationship between gardens and the larger landscape throughout the nineteenth and into the twentieth century.

FROM ORNAMENTAL FARM TO LAND EMBELLISHMENT IN THE GERMAN STATES

In Europe, the taming of nature and the gradual progression from what was considered wilderness to nature as art had been observed from the seventeenth century and in particular from the eighteenth century onward by artists, architects, and wealthy upper-class men from Great Britain, France, the Netherlands, and the German states on their "Grand Tour," a trip through France and Italy. While the phenomenon was first described as such in the volume *Voyage of Italy or a Complete Journey through Italy*, published in 1670 by the Catholic priest and traveling tutor Richard Lassels,[1] David Watkin and others have pointed out that "the Grand Tour proper coincided with the eighteenth-century Enlightenment." Whereas before then, travels were often undertaken for diplomatic reasons, in the eighteenth-century visitors to Italy had a more varied agenda that was based on "intellectual and moral improvement."[2] Thus, besides studying Greek, Roman, medieval, and Renaissance architecture and art and experiencing the varied Italian countryside, many English, French, Dutch, and German travelers also visited Italian Renaissance, baroque, and mannerist villas. There, they could perceive how nature had been formed to display the relationship between gardens and the larger landscape as a progression from wooded hunting parks and agricultural lands to artfully laid out gardens nearer the villa. By the time the first men embarked on their Grand Tour, landscape painting had emerged as a new genre. Returning from their travels and familiar with the new landscape art by Poussin, Lorrain, and Rosa, the British landed gentry embellished the interiors of their mansions with landscape paintings, while at the same time commissioning architects and landscape gardeners to improve their parkland so that it would resemble the classical landscapes in the paintings. The increasing interest in landscape painting and its pastoral scenes from the second half of the seventeenth century onward was reflected in the development of the ornamented farm, the *ferme ornée*, and in the German states in land embellishment (*Landesverschönerung*), an idea based on the desire to turn entire territories into a garden. On the one hand, the conception of many eighteenth-century landscape gardens in the German states included the idea of a civilized wilderness. Examples are the *Sanspareil Rock Garden* begun in the mid-eighteenth century near Bayreuth[3] and the *Rehgarten* ("Deer Garden"), a wooded area cut by straight allees, enclosing wildernesses, clumps of trees, and serpentine walks at Potsdam-Sanssouci. At the same time, however, the interest to shape the land in an aesthetically pleasing way began to go far beyond the garden. The idea of "leaping the garden fence" was not new.[4] Many baroque gardens across Europe had been designed along a central axis that continued beyond the garden into the distant countryside, and some early English landscape gardens were laid out as ornamented farms, including agricultural land within their garden boundaries and offering views into the surrounding countryside. The ornamented farm, a design concept first described in England by Stephen Switzer in 1715 and further popularized by Thomas Whately in 1770, attracted French and German visitors. In Germany, the English idea of the ornamented farm was extended to encompass not only one but many farms. This so-called land embellishment could even involve the beautification of an entire state territory.

Besides the English ornamented farm, land embellishment in the German states had an early seventeenth-century precedent near the town of Cleve on the Rhine where Johann von Nassau-Siegen laid out parks and gardens and embellished the countryside with allees. As general-governor and commander in chief of the Dutch West-Indian Company's possession Nieuw-Holland in the northeast of Brazil, he had had his first experiences with the cultivation of nature and wilderness on the South American continent before he returned to the Netherlands in 1644, and in 1647 was appointed governor of Brandenburg in Cleve by Archduke Friedrich Wilhelm.[5] His initiatives were followed by

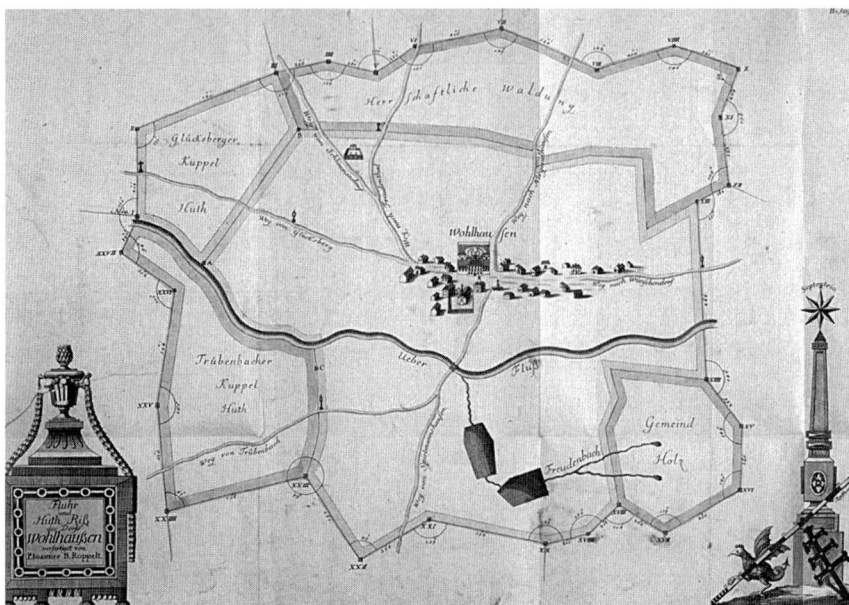

FIGURE 8.1: Plan of the ideal village "Wohlhausen." From Johann Baptist Roppelt, *Practischer Entwurf eines neu zu errichtenden Urbariums ...*, 1790. Dumbarton Oaks Research Library and Collection, Washington, DC.

Prince Leopold Friedrich Franz von Anhalt-Dessau's beautification schemes, which over a fifty-year period beginning in 1764 turned his state territory into the so-called Dessau-Wörlitz garden empire (Dessau-Wörlitzer Gartenreich). The prince tamed the wilderness of his lands both in a literal and figurative sense: The humanist education offered to his subjects, the land embellishment, and the creation of Wörlitz Park that included a miniature reconstruction of Mount Vesuvius with a tamed volcano (1788–94), were to create an electorate upon sound aesthetic and economic foundations.[6] After the Benedictine monk Johann Baptist Roppelt had described his ideal land embellishment program for an imaginary location, stressing the utilitarian and aesthetic benefits of a well-cultivated landscape in his 1790 treatise *Practischer Entwurf eines neu zu errichtenden Urbariums, Saal-oder Lager-Buchs*, many more land embellishment programs were begun in the first decades of the nineteenth century. "The whole of Germany" was, as Jonathan Schuderoff wrote in his 1825 pamphlet for land embellishment, to become "a huge garden."[7] At this time, both Bavaria and Prussia engaged in extensive land improvement initiatives.

The civil servant Gustav Vorherr promoted the embellishment of his state Bavaria in a journal he edited from 1821 to 1829, entitled the *Monthly for Improvement of Rural Architecture and Appropriate Embellishment of the*

State of Bavaria (*Monatsblatt für die Verbesserung des Landbauwesens und für zweckmäßige Verschönerung des baierischen Landes*).[8] Vorherr aspired to improve private and public life through "pleasant design and improvement of towns, markets and villages, including their territories";[9] the continuation in the United States of this social mission for landscape design is considered by Daniel Nadenicek in Chapter 4 of this volume. Vorherr's idea was realized in the environs of the Bavarian city of Regensburg. There, previous initiatives that included plantings on the grounds of former ramparts and the opening of vistas onto distant church towers and villages provided suitable starting points for the creation of new gardens, and allees, and the establishment of a beautification commission in charge of their maintenance and development.[10] Not only did Vorherr want to see his state turned into a garden, but the state's military outposts were to be equally beautified. In order for these sites to resemble "English garden[s]," Vorherr strove for land embellishment to become a part of the military education at the royal corps of cadets in Munich.[11] His ideas for land embellishment were, in fact, very much concerned with the desire "to ban disorder, sloppiness and arbitrariness" and to promote "order, cleanliness, and expediency,"[12] attributes commonly associated with the military. It might, therefore, not come as a surprise that Vorherr increasingly resorted to law and order to realize his ideals. In 1823, his proposal for a leaflet on "land embellishment, a highly important matter for all civilized nations on earth" turned into a demand for "building and land embellishment regulations" for each German state,[13] and he promoted the establishment of a building police to enforce rules and regulations.[14] Whereas Vorherr's Bavarian land embellishment programs especially aimed at improving living conditions in small villages, the Prussian programs addressed wealthy gentleman farmers.[15]

On his estate at Brusenfeld, Karl Cranz, a founding member of the Berlin association for the promotion of horticulture in the royal Prussian states (Verein zur Beförderung des Gartenbaues in den Königlich Preußischen Staaten), cultivated vast sandy areas on the basis of an economic plan. Cranz turned a sandy desert into a *Naturgarten*, a nature garden, by planting "beautiful pines and birches alternating with various groups, […] of indigenous and north-American deciduous and coniferous tree species and beautifully blossoming shrubs and perennials" and by "opening up paths." This way, his entire property "allow[ed] for] a more pleasant sight."[16]

On an even larger scale, Karl Friedrich Schinkel and Peter Joseph Lenné implemented a land embellishment program around Potsdam in the first decades of the nineteenth century, and in 1826 Lenné and Carl Gottlieb Bethe developed a respective program for the Reichenbach estate, about 100 miles east

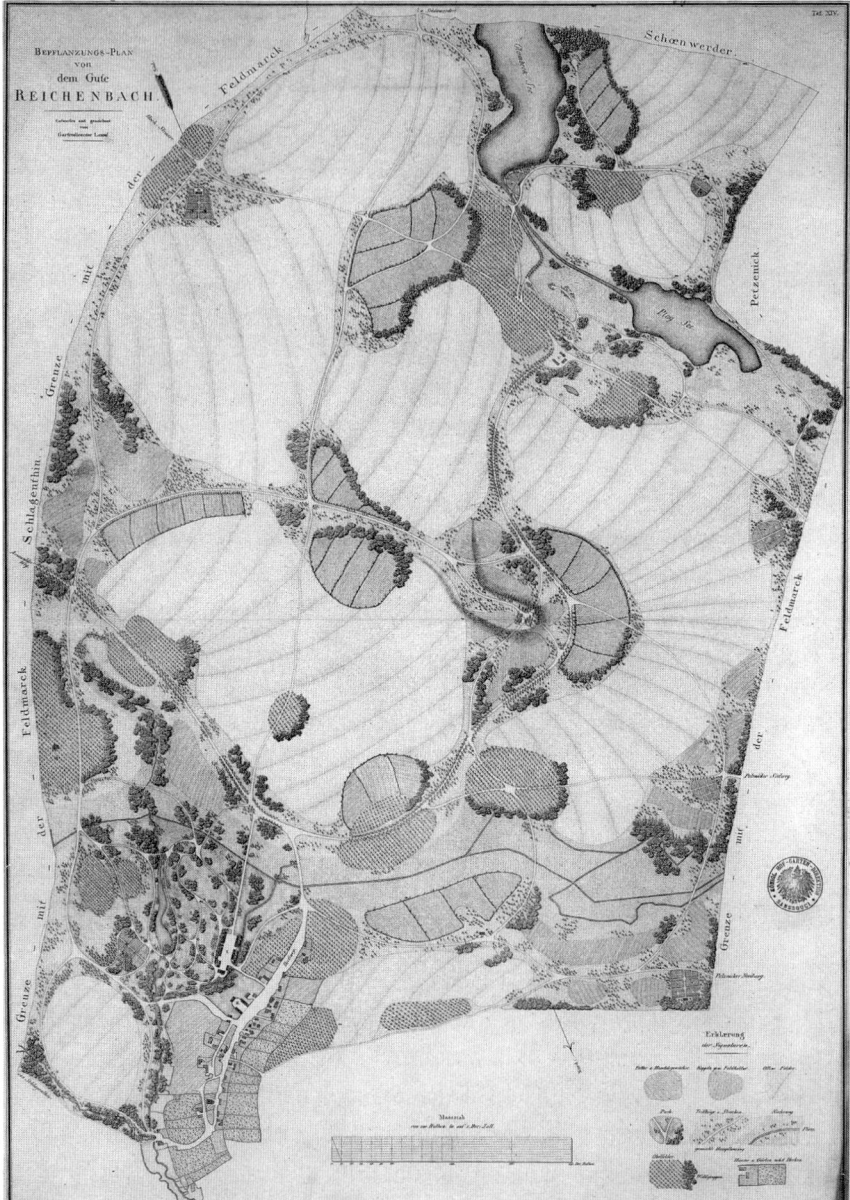

FIGURE 8.2: "Bepflanzungs-Plan," planting plan by Lenné. Plansammlung der Staatlichen Schlösser und Gärten, Inventarnummer 3548, Potsdam.

of Potsdam, shown in Figure 8.2. The embellishment of Bethe's estate, some 4.500 acres, was also intended to raise agricultural yield.[17] In contrast to the English landscape gardens created at the time, agricultural land and buildings were included as part of the scenery, rather than hidden by it. As Olmsted observed, "the grounds of an old English manorial seat" were "usually divided into two parts, one enclosed within the other and separated from it by some form of fence. The interior part, immediately around the dwelling, is distinguished as the pleasure ground or kept ground, the outer as the park. The park is commonly left open to the public, and frequently the public have certain legal rights in it, especially rights of way."[18] According to Olmsted, "The aim of the new art [of landscape architecture] was … to manage the pleasure grounds in such a way that they would provide a harmonious and appropriate foreground to landscapes extending over the park, and to make such changes in the park itself as would improve the composition of these landscapes."[19] However, at Reichenbach, the estate was as much designed for its picturesque views as it was for enhancing its agricultural production.

Although not all German states engaged in land embellishment projects, the idea to beautify wide stretches of countryside and turn wilderness into gardens spread further, across national borders. In 1855, the Swedish garden author Joachim Daniel Andreas Müller had a dream "to turn entire landscapes and even the entire world into a great garden."[20] Referring to land embellishment concepts in England and Germany, he pointed out that Sweden "with its beautiful nature […] would compare to a great garden—with less efforts and sacrifice—if only we ourselves would not disfigure our regions or disguise the beautiful."[21]

The nineteenth-century concepts of land embellishment were influenced by physiocracy, an economic theory developed by the Frenchman François Quesnay in his *Tableau économique* in 1758. In this book, Quesney presented a natural law of economy based on the soil and agriculture as the only sources of wealth. Physiocratism provided the philosophical rationale not only for turning entire estates into a working farm landscape, but also for the respective state governments to maintain the "natural order" established by the ruling class.[22]

WILDERNESS, GARDENS, AND LANDSCAPE IN THE UNITED STATES

"Wilderness [in] the American mind,"[23] so it seems, had, stronger, if not deeper, roots than in Europe. In the United States, the 1803 Louisiana Purchase made available to American and European settlers a huge tract of land west of the Mississippi. Although Native American tribes had lived there for centuries, the settlers perceived it for the most part as wilderness. Land cultivation was initiated in this part of the United States by the Lewis and Clark Expedition between 1804 and 1806. Almost two generations later, the 1864 Civil War engagement known as the Battle of the Wilderness (the Overland Campaign) was fought in a region of Virginia that even then was still referred to as wilderness. However, although concern for the preservation of wilderness led the United States to pioneer a national park system, the relationship of gardens and the larger landscape in the centuries following European settlement in North America and into the antebellum years followed or paralleled developments in Europe. Most gardens and designed landscapes in the United States were located in the north- and south-eastern states and their designs followed English gardens, in particular. At George Mason's eighteenth-century plantation home Gunston Hall, wilderness was incorporated via a visual axis toward the Potomac River. Thomas Jefferson, who while serving as minister to France between 1785 and 1790 had visited the ornamental farm at The Leasowes in England, used this idea in the design of his estates at Monticello and Poplar Forest in Virginia.[24]

In the first half of the nineteenth century, the slowly evolving field of landscape architecture received new impulses from landscape painting. Niagara Falls, the "wild" lands along the new frontier including the Yosemite Valley, and the Hudson River Valley—a celebrated landscape of what was establishing itself as the American Grand Tour—[25]in particular attracted many landscape painters.[26] Their depictions of awe-inspiring as well as pleasing river and mountain scenery in turn influenced the work of the first professional landscape gardeners and landscape architects. Like the Hudson River school painter Frederic Church, the landscape gardener Andrew Jackson Downing lived along the Hudson River. In contrast to Church's precursor Thomas Cole and the writers Washington Irving and James Fenimore Cooper, Downing was less perturbed by the lingering changes in the landscape. Although he appreciated the natural and native American history of the valley, he also proclaimed "the superiority of cultivated nature over the sublime" and "of pastoral landscape over wilderness."[27] Downing described the significance of the Hudson Valley for landscape design in America in his 1850 edition of the *Treatise on the Theory and Practice of Landscape Gardening* as follows:

> There is no part of the Union where the taste in Landscape Gardening is so far advanced, as on the middle portion of the Hudson. The natural

scenery is of the finest character, and places but a mile or two apart often possess, from the constantly varying forms of the water, shores, and distant hills, widely different kinds of home landscape and distant view. Standing in the grounds of some of the finest of these seats, the eye beholds only the soft foreground of smooth lawn, the rich groups of trees shutting out all neighboring tracts, the lake-like expanse of water, and, closing the distance, a fine range of wooded mountain.[28]

Here, wilderness is pushed into "the distance." It served Downing and other landscape architects as a backdrop of romantic garden views. For European landscape gardeners of the first half of the nineteenth century, the Hudson River Valley provided what was considered the foremost example of a landscape garden in the United States: Hyde Park. This garden, property of the botanist Dr. David Hosack, was designed by André Parmentier from Belgium, one of the many European garden designers who in the nineteenth century emigrated to the United States and propagated the design ideal of the landscape garden.[29] In John Claudius Loudon's description of Hyde Park in the eighth edition of his *An Encyclopaedia of Gardening,* wilderness again only served as a background in picturesque views of the garden. He wrote: "The natural capacity of this seat for improvement has been taken advantage of in a very judicious manner …The park is extensive, the rides numerous, and the variety of delightful distant views embrace every kind of scenery … 'here the misty summit of the distant Kaatskill begins to form the outline of the landscape; and it is hardly possible to imagine a more beautiful place.' "[30]

The beauty of the Hudson River Valley was also known to Prince Hermann von Pückler-Muskau. Pückler, who had included large areas of wilderness into his plan for the city of Muskau, Saxony, planned a trip to North America—along the banks of the Hudson River, and to Niagara Falls—that he never realized.[31] Despite Pückler's interest in recreating wilderness, and despite the similarity between the Muskau waterfalls, shown in Figure 8.3, and the falls depicted in paintings published by the Hudson River school painter William Gay Wall, it remains open to speculation as to whether Pückler was influenced in his designs by the American landscape paintings, as claimed by Martin Sperlich.[32]

With certainty, the Bridal Veil Falls near Niagara impressed the landscape architect Frederick Law Olmsted, who in 1864 pleaded with United States President Abraham Lincoln to set this piece of wilderness aside as a nature reserve. Due to increasing urbanization in the last decades of the nineteenth century, wilderness was encroached on by industry, agriculture, buildings, gardens, and

FIGURE 8.3: Etching illustrating the design of a water fall. From Hermann Fürst von Pückler-Muskau, *Atlas zu den Andeutungen über Landschaftsgärtnerei*, 1834, plate 8. Dumbarton Oaks Research Library and Collection, Washington, DC.

parks. Wilderness was discovered as a precious resource that needed to be protected. Although the rising concern for nature and wilderness that had until then defined the United States as "nature's nation" facilitated the establishment of Yellowstone National Park in 1872, its initial advocates were less concerned with wilderness than they were with the prevention of "private acquisition and exploitation of geysers, hot springs, waterfalls and similar curiosities."[33] However, Yellowstone was the first of a series of national parks that has since become established in order to preserve nature and wilderness. Ideological concern about the nation's natural heritage on the one hand, and more practical concerns for public health and recreation in an increasingly urbanized country on the other hand led to a variety of wilderness preservation efforts on various scales.

The establishment of national and state parks throughout the country involved landscape architects in the design of roads, trails, and other visitor facilities. In fact, as Ethan Carr has pointed out, it is the "designed landscapes" that guide the experience of many park visitors and enhance their appreciation of the vast wilderness beyond."[34] It was believed that to preserve and uphold the value attributed to the protected landscapes, they needed to be made accessible through carefully thought-out design interventions. Having proven their worth as park planners on a municipal scale, landscape architects played an

important role in the conservation of scenery and nature in the state and national parks, especially after the National Park Service had been established
within the Department of the Interior in 1916. Through the use of the same
nineteenth-century aesthetic concepts of the pastoral and picturesque they had
used in urban park design, landscape architects designed roads, trails, and
overlooks that opened the wilderness areas to an increasing flow of vehicular
traffic in the first decades of the twentieth century. Thus, state and national
parks became "neither pure wilderness nor mere artifact."[35]

After Frederick Law Olmsted Sr. had backed the protection of the Yosemite
Valley as a landscape park and had pleaded for the preservation of Niagara
Falls in 1864, it fell to one of his apprentices to carry out the plans to protect
the first metropolitan system of reservations outside Boston. In the 1880s, the
landscape architect Charles William Eliot fought for the preservation of Wa-
verly Oaks, a tract of wilderness in Belmont near Boston, Massachusetts. His
initiative not only led in 1891 to the establishment of the first nature protection
agency, The Trustees of (Public) Reservations, but also to the Boston Metropolitan Park System established two years later.

As mentioned above, the preoccupation with native scenery and wilderness
had precedents in the urban landscape on the municipal scale. Largely based
on the aesthetic of the landscape garden, many designs of the first public urban
parks created in the second half of the nineteenth century in the United States
also included wilderness. Using the examples of Central and Prospect Parks in
New York City, John Dixon Hunt has shown that the "notion—that the garden could represent versions of a tripartite nature within its own articulation
of the third one—is not lost, as might be expected, after the Baroque period.
For example, designs by Frederick Law Olmsted and Calvert Vaux for both
Central Park […] and Prospect Park in Brooklyn include within the overall
designed landscape the same scale of 'natures' that were laid out at Wilton.
Here again they are not in a sequence, but nonetheless clearly differentiated
(regular, pastoral, wild)."[36] Park planners aimed at recreating a piece of the
countryside in the city. As much as the perception of these designed landscapes
depended on the types of scenery they provided, that is, pastoral, picturesque,
and sublime, or "wild," it also depended on the visitor's personal experience
and background. Thus, whereas a New York citizen probably perceived of
Central Park as the country in the city, the same park with its artfully contrived
wilderness would likely appear as an artfully contrived wilderness to a visitor
from the Western frontier, for whom Central Park possibly also lacked any
exciting allure of the "wild."

In 1868, eleven years after the design for Central Park and four years after
Olmsted had initiated the enactment for the first nature reserve and drawn up a

plan for the Yosemite Valley, he designed his first garden suburb together with the architect Calvert Vaux. In Riverside, Chicago, Olmsted and Vaux provided for private gardens, public parks, and wilderness as nature reserves.[37] In their 1869 plan for Riverside, they deliberately included wilderness along the banks of the Des Plaines River. Olmsted and his sons who followed him in his office continued to plan garden suburbs for various cities into the early twentieth century, and many other landscape architects and reformers followed in Olmsted Sr.'s footsteps. The English court stenographer Ebenezer Howard, who likely knew of Riverside due to his sojourn in Chicago in the 1870s, published his idea of the garden city in the 1898 book *To-morrow: A Peaceful Path to Real Reform.* Howard's text and concept drawings formed the basis of the garden city movement that inspired many planners, architects, and landscape architects and led to the construction of garden cities, garden suburbs, and villa colonies throughout the United States and Europe during the first decades of the twentieth century. Letchworth and Welwyn Garden City outside London; Suresnes outside Paris; Schlachtensee, Nikolassee, and Wannsee in Berlin; Hellerau in Dresden; Palos Verdes in Los Angeles; and Mariemont in Cincinnati are only a few examples. Although there was no room for wilderness in Howard's concept, parks, gardens, allotments, forests, and agricultural lands structured the ideal circular network of garden cities. In the realized garden suburbs, attempts were made to blend them into the larger landscape through individual and communal garden spaces. The majority of inhabitants of these European and North American garden cities and suburbs belonged to the increasingly potent middle class, made up of industrialists, entrepreneurs, merchants, clergymen, bureaucrats, and professionals such as doctors, lawyers, architects, and engineers. They built houses and gardens with professional help from architects and landscape architects. The latter had established themselves as a profession first in Germany, where the Association of German Garden Architects (Verein Deutscher Gartenkünstler) was founded in 1887,[38] and next in the United States, where the American Society for Landscape Architects was established in 1899. Many designs for villa gardens commissioned around the turn of the century included areas that were labeled "wild gardens" or "nature gardens."

WILDERNESS AND NATURE IN GARDEN DESIGN IN LATE NINETEENTH AND EARLY TWENTIETH-CENTURY ENGLAND AND GERMANY

In England, the relationship between gardens and the larger landscape assumed a particular character when the Irish garden writer William Robinson advocated

FIGURE 8.4: Daffodils planted in a natural and picturesque way, Upper Pool, Gravetye. From Wilhelm Miller, *What England Can Teach Us about Gardening*, 1911.

FIGURE 8.5: Carpet of Sedum spurium in Lange's "garden home" in Berlin-Wannsee. From Willy Lange, *Gartengestaltung der Neuzeit*, 1928, plate 13.

the "wild garden." Robinson published his ideas in numerous books, amongst them his influential 1870 publication *The Wild Garden*. In Germany, the landscape architect and prolific writer Willy Lange published similar ideas using a term that had variously been used already throughout the nineteenth century: *Naturgarten*, nature garden.[39]

Although industrialization and urbanization resulting in air and water pollution and the destruction of (wild) nature provided the necessary climate for the emergence of these garden concepts,[40] Robinson's wild garden and Lange's nature garden were no pleas for wilderness in the garden.

Robinson's call for the wild garden referred to the transition zone between the geometrically designed parts of the garden near the country house and the surrounding landscape. According to Robinson, this particular zone was to be developed into a naturally looking garden landscape by using native plants or hardy foreign plants. One of Robinson's most popular motifs for the wild garden was the planting of narcissi, crocuses, and other spring bulbs that offered spectacular colorful effects in meadows and shrubberies, and that could blend the garden into the larger landscape.

It seems as if the explorations and plant hunting expeditions to other continents undertaken by Alexander von Humboldt, Georg Forster, and others in the late eighteenth and early nineteenth centuries and the resulting literary descriptions and paintings[41] had not only made wilderness accessible and less threatening to the Western world at large; in view of the experience of genuine wilderness, the creation of artificial wilderness may also have lost its power of persuasion in European garden art. In fact, other preoccupations than primarily the domestication of nature and the introduction and use of exotic plant species seem to have played a role in Lange's and Robinson's garden schemes.

Both Robinson and Lange developed their garden concepts at a time when the profession of landscape architecture was still in its early years and had to struggle for its very existence. Architects were rivaling landscape architects and had taken over large parts of the field of garden design. With their design concepts that required specialist botanical and ecological knowledge that architects did not possess, Robinson and Lange reacted to the claims of the architecture profession. Architects like Reginald Blomfield and Hermann Muthesius promoted architectural garden designs based on the idea that gardens provided open-air rooms that functioned as an extension of the house.[42] The individual garden designs were to react to the owners' interests in various outdoor activities.

Lange's concept of the nature garden was influenced by scientific developments in the second half of the nineteenth century. In Germany, Charles Darwin's theory of evolution, published in his book *The Origin of Species*, was applied not only to natural, but also to social phenomena and gained considerable ideological influence in various fields. The principles of the survival of the fittest and of natural selection and adaptation became fundamental parts of *völkisch*, nationalist ideology, and provided Lange with arguments for a German nature garden based on the indigenous plant communities and plant physiognomies found in the German countryside.[43] Indeed, with his writings on nature gardens, Lange contributed to the racist ideology that was later promoted by the Nazi regime. Lange considered the nature garden to be the highest evolutionary form of garden art,[44] and the architectonic garden style as a product of the lower stages of cultural evolution. Lange's garden concept was also influenced by the ideas of the German scientist Ernst Haeckel.[45] Like Haeckel, he argued against the Judeo-Christian "anthropocentric world view," and for the right "of plants to enjoy life as we do [...] ourselves."[46] Consequently, Lange postulated that the nature garden was non-anthropocentric and based on the laws of nature.

Both Robinson and Lange based their ideas on ethical considerations, and a pantheist worldview.[47] In their writings, wild and nature gardens became an ecological paradise, and private nature preserves subordinated to the larger landscape and allegories for the harmonious relationship between man and nature. Robinson's and Lange's knowledge of plant ecology and naturally occurring plant communities provided a scientific basis and method for realizing their paradise, which they considered not an imitation of nature but its artistic improvement.[48] Corresponding to John Ruskin's idea of art portraying the appearance of things,[49] Lange postulated that gardens should be made of "plant communities modeled on the respective home environment of the garden, but heightened by art that is guided by the physiognomic similarities between German and foreign plants of corresponding habitats."[50] While Robinson accepted all hardy plants in his wild garden, Lange was influenced by Alexander von Humboldt's observations on plant physiognomy and geography, and consequently stressed physiognomy as the decisive criterion for use of a plant species in the nature garden.[51] Despite a much larger variety of existing habitats, Lange considered three landscape types sufficient for natural garden design in Germany: "mountain landscapes," "middle landscapes," and "plain landscapes."[52] In his landscape typology, Lange could have followed the categories put forth by the English landscape painter and gardener George Isham Parkyns in "An Essay on the Different Natural Situations of Gardens," published more than 100 years earlier, in 1774. Parkyns would not have known about the studies in plant physiognomy and phytosociology that were readily available to Lange, but he already defined landscape types similar to Lange's. Parkyns differentiated between highlands and mountains, highland offering romantic scenery, undulating country, and flat country, and likened these four landscapes to the four temperaments. He referred to the arts as the appropriate means to strengthen the specific character traits of the respective landscape types and to evoke corresponding emotions.[53] Parkyn's conception of gardens resembled some of the ideas set forth by the French landscape architect Jean-Marie Morel two years later in his 1776 *Théorie des jardins*. As Joseph Disponzio has shown, Morel, who despite his important oeuvre, fell into relative obscurity after his death in 1810, promoted garden design based both on the "activation of the senses" and on the laws of nature.[54] While no direct connection can, of course, be drawn between the writings of these early landscape gardeners and Lange's design approach, it was certainly only possible for Lange to develop his ideas because of the eighteenth- and nineteenth-centuries development of natural philosophy and history, and their impact on garden design, as revealed in Parkyns and Morel. As these two designers long before him, Lange sought to apply to landscape architecture the knowledge about natural systems available to him at the time.

THE "NATURAL STYLE IN LANDSCAPE GARDENING" IN THE UNITED STATES

In many cases, the concern for a natural garden style was at the same time a concern for a national style of garden design. This was not only evident in Europe, but in the United States as well. Claims for regional and national garden styles were made most emphatically by Jens Jensen, Wilhelm Miller, and Frank A. Waugh. Waugh was strongly influenced by Willy Lange's ideas. He had studied garden design with Lange at the Royal Horticultural School in Dahlem near Berlin in 1910.[55] In the same year, Waugh enthusiastically endorsed Lange's work and its significance for landscape architecture in an article on "German Landscape Gardening:"

> The best recent book on landscape gardening written in any language (and I cannot conscientiously except my own) is by a German. This man is Willy Lange, a landscape gardener in the suburbs of Berlin and a teacher in the Horticultural School in Dahlem […] Herr Lange believes in what we in America call the natural style of gardening. In actual practice his work comes nearest to that of Mr. Warren H. Manning of Boston of any in our country. He has a method, fully worked out in scientific lines, in thoroughgoing German fashion. He calls it the biological-physiognomic method; but it would fit better to our use of language to call it the ecological method.[56]

Waugh was a prolific writer. In one of his most important books, *The Natural Style in Landscape Gardening*, published in 1917, he repeated many ideas prevalent in Lange's garden ideology. While Waugh understood "the landscape in spiritual terms" was important, he also promoted plant ecology as the basis of garden designs that "preserve[d] the whole aspect of nature, with all its forms intact."[57] The way to "preserve the whole aspect of nature" in the garden was, according to Waugh, the "native flora cult," which meant that "the ideas, motives, and methods [for landscape gardening] must come mainly from nature."[58] For Waugh, the natural style was "a method of landscape gardening in which the natural forms of landscape are used and imbued with the spirit of the native landscape."[59] Thus, like Lange, Waugh considered the larger landscape a determining factor for the design of the natural garden. In Germany, this landscape was to a large extent an agricultural landscape, called *Kulturlandschaft* in discussions at the time. With this in mind, Waugh attempted to imbue his countrymen and women with "a similar understanding of the beauty of well farmed country." Americans, he was confident, would "learn to love the farm landscape and to realize its deeper spiritual significance."[60]

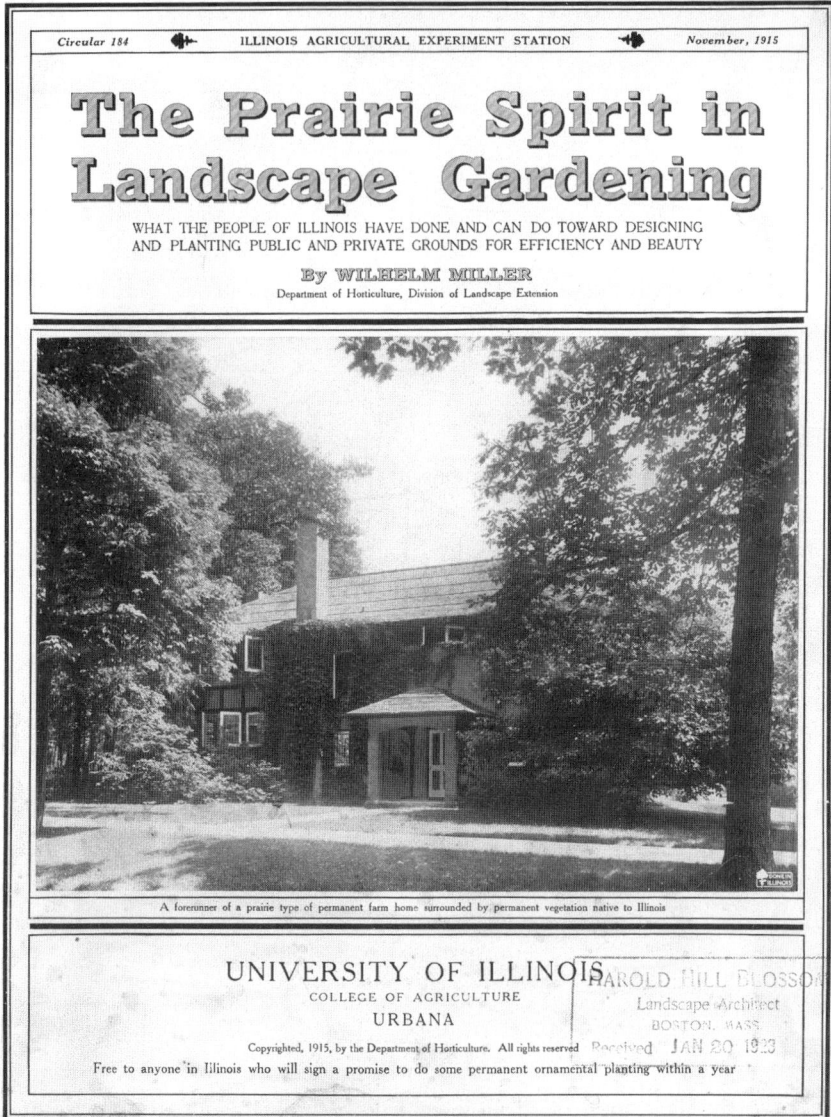

Circular 184   ILLINOIS AGRICULTURAL EXPERIMENT STATION   November, 1915

The Prairie Spirit in Landscape Gardening

WHAT THE PEOPLE OF ILLINOIS HAVE DONE AND CAN DO TOWARD DESIGNING
AND PLANTING PUBLIC AND PRIVATE GROUNDS FOR EFFICIENCY AND BEAUTY

By WILHELM MILLER

Department of Horticulture, Division of Landscape Extension

A forerunner of a prairie type of permanent farm home surrounded by permanent vegetation native to Illinois

UNIVERSITY OF ILLINOIS

COLLEGE OF AGRICULTURE

URBANA

Copyrighted, 1915, by the Department of Horticulture. All rights reserved

Free to anyone in Illinois who will sign a promise to do some permanent ornamental planting within a year

FIGURE 8.6: Wilhelm Miller, *The Prairie Spirit in Landscape Gardening*, 1915, cover.

In Waugh's American words in the early twentieth century, land embellishment became "rural improvement."[61] In his scheme for rural improvement in the United States, he added one landscape type to the three originally identified by Lange. Waugh's landscape types were "the sea, the mountains, the plains, and the forests."[62] Underlying his work was the attempt to further the development of a genuinely American garden style. In Waugh's eyes, a number of different "national" or "racial" garden styles existed that adequately expressed the respective "national, racial or ethnic quality in landscape gardening."[63] In his search for an American garden style, Waugh was joined by his German-born friend Wilhelm Miller. Miller's interest focused on the establishment of a distinctly regional garden style representative of what he described as midwestern landscapes.[64] He considered the "prairie style of landscape gardening" an "American mode of design based upon the practical needs of the middle-western people and characterized by preservation of typical western scenery, by restoration of local color, and by repetition of the horizontal line of land or sky which is the strongest feature of prairie scenery."[65] The prairie style was to be based on the principles of systematic botany and ecology, and on state and local history. With his proposal for a regional garden style for the Midwest, Miller reacted against the garden design that had become popular among wealthy garden owners in the north-eastern Atlantic seaboard. He was critical of the estate designs that were often inspired by Italian and French gardens of earlier periods and feared that the neoclassic garden forms would become the prevailing style in the United States. He complained, for instance, about "great excesses of artificiality, especially in the East, where rich men's gardens are often loaded with globes, cones, pyramids, cubes, and columns of evergreen foliage."[66] Miller wanted the design of gardens to correspond to what he believed were the more modest means of the Midwest. Like his colleague and fellow-advocate of prairie-style gardens Jens Jensen, who had designed a lagoon imitating a "prairie-river" in Chicago's Columbus Park, Miller aimed at creating gardens that would be recognizable as a distilled regional landscape.

As these examples have shown, the larger national and regional landscape began to influence garden design ideas more thoroughly in the second half of the nineteenth and in the first decades of the twentieth century. Using the new scientific knowledge at hand, the designers of wild, nature, and prairie-style gardens aimed at drawing the atmosphere and visual character of the larger landscape into their gardens. In doing so, they displayed their ideologies and ideas of nature. Wild, nature, and prairie-style gardens were intended to merge with the surrounding countryside, and although they were expressly considered works of art, the gardens were to be subordinated to the "more natural" larger landscape through the use of plants selected on the basis of their hardiness, site-adaptive qualities, and physiognomic character. In contrast, the eighteenth- and early nineteenth-century land embellishment programs attempted to reach out from gardens into the larger landscape, so that expansive stretches of land and entire states were subject to embellishment schemes. They were based on the physiocratic ideal of agriculture as the foundation of all wealth on the one hand, and on enlightenment philosophy that combined utilitarian and aesthetic concerns for the enhancement of public moral and physical health on the other hand.

When expansionist politics increased during the early decades of the twentieth century, garden design again influenced programs for entire territories and landscapes. In Germany, expansionist politics were to peak during the Nazi dictatorship, with ideas about natural and regional garden and landscape design adopting an increasingly racist and ideological slant during the 1930s and '40s. The subordination of the garden to the surrounding landscape through the use of so-called native plants became a fundamental criterion of garden design for the creation of "German" landscapes according to the Nazi's racist ideas.[67] Thus, the totalitarian regime would employ landscape architects to design entire landscapes for the so-called "Annexed Eastern Territories," and to participate in nationwide infrastructure projects like the Reichsautobahnen.

NOTES

Introduction

I would like to thank Dumbarton Oaks Research Library and Collection of Harvard University and its Director of Garden and Landscape Studies at the time, Michel Conan, who granted me a 2007 summer readership that enabled me to prepare this chapter and edit parts of this book.

1. Cited in S. Daniels, *Fields of Vision: Landscape Imagery and National Identity in England and the United States* (Princeton, NJ: Princeton University Press, 1993), 83.
2. Daniels, *Fields of Vision*, 84–89.
3. Repton was very concerned that the status of his clients should be reflected in the landscape. At Sheringham in 1812, when the price of wheat reached a peak, he did not screen the ploughed land but framed it instead. See Daniels, *Fields of Vision*, 94.
4. M. Conan, "L'utopie révolutionnaire d'André Thouin: le projet d'une ferme expéri-mentale dans la zone torride (1747–1824)," in *Essais de poétique des jardins,* ed. M. Conan (Florence: Leo S. Olschki, 2004), 413.
5. É. André, *L'art des jardins: traité général de la composition des parcs et jardins* (Marseille: Lafitte Reprints, [1879] 1992), 184–200.
6. For the influence of the French style of urbanization, also see H. W. Lawrence, *City Trees: A Historical Geography from the Renaissance through the Nineteenth Century* (Charlottesville: University of Virginia Press, 2006), 134–45.
7. K. Appelshäuser, *Die öffentliche Grünanlage im Städtebau Napoleons in Italien als politische Aussage* (Frankfurt am Main: Pollinger Schnelldruck, 1994).
8. A. La Padula, *Roma, 1809–1814: contributo alla storia dell'urbanistica* (Rome: Fratelli Palombi, 1958), 13–22, 38–39, 49–64; M. De Vico Fallani, *Storia dei giardini*

pubblici di Roma nell'Ottocento: dalle importanti sistemazioni del Pincio, del Parco del Celio e della Passeggiata archeologica al Gianicolo (Roma: Newton Compton, 1992), 88–91; A. Tagliolini, *I giardini di Roma* (Rome: Newton Compton, 1992), 263–69.

9. Appelhäuser, *Die öffentliche Grünlage*, 89–102. As soon as Napoleon had retreated from Rome in 1814, the gardens were simply referred to as "Monte Pincio," or "Giardino del Popolo." See De Vico Fallani, *Storia dei giardini pubblici*, 97. Napoleon founded a democratic republic in Italy in 1797 and turned it into a monarchy in 1805.

10. E. Silva, *Dell'Arte dei Giardini Inglesi* (Milano: Stamparia e Fonderia al Genio Tipografico; Sala Bolognese: Arnaldo Forni Editore S.p.A, [1801] 1985), 255–60, 319–20; L. Mabil, *Teoria dell'arte dei giardini* (Bassano: [s.n.], 1801), 184–87, 265–67; V. Marulli, *L'arte di ordinare i giardini* (Napoli: Stamperia Simoniana, 1804), 21–26, 40–44, and appendix V: 27–31, 36.

11. De Vico Fallani, *Storia dei giardini pubblici,* 15–18.

12. D. P. McCracken, *Gardens of Empire: Botanical Institutions of the Victorian British Empire* (London: Leicester University Press, 1997), 1–16.

13. A. Thouin, *Cours de culture et de naturalisation des végétaux*, vol. 3 (Paris: Huzard, 1827), 459–60; Conan, "L'utopie révolutionnaire d'André Thouin," 402.

14. G. Thouin, *Plans raisonnés de toutes les espèces de jardins* (Paris: De Lebégue, 1819), 53–55.

15. M. Nicolson, "Alexander von Humboldt, Humboldtian Science and the Origins of the Study of Vegetation," *History of Science* 25 (1987): 178.

16. For Humboldt's worldview and its influence on his development of plant geography see Nicolson, "Alexander von Humboldt," and J. Browne, *The Secular Ark* (New Haven, CT: Yale University Press, 1983), 32–57.

17. Conan, "L'utopie révolutionnaire d'André Thouin," 412–13.

18. McCracken, *Gardens of Empire*, 9, 17–19, 74–78.

19. Antrobus cit. in J. Sharma, "British Science, Chinese Skill and Assam Tea: Making Empire's Garden," *The India Economic and Social History Review* 43, no. 4 (2006): 437.

20. M'Cosh cit. in Sharma, "British Science," 449.

21. McCracken, *Gardens of Empire*, 30.

22. R.T.M. Pescott, *The Royal Botanic Gardens Melbourne: A History from 1845 to 1970* (Melbourne: Oxford University Press, 1982); McCracken, *Gardens of Empire*, 31; R. H. Drayton, *Nature's Government: Science, Imperial Britain, and the "Improvement" of the World* (New Haven, CT: Yale University Press, 2000), 180–83.

23. R. Desmond, *Kew: The History of the Royal Botanic Gardens* (London: Harvill Press, 1995), 223–38.

24. McCracken notes, "Colonial botanical gardens were not noted for their flowerbeds. It is true that some of the Australian and Indian botanic gardens did indulge in carped bedding, and mass displays of anthuriums, mesembryanthemums, … did appear in most botanic gardens from time to time, but as a rule colonial curators found flowerbeds to be a tiresome nuisance." Most likely, the Hookers' dislike of flowerbeds influenced the colonial garden directors. See McCracken, *Gardens of Empire*, 123.

25. Pescott, *The Royal Botanic Gardens*, 91–147; McCracken, *Gardens of Empire*, 116–17, 124.

26. Drayton, *Nature's Government*, 272.

27. McCracken, *Gardens of Empire*, 168.

28. This has induced Henry Lawrence to suggest that the colonies might have influenced the cities in the home countries to plant more trees. See Lawrence, *City Trees*, 131.

29. J. Reps, "The Green Belt Concept," *Town and Country Planning* 28, no. 7 (1960): 246–50; A. King, *Colonial Urban Development: Culture, Social Power and Environment* (London: Routledge & Kegan Paul, 1976), 271–73; D. Jones, "Designing the Adelaide Parklands in the 1880s: The Proposals of John Ednie Brown," *Studies in the History of Gardens & Designed Landscapes* 18, no. 4 (1998): 287–99; R. Freestone, "Greenbelts in City and Regional Planning," in *From Garden City to Green City*, ed. K. C. Parsons and D. Schuyler (Baltimore: Johns Hopkins University Press, 2002).

30. G. Whitehead, *Civilizing the City: A History of Melbourne's Public Gardens* (Melbourne: State Library of Victoria and the City of Melbourne, 1997).

31. A. Neale, "The Garden Designs of E. L. Bateman," *Garden History* 33, no. 2 (2006): 225–55.

32. J. Roberts, "English Gardens in India," *Garden History* 26, no. 2 (1998): 128.

33. E. W. Herbert, "The Taj and the Raj: Garden Imperialism in India," *Studies in the History of Gardens & Designed Landscapes* 25, no. 4 (2005): 266–67.

34. W. Sonne, *Representing the State: Capital City Planning in the Early Twentieth Century* (Munich: Prestel, 2003), 202–3, 214, 231.

35. British supremacy according to the viceroy was also to be expressed in the elevated position of the Governmental Palace. Indians were supposed to look upward toward it. See Sonne, *Representing the State*, 208; for the role of architecture (and some parks and gardens) in the building of the British Empire on the Indian subcontinent, also see T. R. Metcalf, *An Imperial Vision: Indian Architecture and Britain's Raj* (Berkeley: University of California Press, 1989).

36. On Villiers-Stuart and the historiography of gardens in India, see J. L. Wescoat Jr. and J. Wolschke-Bulmahn, "Sources, Places, Representations, and Prospects: A Perspective of Mughal Gardens," in *Mughal Gardens: Sources, Places, Representations, and Prospects,* ed. J. L. Wescoat Jr. and J. Wolschke-Bulmahn (Washington, D.C.: Dumbarton Oaks, 1996), 17; and J. L. Wescoat Jr., "Mughal Gardens: The Re-emergence of Comparative Possibilities and the Wavering of Practical Concern," in *Perspectives on Garden Histories*, ed. M. Conan (Washington, D.C.: Dumbarton Oaks Research Library and Collection, 1999), 128–29, 132–33.

37. C. M. Villiers-Stuart, *Gardens of the Great Mughals* (London: A. & C. Black, 1913), 268–69.

38. R. G. Irving, *Indian Summer: Lutyens, Baker, and Imperial Delhi* (New Haven, CT: Yale University Press, 1981), 215–26.

39. Villiers-Stuart, *Great Mughals*, 275.

40. Irving, *Indian Summer*, 80–82.

41. For the symbolism inherent in the city plan for New Delhi, see Sonne, *Representing the State*, 222.

42. H. Ritvo, "At the Edge of the Garden: Nature and Domestication in Eighteenth-and Nineteenth-Century Britain," in *An English Arcadia: Landscape and Architecture in Britain and America*. Papers delivered at a Huntington symposium (San Marino, CA: Huntington Library, 1992), 373.

43. Ritvo, "At the Edge of the Garden."

44. For Biddulph Grange, see B. Elliott, *Victorian Gardens* (London: B. T. Batsford, 1986), 102–6, 121 22; J. MacKenzie, *Orientalism: History, Theory and the Arts* (Manchester: Manchester University Press, 1995), 75; and M. Charlesworth, *Landscape and Vision in Nineteenth-Century Britain and France* (Aldershot: Ashgate, 2008), 68–69.

45. J. C. Loudon, *Remarks on the Construction of Hothouses* (London: Richard and Arthur Taylor, 1817), 49.

46. P. Greenhalgh, *Ephemeral Vistas: The Expositions Universelles, Great Exhibitions, and World's Fairs, 1851–1939* (Manchester: Manchester University Press; New York: St. Martin's Press, 1988), 85.

47. For panoramas, and their use in educating the public about the colonies, see Charlesworth, *Landscape and Vision*, 12–34.

48. R. Rees, *Interior Landscapes: Gardens and the Domestic Environment* (Baltimore: Johns Hopkins University Press, 1993), 155; G. King, *The Mad King: The Life and Times of Ludwig II of Bavaria* (Secaucus: Birch Lane Press, 1996), 229–30.

49. S. Koppelkamp, *Glasshouses and Wintergardens of the Nineteenth Century* (New York: Rizzoli, 1981), 42.

50. MacKenzie, *Orientalism*, 90.

51. H. Strehlow, "Zoos and Aquariums of Berlin," in *New Worlds, New Animals: From Menagerie to Zoological Park in the Nineteenth Century*, ed. R. J. Hoage and W. A. Deiss (Baltimore: Johns Hopkins University Press, 1996), 66–67.

52. N. Rothfels, *Savages and Beasts: The Birth of the Modern Zoo* (Baltimore: Johns Hopkins University Press, 2002), 37.

53. Elliott, *Victorian Gardens*, 110.

54. J. Hyson, "Jungles of Eden: The Design of American Zoos," in *Environmentalism in Landscape Architecture*, ed. M. Conan (Washington, D.C.: Dumbarton Oaks, 2000), 29–31.

55. Hyson, "Jungles of Eden"; Rothfels, *Savages and Beasts*, 161–88.

56. Elliott, *Victorian Gardens*, 190.

57. Elliot, *Victorian Gardens*, 193. For a short iconographic and cultural history of the garden gnome, see G. F. Hartlaub, *Der Gartenzwerg und seine Ahnen* (Heidelberg: Heinz Moos Verlag, 1962). For more recent popular accounts on garden gnomes and their history, see F. Friedmann, *Zipfel auf! Alles über Gartenzwerge: ein rein wissenschaftliches Lehr- und Lesebuch* (Schaffhausen: Meier Verlag, 1994); F. Crestin-Billet, *Les nains de jardin* (Paris: Editions Solar, 1997); and L. Le Bon and D. Lavergne, *Des nains, des sculptures*, catalog of the exhibition "2000 nains à Bagatelle" (Paris: Publications Artistiques Françaises, 2000).

58. W. Robinson, *The Wild Garden* (London: John Murray, 1870), 9–10.

59. Elliott, *Victorian Gardens*, 46–48, 94–99, 123, 176–79, 187–92; Charlesworth, *Landscape and Vision*, 68–69.

60. U. Strohmeyer, "Urban Design and Civic Spaces: Nature at the Parc des Buttes-Chaumont in Paris," *Cultural Geographies* 13 (2006): 564.

61. A. Komara, "Concrete and the Engineered Picturesque: The Parc des Buttes Chaumont (Paris, 1867)," *Journal of Architectural Education* 58, no. 1 (2004): 5–12.

62. Komara, "Concrete and the Engineered Picturesque," 6.

63. H. Schenker, "Central Park and the Melodramatic Imagination," *Journal of Urban History* 29, no. 4 (2003): 375–93.

64. In his book The *Parks, Promenades & Gardens of Paris* (London: John Murray, 1869), William Robinson, critical of what he thought a lost opportunity for rock gardening, considered "the face of the high rocks [...] suggestive of little but suicide," 62.

65. Strohmeyer, "Urban Design and Civic Spaces," 564.

66. L. Lieberman, "Romanticism and the Culture of Suicide in Nineteenth-Century France," *Comparative Studies in Society and History* 33, no. 3 (1991): 614.

67. For the designs of Highgate and Nunhead, and other nineteenth-century cemeteries in Britain, see J. S. Curl, *A Celebration of Death* (London: B. T. Batsford, 1993), 206–43; and J. S. Curl, *The Victorian Celebration of Death* (Stroud, Gloucestershire: Sutton Publishing, 2000), 86–95. For Mount Auburn Cemetery in Cambridge, see R. Etlin, *The Architecture of Death: The Transformation of the Cemetery in Eighteenth-Century Paris* (Cambridge, MA: MIT Press, 1984), 358–68; and B.M.G. Linden, *Silent City on a Hill: Picturesque Landscapes of Memory and Boston's Mount Auburn Cemetery* (Amherst: University of Massachusetts Press in association with Library of American Landscape History, 2007). For rural cemeteries in the United States, also see D. C. Sloane, *The Last Great Necessity: Cemeteries in American History* (Baltimore: Johns Hopkins University Press, 1991); and D. Schuyler, *The New Urban Landscape: The Redefinition of City Form in Nineteenth-Century America* (Baltimore: Johns Hopkins University Press, 1986), 37–56. For the forerunner of these rural cemeteries, the cemetery of Père Lachaise in Paris and the history of commemoration and burials in the landscape, see Etlin, *The Architecture of Death*, 163–368.

68. For an account of "The Genesis of Victorian Attitudes to Death," see Curl, *Victorian Celebration of Death*, 1–22. For the influence of transcendentalism on cemetery design, see D. J. Nadenicek, "Emerson's Aesthetic and Natural Design: A Theoretical Foundation for the Work of Horace William Shaler Cleveland," in *Nature and Ideology: Natural Garden Design in the Twentieth Century*, ed. J. Wolschke-Bulmahn (Washington, D.C.: Dumbarton Oaks, 1997).

69. Curl, *A Celebration of Death*, 244–64; Curl, *Victorian Celebration of Death*, 128–29.

70. Linden, *Silent City*, 155–79.

71. J. C. Loudon, "The Principles of Landscape-Gardening and of Landscape-Architecture applied to the Laying out of Public Cemeteries and the Improvement of Churchyards [...]," *Gardener's Magazine* 19 (March 1843): 104–5; Curl, *A Celebration of Death*, 249.

72. A. T. Scull, *The Most Solitary of Afflictions: Madness and Society in Britain, 1700-1900* (New Haven, CT: Yale University Press, 1993), 87–114, 155–69; L. D. Smith,

Cure, Comfort, and Safe Custody: Public Lunatic Asylums in Early Nineteenth-Century England London (New York: Leicester University Press, 1999), 12–51.

73. Smith, *Cure, Comfort and Safe Custody*, 228–39; C. Hickman, "The Picturesque at Brislington House, Bristol: The Role of Landscape in Relation to the Treatment of Mental Illness in the Early Nineteenth-Century Asylum," *Garden History* 33, no. 1 (2005): 48. For an account of the connection between nineteenth-century health theories and landscape architecture, also see K. Hawkins, "The Therapeutic Landscape: Nature, Architecture, and Mind in Nineteenth-Century America" (Ph.D. diss., University of Rochester, 1991). In order to disprove the image of lunatic asylums as confined, controlled, and prison-like institutions, at the end of the nineteenth century, psychiatric authorities in Germany and Austria promoted so called "free treatment" in environments that consisted of villas or cottages freely distributed amid ample agricultural and park land. In many cases, these psychiatric villages merged with existing villages or used extant buildings. For more on "psychiatric space and images of freedom and control," see L. Topp, "The Modern Mental Hospital in Late Nineteenth-Century Germany and Austria," in *Madness, Architecture and the Built Environment*, ed. L. Topp, J. E. Moran, and J. Andrews (New York: Routledge, 2007).

74. A. J. Downing, *Rural Essays*, ed. G. W. Curtis (New York: George P. Putnam, [1848] 1853), 269.

75. B. Edginton, "The Design of Moral Architecture at the York Retreat," *Journal of Design History* 16, no. 2 (2003): 103–17; Hawkins, "The Therapeutic Landscape," 37, 73–74.

76. J. MacDonald, "Statistics of the Bloomingdale Asylum for the Insane," *New York Journal of Medicine and Surgery* 1 (1839): 310–11.

77. S. Rutherford, "Landscapers for the Mind: English Asylum Designers, 1845–1914," *Garden History* 33, no. 1 (2005): 61–86. For the siting and landscape design at American nineteenth-century asylums, also see C. Yanni, *The Architecture of Madness: Insane Asylums in the United States* (Minneapolis: University of Minnesota Press, 2007), 36–38, 43–44, 56–58, 107–8, 110, 142.

78. J. Weidenmann, *Beautifying Country Homes* (New York: Orange Judd, [1870] 1978), plate 18.

79. Schuyler, *The New Urban Landscape*, 59–76; B. Szczygiel and R. Hewitt, "Nineteenth-Century Medical Landscapes: John H. Rauch, Frederick Law Olmsted, and the Search for Salubrity," *Bulletin of the History of Medicine* 74 (2000): 7734.

80. F. L. Olmsted, "Public Parks and the Enlargement of Towns," *Journal of Social Science* 3 (1871): 32.

81. E.R.L. Gould, "Park Areas and Open Spaces in Cities," *American Statistical Association* 2–3 (1888): 51.

82. S. Lasdun, *The English Park: Royal, Private and Public* (New York: Vendome Press, 1992), 142.

83. G. Davison, "The City as a Natural System: Theories of Urban Society in Early Nineteenth-Century Britain," in *The Pursuit of Urban History*, ed. by D. Fraser and A. Sutcliffe (London: Edward Arnold, 1983), 349–70.

84. Simo, *Loudon and the Landscape*, 227–42.

85. T. Hunt, *Building Jerusalem: The Rise and Fall of the Victorian City* (New York: Henry Holt, 2005), 433; E. Howard, *To-morrow: A Peaceful Path to Real Reform* (London: Routledge, [1898] 2003); S. V. Ward, "Ebenezer Howard: His Life and Times," in *From Garden City to Green City*, ed. D. Schuyler (Baltimore: Johns Hopkins University Press, 2002).

86. M. Wagner, *Das sanitäre Grün der Städte. Ein Beitrag zur Freiflächentheorie* (Berlin: C. Heymann, 1915).

87. J. C. Nicolas Forestier, *Grandes Villes et Systèmes de Parcs* (Paris: Hachette Et Cie., 1906), 24, 32–36.

88. H. Koch, *Gartenkunst im Städtebau* (Berlin: E. Wasmuth, 1914), 242.

89. W. Morris, *Art and Beauty of the Earth*, lecture delivered at Burslem Town Hall on October 13, 1881 (London: Longmans, 1898), 26, 28.

90. D. Schubert, *Die Gartenstadtidee zwischen reaktionärer Ideologie und pragmatischer Umsetzung: Theodor Fritschs völkische Version der Gartenstadt* (Dortmund: Institut für Raumplanung, Universität Dortmund, Fakultät Raumplanung, 2004).

91. L. Migge, *Die Gartenkultur des 20. Jahrhunderts* (Jena: E. Diederichs, 1913), 7.

92. P. Warnecke, *Laube Liebe Hoffnung. Kleingartengeschichte* (Berlin: Verlag W. Wächter GmbH, 2001), 10–44; S. Herrington, "Kindergartens: Shaping Childhood from Bad Blankenburg to Boston," *Die Gartenkunst* 18, no. 1 (2006): 81–95.

93. Migge, *Gartenkultur*, 7.

94. R. Brettell, "The Impressionist Landscape and the Image of France," in *A Day in the Country: Impressionism and the French Landscape* (New York: Abradale Press, 1990), 46.

95. J. R. Stilgoe, "The Railroad Beautiful: Landscape Architecture and the Railroad Gardening Movement, 1867–1930," *Landscape Journal* 1, no. 2 (1982): 57–58.

96. A. Freytag, "When the Railway Conquered the Garden: Velocity in Parisian and Viennese Parks," in *Landscape Design and the Experience of Motion*, ed. M. Conan (Washington, D.C.: Dumbarton Oaks Trustees for Harvard University, 2003), 233.

97. Stilgoe, "The Railroad Beautiful."

98. C. M. Robinson, "A Railroad Beautiful," *House & Garden* 2 (1902): 570.

99. J. Richards, "The Role of the Railways," and J. K. Walton, "The National Trust: Preservation or Provision?" in *Ruskin and Environment*, ed. M. Wheeler (Manchester: Manchester University Press, 1995).

100. J. H. Rauch, *Public Parks: Their Effects upon the Moral Physical and Sanitary Condition of the Inhabitants of Large Cities* (Chicago: Griggs, 1869), 21.

101. C. R. Bardelli, "Modelli per una capitale europea," in *Torino città di loisir. Viali, parchi e giardini tra Otto e Novecento*, ed. V. C. Mandracci and R. Roccia (Turin: Archivio storico della città di Torino, 1996), 123–25.

102. C. Paolini. *Il sistema del verde. Il viale dei colli e la Firenze di Giuseppe Poggi nell'Europa dell'Ottocento* (Florence: Edizione Polistampa, 2004).

103. De Vico Fallani, *Storia dei giardini pubblici*, 88–126; A. Cremona, "Il giardino della memoria," in *Il Giardino della Memoria: I busti dei grandi italiani al Pincio*, ed. A. Cremona and A. Ponente (Rome: Artemide Edizioni S.r.l., 1999), 11–20.

104. De Vico Fallani, *Storia dei giardini pubblici*, 196–222; A. M. Racheli, "Ville e giardini nei primi piani urbanistici di Roma capitale: i progetti e le trasformazioni," in *La memoria, il tempo, la storia nel giardino italiano fra '800 e '900*, ed. V. Cazzato (Rome: Istituto poligrafico e Zecca dello Stato, 1999), 395.

105. Elliott, *Victorian Gardens*, 58, 179–80.

106. F.-M. Granet, "Memoirs of the Painter Granet," trans. and ann. J. Focarino, in *François-Marius Granet: Watercolors from the Musée Granet at Aix-en-Provence*, ed. E. Munhall (New York: The Frick Collection, [1802] 1988), 21.

107. R. Deakin, *Flora of the Colosseum of Rome* (London: Broombridge, 1855). For a first presentation of historical and contemporary studies of the Roman colosseum's flora, see G. Caneva, ed., *Amphitheatrum Naturae* (Milano: Mondadori Electa S.p.A., 2004).

108. Deakin, *Flora of the Colosseum*, vi–vii.

109. For an account of the development of phytogeography, natural regions, and the nineteenth-century study of "plant nations," see Browne, *The Secular Ark*, 32–57. For William Hooker's "Colonial Floras" scheme, see Drayton, *Nature's Government*, 201–6.

110. For the polemical debates surrounding the *passeggiata archeologica*, see De Vico Fallani, *Storia dei giardini pubblici*, 196–222. For Boni's *flora dei monumenti* and the opposition against his initiatives, see M. De Vico Fallani, *I parchi archeologici di Roma* (Rome: Nuova Editrice Spada, 1988). Although he was able to carry out many plantings and led the excavations on the forum and Palatine from 1898 to 1914, governmental opposition finally prevented the continuation of Boni's patriotic scheme.

111. T. O'Malley, "'Your Garden Must Be a Museum to You': Early American Botanic Gardens," in *Art and Science in America: Issues of Representation*, ed. A.R.W. Meyers (San Marino, CA: Huntington Library, 1998), 57; T. O'Malley, "'A Public Museum of Trees': Mid-Nineteenth Century Plans for the Mall," in *The Mall in Washington, 1791–1848*, ed. R. Longstreth, National Gallery of Art, Studies in the History of Art 30 (Washington, D.C.: Trustees of the National Gallery of Art, 1991), 61–76; J. S. Ackerman, "On Public Landscape Design before the Civil War," in *Regional Garden Design in the United States*, ed. T. O'Malley and M. Treib (Washington, D.C.: Dumbarton Oaks Research Library and Collection, 1995), 197–201.

112. F. Kirchner, *Der Central Park in New York und der Einfluss der deutschen Gartentheorie und –praxis auf seine Gestaltung* (Worms: Wernersche Verlagsgesellschaft, 2002), 157–91.

113. M. C. Robbins, "Park-Making as a National Art," *The Atlantic Monthly* 79, no. 471 (January 1897): 92.

114. C. Gatchell, "Movie Pilferers in Parks," *The Park International* 1 (1920): 149–52.

115. J. Major, *To Live in the New World: A. J. Downing and American Landscape Gardening* (Cambridge, MA: MIT Press, 1997), 137–41.

116. Mrs. S. Van Rensselaer, *Art Out-of-Doors* (New York: Scribner's Sons, 1893), 63.

117. The exceptional beauty of the Rhine Valley that attracted nineteenth-century artists and writers from Britain and Germany alike and the growth of industry along the river in the Rhine province led to the foundation of the country's oldest preservation organizations. For the nature protection movement in this region, see T. M. Lekan, *Imagining the Nation in Nature: Landscape Preservation and German Identity, 1885–1945* (Cambridge, MA: Harvard University Press, 2004), 9, 24–49; see A. Knaut, *Zurück zur Natur! die Wurzeln der Ökologiebewegung* (Greven: Kilda-Verlag, 1993) for an overview of the German conservation and nature protection movements.

118. F. Encke, "Der Volkspark," *Die Gartenkunst* 13, no. 8 (1911): 157–58.

119. Fr. Saftenberg, "Ein Vorschlag," *Die Gartenwelt* 16, no. 5 (1912): 62.

120. D. Land and J. Wenzel, *Heimat, Natur und Weltstadt. Leben und Werk des Gartenarchitekten Erwin Barth* (Leipzig: Koehler und Amelang, 2005), 200–4, 233–40.

121. G. Heick, "Der Naturschutzpark in den Parkanlagen," *Die Gartenkunst* 13, no. 12 (1911): 223.

122. J. Conder, *Landscape Gardening in Japan* (Tokio: Hakubunsha, Ginza, 1893), v–vi. For Japanese gardens in England, see Elliott, *Victorian Gardens*, 199–201.

123. A. Helmreich, *The English Garden and National Identity: The Competing Styles of Garden Design, 1870–1914* (Cambridge: Cambridge University Press, 2002), 30.

124. J. Ruskin, *Sesame and Lilies*, in *The Works of John Ruskin*, ed. E. T. Cook and A. Wedderburn (London: George Allen; New York: Longmans, Green, [1865] 1905), 122; J. Illingworth, "Ruskin and Gardening," *Garden History* 22, no. 2 (1994): 232; A. Helmreich, *The English Garden and National Identity: The Competing Styles of Garden Design, 1870–1914* (Cambridge: Cambridge University Press, 2002), 22, 24, 231.

125. M. S. Morris, "'Tha'lt Be Like a Blush-Rose When Tha' Grows Up, My Little Lass': English Cultural and Gendered Identity in *The Secret Garden*," *Environment and Planning D: Society and Space*, 14, no. 1 (1996): 61.

126. Morris, "Tha'lt Be Like a Blush-Rose," 66.

127. Helmreich, *The English Garden*, 90.

128. Helmreich, *The English Garden*, 35, 47, 72–77, 231.

129. E. Hobsbawm, "Introduction: Inventing Traditions," in *The Invention of Tradition*, ed. E. Hobsbawm and T. Ranger (Cambridge: Cambridge University Press, 1983), 1, 6, 9, 11, 13–14; Helmreich, *The English Garden*, 73, 106.

130. Helmreich, *The English Garden*, 93–97, 100–106.

131. J. D. Sedding, *Garden-Craft Old and New* (London: Kegan Paul, Trench, Trübner, 1891), 154.

132. Sedding, *Garden-Craft Old and New*, 154; Helmreich, *The English Garden*, 137, 189–222.

133. J. Brown, *Gardens of a Golden Afternoon* (London: Penguin Books, 1982), 136–38.

134. R. Rotenberg, *Landscape and Power in Vienna* (Baltimore: Johns Hopkins University Press, 1995), 88–109.

135. Downing, *Rural Essays*, 14–17. Convinced of the political and moral influences of horticultural pursuits, Downing approvingly commented that the "tendency 'to settle' is slowly but gradually on the increase," and there was "growing evidence that the Anglo-Saxon love of home is gradually developing itself out of the Anglo-American love of change" (16).

136. Schenker, "Central Park," 388–90.

137. D. E. Taylor, "Central Park as a Model for Social Control: Urban Parks, Social Class and Leisure Behavior in Nineteenth-Century America," *Journal of Leisure Research* 31, no. 4 (1999): 446–67.

138. B. A. Babcock, ed., *The Reversible World: Symbolic Inversion in Art and Society* (Ithaca, NY: Cornell University Press, 1978), 14, cited in D. Lambert, "Rituals of Transgression in Public Parks in Britain, 1846 to the Present," in *Performance and Appropriation: Profane Rituals in Gardens and Landscapes,* ed. M. Conan (Washington, D.C.: Dumbarton Oaks Research Library and Collection), 206; Lambert, "Rituals of Transgression," 195–210.

139. C. Chaplin, *My Autobiographie* (New York: Simon and Schuster, 1964), 159.

140. Charlie Chaplin's early park films include *Between Showers* (1914), *Star Boarder* (1914), *Caught in the Rain* (1914), *The Fatal Mallet* (1914), *His New Profession* (1914), *The Rounders* (1914), *Those Love Pangs* (1914), *His Trysting Place* (1914), *Getting Acquainted* (1914), and *A Woman* (1915). In *Caught in the Park* (1915), *The Child Needs a Mother* (1915), and *The Magic of Spring* (1917), like in many of the Chaplin films, public parks provide the backdrop for comedy scenes in which the central characters are involved in the pursuit of love or flirtation. In *The Child Needs a Mother,* Gwendolyn's father goes to the park to seek a wife for his unmanageable obese daughter. While he attempts to win the attention of a lady, his daughter falls in love with the lady's escort. In the middle of one of the small fights between the different characters, a park keeper appears and is knocked out. The film ends with nobody realizing his/her wishes and desires. In *The Magic of Spring,* a young man dreams that he is the god Pan pursuing a wood nymph through the forest and awakes to find the girl of his dreams sitting on the park bench beside him. On various occasions before and after his dream, a park keeper is shown to prevent the main character from pursuing his impulses, that is, picking flowers and kissing the girl of his dreams.

141. C. L. Pack, *The War Garden Victorious* (Philadelphia: J. B. Lippincott, 1919), 1–23; L. J. Lawson, *City Bountiful: A Century of Community Gardening in America* (Berkeley: University of California Press, 2005), 117–43.

142. W. A. McKeever, "A Better Crop of Boys and Girls," *Nature-Study Review* 7 (1911).

143. S. G. Kohlstedt, "'A Better Crop of Boys and Girls': The School Gardening Movement, 1890–1920," *History of Education Quarterly* 48, no. 1 (2008): 84–90.

144. Kohlstedt, "A Better Crop of Boys," 87.

145. K. I. Helphand, *Defiant Gardens: Making Gardens in Wartime* (San Antonio, TX: Trinity University Press, 2006), 20, 23, 48.

146. K. Foerster, *Vom Blütengarten der Zukunft* (Berlin: Furche-Verlag, 1917), 5; F. Karl, *Von Landschaft, Garten, Mensch* (Berlin: Heinrich Beenken, 1941), 2.

147. Villiers-Stuart, *Great Mughals*, 275.

148. F. Steele, *Design in the Little Garden* (Boston: The Atlantic Monthly Press, 1924), 116.

149. C. Fuhrmeister, "Klatschmohn und Ochsenblut. Zur Ikonographie der Kriegs-gräberstätten des Volksbundes Deutsche Kriegsgräberfürsorge," in *Gartenkultur und nationale Identität*, ed. G. Gröning and U. Schneider (Worms: Wernersche Verlagsgesellschaft, 2001).

1 Design

1. See, for example, H. H. Kames, *Elements of Criticism*, vol. 3 (Edinburgh: A. Millar, 1762), 313.

2. For a discussion of the significance of Herder for the beginnings of cultural relativism, see M. Peckham, *The Birth of Romanticism* (Greenwood, FL: Penkevill Publishing, 1986), 1–15.

3. J. C. Loudon, *The Landscape Gardening and Landscape Architecture of the Late Humphry Repton* (London: privately published, 1840), v–vi.

4. H. Repton, *An Enquiry into the Changes of Taste in Landscape Gardening* (London: J. Taylor, 1806). Thomas Rickman's *Attempt to Distinguish the Styles of Architecture in England* (1817) established the chronology of Gothic styles. Also see A. J. Downing, *A Treatise on the Theory and Practice of Landscape Gardening* (New York: George P. Putnam, 1850), 92–93.

5. B. Elliott, *Victorian Gardens* (London: B. T. Batsford, 1986), 55–63; J. Sales, "Garden Restoration Past and Present," *Garden History* 23, no. 1 (1995): 1–9.

6. The estimate was provided by David Jacques, in a lecture on "The Impact of English Eighteenth-Century Taste on European Gardens" at the 2006 Europa Nostra (UK) conference in Oxford, entitled "Designed Gardens & Landscapes in Britain: The Influence from and upon Other European Countries."

7. A. Alphand, *Les promenades de Paris*. (Paris: J. Rothschild, 1892; reprint, Princeton, NJ: Princeton University Press, 1984), xxv. For the development of the landscape garden in France during the early nineteenth century, see M.-B. D'Arneville, *Parcs et jardins sous le premier empire: reflets d'une société* (Paris: Librairie Jules Tallandier, 1981).

8. For Germany, see D. Hennebo and A. Hoffmann, *Geschichte der deutschen Gartenkunst. Vol. 3. Der Landschaftsgarten* (Koenigstein: Otto Koeltz Science Publishers, [1965] 1981); for Austria, S. Gerndt, *Idealisierte Natur: die literarische Kontroverse um den Landschaftsgarten des 18. und frühen 19. Jahrhunderts in Deutschland* (Stuttgart: J.B. Metzlersche Verlagsbuchhandlung, 1981). For a case study of the arrival of geometric gardening, see C. A. Wimmer, "Victoria, the Empress Gardener, or the Anglo-Prussian Garden War, 1858–88," *Garden History* 26, no. 2 (1997): 192–207.

9. A. Tagliolini, ed., *Il giardino italiano dell'ottocento: nelle immagini, nelle lettera-tura, nelle memorie* (Milano: Guerini e Associati, 1990).

10. Elliott, *Victorian Gardens*, 74–78.

11. Elliott, *Victorian Gardens*, 71–74, 138–47; C. Ridgway, "William Andrews Nes-field: Between Uvedale Price and Isambard Kingdom Brunel," *Journal of Garden History* 13 (1993): 69–89.

12. J. Lindley, "On the Arrangement of Gardens and Pleasure-Grounds in the Elizabe-than Age," *Journal of the Horticultural Society* 3 (1848): 1–15; Elliott, *Victorian Gardens*, 66–70, 83–87, 118–21.

13. Elliot, *Victorian Gardens*, 221–42; B. Elliott, "Historical Revivalism in the Twen-tieth Century," *Garden History* 28, no. 1 (2000): 17–31.

14. B. Elliott, "Mosaiculture: Its Origins and Significance," *Garden History* 9, no. 1 (1981): 76–98.

15. F. André and S. de Courtois, *Edouard André (1840–1911): un paysagiste bota-niste sur les chemins du monde* (Besançon: Éditions de l'Imprimeur, 2001).

16. M. Mosser, M. Duchêne, C. Frange, M. Baridon, J. Frange, and J. Moulin, *Le style Duchêne: Henri & Achille Duchêne: architectes paysagistes 1841–1947* (Neuilly: Editions du Labyrinthe, 1998).

17. G. Bresc-Bautier, D. Caget, and E. Jacquin, *Jardins du Carrousel et des Tuileries*, ([S.l.]: Réunion des Musées Nationaux/Caisse nationale des monuments histo-riques et des sites, 1996).

18. For the apogee of Le Nôtre's fame, see L. Corpechot, *Les jardins de l'intelligence* (Paris: Émile Paul, 1912), later revised as *Parcs et jardins de France* (Paris: Li-brairie Plon, 1937), and L. Corpechot, *La renaissance du jardin français* (Paris: Nouvelle Librairie Nationale, 1913).

19. G. Allinger, *Das Hohelied von Gartenkunst und Gartenbau: 150 Jahre Garten-bau-Ausstellungen in Deutschland* (Berlin: Verlag Paul Parey, 1963); B. Zijlistra, *Nederlandse tuinarchitectuur 1850–1940* (Zutphen: Walburg Pers., 1991); C. Quest-Ritson, *The English Garden Abroad* (London: Viking, 1992).

20. D. Green. *Gardener to Queen Anne: Henry Wise (1653–1738) and the Formal Garden* (London: Oxford University Press, 1956).

21. D. Stroud, *Capability Brown* (London: Faber, 1975); F. J. Ladd, *Architects at Corsham Court* (Bradford-on-Avon: Moonraker Press, 1978).

22. G. Carter, P. Goode, and K. Laurie, *Humphry Repton, Landscape Gardener 1752–1818* (Norwich: Sainsbury Centre, 1982); S. Daniels, *Humphry Repton: Landscape Gardening and the Geography of Georgian England* (New Haven, CT: Yale University Press, 1999).

23. A. Rogger, *Landscapes of Taste: The Art of Humphry Repton's Red Books* (Lon-don: Routledge, 2007).

24. Carter et al., *Humphry Repton*; K. Laurie, "Humphry Repton 1752–1818: New Discoveries," *The Garden (Journal of the Royal Horticultural Society)* 108 (1983): 365–66. Repton's insistence that the Red Books not be printed lasted until 1976, when Charlene Garry of the Basilisk Press reasoned that, as offset photoli-thography was unknown to Repton, by his standards it did not count as printing. Garry consequently published three Red Books in facsimile.

25. No one has made a search, let alone a tally, of quasi–Red Books produced in the wake of Repton, and those that I have seen or have been told about are in private hands.

26. For the history of the term "landscape architect," see J. Disponzio, "Jean-Marie Morel and the Invention of Landscape Architecture," *Tradition and Innovation in French Garden Art: Chapters of a New History*, ed. J. D. Hunt and M. Conan (Philadelphia: University of Pennsylvania Press, 2002), 135–59, especially 151–54.

27. W. J. Bean, "Mr. William Goldring," *Journal of Horticulture* 66 (1913): 509.

28. See William Robinson's polemic in *Garden Design and Architects' Gardens* (London: John Murray, 1892).

29. See Simeon Marshall's obituary in *Gardeners' Chronicle* 2 (August 27, 1910), 169.

30. N. D. G. James, *A History of English Forestry* (Oxford: Basil Blackwell, 1990), 189–206. For the United States, see S. E. Cohen, *Planting Nature: Trees and the Manipulation of Environmental Stewardship in America* (Berkeley: University of California Press, 2004), 39–45. For a categorization of early park professionals in America, see G. Cranz, *The Politics of Park Design: A History of Urban Parks in America* (Cambridge, MA: MIT Press, 1982), 168–72.

31. James Mean, in his introduction in J. Abercrombie, *Abercrombie's Practical Gardener*, 2nd ed. (London: Cadell & Davies, 1817), xi.

32. See "British Gardeners: David T. Fish," *Gardeners' Chronicle* 1 (May 22, 1875), 655–56.

33. For the career of Paxton, see G. Chadwick, *The Works of Sir Joseph Paxton* (London: Architectural Press, 1961), a work superseded in various respects by K. Colquhoun, *A Thing in Disguise: The Visionary Life of Joseph Paxton* (London: Fourth Estate, 2003).

34. A. J. Beresford Hope, "The International Exhibition," *Quarterly Review* 112 (1862): 180.

35. J. Wright, "Heckfield Place," *Journal of Horticulture* 5 (1882): 430–32.

36. B. Elliott, *The Royal Horticultural Society: A History 1804–2004* (Chichester: Phillimore, 2004). For Carl August Sckell, see J. Woudstra, "The Sckell Family in England (1770–1830)," *Die Gartenkunst* 14, no. 2 (2002): 211–20.

37. On the founding of the school, see G. Hinz, *Peter Josef Lenné* (Berlin: Deutscher Kunstverlag, 1937), 17–18. In 1872, F. Jühlke published an illustrated book based on the course content; see F. Jühlke, *Die Königliche Landesbaumschule und Gärtnerlehranstalt zu Potsdam* (Berlin: Weigandt & Hempel, 1872).

38. For McKenzie's hopes regarding Alexandra Palace, see D. Deal [H. H. Dombrain], "Alexandra Palace and Park, Muswell Hill," *Journal of Horticulture* 26 (1874): 444–45. For the Crystal Palace School, see the prospectus announcement in *Gardeners' Chronicle* 1 (April 2, 1881): 437, and correspondence (May 7, 1881): 603–4, (May 14, 1881): 636.

39. Elliott, *Victorian Gardens*, 317–24.

40. D. T. Fish, "Trentham, the Seat of the Duke of Sutherland," *Gardeners' Chronicle,* April 20, 1872, 540.

41. L. Limido, "Un paysagiste français d'envergure internationale: Jean-Pierre Baril-let-Deschamps, maître d'Édouard André," in *Édouard André (1840–1911) un paysagiste botaniste sur les chemins du monde*, ed. F. André and S. de Courtois (Besançon: Éditions de l'Imprimeur, 2001), 55–66; L. Limido, *L'art des jardins sous le second empire: Jean-Pierre Barillet-Deschamps* (Seyssel: Éditions Champ Vallon, 2002).

42. J. C. Loudon, *The Suburban Gardener and Villa Companion* (London: Longman, Orme, Brown, Breen, and Longmans; Edinburgh: W. Black, 1838), 136–70.

43. K. Woodbridge, *Princely Gardens* (London: Thames and Hudson, 1986), 227–28.

44. S. Bending, "William Mason's 'An Essay on the Arrangement of Flowers in Plea-sure-Grounds,'" *Journal of Garden History* 9 (1989): 217–20.

45. R. Gorer, *The Growth of Gardens* (London: Faber and Faber, 1978), 128–36, 188–91; Elliott, *The Royal Horticultural Society*, 197–211.

46. Elliott, *Victorian Gardens*, 11–13; B. Elliott, "Gardening Times," *The Garden (Journal of the Royal Horticultural Society)* 118 (1993): 411–13. A comprehensive history of gardening magazines, even for Britain, has yet to be written, but in the meantime, see R. Desmond, "Victorian Gardening Magazines," *Garden History 5*, no. 3 (1977): 47–66; R. Desmond, "Loudon and Nineteenth-Century Horticultural Journalism," in *John Claudius Loudon and the Early Nineteenth Century in Great Britain*, ed. E. B. MacDougall (Washington, D.C.: Dumbarton Oaks, 1980), 79–97.

47. Elliott, *Victorian Gardens*, 48–51, 87–90, 123–40, 148–58, 203–11, 216–20.

48. Robinson, *Garden Design and Architects' Gardens*.

49. Elliott, *Victorian Gardens*, 46–48, 94–99, 176–78, 187–92; G. Thomas, *The Rock Garden and Its Plants* (London: J. M. Dent, 1989).

50. Gorer, *Growth of Gardens*, 187–88. The water garden reached its peak of popularity later than the other planting genres; for the classic work, see F. Perry, *Water Gardening* (London: Country Life, 1938).

51. Elliott, *Victorian Gardens*, 180–84; B. Elliott, *Waddesdon Manor: The Garden* (Waddesdon Manor, Bucks: National Trust, 1994), 15–16.

52. There has yet to be a decent study of the international spread of Robinson's ideas. For André, see J. Christiany, "Échanges et relations amicales entre Édouard André et William Robinson," in *Édouard André (1840–1911) un paysagiste botaniste sur les chemins du monde*, ed. F. André and S. de Courtois (Besançon: Éditions de l'Imprimeur, 2001), 121–27. For Wilhelm Miller, see W. Miller, *What England Can Teach Us about Gardening* (Garden City, NY: Doubleday, Page, 1911); and C. Vernon, "Wilhelm Miller and *The Prairie Spirit in Landscape Gardening*," in *Regional Garden Design in the United States*, ed. T. O'Malley and M. Treib, Dumbarton Oaks Colloquium on the History of Landscape Architecture 15 (Washington, D.C.: Dumbarton Oaks, 1995), 271–75; and in the same volume, R. E. Grese, "The Prairie Gardens of O. C. Simonds and Jens Jensen," 99–123, esp. 99–105. For Germany, see K. Foerster, *Vom Blütengarten der Zukunft* (Berlin: Furche-Verlag, 1917), and the second edition of the same volume (Berlin: Verlag der Gartenschön-heit, 1922); E. E. Silva Tarouca and C. Schneider, *Unsere Freiland-Stauden* (Wien: Tempsky, 1913) and its companion works; W. Lange, *Gartengestaltung der Neuzeit*

(Leipzig: J. J. Weber, 1907), in which he cited Robinson and Gertrude Jekyll. Lange also used plates from Elgood and Jekyll's *Some English Gardens* in this work.

2 Types of Gardens

1. R. Desmond, "The Transformation of the Royal Gardens at Kew," in *Sir Joseph Banks: A Global Perspective*, ed. R.E.R. Banks et al. (Richmond: Royal Botanic Gardens Kew, 1994); B. Elliott, "The Promotion of Horticulture," in Banks et al., *Sir Joseph Banks*.
2. É. André, *Le potager de Versailles. L'École Nationale d'Horticulture de Versailles* (Paris: Librairie Agricole et Maison Rustique, 1890). For a good web-based summary of the history of the Potager du Roi, see http://www.potager-du-roi.fr/histoire/his toire1.html (accessed June 1, 2007).
3. J. C. Loudon, *The Suburban Gardener and Villa Companion* (London: Longman, Orme, Brown, Breen, and Longmans; Edinburgh: W. Black, 1838), 170–71.
4. A. J. Downing, *A Treatise on the Theory and Practice of Landscape Gardening* (New York: George P. Putnam, 1850), 40–60.
5. On the organization of garden departments in the nineteenth century, see J. Morgan and A. Richards, *A Paradise Out of a Common Field* (London: Century, 1990).
6. Loudon's *Gardener's Magazine* is a good source of such plans, especially volumes 11–12 (1835–36), in which Thomas Rutger published a series of plans for suburban villa gardens that explored many different locations for various functions.
7. Robinson's planting concept is apparent in all his publications, but nowhere more so than in Robinson. W. Robinson, *The Subtropical Garden* (London: John Murray, 1871). His recommendations in this book to use pampas grass, bamboos, and so forth as the counterparts to bananas and other tender woody-stemmed plants for summer bedding would indeed have created a distinct visual effect.
8. T. Longstaffe-Gowan, *The London Town Garden 1740–1840* (New Haven, CT: Yale University Press, 2001); S. T. Marcus, "Town Gardens of London 1820–1914: A Study of Domestic Horticulture" (Thesis, Architectural Association, London, 1990). A decent study of town gardens on the continent of Europe is still lacking. For the garden squares of London, see C. Sumner and S. T. Marcus, "The History, Design and Planting of London Squares," in *London Squares: The Proceedings of the London Squares Conference* (London: Historic Parks and Gardens Trust, 1995), 10–16. The communal gardens of the Kensington area of west London have become familiar internationally through the film *Notting Hill*.
9. Air pollution was not only caused by industry. The effect of domestic coal fires was sufficient to kill plants and cause structural damage to greenhouses. For the effects on the gardens of the Royal Horticultural Society, see B. Elliott, *The Royal Horticultural Society: A History 1804–2004* (Chichester: Phillimore, 2004), 73–75, 232, 279. To gain an appreciation of the limitations imposed on the planter's palette, see A. D. Webster, *London Trees* (London: Swarthmore Press, 1920); and W. W. Pettigrew, "The Influence of Air Pollution on Vegetation," *Gardeners' Chronicle* 2 (1928), 292, 308–9, 335.

10. The last notable professor of botany at a British medical institution was probably Robert Bentley, whose *Medicinal Plants* (with H. Trimen; London: J. & A. Churchill, [1875]–1880) was the last major work of its genre. Bentley served as Professor of Botany to the Pharmaceutical Society but also held a position in plant taxonomy at King's College London.

11. S. B. Sutton, *The Arnold Arboretum: The First Century* (Jamaica Plain, MA: Arnold Arboretum, 1971); C. Zaitzevsky, *Frederick Law Olmsted and the Boston Park System* (Cambridge, MA: Harvard University Press, 1982).

12. Desmond, *Kew: The History*. There is substantial literature on the imperial role of botanic gardens. See, for example, Drayton, *Nature's Government*.

13. Elliott, *The Royal Horticultural Society*, 60–63.

14. D. Bown, *Westonbirt* (Baltonsborough: Julian Holland, 1990); Sir J. Russell et al., *Rothamsted 1843–1943* (Harpenden: Rothamsted, 1943).

15. J. C. Loudon, *A Manual of Cottage Gardening* (privately published, 1830); R. Adamson, *The Cottage Garden* (Leven: Robert Reid, 1851); J. Floyd, *The Book of Cottage & Villa Gardening* (London: Aldine Publishing, 1900).

16. B. Elliott, *Victorian Gardens* (London: B. T. Batsford, 1986), 63–64; A. Clayton-Payne and B. Elliott, *Victorian Flower Gardens* (London: Weidenfeld & Nicolson, 1988), 13–73; A. Scott-James, *The Cottage Garden* (London: Allen Lane, 1981).

17. N. Kent, *Hints to Gentlemen of Landed Property* (London: J. Dodsley, 1775), 223–27; Sir T. Bernard, *An Account of a Cottage and Garden, Near Tadcaster* (London: T. Becket, 1797).

18. D. M. Moran, *The Allotment Movement in Britain* (New York: Peter Lang, 1990); D. Crouch and C. Ward, *The Allotment: Its Landscape and Culture* (Nottingham: Five Leaves Publications, 1997); J. Burchardt, *The Allotment Movement in England 1793–1873* (Woodbridge: Boydell Press, 2002). The provision of allotments by Tory landowners has been underplayed in recent historiography. For the first attempt at a correction, see J. Ward, *W. G. Ferrand: "The Working Man's Friend" 1809–1889* (East Linton: Tuckwell Press, 2002)

19. J. Curé, "Les jardins d'ouvriers et l'oeuvre de M. Renaudin, à Sceaux," *Revue Horticole* (1901): 211–12. Also see related articles by Curé and others over the ensuing years, esp. J. Curé, "L'oeuvre Marguerite Renaudin," *Revue Horticole* (1902): 454–56; and G. T. Grignan's report "Le Congrès International des Jardins Ouvriers," *Revue Horticole* (1903): 531–32.

20. S. Sidblad, "Swedish Perspectives of Allotment and Community Gardening," *Acta Horticulturae* 523 (2000): 151–60.

21. J. C. Loudon, *Encyclopaedia of Gardening* (London: Longman, Hurst, Rees, Orme, and Brown, 1822), 1186.

22. W. Wroth, *The London Pleasure Gardens of the Eighteenth Century* (London: Macmillan, 1896); R. Altick, *The Shows of London* (Cambridge, MA: Harvard University Press, 1978), 317–31; J. S. Curl, "Spas and Pleasure Gardens of London," *Garden History* 7, no. 2 (1979): 27–68; J. Harding and A. Taigel, "An Air of Detachment: Town Gardens in the Eighteenth and Nineteenth Centuries," *Garden History* 24, no. 2 (1996): 237–54.

23. J. C. Loudon, *On the Laying Out, Planting, and Managing of Cemeteries* (London: Longman, 1843); J. S. Curl, *A Celebration of Death* (London: Constable, 1980); C. Brooks et al., *Mortal Remains: The History and Present State of the Victorian and Edwardian* Cemetery (Exeter: Wheaton, 1989).

24. Elliott, *Victorian Gardens*, 51–54, 134–35; H. Conway, *People's Parks: The Design and Development of Victorian Parks in Britain* (Cambridge: Cambridge University Press, 1991).

25. For the debate about the future of the fortifications of Paris, and the loss of an opportunity to create a *parc périphérique*, see N. Evenson, *Paris: A Century of Change 1878–1978* (New Haven, CT: Yale University Press, 1979), 272–76.

26. F. Baltazavek and R. Schediwy, "The Economic Origins of Europe's Largest City Parks," *Parks and Recreation*, July 1981, 15–20; August 1981, 35–42; F. Debié, *Jardins de capitales: une géographie des parcs et jardins public de Paris, Londres, Vienne et Berlin* (Paris: Éditions du Centre National de la Recherche Scientifique, 1992). For parks in Paris, G. F. Chadwick, *The Park and the Town* (London: Architectural Press, 1966), 52–62, is still a good account, but see also Limido, *L'art des jardins sous le second empire*. For Sweden, see C. Nolin, *Till stadsbornas nytta och förlustande: den offentliga parken i Sverige under 1800-talet* (Stockholm: Byggförlaget, 1999), with an English summary on 320–26; and C. Nolin, "Public Parks in Gothenburg and Jönköping: Secluded Idylls for Swedish Townfolk," *Garden History* 32, no. 2 (2004): 197–212.

27. Cited in Evenson, *Paris*, 270.

28. Zaitzevsky, *Frederick Law Olmsted*; G. Cranz, *The Politics of Park Design: A History of Urban Parks in America* (Cambridge, MA: MIT Press, 1982). For the park system in Seattle, see J. Hockaday, *Greenscapes: Olmsted's Pacific Northwest* (Pullman, WA: Washington State University Press, 2009).

29. Elliott, *Victorian Gardens*, 211–14; H. Jordan, "Public Parks, 1885–1914," *Garden History* 22, no. 1 (1994): 85–113; H. Taylor "Urban Public Parks 1840–1900: Design and Meaning," *Garden History* 23, no. 2 (1995): 201–21.

30. F. Janson, *Pomona's Harvest* (Portland, OR: Timber Press, 1996), 241.

31. R. Webber, *Market Gardening* (Newton Abbot: David & Charles, 1972); C. W. Shaw, *The London Market Gardens*, 2nd ed. (London: The Garden, 1880).

32. J. Curé, *Les jardiniers de Paris et leur culture à travers les siècles* (Paris: Librairie Agricole et Maison Rustique, 1900). For the brief vogue of culture maraichère in England, see C. D. McKay, *The French Garden in England* (London: Daily Mail, 1909).

33. D. Faucher, "Les jardins familiaux et la technique agricole," *Annales: Economies, Sociétés, Civilisations,* 14 (1959): 297–307; T. Stovall, *The Rise of the Paris Red Belt* (Berkeley: University of California Press, 1990), 10–17; M. Conan, "The *Hortillonages*: Reflections on a Vanishing Gardeners' Culture," in *The Vernacular Garden*, ed. J. D. Hunt and J. Wolschke-Bulmahn (Washington, D.C.: Dumbarton Oaks, 1993).

34. R. Webber, *Covent Garden: Mud-Salad Market* (London: J. M. Dent, 1969); N. Pevsner, *A History of Building Types* (London: Thames and Hudson, 1976), 235–56.

35. N. E. Hoffmann and J. C. Van Horne, eds., *America's Curious Botanist: A Tercentennial Reappraisal of John Bartram* (Philadelphia, PA: American Philosophical Society, 2004); D. Sox, *Quaker Plant Hunters* (York: Sessions Book Trust, 2004).

36. E. J. Willson, *West London Nursery Gardens* (Fulham & Hammersmith Historical Society, 1982); B. Elliott, "Commercial Horticulture," in *London's Pride: The Glorious History of the Capital's Gardens*, ed. M. Galinou (London: Anaya Publishers, 1990); D. Solman, *Loddiges of Hackney* (London: Hackney Society, 1995); S. Heriz-Smith, *The House of Veitch* (privately published, 2000).

3 Plantings

1. "Picturesque" is a term of complex meanings as John Dixon Hunt makes clear in several publications. See, for example, J. D. Hunt, *The Picturesque Garden in Europe* (London: Thames and Hudson, 2002). It is particularly problematic when applied to "plantings." See, for example, M. Laird, "Ornamental Planting and Horticulture in English Pleasure Grounds, 1700–1830," in *Garden History: Issues, Approaches, Methods*, ed. J. D. Hunt (Washington, D.C.: Dumbarton Oaks, 1992), 243–77, and especially 247: "In this essay, I would like to shift the discussion away from stylistic labels—*formal/informal*, *picturesque*, *Gardenesque*—to evidence of continuity in planting systems." This essay established for the first time the idea of a picturesque/baroque continuum: geometry and linearity structuring features of the landscape garden—the flower border as much as the *plate-bande*, the shrubbery as much as the *bosquet*. Later publications by Laird confirmed and refined a clutch of other defining characteristics of plantings in the Georgian pleasure ground: mixing, theater, gradation, and so forth. Despite the revisionist work of the past twenty years (including the replanting of Painshill), the label picturesque remains valid as a convenient way of defining the period of the dominant landscape garden and the shifting styles within that period (roughly 1720s to 1820s). Hence, when drifts first appeared in the 1820s as an alternative to the matrix that had structured the flower border and the shrubbery, it fell within the picturesque period and drew upon picturesque writings (for example, the "forest lawns" of William Gilpin's *Remarks on Forest Scenery* [London: Printed for R. Blamire, 1791]), yet it also anticipated the "gardenesque." While this picturesque/gardenesque continuum adds another area of complexity to another problematic term, the label gardenesque remains a valid shorthand for defining the period of shifting styles (roughly 1820s to 1830s). Picturesque as a way of seeing and of representation is occasionally used here—in distinction to broad stylistic periodization—to indicate how an artist, as opposed to a designer, perceived plantings (e.g., Thomas Daniell and William Daniell's *Oriental Scenery*, 6 parts [London, 1795–1808]).

2. J. Roberts, "English Gardens in India," *Garden History* 26, no. 2 (Winter 1998): 115–35.

3. S. Daniels, *Humphry Repton: Landscape Gardening and the Geography of Georgian England* (New Haven, CT: Yale University Press, 1999), 191–205; V. Hinze,

"The Re-Creation of John Nash's Regency Gardens at the Royal Pavilion, Brighton," *Garden History* 24, no. 1 (1996): 45–53.

4. B. Elliott, *Victorian Gardens* (London: B. T. Batsford, 1986), 28.

5. M. Batey, *Regency Gardens* (Princes Risborough, Buckinghamshire: Shire Publications, 1995), 43–45.

6. Daniels, *Humphry Repton*, 180–83.

7. Daniels, *Humphry Repton*, 192.

8. Daniels, *Humphry Repton*, 194; M. Archer, *Early Views of India: The Picturesque Journeys of Thomas and William Daniell 1786–1794* (London: Thames and Hudson, 1980).

9. Repton cit. in Daniels, *Humphry Repton*, 197.

10. Elliott, *Victorian Gardens*, 102–6.

11. Repton cit. in Daniels, *Humphry Repton*, 197.

12. Repton cit. in Daniels, *Humphry Repton*, 197.

13. M. Laird, *The Flowering of the Landscape Garden: English Pleasure Grounds, 1720–1800* (Philadelphia: University of Pennsylvania Press, 1999), 341–60.

14. Batey, *Regency Gardens*, 41–42, 66.

15. Laird, *The Flowering of the Landscape Garden*; M. Laird, "From Bouquets to Baskets," *The Magazine Antiques, "England"* (2000): 932–39.

16. Laird, *The Flowering of the Landscape Garden*, 363–76.

17. K. N. Sanecki and M. Thompson, *Ashridge* (Norwich: Jarrold, 1998), 16–27.

18. Laird, "Ornamental Planting," 268–71; M. Laird, "Rekonstruktion des Herrengartens entsprechend der Pücklerschen Grundkonzeption," unpublished report for the Stiftung "Fürst-Pückler-Park Bad Muskau" (November 2001); C. A. Wimmer, *Bäume und Sträucher in historischen Gärten: Gehölzverwendung in Geschichte und Denkmalpflege* (Dresden: Verlag der Kunst Dresden, 2001), 185–88.

19. Daniels, *Humphry Repton*, 168; M. Laird, "*Corbeille, Parterre* and *Treillage*: The Case of Humphry Repton's Penchant for the French Style of Planting," *Journal of Garden History* 16, no. 3 (1996): 165.

20. Batey, *Regency Gardens*, 71.

21. R. H. Drayton, *Nature's Government: Science, Imperial Britain, and the "Improvement" of the World* (New Haven, CT: Yale University Press, 2000); B. Elliott, *The Royal Horticultural Society: A History 1804–2004* (Chichester: Phillimore, 2004).

22. Laird, *The Flowering of the Landscape Garden*, 221–24; M. Laird, "The Culture of Horticulture: Class, Consumption, and Gender in the English Landscape Garden," in *Bourgeois and Aristocratic Cultural Encounters in Garden Art, 1550–1850*, ed. M. Conan (Washington, D.C.: Dumbarton Oaks, 2002), 254.

23. T. O'Malley, "Art and Science in the Design of Botanic Gardens, 1730–1830," in *Garden History: Issues, Approaches, Methods*, ed. J. D. Hunt (Washington, D.C.: Dumbarton Oaks, 1992); M. Laird, "From Callicarpa to Catalpa: The Impact of Mark Catesby's Plant Introductions on English Gardens of the Eighteenth Century," in *Empire's Nature: Mark Catesby's New World Vision*, ed. A. R. W. Meyers and M. B. Pritchard (Chapel Hill: University of North Carolina Press, 1998), 199–201, 212.

24. J. C. Loudon, *Observations on the Formation and Management of Useful and Ornamental Plantations* (Edinburgh: Constable; London: Longman Hurst Rees & Orme, 1804).

25. Elliott, *Victorian Gardens*, 46–47; C. A. Shoemaker and P. Miles, "Alpine Garden," in *Chicago Botanic Garden Encyclopedia of Gardening: History and Design* vol. 1, ed. C. A. Shoemaker (Chicago: Fitzroy Dearborn Publishers, 2001), 38–39.

26. C. A. Wimmer, *Bäume und Sträucher in historischen Gärten: Gehölzverwendung in Geschichte und Denkmalpflege* (Dresden: Verlag der Kunst Dresden, 2001), 164–65.

27. Elliott, *Victorian Gardens*, 44, 58–59, 74–78, 238–40.

28. Wimmer, *Bäume und Sträucher,* 158–60.

29. Daniels, *Humphry Repton,* 175.

30. H. Repton, *Fragments on the Theory and Practice of Landscape Gardening* (London: T. Bensley and Son, 1816), 99.

31. C. Clunas, "Nature and Ideology in Western Descriptions of the Chinese Garden," in *Nature and Ideology: Natural Garden Design in the Twentieth Century*, ed. J. Wolschke-Bulmahn (Washington, D.C.: Dumbarton Oaks, 1997).

32. Hibberd cited in Elliott, *Victorian Gardens,* 19.

33. Repton, *Fragments,* 99.

34. M. Laird, "Approaches to Planting in the Late Eighteenth Century: Some Imperfect Ideas on the Origins of the American Garden," *Journal of Garden History* 11, no. 3 (1991): 154–72; M. Laird, "American Gardens," in *Chicago Botanic Garden Encyclopedia of Gardening: History and Design*, vol. 1, ed. C. A. Shoemaker (Chicago: Fitzroy Dearborn Publishers, 2001), 39–41.

35. Wimmer, *Bäume und Sträucher,* 160, 162.

36. Elliott, *Victorian Gardens*, 40; Daniels, *Humphry Repton,* 180; Wimmer, *Bäume und Sträucher,* 162.

37. Repton, *Fragments,* 98–99.

38. Cited in D. Jacques, *Georgian Gardens: The Reign of Nature* (London: B. T. Batsford, 1983), 196.

39. N. C. Johnson, "Names, Labels and Planting Regimes: Regulating Trees at Glasnevin Botanic Gardens, Dublin, 1795–1850," *Garden History* 35, suppl. 2 (2007): 56.

40. Laird, "Approaches to Planting in the Late Eighteenth Century," 169; B. Elliott, "From the Arboretum to the Woodland Garden," *Garden History* 35, suppl. 2 (2007): 71–83.

41. See the respective discussions in P. Elliott, C. Watkins, and S. Daniels, " 'Combining Science with Recreation and Pleasure': Cultural Geographies of Nineteenth-Century Arboretums," 6–27; B. Hartley, "Sites of Knowledge and Instruction: Arboretums and the Arboretum et Fruticetum Britannicum," 28–52; and B. Elliott, "From the Arboretum to the Woodland Garden," 71–83, in *Garden History* 35, suppl. 2 (2007).

42. Wimmer, *Bäume und Sträucher,* 155–58. See also T. J. Schlereth, "Early North American Arboreta," *Garden History* 35, suppl. 2 (2007): 196–216. Schlereth discusses John Quincy Adams's "White House Arboretum" of the 1820s, as well as A. J. Downing's work, 1841–51, clearly inspired by Loudon.

43. Wimmer, *Bäume und Sträucher,* 141–43.

44. Wimmer, *Bäume und Sträucher,* 140.

45. M. L. Simo, *Loudon and the Landscape: From Country Seat to Metropolis* (New Haven, CT: Yale University Press, 1988), 12.

46. Repton, *Fragments*, 198.

47. Wimmer, *Bäume und Sträucher*, 183.

48. Cited in Elliott, *Victorian Gardens*, 34.

49. Elliott, *Victorian Gardens*, 32–34.

50. Cited in Elliott, *Victorian Gardens*, 36.

51. H. Schenker, "Women, Gardens and the English Middle Class, 1790–1850," in *Bourgeois and Aristocratic Cultural Encounters in Garden Art, 1550–1850*, ed. M. Conan (Washington, D.C.: Dumbarton Oaks, 2002).

52. Simo, *Loudon and the Landscape*, 148–49; C. A. Wimmer, *Die Preußischen Hofgärtner*, ed. Stiftung Preussische Schlösser and Gärten Berlin-Brandenburg (Berlin: Druckhaus Hentrich, 1996).

53. Elliott, *Victorian Gardens*, 12.

54. This unpublished manuscript is held in the Garden Library at Dumbarton Oaks, Washington, D.C.

55. Dianne Harris, "Women as Gardeners," in C. A. Shoemaker, ed., *Chicago Botanic Garden Encyclopedia of Gardening: History and Design*, vol. 1. (Chicago: Fitzroy Dearborn Publishers, 2001); L. T. Tomasi, *An Oak Spring Flora: Flower Illustration from the Fifteenth Century to the Present Time* (Upperville, VA: Oak Spring Garden Library and Yale University Press, 1997), 307–31.

56. A. B. Shteir, *Cultivating Women, Cultivating Science: Flora's Daughters and Botany in England, 1760 to 1860* (Baltimore: Johns Hopkins University Press, 1996).

57. Laird, "The Culture of Horticulture," 247–48.

58. M. Laird, "Rekonstruktion des Herrengartens entsprechend der Pücklerschen Grundkonzeption." Hermann Jäger, for example, claimed that Pückler turned away from his artificial flowerbeds at Muskau, blaming the excess on his wish to please a lady; see H. Jäger, *Die Verwendung der Pflanzen in der Gartenkunst, oder Gehölz, Blumen und Rasen* (Gotha: Scheube; Darmstadt: Leske, 1858).

59. Schenker, "Women, Gardens and the English Middle Class," 349.

60. Cited in D. Stuart, *The Garden Triumphant: A Victorian Legacy* (London: Viking, 1988), 116; C. A. Wimmer, "Bed and Bedding System," in *Chicago Botanic Garden Encyclopedia of Gardening: History and Design*, vol. 1, ed. C. A. Shoemaker (Chicago: Fitzroy Dearborn Publishers, 2001), 117.

61. Cited in Elliott, *Victorian Gardens*, 28; Elliott, *Victorian Gardens*, 28–32.

62. Simo, *Loudon and the Landscape*, 112–16.

63. T. O'Malley, *Glasshouses: The Architecture of Light and Air* (New York: The New York Botanical Garden, 2005), 20–25.

64. M. F. Darby, "Joseph Paxton's Water Lily," in *Bourgeois and Aristocratic Cultural Encounters in Garden Art, 1550–1850*, ed. M. Conan (Washington, D.C.: Dumbarton Oaks Research Library and Collection, 2002), 255–83.

65. Elliott, *Victorian Gardens*, 125.

66. Stuart, *The Garden Triumphant*, 129.

67. Elliott *Victorian Gardens*, 125–26.

68. Elliott, *Victorian Gardens*, 132–34.

69. Cited in Elliott, *Victorian Gardens*, 33.

70. Elliott, *Victorian Gardens*, 93.

71. Cited in Elliott, *Victorian Gardens*, 51; Elliott, *Victorian Gardens*, 44, 88.

72. Elliott, *Victorian Gardens*, 87.

73. M. Sutherill, *The Gardens of Audley End* (London: English Heritage, 1995), 14–15, 34–35.

74. Wimmer, "Bed and Bedding System," 117.

75. M. Laird, "'A Cloth of Tissue of Divers Colours': The English Flower Border, 1660–1735," *Garden History* 21, no. 2 (1993): 158–205 (with appendix by J. Harvey).

76. Laird, "Rekonstruktion des Herrengartens entsprechend der Pücklerschen Grundkonzeption."

77. Elliott, *Victorian Gardens*, 154–55.

78. B. Elliott, "Mosaiculture: Its Origins and Significance," *Garden History* 9, no. 1 (Spring 1981): 76–98; Wimmer, "Bed and Bedding System," 117.

79. Elliott, *Victorian Gardens*, 155; Wimmer, "Bed and Bedding System," 117.

80. Elliott, *Victorian Gardens*, 138–40.

81. Elliott, *Victorian Gardens*, 148–52.

82. J. Sim, "Fernery," in *Chicago Botanic Garden Encyclopedia of Gardening: History and Design*, vol. 1, ed. C. A. Shoemaker (Chicago: Fitzroy Dearborn Publishers, 2001).

83. Elliott, *Victorian Gardens*, 152–54.

84. M. Seiler, *Das Palmenhaus auf der Pfaueninsel: Geschichte seiner baulichen und gärtnerischen Gestaltung* (Berlin: Haude & Spencer, 1989), 101.

85. Elliott, *Victorian Gardens*, 153.

86. Elliott, *Victorian Gardens*, 93–94.

87. Elliott, *Victorian Gardens*, 201.

88. Cited in Elliott, *Victorian Gardens*, 183.

89. Elliott, *Victorian Gardens*, 148–49.

90. S. Garfield, *Mauve: How One Man Invented a Color That Changed the World* (New York: W. W. Norton, 2001).

91. S. W. Lanman, "Colour in the Garden: 'Malignant Magenta,'" *Garden History* 28, no. 2 (2000): 209–21.

92. Lanman, "Colour in the Garden," 215.

93. H. H. Lamb, *Climate, History and the Modern World*, 2nd ed. (New York: Routledge, 1995), 247.

94. J. B. Tankard and M. A. Wood, *Gertrude Jekyll at Munstead Wood* (Gloucestershire: Sutton; Sagaponack, NY: Sagapress, 1996); J. B. Tankard, "Jekyll, Gertrude 1843–1932: English Horticulturist and Garden Designer," in *Chicago Botanic Garden Encyclopedia of Gardening: History and Design*, vol. 1, ed. C. A. Shoemaker (Chicago: Fitzroy Dearborn Publishers, 2001), 664–67; M. R. Van Valkenburgh and C. D. Van Valkenburgh, "A Contemporary View of Gertrude Jekyll's Herbaceous Border," in *Getrude Jekyll: A Vision of Garden and Wood*, ed. J. B. Tankard and M. R. Van Valkenburgh (New York: H. N. Abrams, 1989), 14.

95. Lanman, "Colour in the Garden," 210–14.

96. For watering systems, see A. Alphand, *Les promenades de Paris*, vol. 1 (Paris: J. Rothschild, 1870), 15–26.

97. Lanman, "Colour in the Garden," 214, 216.

98. Van Valkenburg and Van Valkenburg, "A Contemporary View," 11; Laird, *The Flowering of the Landscape Garden*, 191–92, plates 27, 28.

99. Elliott, *Victorian Gardens*, 205–9.

100. Elliott, *Victorian Gardens*, 206.

101. Elliott, *Victorian Gardens*, 208–9.

102. Elliott, *Victorian Gardens*, 207.

103. Harris, "Women as Gardeners," 1448.

104. J. B. Tankard, "Munstead Wood: Heath Lane, Busbridge, Surrey, England," in *Chicago Botanic Garden Encyclopedia of Gardening: History and Design*, vol. 1, ed. C. A. Shoemaker (Chicago: Fitzroy Dearborn Publishers, 2001), 922–24.

105. Elliott, *Victorian Gardens*, 93.

106. A. Helmreich, *The English Garden and National Identity: The Competing Styles of Garden Design, 1870–1914* (Cambridge: Cambridge University Press, 2002), 164–71.

107. Laird, *The Flowering of the Landscape Garden*, 289; Helmreich, *The English Garden*, 94. The idea of "enameling" and "garnishing" will be further elaborated on in a chapter of Laird's forthcoming book *A Natural History of English Gardening*, 1650–1800 (New Haven and London: Yale University Press, 2014).

108. Laird, *The Flowering of the Landscape Garden*, 359; J. Hermand, "Rousseau, Goethe, Humboldt: Their Influence on Later Advocates of the Nature Garden," in *Nature and Ideology: Natural Garden Design in the Twentieth Century*, ed. J. Wolschke-Bulmahn (Washington, D.C.: Dumbarton Oaks, 1997), 36–37.

109. L. Parshall, "C. C. L. Hirschfeld's Concept of the Garden in the German Enlightenment," *Journal of Garden History* 13, no. 13 (1993): 125–71.

110. J. Woudstra, "The Changing Nature of Ecology: A History of Ecological Planting (1800–1980)," in *The Dynamic Landscape: Design, Ecology and Management of Naturalistic Urban Planting*, ed. N. Dunnett and J. Hitchmough (London: Spon, 2004).

111. Cited in Woudstra, "The Changing Nature of Ecology," 26.

112. Clunas, "Nature and Ideology," 25.

113. Clunas, "Nature and Ideology," 27.

114. Helmreich, *The English Garden*, 66–90.

115. Helmreich, *The English Garden*, 8, 10, 89.

116. Helmreich, *The English Garden*, 47–52.

117. Elliott, *Victorian Gardens*, 94.

118. R. Flenley, "The Avenue Gardens, Regent's Park," in *William Andrews Nesfield: Victorian Landscape Architect*, ed. C. Ridgway (York: Institute of Advanced Architectural Studies, 1996).

119. *The Gardeners' Chronicle and Agricultural Gazette*, August 15, 1863, 771.

120. *The Gardeners' Chronicle and Agricultural Gazette*, September 17, 1864, 889.

121. *The Gardeners' Chronicle and Agricultural Gazette*, September 30, 1865, 915.

122. Elliott, *Victorian Gardens*, 152.

123. W. Robinson, *Gleanings from French Gardens* (London: F. Warne; New York: Scribner, Welford, 1868); W. Robinson, *The Parks, Promenades, and Gardens of Paris* (London: John Murray, 1869); W. Robinson, *The Subtropical Garden* (London: John Murray, 1871).

124. Cited in Judith B. Tankard's introduction to W. Robinson, *The Wild Garden* (facsimile of 1895 edition, Sagaponack, NY: Sagapress, 1994), xiii–iv.

125. Robinson, *The Wild Garden*, 6–7.

126. Helmreich, *The English Garden*, 4.

127. R. Williams, "Edwardian Gardens, Old and New," *Journal of Garden History* 13, nos. 1 and 2 (1993): 90–103.

128. Cited in Helmreich, *The English Garden*, 149.

129. J. Wolschke-Bulmahn, "The 'Wild Garden' and the 'Nature Garden': Aspects of the Garden Ideology of William Robinson and Willy Lange," *Journal of Garden History*, 12, no. 3 (1992): 183–206.

130. J. Wolschke-Bulmahn and G. Gröning, "Lange, Willy 1864–1941: German Garden Writer, Garden Theorist, and Landscape Architect," in *Chicago Botanic Garden Encyclopedia of Gardening: History and Design*, vol. 1, ed. C. A. Shoemaker (Chicago: Fitzroy Dearborn Publishers, 2001), 757–60.

131. Woudstra, "The Changing Nature of Ecology," 32–33; G. Gröning, "Barth, Erwin 1880–1933: German Landscape Architect," in *Chicago Botanic Garden Encyclopedia of Gardening: History and Design*, vol. 1, ed. C. A. Shoemaker (Chicago: Fitzroy Dearborn Publishers, 2001), 110–12.

132. See L. Dicaire, E. von Baeyer, and M. Laird, "Rideau Hall Landscape Conservation Study," unpublished report for PWGSC Heritage Conservation Program for the National Capital Commission, 1990.

133. E. W. Herbert, "The Taj and the Raj: Garden Imperialism in India," *Studies in the History of Gardens & Designed Landscapes* 25, no. 4 (2005): 250–72. Lord Curzon was Viceroy of India from 1899 to 1905.

134. I. van Groeningen, "Hidcote Manor Garden: Hidcote Bartrim, Gloucerstershire, England," in *Chicago Botanic Garden Encyclopedia of Gardening: History and Design*, vol. 1, ed. C. A. Shoemaker (Chicago: Fitzroy Dearborn Publishers, 2001).

135. D. Imbert, *The Modernist Garden in France* (New Haven, CT: Yale University Press, 1993), 128.

136. C. Tunnard, *Gardens in the Modern Landscape* (London: The Architectural Press, 1938), 110–11.

137. Van Valkenburg and Van Valkenburg, "A Contemporary View," 25.

4 Use and Reception

1. Sociologists, anthropologists, and psychologists use the term "impression management." While the term was not of the historic period, it describes the intent of those designed places better than any other.

2. The *New York Herald* expressed this concern about a lack of legal or formal class distinctions in America and the way such lack of distinctions might influence behavior in public parks. Prior to the construction of Central Park, the paper commented on how, while people knew their place in Europe, in America, cultivated citizens would certainly be harassed in parks by "the lowest denizens of the city"; R. Rosenzweig and E. Blackmar, *The Park and the People: A History of Central Park* (Ithaca, NY: Cornell University Press, 1992), 211.

3. G. F. Chadwick, *The Park and the Town* (London: Architectural Press, 1966), 68.

4. G. Blodgett, "Frederick Law Olmsted: Landscape Architecture as Conservative Reform," *Journal of American History* 62 (1976): 869–89.

5. During the French Second Empire, moves reminiscent of the techniques of "impression management," once employed by absolute monarchs, were incorporated into new urban designs for Paris by Baron Haussmann.

6. For an in-depth study of how reception theory adapted from literary research can be applied to the study of landscapes, see J. D. Hunt, *The Afterlife of Gardens* (Philadelphia: University of Pennsylvania Press, 2004), 7–32.

7. H. R. Jauss, *Toward an Aesthetic of Reception*, tr. T. Bahti (Minneapolis: University of Minnesota Press, 1982); S. Hall and P. Du Gay, eds., *Questions of Cultural Identity* (Thousand Oaks, CA: Sage, 1996).

8. M. P. Thomas, "Reception Theory and the Interpretation of Historical Meaning," *History and Theory* 32 (1993): 248–72.

9. Harold Marcuse has introduced the term "reception history" to describe how varied meanings have been attached to historical events over time by participants, authors, and other interpreters of the past. In a similar manner, James Lowen in *Lies across America* has applied pragmatic theory (though he did not directly use that term) in explaining gaps between the interpretation of historical events at their occurrence and the way those events were memorialized years later. In exploring reception, Lowen identifies three groups: those involved in the event, those who memorialize the event, and all of the various audiences from the memorial's construction forward in time. H. Marcuse, *Legacies of Dachau: The Use and Abuse of a Concentration Camp, 1933–2001* (Cambridge, New York: Cambridge University Press, 2001); J. W. Lowen, *Lies across America: What Our Historic Sites Get Wrong* (New York: The New York Press, 1999).

10. A. J. Downing, *Rural Essays*, ed. G. W. Curtis (New York: Leavitt and Allen, 1857), 147.

11. Downing, *Rural Essays*, 152.

12. For an idealistic perspective on Olmsted's theories, see A. Fein, *Frederick Law Olmsted and the American Environmental* Tradition (New York: George Braziller, 1972), 18–28.

13. T. L. Haskell, *The Emergence of Professional Social Science: The American Social Science Association and the Nineteenth-Century Crisis of Authority* (Baltimore: Johns Hopkins University Press, 2000), 1–4.

14. E. Ewen and S. Ewen, *Typecasting: On the Arts and Sciences of Human Inequality, A History of Dominant Ideas* (New York: Seven Stories Press, 2006).

15. Ewen and Ewen, *Typecasting*, 142–43; D. J. Nadenicek, "Nature in the City: Horace Cleveland's Aesthetic," *Landscape and Urban Planning* 26 (1993): 7–9.

16. Blodgett, *Frederick Law Olmsted*, 875.

17. R. W. Emerson, "The Young American," in *Nature, Addresses, and Lectures* (Boston: Houghton Mifflin, 1895), 367–68.

18. Haskell, *The Emergence of Professional Social Science*, 24–39.

19. D. J. Nadenicek, "Frederick Billings: The Intellectual and Practical Influences on Forest Planting, 1823–1899," unpublished Report to Marsh-Billings-Rockefeller National Historical Park, 2003, 43–47.

20. He saw doctors often for a type of anxiety disorder that visits to Central Park or his home landscape seemed to quiet.

21. H. W. S. Cleveland, *The Aesthetic Development of the United Cities of St. Paul and Minneapolis* (Minneapolis: A. C. Baussman, 1888), 12.

22. H. W. S. Cleveland, *Landscape Architecture as Applied to the Wants of the West with an Essay on Forest Planting on the Great Plains* (Chicago: Jansen, McClurg, 1873), 93–147.

23. F. Billings, "Report to Land Committee, March 1, 1871," *Northern Pacific Railroad Archives* (Minnesota Historical Society).

24. Both Olmsted and Cleveland suggested design solutions at a range of scales from small sites to vast regions. Both also saw forest planting within the prevue of landscape architecture.

25. R. Lewis, "Frontier and Civilization in the Thought of Frederick Law Olmsted," *American Quarterly* 29 (1977): 395.

26. Cited in L. W. Roper, "Frederick Law Olmsted and the Port Royal Experiment," *Journal of Southern History* 31 (1965): 279. Olmsted's experiment involved a plan for the care and education of African Americans located on the Sea Islands near Charleston, S. C.

27. Cited in Lewis, "Frontier and Civilization," 394.

28. Olmsted's 1870 paper titled "Public Parks and the Enlargement of Towns" to the ASSA in S. B. Sutton, *Civilizing American Cities: A Selection from Frederick Law Olmsted's Writings on City Landscapes* (Cambridge, MA: MIT Press, 1971), 74.

29. Cited in Sutton, *Civilizing American Cities*, 76–77.

30. Cited in Sutton, *Civilizing American Cities*, 81–82.

31. Cited in F. L. Olmsted Jr. and T. Kimball, eds., *Forty Years of Landscape Architecture, Central Park* (Cambridge, MA: MIT Press, 1973), 250.

32. Cited in Olmsted Jr. and Kimball, *Forty Years*, 249–50.

33. R. M. Copeland and H. W. S. Cleveland, *A Few Words on the Central Park* (Boston: publisher unnamed, 1856), 3–4.

34. Copeland and Cleveland, *A Few Words*, 3.

35. The phrase was probably first coined by the Pulitzer Prize–winning New England scholar Van Wyck Brooks and was later used as a book title by Perry Miller.

36. To be fair to Olmsted, little existed in Central Park to be saved. I am referring to the numerous times native trees that were allowed to grow only as long as they did not interfere with Olmsted's intended design effects.

37. D. J. Nadenicek, "Emerson's Aesthetic and Natural Design: A Theoretical Foundation for the Work of Horace William Shaler Cleveland," in *Nature and Ideology: Natural Garden Design in the Twentieth Century*, ed. J. Wolschke-Bulmahn (Washington, D.C.: Dumbarton Oaks, 1997), 72–78.

38. H. W. Longfellow, *The Song of Hiawatha* (Rutland, VT: Charles E. Tuttle Co., 1975), 208–9.

39. Longfellow, *The Song of Hiawatha*, 22.

40. Cited in Olmsted Jr. and Kimball, *Forty Years*, 525.

41. "With Apologies to Longfellow," *Minneapolis Journal*, May 17, 1904.

42. "A Minnehaha Improvement," *Minneapolis Tribune*, September 15, 1889.

43. D. J. Nadenicek, "Commemoration in the Landscape of Minnehaha: 'A Halo of Poetic Association,'" in *Places of Commemoration: Search of Identity and Landscape Design*, ed. J. Wolschke-Bulmahn (Washington, D.C.: Dumbarton Oaks, 2001), 74.

44. The incident was discussed by Olmsted in a letter to Stebbins; see Rosenzweig and Blackmar, *The Park and the People*, 319.

45. Cited in Olmsted Jr. and Kimball, *Forty Years*, 529.

46. Rosenzweig and Blackmar, *The Park and the People*, 234.

47. A. von Hoffman, "'Of Greater Lasting Consequence'?: Frederick Law Olmsted and the Fate of Franklin Park, Boston," *Journal of the Society of Architectural Historians* 47 (1988): 345.

48. Horace Cleveland to William Watts Folwell, May 14, 1889, *Folwell Papers*, Minnesota Historical Society.

49. C. Lasch ed., *The Social Thought of Jane Addams* (New York: Bobbs-Merrill), 1965.

50. It is important to acknowledge the body of scholarship that suggests that these Progressive Era reforms were also ultimately about control. The difference between the two eras, however, is that the recreational desires of lower class citizens were taken into consideration in the early years of the twentieth century. See S. Hardy and A. G. Ingham, "Games, Structures, and Agency: Historians on the American Play Movement," *Journal of Social Science* 17 (1983): 290.

51. G. R. Taylor, "Recreation Developments in Chicago," *Annals of the American Academy of Political and Social Science* 35 (1910): 88–105.

52. H. S. Jones, "Recreation Tendencies in America," *Annals of the American Academy of Political and Social Science* 105 (1923): 244–45.

53. The landscape architect and urban planner John Nolen explained all those period perspectives on the design and use of parks, including National Parks. See J. Nolen, "Parks and Recreational Facilities in the United States," *Annals of the American Academy of Political and Social Science* 35 (1910): 1–12.

54. R. E. Foglesong, *Planning the Capitalist City: The Colonial Era to the 1920s* (Princeton, NJ: Princeton University Press, 1986), 89–123.

55. By the twentieth century, the down-side of greater reliance on science and pseudo-science led many to a more ridged social theory, including the belief in genetic inferiority, which, as some believed, could not be overcome under any circumstances.

5 Meaning

1. R. Williams, *The Country and the City* (New York: Oxford University Press, 1973), 17.

2. Williams, *The Country and the City*, 152.

3. M. Girouard, *Cities and People: A Social and Architectural History* (New Haven, CT: Yale University Press, 1985), 286.

4. Williams, *The Country and the City*, 186.

5. Williams, *The Country and the City*, 217.

6. G. P. Marsh, *Man and Nature* (Cambridge, MA: The Belknap Press of Harvard University Press, [1864] 1965), 36.

7. R. W. Emerson, *Journals of Ralph Waldo Emerson*, ed. E. W. Emerson and W. E. Forbes (Cambridge: Riverside Press, 1909–14), 322.

8. Schenker, "Central Park and the Melodramatic Imagination," *Journal of Urban History* 29, no. 4 (2003): 375–93.

9. McCracken, *Gardens of Empire: Botanical Institutions of the Victorian British Empire* (London: Leicester University Press, 1997), 17.

10. Williams, *The Country and the City*, 281.

11. A. J. Downing, *Landscape Gardening and Rural Architecture* ([New York: Orange Judd Agricultural Book Publisher] New York: Dover Publications, [1865] 1991); J. C. Loudon, *The Suburban Gardener and Villa Companion* (London: Longman, Orme, Brown, Breen, and Longmans; Edinburgh: W. Black, 1838); Gertrude Jekyll, *Gardens for Small Country Houses* (London: Country Life; New York: C. Scribner's Sons, 1913).

12. A. Helmreich, *The English Garden and National Identity: The Competing Styles of Garden Design, 1870–1914* (Cambridge: Cambridge University Press, 2002), 67.

13. G. Taylor, *The Victorian Flower Garden* (London: Skeffington, 1952), 114.

14. H. Schenker, *Melodramatic Landscapes: Urban Parks in the Nineteenth Century* (Charlottesville: University of Virginia Press, 2009).

15. S. Lasdun, *The English Park: Royal, Private and Public* (London: Andre Deutsch, 1991), 125–34.

16. Alphand, *Les promenades de Paris* ([Paris: J. Rothschild] Princeton, NJ: Princeton University Press, [1892] 1984), 59.

17. F. L. Olmsted, *Writings on Public Parks, Parkways and Park Systems*, eds. C. E. Beveridge and C. F. Hoffman (Baltimore: Johns Hopkins University Press, 1997); Schenker, *Melodramatic Landscapes*.

18. T. Veblen, *The Theory of the Leisure Class* (New York: Dover, 1899), 29.

19. Taylor, *The Victorian Flower Garden*, 180–90.

20. L. H. Brockway, *Science and Colonial Expansion: The Role of the British Royal Botanic Gardens* (New York: Academic Press, 1979); McCracken, *Gardens of Empire*.

21. R. R. Gutowski, ed., *Victorian Landscape in America: The Garden as Artifact*, Proceedings from the Centennial Symposium, Morris Arboretum of the University of Pennsylvania, 1988.

22. F. M. L. Thompson, *English Landed Society in the Nineteenth Century* (London: Routledge and Kegan Paul, 1963); A. Kidd and D. Nicholls, eds., *The Making of the British Middle Class* (Stroud, Gloucestershire: Sutton Publishing, 1998).

23. A. Leighton, *American Gardens of the Nineteenth Century* (Amherst: University of Massachusetts Press, 1987); A. Wilkinson, *The Victorian Gardener: The Growth of Gardening and the Floral World* (Stroud, Gloucestershire: Sutton Publishing, 2006).

24. G. Taylor, *Some Nineteenth-Century Gardeners* (London: Skeffington, 1951), 17–67.

25. M. L. Simo, *Loudon and the Landscape: From Country Seat to Metropolis* (New Haven, CT: Yale University Press, 1988), 257.

26. Loudon, *The Suburban Gardener*, 171, 622.

27. Loudon, *The Suburban Gardener*, 9.

28. L. Davidoff and C. Hall, *Family Fortunes: Men and Women of the English Middle Class, 1780–1850* (Chicago: University of Chicago Press, 1987), 23.

29. Loudon, *The Suburban Gardener*, 169.

30. Simo, *Loudon and the Landscape*, 170.

31. Schenker, "Women, Gardens and the English Middle Class, 1790–1850," in *Bourgeois and Aristocratic Cultural Encounters in Garden Art, 1550–1850*, ed. M. Conan (Washington, D.C.: Dumbarton Oaks, 2002).

32. Downing, *Landscape Gardening*, 7–8.

33. F. J. Scott, *Victorian Gardens: The Art of Beautifying Suburban Home Grounds* (New York: D. Appleton, American Life Foundation, [1870] 1982); J. Weidenmann, *Beautifying Country Homes* (New York: Orange Judd; Watkins Glen, NY: The American Life Foundation for the Athenaeum Library of Nineteenth Century America, [1870] 1978); D. J. Berg, ed., *Country Patterns, 1841–1883: A Sampler of Nineteenth Century Rural Homes and Gardens* (Rockville Center, NY: Antiquity Reprints, 1982).

34. T. Carter, *The Victorian Garden* (London: Bell and Hyman, 1984), 10.

35. J. Ruskin, *Sesame and Lilies* (New York: Charles E. Merrill, 1891), 173.

36. N. Fraser, "Rethinking the Public Sphere: A Contribution to the Critique of Actually Existing Democracy," in *Habermas and the Public Sphere*, ed. C. Calhoun (Cambridge, MA: MIT Press, 1994), 125.

37. Loudon, *The Suburban Gardener*, 7.

38. Loudon, *The Suburban Gardener*, 562.

39. A. Shteir, *Cultivating Women, Cultivating Science: Flora's Daughters and Botany in England, 1760 to 1860* (Baltimore: Johns Hopkins University Press, 1996), 61.

40. Taylor, *The Victorian Flower Garden*, 156, 161.

41. J. W. Loudon, *The Ladies' Companion to the Flower Garden* (London: W. Smith, 1841); J. W. Loudon, *The Lady's Country Companion; or, How to Enjoy a Country Life Rationally* (London: Longman, Brown, Green and Longmans, 1845).

42. Schenker, "Women, Gardens and the English Middle Class."

6 Verbal Representations

1. B. von Arnim, *Goethe's Briefwechsel mit einem Kinde*, 3rd ed. (Berlin: Hertz Verlag, 1881), xxviii–xxix. All translations are mine unless otherwise noted.

2. J. Austen, *The Complete Novels of Jane Austen* (London: Wordsworth Editions, 2007), 382 (chapter 43).

3. J. Austin, *Pride and Prejudice* (London: T. Egerton, 1813).

4. See the major and indispensable study by G. Finney, *The Counterfeit Idyll. The Garden Ideal and Social Reality in Nineteenth-Century Fiction* (Tübingen: M. Niemeyer,

1984). Finney distinguishes the gardens in nineteenth-century French, German, and English fiction as realistic, idealistic, and elegiac, respectively. H. Volkmann (*Unterwegs nach Eden. Von Gärtnern und Gärten in der Literatur* [Göttingen: Vandenhoeck & Ruprecht, 2000]) includes gardens in world literature from classical Greece to the late twentieth century and arranges the material thematically.

5. The remaining volumes appeared quickly thereafter: *Briefe eines Verstorbenen* (Munich: G. F. Franckh; Suttgart: Hallberger, 1830–1831); new ed. by H. Ohff in one volume (Berlin: Kupfergraben, 1986). Pückler was much read in England and America in Sarah Austin's translation: *Tour in England, Ireland, and France in the Years 1826, 1827, 1828 & 1829* (London: Effinham Wilson, 1832; Philadelphia: Carey, Lea & Blanchard, 1833). Different editions of both the German and English letters have slight variations in their titles. On his influence in America, see the articles in S. Duempelmann, ed., *Pückler and America* (Bulletin of the German Historical Institute, Washington, D.C., Supplement 4, 2007).

6. H. F. von Pückler-Muskau, *Andeutungen über Landschaftsgärtnerei* (Stuttgart: Hellberger'sche Verlagshandlung). English translation by B. Sickert and edited by S. Parsons, *Hints on Landscape Gardening* (Boston: Houghton Mifflin, [1834] 1917). For some of the unpublished material related to his journey, see Stiftung Fürst-Pückler-Park Bad Muskau, ed., *Englandsouvenirs. Fürst Pücklers Reise 1826–1829* (Zittau: Graphische Werkstätten, 2005), with several important, revisionist essays. See also H. Tausch, "Vom Bild der Natur zum imaginären Bilderbogen der Vergangenheit. Hermann von Pückler-Muskaus *Andeutungen über Landschaftsgärtnerei* und die Literarisierung des englischen Landschaftsgartens," *Archiv für das Studium der neueren Sprachen und Literaturen* 233 (1996): 1–19.

7. On the appreciation of his style (and its relationship to Poe), see L. Parshall, "Hirschfeld, Pückler, Poe—The Literary Modeling of Nature," in *Pückler and America*, ed. S. Duempelmann (Bulletin of the German Historical Institute Washington, D.C., Supplement 4, 2007), 149–69.

8. See D. Wordsworth, *The Grasmere and Alfoxden Journals*, ed. P. Woof (Oxford: Oxford University Press, 2002). Wordsworth kept these diaries between 1797 and 1803.

9. Published in 1846 in N. Hawthorne, *Mosses from an Old Manse*, new ed. (New York: Modern Library, 2003), 3–27, which also includes "Rappuccini's Daughter."

10. E. von Armin, *Elizabeth and Her German Garden* (London: Virago, [1898] 1985).

11. Armin, *Elizabeth and Her German Garden*, 33.

12. Armin, *Elizabeth and Her German Garden*, 25–26.

13. Many other names could be listed here, of course, including the Czech writer Karel Capek (1890–1938), whose charming book *The Gardener's Year* was originally published in 1929 and is available in a recent paperback edition with an introduction by V. Klinkenburg (New York: Modern Library, 2002).

14. Italian gardens are found in "The Muse's Tragedy," "Roman Fever," "A Venetian Night's Entertainment," "The Letter," and so forth. Many believe the model for Bellomont was the Mills estate on the Hudson. The gardens of her travels also influenced Wharton's designs for her own gardens at the Mount in the Berkshires.

15. H. Hesse, *Siddhartha* (Berlin: S. Fischer, 1922).

16. Finney argues that these gardens represent divergent conceptions of self-cultivation (*The Counterfeit Idyll*, 64–74). The notes to the Deutscher Taschenbuch Verlag edition include a valuable excursus, with bibliography, of the depiction of the landscape; see J. W. von Goethe, *Die Wahlverwandtschaften* (Munich: Deutscher Taschenbuch Verlag, 1977), 325–30. The bibliography of scholarly studies on this novel is enormous.

17. W. Benjamin, "Goethes "Wahlverwandtschaften" in *Spiegelungen Goethes in unserer Zeit*, ed. H. Meyer (Wiesbaden: Limes-Verlag, 1949), 11–93.

18. Quotations are from the English translation, *Elective Affinities*, trans. R. J. Hollingdale (London: Penguin, 1971), 218–19.

19. Finney, who discusses Stifter at length, sees this novel as another instance of the German mode of self-cultivation (*The Counterfeit Idyll*, 83–96).

20. Originally published in the *Atlantic Monthly*. The plot was inspired by actual events concerning an English admirer of Shelley who sought to retrieve the writer's papers from Byron's former mistress. See the preface to vol. 12 of H. James, *The Aspern Papers*, in *The Novels and Tales of Henry James* (New York: C. Scribner's Sons, [1908] 2001), v–xii.

21. James, *The Aspern Papers*, 26.

22. Such as in Austin, *Pride and Prejudice*, above, or C. Brontë's *Jane Eyre* (London: Smith, Elder, 1847) where the garden and the natural are opposed to society and the artificial.

23. J. F. von Eichendorff, *Aus dem Leben eines Taugenichts* ([Berlin: Vereinsbuchhandlung] Stuttgart: Reclam, [1826] 1992), 9. Eichendorff himself grew up on a large estate in Silesia, and his affinity for such environs is apparent throughout his oeuvre; see also J. F. von Eichendorff, "Das Marmorbild," *Frauentaschenbuch* (Nuremberg: J. L. Schrag, 1819).

24. There have been many adaptations for the stage and screen.

25. This fairy tale is a concentrated version of the novel's plot, albeit with a happy ending, for *Die Lehrlinge* tells of the original state of the world when nature was still understandable to mankind; but humanity is inadequate, and Nature herself bemoans mankind's indifference to the lost unity that could have been regained, but was not.

26. L. Carroll, *Alice's Adventures in Wonderland* and *Through the Looking-Glass*, ed. H. Haughton (London: Penguin, [1865, 1871] 1998), 12.

27. The pastoral interlude in *Looking-Glass* (*Alice's Adventures*, 135–40) has been identified as an allusion to Alfred Tennyson's *Maud* (Boston: Ticknor and Fields, 1855). See 333, 34n2 of the Penguin edition.

28. Carroll, *Alice's Adventures*, 69.

29. Carroll, *Alice's Adventures*, 140.

30. Originally in *Columbia Magazine*, March 1846; an early version was published in 1842 as "The Landscape Garden." Quoted from *The Complete Tales and Poems of Edgar Allan Poe* (Vintage Books Edition, 1975), 604–15. This tale was inspired by passages in Pückler's *Tour*; see Parshall, "Hirschfeld, Pückler, Poe," 149–69.

31. Musings about nature and the superiority of the natural style of gardening recall A. J. Downing's *A Treatise on the Theory and Practice of Landscape Gardening*

Adapted to North America (Washington, D.C.: Dumbarton Oaks Research Library and Collection, [1841] 1991), although the garden theorist whom Poe names in the text is Joseph Addison.

32. Poe, *The Complete Tales*, 615.

33. Poe's description of the flawless "composition" of this garden reflects his familiarity with current theories of landscape design, such as Downing, Addison, and William Howitt. Poe's horticultural expertise is revealed in many plant descriptions, including an enthusiastically detailed look at a huge *Liriodendron tulipifera* (that he errs in calling a "Liriodendron Tulipiferum"), a tree that also features prominently in "The Gold Bug." The idealized cottage recalls the humble dwelling in which Poe and his wife lived from 1846 to his death in 1849. His wife died there in 1847.

34. First published in the *Daily Chronicle*, then in 1911, in H. G. Wells, *The Door in the Wall, and Other Stories* (New York: Mitchell Kennerley, 1911).

35. Both the skepticism and the naming of the protagonist add credibility to the tale. As Poe's "Arnheim" and other frame stories show, this was a popular literary form in the nineteenth century.

36. H. G. Wells, *The Door in the Wall, and Other Stories* (New York: Mitchell Kennerley, 1911), 10.

37. Available online: http://hca.gilead.org.il/paradise.html.

38. *Adam's Diary* was first published in 1893 as part of a souvenir book about Niagara Falls. A new edition appeared in *Harper's Magazine*, 1904. *Eve's Diary* was published in 1906. See the combined edition, M. Twain, *The Diaries of Adam and Eve*, ed. S. F. Fishkin, with an introduction by U. K. Le Guin (New York: Oxford University Press, 1996).

39. "When I look back, the Garden is a dream to me. It was beautiful, surpassingly beautiful, enchantingly beautiful ... The Garden is lost, but I have found HIM, and am content." M. Twain, *The Complete Short Stories of Mark Twain,* ed. C. Neider (New York: Bantam Books, 1981), 210. Available online: http://www.online-literature.com/twain/3265/.

40. In J. Milton, *Paradise Lost* (London: John Bumpus, 1821), book 12, 382. Adam is reassured of love's importance: "then wilt thou not be loth / To leave this Paradise, but shalt possess /A Paradise within thee, happier far."

41. Hawthorne, *Mosses from an Old Manse*, 71–99.

42. Hawthorne, *Mosses from an Old Manse*, 99.

43. Émile Zola, *La Faute de l'Abbé Mouret* (Paris: Charpentier et Cie.), English translation by E. A. Vizetelly, *Abbé Mouret's Transgression* (London: Mondial, [1875] 2005), 18.

44. Zola, *Abbé Mouret's Transgression*, 36.

45. Zola, *Abbé Mouret's Transgression*, 113.

46. Zola, *Abbé Mouret's Transgression*, 120.

47. Zola, *Abbé Mouret's Transgression*, 148. As Serge and Albine search for the secret spot, one hears numerous echoes of the grotto of love episode in the Tristan and Isolde story, where the lovers' oneness with nature and each other is disturbed by the intervention of the outside world, which they themselves have allowed to enter. See G. von Strassburg, *Tristan*, tr. A. T. Hatto (Harmondsworth: Penguin Books, 1967), 261–68.

48. Zola, *Abbé Mouret's Transgression*, 157. This is part of an extended encounter with monstrous plants, mostly of the cactus family (157–59). It is known that Zola drew from his own experience in depicting Paradou's wonders—from his then-present garden and those of his childhood in Provence. He also consulted horticultural publications; indeed, his descriptions have been unjustly criticized as "a mere florist's catalogue"; see introduction in Zola, *Abbé Mouret's Transgression*, iii.

49. The full title is *Aus meinem Leben. Dichtung und Wahrheit*, usually translated: "From my Life. Poetry and Truth." But *Dichtung* means fiction as well as poetry, an ambiguity that was surely intentional. Written between 1808 and 1831—the final volume appeared after Goethe's death—it covers his early years from birth to the age of twenty-six, and its mellow tone and insightful recollections of youth were an important influence on Proust.

50. The author's true name was Louis Marie Julien Viaud. P. Loti, *Le roman d'un enfant* (Paris: Calmann-lévy), English translation by C. F. Smith, *The Story of a Child* (Boston: C. C. Birchard, 1901).

51. Loti, *The Story of a Child*, 12.

52. Loti, *The Story of a Child*, 41.

53. Originally published in seven volumes from 1913 to 1927. English translation by C.K.S. Moncrieff, *Remembrance of Things Past* (1922–1930; New York: Random House, 1970). The floral and garden imagery is already present in Proust's unfinished novel *Jean Santeuil* (1896–1899), which was not published until 1952. English translation by Gerard Hopkins (London: Simon and Schuster, 1956).

54. *Swann's Way*, vol. 1 of Proust, *Remembrance*, 106.

55. M. Proust, *Sodom and Gomorrah*, vol. 4, trans. with an introduction by John Sturrock (London: Penguin, 2002), part I, 3–33.

56. They invent a metaphor for their love-making: to "do a cattleya," Proust, *Swann's Way*, 169–79.

57. Proust, *Swann's Way*, 36.

58. Proust, *Swann's Way*, 104–5.

59. Proust, *Swann's Way*, 106.

60. Proust, *Swann's Way*, 108.

61. Her name, "uttered across the heads of the stocks and jasmines, pungent and cool as the drops which fell from the green watering-pipe; impregnating and irradiating the zone of pure air through which it had passed, which it set apart and isolated from all other air, with the mystery of the life of her whom its syllables designated to the happy creatures that lived and walked and traveled in her company; unfolding through the arch of the pink hawthorn, which opened at the height of my shoulder, the quintessence of their familiarity—so exquisitely painful to myself—with her, and with all that unknown world of her existence, into which I should never penetrate" (Proust, *Swann's Way*, 109).

62. Proust, *Swann's Way*, 325. *Swann's Way* concludes with Marcel walking in an autumnal Bois de Bologne (321–25) where he searches in vain to recapture his youthful experiences.

63. James, *The Aspern Papers*, ix.

7 Visual Representations

1. H. Haddad, *Le jardin des peintres* (Paris: Hazan, 2000); S. Schulze, ed., *Gärten: Ordnung Inspiration Glück* (Ostfildern: Hatje Cantz, 2006); A. Husslein-Arco, ed., *Gartenlust. Der Garten in der Kunst* (Vienna: Brandstätter, 2007).

2. 1609, Munich, Alte Pinakothek.

3. V. Royet, *Georges Louis Le Rouge: jardins anglo chinois, Inventaire du fonds français: graveurs du XVIII siècle*. 15 (Paris : Bibliothèque Nationale de France, 2004); I. Lauterbach, "Introduction," in *Georges-Louis Le Rouge, Détail des nouveaux jardins à la mode* (reprint, Nördlingen: Dr. Alfons Uhl, 2009).

4. G. Flaubert, *Bouvard et Pécuchet* (Paris: Garnier Flammarion, 1966), 71–79.

5. J. W. von Goethe, "Wilhelm Meister's Journeyman Years," trans. K. Winston, in *Goethe The Collected Works*, vol. 10, ed. J. K. Brown (New York: Princeton University Press, [1829] 1995), 159.

6. G. Huth, ed., *Allgemeines Magazin für die bürgerliche Baukunst* 1(2) (Weimar: Hoffmann, 1790), 78.

7. E. Börsch-Supan, *Garten-, Landschafts- und Paradiesmotive im Innenraum* (Berlin: Hessling, 1967).

8. C. C. Oman and J. Hamilton, *Wallpapers: A History and Illustrated Catalogue of the Collection of the Victoria and Albert Museum* (London: Sotheby Publ., 1982); O. Nouvel-Kammerer, ed., *Papiers peints panoramiques* (Paris: Flammarion, 1990); S. Thümmler, *Geschichte der Tapete* (Eurasburg: Edition Minerva, 1998).

9. G. Pastiaux-Thiriat and J. Pastiaux, *Un créateur de papiers peints, Joseph Dufour 1754–1827* (Tramayes: Syndicat d'initiative de Tramayes, 2000).

10. G. Cogeval and K. Jones, *Édouard Vuillard* (New Haven, CT: Yale University Press, 2003), cat. 111–24.

11. K. Henkel and C. Bohlmann, *Garten des Lebens: ein Wandschirm von Pierre Bonnard* (Köln: DuMont, 2002).

12. A. van Dülmen, *Das irdische Paradies. Bürgerliche Gartenkultur der Goethezeit* (Köln: Böhlau, 1999).

13. Weimar, Schlossmuseum, 1811.

14. F. L. von Sckell, *Beiträge zur bildenden Gartenkunst*, 2nd ed. (München: Lindauer, 1825), 76–78.

15. K. F. Schinkel, *Entwurf zu dem kaiserlichen Palast Orianda in der Krimm*, 4th ed. (Berlin: Ernst & Korn, 1873); K. J. Philipp, *Karl Friedrich Schinkel: Späte Projekte/ Karl Friedrich Schinkel: Late Projects* (Stuttgart: A. Menges, 2000).

16. H. Börsch-Supan, *Karl Friedrich Schinkel: Lebenswerk, begründet von Paul Ortwin Rave*, vol. 20, *Bild-Erfindungen* (München: Deutscher Kunstverlag, 2007).

17. J. W. von Goethe, *Wilhelm Meister's Apprenticeship*, vol. 14. Harvard Classics Shelf of Fiction (New York: P. F. Collier & Son, 1917). Available online: http://www.bartleby.com/314/ (accessed July 18, 2008).

18. C. Percier and P.-F.-L. Fontaine, *Choix des plus célèbres maisons de plaisance de Rome et de ses environs* (Paris: P. Didot l'aîné: Discours préliminaire, 1809), 4.

19. G. Noehles-Doerk, ed., *Kunst in Spanien im Blick des Fremden. Reiseerfahrungen vom Mittelalter bis in die Gegenwart* (Frankfurt am Main: Vervuert, 1996).

20. H. Swinburne, *Travels through Spain, in the Years 1775 and 1776*, 2nd ed. (London: Elmsly, 1787), 1, 293.

21. T. Gautier, *Voyage en Espagne* (Paris: G. Charpentier & Cie., 1890), 222.

22. Berlin, Alte Nationalgalerie.

23. *A Day in the Country: Impressionism and the French Landscape* (New York: Los Angeles County Museum of Art, Chicago Art Institute, and Réunion des Musées Nationaux, 1984), 207–39; J. D. Hunt, *Gardens and the Picturesque* (Cambridge, MA: The MIT Press, 1997), 243–83.

24. 1862, London, The National Gallery.

25. 1805–06, Hamburger Kunsthalle.

26. 1826–27, Berlin, Alte Nationalgalerie.

27. 1877–78; I. Pfeiffer, *Impressionistinnen—Berthe Morisot, Mary Cassatt, Eva Gonzalès, Marie Bracquemond* (Ostfildern: Hatje Cantz, 2008), 231.

28. P. Wittmer, *Caillebotte au jardin: la période d'Yerres (1860–1879)* (Saint-Rémy-en-l'Eau: Hayot, 1990); C.A.P. Willsdon, *In the Gardens of Impressionism* (London: Thames and Hudson, 2004).

29. 1867, Paris, Musée d'Orsay.

30. G. Clemenceau, *Claude Monet: Les Nymphéas* (Paris: Terrain Vague, 1990), 60.

31. Clemenceau, *Claude Monet*, 60.

32. K. Ireland, *Cythera Regained? The Rococo Revival in European Literature and the Arts, 1830–1910* (Cranbury, NJ: Fairleigh Dickinson University Press, 2006).

33. C. Baudelaire, *Curiosités esthétiques. L'Art romantique et autres Œuvres critiques* (Paris: Éditions Garnier Frères, 1962), 133, 178.

34. E. and J. de Goncourt, *L'Art du XVIIIme siècle* (Paris: G. Charpentier, 1881), 3, 7.

35. G. Farou and S. Eloy, eds., *La Collection La Caze. Chefs-d'oeuvre des peintures des XVIIe et XVIIIe siècles* (Paris: Hazan, 2007).

36. Édouard Duc de Trévise, "Le Pèlerinage de Giverny," *Revue de l'art* 51 (1927): 42–50, 121–34.

37. 1876, Musée d'Orsay, Paris.

38. G. Rivière, "Les Intransigeants et les impressionnistes: Souvenirs du salon libre de 1877," *L'Artiste* (1877); reprinted in R. Berson, ed., *The New Painting: Impressionism 1874–1886; Documentation*, 2 vols. (San Francisco, CA: Fine Arts Museums of San Francisco; Seattle: Distributed by the University of Washington Press, 1996), vol. 1, 186.

39. E. Hoschedé, "Les Femmes artistes," *L'Art de la mode* (April 1881), reprinted in Berson, *The New Painting*, vol. 1, 348; Pfeiffer, *Impressionistinnen*, 255, 257.

40. *A Day in the Country* 1984: 79–107.

41. Jacques, "Menus propos: Exposition impressionniste," *L'Homme libre* (1877), reprinted in Berson, *The New Painting*, vol. 1, 156.

42. J. E. Howoldt and U. M. Schneede, *Im Garten von Max Liebermann* (Berlin: Nicolai, 2004).

43. H. Guratzsch and H. Joachim Neyer, *Wilhelm Busch. Die Bildergeschichten. Historisch-kritische Gesamtausgabe in drei Bänden* (Hannover: Schlütersche, 2002), 548–59, 1487–88; English translation by G. Kahn, available online: http://river-text.com/mole_fr.shtml (accessed November 11, 2012).

44. Clemenceau, *Claude Monet*; Trévise, "Le Pèlerinage de Giverny," 42–50, 121–34; Willsdon, *In the Garden of Impressionism*.

45. É. Blément, "Les Impressionistes," *Le Rappel* (April 9, 1876), reprinted in Berson, *The New Painting*.

46. Clemenceau, *Claude Monet*, 30.

47. P. Georgel, *Monet: Le cycle des Nymphéas; Catalogue sommaire* (Paris: Edition de la Réunion des musées nationaux, 1999).

48. Clemenceau, *Claude Monet*, 37, 86.

8 Gardens and the Larger Landscape

1. D. Watkin, "The Architectural Context of The Grand Tour: The British as Honorary Italians," in *The Impact of Italy: The Grand Tour and Beyond*, ed. C. Hornsby (London: The British School at Rome, 2000), 55.

2. Watkin, "The Architectural Context of The Grand Tour," 55.

3. For the *Sanspareil Rock Garden*, see S. Habermann, *Bayreuther Gartenkunst, Die Gärten der Markgrafen von Brandenburg-Culmbach im 17. und 18. Jahrhundert*. Grüne Reihe, Quellen und Forschungen zur Gartenkunst. Vol. 6 (Worms: Wernersche Verlagsgesellschaft, 1982), 147–72.

4. Adopted from Horace Walpole, who in the last quarter of the eighteenth century in *The History of the Modern Taste in Gardening 1771–80* described William Kent as having "leaped the fence" and having seen "that all nature was a garden." See H. Walpole, *The History of the Modern Taste in Gardening 1771–80* (New York: Ursus Press, [1780] 1995), 43.

5. For more detail on Johann Moritz von Nassau-Siegen and his gardens and parks in Cleve, see W. A. Diedenhofen, *Klevische Gartenlust. Gartenkunst und Badebauten in Kleve* (Kleve: Freunde des Städtischen Museums Haus Koekkoek, 1994).

6. For more details on the Dessau-Wörlitz garden empire, see Hirsch, E. *Dessau-Wörlitz, Zierde und Inbegriff des 18. Jahrhunderts*. (München: Verlag C.H. Beck, 1988). A. Dorgerloh, " 'Er ist ein Effektstück'—Der Vesuv in der Kunst und Gartenkunst um 1800," *Anzeiger des Germanischen National-Museums* (1997), 71–86.

7. Schuderoff, cited in G. Gröning, "The Idea of Land Embellishment," *Journal of Garden History* 12 (1992): 176.

8. Gröning, "The Idea of Land Embellishment"; G. Gröning, "Anmerkungen zu Gustav Vorherrs Idee der Landesverschönerung," in *Umweltgeschichte. Methoden, Themen, Potentiale*, Cottbuser Studien zur Geschichte von Technik, Arbeit und Umwelt, vol. 1, eds. G. Bayerl, N. Fuchsloch, and T. Meyer (New York: Waxmann, 1996).

9. G. Vorherr, "Ueber Entstehung und Zweck der Deputation für Verbesserung des Landbauwesens und für zweckmäßige Verschönerung des baierischen Landes, dann Nachricht über die Herausgabe dieses Blattes," *Monatsblatt für die Verbesserung des Landbauwesens und für zweckmäßige Verschönerung des baierischen Landes* 1, no. 1 (1821): 1–3.

10. G. Felix, "Die nächsten Umgebungen von Regensburg," *Monatsblatt für die Verbesserung des Landbauwesens und für zweckmäßige Verschönerung des baierischen Landes*, 1, no. 4 (1826): 13–15.

11. G. Vorherr, "Sparcassen zur Beförderung der Landesverschönerung in Europa," *Monatsblatt* 6, no. 9 (1826): 45–46.

12. G. Vorherr, "Anmerkung zum Beitrag Nachricht von der königl. Baugewerkschule zu München," *Monatsblatt für die Verbesserung des Landbauwesens und für zweckmäßige Verschönerung des baierischen Landes* 4, no. 8 (1824): 49.

13. Anonymous, "Auszug des Sitzungsprotokolls der Baudeputation zu München," *Monatsblatt für die Verbesserung des Landbauwesens und für zweckmäßige Verschönerung des baierischen Landes* 5, no. 1 (1824): 3–4.

14. G. Vorherr, "Baupolizei," *Monatsblatt für die Verbesserung des Landbauwesens und für zweckmäßige Verschönerung des baierischen Landes* 5, no. 7 (1825): 33–36.

15. Gröning, "Anmerkungen zu Gustav Vorherrs Idee der Landesverschönerung," 161.

16. K. Cranz, "Zweckmäßige Boden-Kultur und Landes-Verschönerung in Preußen," *Wochenblatt des landwirthschaftlichen Vereins in Baiern* 13, no. 3 (1822): 33.

17. G. Gröning and U. Schneider, "Gut Reichenbach (Radaczewo), Pommern—Modellhafte landwirtschaftliche Einflüsse bei einer Gutsanlage der ersten Hälfte des 19. Jahrhunderts," in *Landgüter in den Regionen des gemeinsamen Kulturerbes von Deutschen und Polen—Entstehung, Verfall und Bewahrung, Majątki ziemskie na obszarze wspólnego dziedzictwa polsko-niemieckiego—problemy rozwoju, degradacji i konserwacji, Das Gemeinsame Kulturerbe—Wspólne Dziedzictwo*, Vol. 4/Tom IV, Instytut Sztuki PAN, eds. B. Pusback and J. Skuratowicz (Warszawa: Instytut Sztuki PAN, 2007); G. Gröning, "Das Gut Reichenbach (Radaczewo), Pommern—eine musterhaft verschönerte Feldflur?" in *Die "Ornamental Farm," Gartenkunst und Landwirtschaft*, ed. Stiftung Fürst-Pückler-Park Bad Muskau (Zittau: Graphische Werkstätten, 2010), 73–90. G. Gröning, "Peter Joseph Lenné, Eine Gartenreise im Rheinland," *Rheinische Vierteljahrsblätter* 76 (2012): 430–33.

18. F. L. Olmsted, "Park," in *American Cyclopedia*, reprinted in *The Papers of Frederick Law Olmsted*, Supplementary Series, vol. 1, ed. C. E. Beveridge, C. F. Hoffman, and K. Hawkins (Baltimore: Johns Hopkins University Press, [1875] 1997), 308.

19. Olmsted, "Park," 308–9.

20. Müller cited in J. Schnitter. For land embellishment projects in Sweden, see J. Schnitter, *Anguis in herba, Gartenpädagogik und Weltveredlung im Lebenswerk des schwedischen Agitators Olof Eneroth* (Hamburg: disserta Verlag, 2011).

21. D. Müller, "Ackerbau und Gärtnerei," *Hamburger Garten- und Blumenzeitung* (1855), 433–41.

22. P. D. Groenewegen, *The French Connection: Some Case Studies of French Influence on British Economics in the Eighteenth Century*, report no. 202 (Sydney: Department of Economics, University of Sydney, 1994); P. D. Groenewegen, "La 'French Connection': Influences Françaises sur l'Economie Politique Britannique," *Dix-Huitième Siècle*, 26 (1994):15–36; B. Klein, *Die physiokratische Verlandschaftung der Stadt um 1800: Städtebau und Stadtauflösung in der Realität von Freiburg im Breisgau sowie in der Utopie des französischen Revolutionsarchitekten Ledoux*. Beiträge zur Kunstwissenschaft. Vol. 46 (Munich: Scaneg, 1993).

23. R. F. Nash, *Wilderness & the American Mind* (New Haven, CT: Yale University Press, [1967] 2001).

24. C. A. Brown, "Thomas Jefferson's Poplar Forest: The Mathematics of an Ideal Villa," *Journal of Garden History* 10, no. 2 (1990): 117–39. S. Schulz, "Gartenkunst, Landwirtschaft und Dichtung bei William Shenstone und seine Ferme Ornée 'The Leasowes' im Spiegel seines literarischen Zirkels," Dr. phil. diss., Freie Universität Berlin, 2005.

25. D. Schuyler, "The Mid-Hudson Valley as Iconic Landscape: Tourism, Economic Development, and the Beginnings of a Preservationist Impulse," in *Within the Landscape*, ed. P. Earenfight and N. Siegel (University Park: The Pennsylvania State University Press, 2005).

26. A. Wallach, "Some Further Thoughts on the Panoramic Mode," in *Within the Landscape*, ed. P. Earenfight and N. Siegel (University Park: The Pennsylvania State University Press, 2005); A. Wallach, "Thomas Cole: Landscape and Course of American Empire," in *Thomas Cole: Landscape into History*, ed. W. H. Truttner and A. Wallach (New Haven, CT: Yale University Press; Washington, D.C.: National Museum of American Art, Smithsonian Institution, 1994); W. Born, *American Landscape Painting: An Interpretation* (Westport, CT: Greenwood Press, 1970), 36ff.

27. Schuyler, "The Mid-Hudson Valley," 23, 32–37.

28. A. J. Downing, *A Treatise on the Theory and Practice of Landscape Gardening adapted to North America* (New York: G. P. Putnam; London: Longman, Brown, Green & Longmans, 1850), 44.

29. C. Zaitzevski, "André Parmentier: A Bridge between Europe and America," in *The Landscape Universe: Historic Designed Landscapes in Context*, ed. C. Birnbaum (Papers from a national symposium, Armor Hall at Wave Hill, New York, 1993), 55.

30. J. C. Loudon, *An Encyclopaedia of Gardening* (London: Longman, Brown, Green, and Longmans, 1850), 329f.

31. L. Assing, *Briefwechsel und Tagebücher des Fürsten Hermann von Pückler-Muskau* (Bern: Herbert Lang, [1873] 1971), 242.

32. M. Sperlich, "Das neue Arkadien. Der Garten als utopische Landschaft," *Neue Heimat Monatshefte* 26, no. 6 (1979): 22. For a critical appraisal thereof, see J. Wolschke-Bulmahn, "Zwischen Hudson-River und Neiße. Fürst Pückler, die Muskauer Wasserfälle und das Hudson-River-Portfolio," *Die Gartenkunst* 10, no. 2 (1998), 300–309.

33. Nash, *Wilderness & the American Mind*, 108–9.

34. E. Carr, *Wilderness by Design: Landscape Architecture & the National Park Service* (Lincoln: University of Nebraska Press, 1998), 1.

35. Carr, *Wilderness by Design*, 9. For state parks, see J. W. Steeley, *Parks for Texas: Enduring Landscapes of the New Deal* (Austin: The University of Texas Press, 1999); for national parks, see C. L. Wirth, *Parks, Politics, and the People* (Norman: The University of Oklahoma Press, 1980).

36. J. D. Hunt, *Greater Perfections: The Practice of Garden Theory* (Philadelphia: University of Pennsylvania Press, 2000), 51.

37. Olmsted, Vaux, and Company, *The Preliminary Report upon the Proposed Suburban Village at Riverside, near Chicago.* (New York: Sutton, Bowne, 1868); A. Levee, "The Olmsted Brothers' Residential Communities: A Preview of a Career Legacy," in *The Landscape Universe: Historic Designed Landscapes in Context*,

ed. C. Birnbaum (Wave Hill, NY: National Park Service and Catalog of Landscape Records in the United States, 1993).

38. G. Gröning and J. Wolschke-Bulmahn, *1887–1987, DGGL Deutsche Gesellschaft für Gartenkunst und Landschaftspflege e.V. Ein Rückblick auf 100 Jahre DGGL*, Schriftenreihe der Deutschen Gesellschaft für Gartenkunst und Landschaftspflege, vol. 10, ed. Deutsche Gesellschaft für Gartenkunst und Landschaftspflege (Berlin: Boskett Verlag, 1987).

39. In 1803, Christian August Semler used the term *Naturgarten* in his book *Ideen zu einer Gartenlogik*. See G. Gröning, "Ideological Aspects of Nature Garden Concepts in Late Twentieth-Century Germany," in *Nature and Ideology: Natural Garden Design in the Twentieth Century*, ed. J. Wolschke-Bulmahn, Dumbarton Oaks Colloquium on the History of Landscape Architecture, vol. 18 (Washington, D.C.: Dumbarton Oaks, 1997). For more details about the wild and the nature garden, see J. Wolschke-Bulmahn, "The 'Wild Garden' and the 'Nature Garden': Aspects of the Garden Ideology of William Robinson and Willy Lange," *Journal of Garden History* 12, no. 3 (1992): 183–206.

40. W. Robinson, *The English Flower Garden and Home Grounds* (London: John Murray, 1900), 36.

41. M. Duval, *La planète des fleurs* (Paris: R. Laffont, 1977); K. Cox, ed., *Frank Kingdon Ward's Riddle of the Tsangpo Gorges* (Woodbridge, Suffolk: Antique Collectors' Club, 2001).

42. U. Schneider, *Hermann Muthesius und die Reformdiskussion in der Gartenarchitektur des frühen 20. Jahrhunderts* (Worms: Wernersche Verlagsgesellschaft, 2000).

43. W. Lange, *Gartengestaltung der Neuzeit* (Leipzig: J. J. Weber, 1907), 358.

44. W. Lange, "Meine Anschauungen über die Gartengestaltung unserer Zeit," *Die Gartenkunst* 7, no. 7 (1905): 114.

45. G. Gröning, "Die goldene Axt. Wachstum und Kontrolle in Pücklers Schriften—autopoietische Kräfte in der Konzeption des Landschaftsgartens," in *Von selbst, Autopoietische Verfahren in der Ästhetik des 19. Jahrhunderts*, ed. F. Weltzien (Berlin: Reimer, 2006), 157–58.

46. W. Lange, *Der Garten und seine Bepflanzung* (Stuttgart: Kosmos, Gesellschaft der Naturfreunde, 1913), 14; W. Lange, "Gartengedanken," *Die Gartenkunst*, 5, no. 6 (1903): 100–102.

47. N. Pevsner, *Some Architectural Writers of the Nineteenth Century* (Oxford: Clarendon Press, 1972), 110.

48. W. Lange, "Die Pflanzung im Garten nach physiognomischen Grundsätzen," *Die Gartenkunst* 6, no. 9 (1904): 169.

49. R. L. Herbert (ed.), *The Art Criticism of John Ruskin* (New York: Da Capo Press, 1987), 16.

50. W. Lange, "In welcher Weise kann der modernen Kunstrichtung in der Gartenkunst praktisch Rechnung getragen werden?" *Die Gartenkunst* 6, no. 5 (1904): 98.

51. See, for example, A. von Humboldt, *Ideen zu einer Physiognomik der Gewächse* (Tübingen: Cotta, 1806).

52. W. Lange, "Bilder aus der Gebirgslandschaft," *Die Gartenwelt* 5, no. 7 (1900): 74.

53. C. A. Wimmer, "Der vergessene Gartenkünstler George Isham Parkyns," *Zandera* 22, no. 1 (2007): 27–36.

54. J. Disponzio, "The Garden Theory and Landscape Practice of Jean-Marie Morel," Ph.D. diss., Columbia University in the City of New York, 2000), 220, 217–76.

55. F. A. Waugh, "A Horticultural School," *The Country Gentleman,* June 23, 1910, 604.

56. F. A. Waugh, "German Landscape Gardening," *The Country Gentleman,* August 25, 1910, 790.

57. F. A. Waugh, *Rural Improvement: The Principles of Civic Art Applied to Rural Conditions, including Village Improvement and the Betterment of the Open Country* (New York: Orange Judd, 1914), 24, 51.

58. Waugh, *Rural Improvement,* 25.

59. Waugh, *Rural Improvement,* 43.

60. Waugh, *Rural Improvement,* 39f.

61. See the title of Waugh's book, *Rural Improvement.*

62. Waugh, *Rural Improvement,* 34, 37.

63. Waugh, *Rural Improvement,* 19

64. For more details about regional garden design in the United States, see T. O'Malley and M. Treib, eds., *Regional Garden Design in the United States,* Dumbarton Oaks Colloquium on the History of Landscape Architecture, vol. 15 (Washington, D.C.: Dumbarton Oaks, 1995).

65. W. Miller, *The Prairie Spirit in Landscape Gardening* (Urbana: University of Illinois Agricultural Experiment Station, 1915), 5.

66. Miller, *The Prairie Spirit,* 32.

67. For landscape planning and garden design during National Socialism, see G. Gröning and J. Wolschke-Bulmahn, *Die Liebe zur Landschaft. Teil III. Der Drang nach Osten, Zur Entwicklung der Landespflege im Nationalsozialismus und während des Zweiten Weltkrieges in den "eingegliederten Ostgebieten,"* Arbeiten zur sozialwissenschaftlich orientierten Freiraumplanung, vol. 9, ed. U. Herlyn and G. Gröning (München: Minerva Publikation, 1987); and J. Wolschke-Bulmahn and G. Gröning, "The National Socialist Garden and Landscape Ideal: *Bodenständigkeit* (Rootedness in the Soil)," in *Art, Culture, and Media under the Third Reich,* ed. R. Etlin (Chicago: The University of Chicago Press, 2002), 73–97.

BIBLIOGRAPHY

Abercrombie, J. *Abercrombie's Practical Gardener*. 2nd ed. London: Cadell & Davies, 1817.

Ackerman, J. S. "On Public Landscape Design before the Civil War." In *Regional Garden Design in the United States*, ed. T. O'Malley and M. Treib. Washington, D.C.: Dumbarton Oaks Research Library and Collection, 1995.

Adamson, R. *The Cottage Garden*. Leven: Robert Reid, 1851.

Allinger, G. *Das Hohelied von Gartenkunst und Gartenbau: 150 Jahre Gartenbau-Ausstellungen in Deutschland*. Berlin: Verlag Paul Parey, 1963.

Alphand, A. *Les promenades de Paris*. [Paris: J. Rothschild] Princeton, NJ: Princeton University Press, [1867–73] 1984.

Altick, R. *The Shows of London*. Cambridge, MA: Harvard University Press, 1978.

Andersen, H. C. *The Garden of Paradise and Other Stories*. Garden City, NY: Doubleday, Page, 1914.

André, É. *Le potager de Versailles: L'École Nationale d'Horticulture de Versailles*. Paris: Librairie Agricole et Maison Rustique, 1890.

André, É. F. *L'art des jardins: traité général de la composition des parcs et jardins*. Marseille: Lafitte Reprints, [1879] 1992.

André, F., and S. de Courtois. *Édouard André (1840–1911): un paysagiste botaniste sur les chemins du monde*. Besançon: Éditions de l'Imprimeur, 2001.

Anonymous. "Auszug des Sitzungsprotokolls der Baudeputation zu München." *Monatsblatt für die Verbesserung des Landbauwesens und für zweckmäßige Verschönerung des baierischen Landes* 5, no. 1 (1824): 3–4.

Appelshäuser, K. *Die öffentliche Grünanlage im Städtebau Napoleons in Italien als politische Aussage*. Frankfurt am Main: Pollinger Schnelldruck, 1994.

Archer, M. *Early Views of India: The Picturesque Journeys of Thomas and William Daniell 1786–1794*. London: Thames and Hudson, 1980.

Arnim, B, von. *Goethes Briefwechsel mit einem Kind*. Berlin: Dümmler, 1835.

Arnim, E, von. *Elizabeth and Her German Garden*. London: Virago, [1898] 1985.

Assing, L. *Briefwechsel und Tagebücher des Fürsten Hermann von Pückler-Muskau.* Bern: Herbert Lang, [1873] 1971.

Austin, J. *Pride and Prejudice.* London: T. Egerton, 1813.

Babcock, B. A., ed. *The Reversible World: Symbolic Inversion in Art and Society.* Ithaca, NY: Cornell University Press, 1978.

Bagatti Valsecchi, P. F., and A. Kipar, eds. *Il giardino paesaggistico tra Settecento e Ottocento in Italia e in Germania. Villa Vigoni e l'opera di Giuseppe Balzaretto.* Milan: Guerini, 1996.

Baltazavek, F., and R. Schediwy. "The Economic Origins of Europe's Largest City Parks." *Parks and Recreation*, July 1981, 15–20; August 1981, 35–42.

Banks, R.E.R., B. Elliot, J. G. Hawkes, D. King-Hele, and G. L. Lucas, eds. *Sir Joseph Banks: A Global Perspective.* Richmond: Royal Botanic Gardens Kew, 1994.

Batey, M. *Regency Gardens.* Princes Risborough, Buckinghamshire: Shire Publications, 1995.

Bean, W. J. "Mr. William Goldring." *Journal of Horticulture* 66 (1913): 509.

Bender, T. *Toward an Urban Vision: Ideas and Institutions in Nineteenth Century America.* Baltimore: Johns Hopkins University Press, 1982.

Bending, S. "William Mason's 'An Essay on the Arrangement of Flowers in Pleasure-Grounds.'" *Journal of Garden History* 9 (1989): 217–20.

Benjamin, W. "Goethes "Wahlverwandtschaften." In *Spiegelungen Goethes in unserer Zeit*, ed. H. Meyer. Wiesbaden: Limes-Verlag, 1949.

Bentley, R., and H. Trimen. *Medicinal Plants.* London: J. & A. Churchill, [1875]–1880.

Beresford Hope, A. J. "The International Exhibition." *Quarterly Review* 112 (1862): 179–219.

Berg, D. J., ed. *Country Patterns, 1841–1883: A Sampler of Nineteenth Century Rural Homes and Gardens.* Rockville Center, NY: Antiquity Reprints, 1982.

Bernard, T. *An Account of a Cottage and Garden, Near Tadcaster.* London: T. Becket, 1797.

Berson, R., ed. *The New Painting: Impressionism 1874–1886; Documentation*, 2 vols. San Francisco, CA: Fine Arts Museums of San Francisco; Seattle: Distributed by the University of Washington Press, 1996.

Blément, É. "Les Impressionistes." *Le Rappel*, April 9, 1876.

Blodgett, G. "Frederick Law Olmsted: Landscape Architecture as Conservative Reform." *Journal of American History* 62 (1976): 869–89.

Born, W. *American Landscape Painting: An Interpretation.* Westport, CT: Greenwood Press, 1970.

Börsch-Supan, E. *Garten-, Landschafts- und Paradiesmotive im Innenraum.* Berlin: Hessling, 1967.

Börsch-Supan, H. *Karl Friedrich Schinkel: Lebenswerk, begründet von Paul Ortwin Rave., Vol. 20, Bild-Erfindungen.* München: Deutscher Kunstverlag, 2007.

Bown, D. *Westonbirt.* Baltonsborough: Julian Holland, 1990.

Bresc-Bautier, G., D. Caget, and E. Jacquin. *Jardins du Carrousel et des Tuileries.* [S.l.]: Réunion des Musées Nationaux/Caisse nationale des monuments historiques et des sites, 1996.

Brettell, R. "The Impressionist Landscape and the Image of France." In *A Day in the Country: Impressionism and the French Landscape*, ed. A.P.A. Belloli. New York: Abradale Press, 1990.

"British Gardeners: David T. Fish." *Gardeners' Chronicle* 1 (1875): 655–56.

Brockway, L. H. *Science and Colonial Expansion: The Role of the British Royal Botanic Gardens*. New York: Academic Press, 1979.

Brontë, C. *Jane Eyre*. London: Smith, Elder, 1847.

Brooks, C., et al. *Mortal Remains: The History and Present State of the Victorian and Edwardian Cemetery*. Exeter: Wheaton, 1989.

Brown, C. A. "Thomas Jefferson's Poplar Forest: The Mathematics of an Ideal Villa." *Journal of Garden History* 10, no. 2 (1990): 117–39.

Brown, J. *Gardens of a Golden Afternoon*. London: Penguin Books, 1982.

Browne, J. *The Secular Ark*. New Haven, CT: Yale University Press, 1983.

Bryant, W. C., ed. *Picturesque America; or, The Land We Live In*, vol. 2. New York: D. Appleton. Publishers, 1874.

Burchardt, J. *Allotment Movement in England 1793–1873*. Woodbridge: Boydell Press, 2002.

Burnett, F. H. *The Secret Garden*. New York: Frederick A. Stokes, 1911.

Buttlar, F., von. *Peter Joseph Lenné: Volkspark und Arkadien*. Berlin: Nicolaische Verlagsbuchhandlung, 1989.

Campanella, T. J. *Republic of Shade: New England and the American Elm*. New Haven, CT: Yale University Press, 2003.

Caneva, G., ed. *Amphitheatrum Naturae*. Milano: Mondadori Electa S.p.A., 2004.

Capek, K. *The Garderner's Year*. Introduction by Verlyn Klinkenburg. New York: Modern Library, [1919] 2002.

Carr, E. *Wilderness by Design: Landscape Architecture & the National Park Service*. Lincoln: University of Nebraska Press, 1998.

Carroll, L. *Alice's Adventures in Wonderland and Through the Looking-Glass*. Edited by. H. Haughton. London: Penguin, [1865, 1871] 1998.

Carter, G., P. Goode, and K. Laurie. *Humphry Repton, Landscape Gardener 1752–1818*. Norwich: Sainsbury Centre, 1982.

Carter, T. *The Victorian Garden*. London: Bell and Hyman, 1984.

Chadwick, G. F. *The Park and the Town*. London: Architectural Press, 1966.

Chadwick, G. F. *The Works of Sir Joseph Paxton*. London: Architectural Press, 1961.

Chaplin, C. *My Autobiographie*. New York: Simon and Schuster, 1964.

Charlesworth, M. *Landscape and Vision in Nineteenth-Century Britain and France*. Aldershot: Ashgate, 2008.

Christiany, J. "Échanges et relations amicales entre Édouard André et William Robinson." In *Édouard André (1840–1911) un paysagiste botaniste sur les chemins du monde*, ed. F. André and S. de Courtois. Besançon: Éditions de l'Imprimeur, 2001.

Clayton-Payne, A., and B. Elliott. *Victorian Flower Gardens*. London: Weidenfeld & Nicolson, 1988.

Clemenceau, G. *Claude Monet: Les Nymphéas*. Paris: Terrain Vague, 1990.

Cleveland, H.W. S. *The Aesthetic Development of the United Cities of St. Paul and Minneapolis*. Minneapolis, MN: A.C. Baussman, 1888.

Cleveland, H.W.S. *Landscape Architecture as Applied to the Wants of the West with an Essay on Forest Planting on the Great Plains*. Chicago: Jansen, McClurg, 1873.

Clunas, C. "Nature and Ideology in Western Descriptions of the Chinese Garden." In *Nature and Ideology: Natural Garden Design in the Twentieth Century*, ed. J. Wolschke-Bulmahn. Washington, D.C. Dumbarton Oaks, 1997.

Cogeval, G., with K. Jones. *Édouard Vuillard*. New Haven, CT: Yale University Press, 2003.

Cohen, S. E. *Planting Nature: Trees and the Manipulation of Environmental Stewardship in America*. Berkeley: University of California Press, 2004.

Colquhoun, K. *A Thing in Disguise: The Visionary Life of Joseph Paxton*. London: Fourth Estate, 2003.

Conan, M. "The *Hortillonages*: Reflections on a Vanishing Gardeners' Culture." In *The Vernacular Garden*, ed. J. D. Hunt and J. Wolschke-Bulmahn. Washington, D.C. Dumbarton Oaks, 1993.

Conan, M. "L'utopie révolutionnaire d'André Thouin: le projet d'une ferme experimentale dans la zone torride (1747–1824)." In *Essais poetique des jardins*, ed. M. Conan. Florence: Leo S. Olschki, 2004.

Conder, J. *Landscape Gardening in Japan*. Tokio: Hakubunsha, Ginza. 1893.

Conway, H. *People's Parks: The Design and Development of Victorian Parks in Britain*. Cambridge: Cambridge University Press, 1991.

Copeland, R. M., and H.W.S. Cleveland. *A Few Words on the Central Park*. Boston, 1856.

Corpechot, L. *La renaissance du jardin français*. Paris: Nouvelle Librairie Nationale, 1913.

Corpechot, L. *Parcs et jardins de France*. Paris: Librairie Plon, 1937.

Cox, K., ed. *Frank Kingdon Ward's Riddle of the Tsangpo Gorges*. Woodbridge, Suffolk: Antique Collectors' Club, 2001.

Cranz, G. *The Politics of Park Design: A History of Urban Parks in America*. Cambridge, MA: MIT Press, 1982.

Cranz, K. "Zweckmäßige Boden-Kultur und Landes-Verschönerung in Preußen." *Wochenblatt des landwirthschaftlichen Vereins in Baiern* 13, no. 3 (1822): 28–36.

Cremona, A. "Il giardino della memoria." In *Il Giardino della Memoria: I busti dei grandi italiani al Pincio*, ed. A. Cremona and A. Ponente. Rome: Artemide Edizioni S.r.l., 1999.

Crestin-Billet, F. *Les nains de jardin*. Paris: Editions Solar, 1997.

Crouch, D., and C. Ward. *The Allotment: Its Landscape and Culture*. Nottingham: Five Leaves Publications, 1997.

Curé, J. *Les jardiniers de Paris et leur culture à travers les siècles*. Paris: Librairie Agricole et Maison Rustique, 1900.

Curé, J. "Les jardins d'ouvriers et l'oeuvre de M. Renaudin, à Sceaux" *Revue Horticole* (1901): 211–12.

Curé, J. "L'Oeuvre Marguerite Renaudin." *Revue Horticole* (1902): 454–56.

Curl, J. S. *A Celebration of Death*. London: B. T. Batsford Ltd., 1993.

Curl, J. S. "Spas and Pleasure Gardens of London." *Garden History* 7, no. 2 (1979): 27–68.

Curl, J. S. *The Victorian Celebration of Death*. Stroud, Gloucestershire: Sutton Publishing, 2000.

Daniell, T., and W. Daniell. *Oriental Scenery*, 6 parts. London, 1795–1808.

Daniels, S. *Fields of Vision: Landscape Imagery and National Identity in England and the United States*. Princeton, NJ: Princeton University Press, 1993.

Daniels, S. *Humphry Repton: Landscape Gardening and the Geography of Georgian England*. New Haven, CT: Yale University Press, 1999.

Darby, M. F. "Joseph Paxton's Water Lily." In *Bourgeois and Aristocratic Cultural Encounters in Garden Art, 1550–1850*, ed. M. Conan. Washington, D.C. Dumbarton Oaks, 2002.

D'Arneville, M. B. *Parcs et jardins sous le premier empire: reflets d'une société*. Paris: Librairie Jules Tallandier, 1981.

Davidoff, L., and C. Hall. *Family Fortunes: Men and Women of the English Middle Class, 1780–1850*. Chicago: University of Chicago Press, 1987.

Davidson, R. W. "Images and Ideas of the Italian Garden in American Landscape Architecture." Ph.D. diss., Columbia University, New York, 1994.

Davison, G. "The City as a Natural System: Theories of Urban Society in Early Nineteenth-Century Britain." In *The Pursuit of Urban History*, ed. D. Fraser and A. Sutcliffe (London: Edward Arnold, 1983).

A Day in the Country: Impressionism and the French Landscape. New York: Los Angeles County Museum of Art, Chicago Art Institute, and Réunion des Musées Nationaux, 1984.

Deakin, R. *Flora of the Colosseum of Rome*. London: Broombridge, 1855.

Deakin, R. *Florigraphia Britannica; or, Engravings and Descriptions of the Flowering Plants & Ferns of Britain*. London: R. Groombridge, 1837.

Debié, F. *Jardins de capitales: une géographie des parcs et jardins public de Paris, Londres, Vienne et Berlin*. Paris: Éditions du Centre National de la Recherche Scientifique, 1992.

Desmond, R. *Kew: The History of the Royal Botanic Gardens*. London: Harvill Press, 1995.

Desmond, R. "Loudon and Nineteenth-Century Horticultural Journalism." In *John Claudius Loudon and the Early Nineteenth Century in Great Britain*, ed. E. B. MacDougall. Washington, D.C.: Dumbarton Oaks, 1980.

Desmond, R. "The Transformation of the Royal Gardens at Kew." In *Sir Joseph Banks: A Global Perspective*, ed. R.E.R. Banks et al. Richmond: Royal Botanic Gardens Kew, 1994.

Desmond, R. "Victorian Gardening Magazines." *Garden History 5*, no. 3 (1977): 47–66.

De Vico Fallani, M. *I parchi archeologici di Roma*. Rome: Nuova Editrice Spada, 1988.

De Vico Fallani, M. *Storia dei giardini pubblici di Roma nell'Ottocento: dalle importanti sistemazioni del Pincio, del Parco del Celio e della Passeggiata archeologica al Gianicolo*. Roma: Newton Compton, 1992.

Diedenhofen, W. A. *Klevische Gartenlust. Gartenkunst und Badebauten in Kleve*. Kleve: Freunde des Städtischen Museums Haus Koekkoek, 1994.

Disponzio, J. "The Garden Theory and Landscape Practice of Jean-Marie Morel." Ph.D. diss., Columbia University, New York, 2000.

Disponzio, J. "Jean-Marie Morel and the Invention of Landscape Architecture." In *Tradition and Innovation in French Garden Art: Chapters of a New History*, ed. J. D. Hunt and M. Conan. Philadelphia: University of Pennsylvania Press, 2002.

Dorgerloh, A. "'Er ist ein Effektstück'—Der Vesuv in der Kunst und Gartenkunst um 1800." *Anzeiger des Germanischen National-Museums* (1997): 71–86.

Downing, A. J. *Landscape Gardening and Rural Architecture*. [New York: Orange Judd Agricultural Book Publisher] New York: Dover Publications, [1865] 1991.

Downing, A. J. *A Treatise on the Theory and Practice of Landscape Gardening*. New York: George P. Putnam, 1850.

Downing, A. J. *A Treatise on the Theory and Practice of Landscape Gardening Adapted to North America*. Introduction by T. O'Malley. Washington, D.C.: Dumbarton Oaks Research Library and Collection, [1841] 1991.

Downing, A. J. *Rural Essays*, ed. G. W. Curtis. New York: Leavitt and Allen, 1857.

Drayton, R. H. *Nature's Government: Science, Imperial Britain, and the "Improvement" of the World*. New Haven, CT: Yale University Press, 2000.

Duempelmann, S., ed. *Pückler and America*. Bulletin of the German Historical Institute, Washington, D.C. Supplement 4, 2007.

Dülmen, A., van. *Das irdische Paradies. Bürgerliche Gartenkultur der Goethezeit*. Köln: Böhlau, 1999.

Duval, M. *La planète des fleurs*. Paris: R. Laffont, 1977.

Edginton, B. "The Design of Moral Architecture at the York Retreat." *Journal of Design History* 16, no. 2 (2003): 103–17.

Eichendorff, J. F., von. *Aus dem Leben eines Taugenichts*. [Berlin: Vereinsbuchhandlung] Stuttgart: Reclam, [1826] 1992.

Elliott, B. "Commercial Horticulture." In *London's Pride: The Glorious History of the Capital's Gardens*, ed. M. Galinou. London: Anaya Publishers, 1990.

Elliott, B. "From the Arboretum to the Woodland Garden." *Garden History* 35, suppl. 2 (2007): 71–83.

Elliott, B. "Gardening Times." *The Garden (Journal of the Royal Horticultural Society)* 118 (1993): 411–13.

Elliott, B. "Historical Revivalism in the Twentieth Century." *Garden History* 28, no. 1 (2000): 17–31.

Elliott, B. "Mosaiculture: Its Origins and Significance." *Garden History* 9, no. 1 (1981): 76–98.

Elliott, B. "The Promotion of Horticulture." In *Sir Joseph Banks: A Global Perspective*, ed. R.E.R. Banks et al. Richmond: Royal Botanic Gardens Kew, 1994.

Elliott, B. *The Royal Horticultural Society: A History 1804–2004*. Chichester: Phillimore, 2004.

Elliott, B. *Victorian Gardens*. London: B. T. Batsford, 1986.

Elliott, B. *Waddesdon Manor: The Garden*. Waddesdon Manor, Bucks: National Trust, 1994.

Elliott, P., C. Watkins, and S. Daniels. "'Combining Science with Recreation and Pleasure': Cultural Geographies of Nineteenth-Century Arboretums." *Garden History* 35, suppl. 2 (2007): 6–27.

Emerson, R. W. *Journals of Ralph Waldo Emerson*, ed. E. W. Emerson and W. E. Forbes. Cambridge, MA: Riverside Press, 1909–14.

Emerson, R. W. "The Young American." In *Nature, Addresses, and Lectures*, ed. R. W. Emerson. Boston: Houghton Mifflin, 1895.

Encke, F. "Der Volkspark." *Die Gartenkunst* 13, no. 8 (1911): 152–58.

Etlin, R. *The Architecture of Death: The Transformation of the Cemetery in Eighteenth-Century Paris*. Cambridge, MA: The MIT Press, 1984.

Evenson, N. *Paris: A Century of Change 1878–1978*. New Haven, CT: Yale University Press, 1979.

Ewen, E., and S. Ewen. *Typecasting: On the Arts and Sciences of Human Inequality, A History of Dominant Ideas*. New York: Seven Stories Press, 2006.

Farou, G., and S. Eloy, eds. *La Collection La Caze. Chefs-d'oeuvre des peintures des XVIIe et XVIIIe siècles*. Paris: Hazan, 2007.

Faucher, D. "Les jardins familiaux et la technique agricole." *Annales: Economies, Sociétés, Civilisations,* 14 (1959): 297–307.

Fein, A. *Frederick Law Olmsted and the American Environmental Tradition*. New York: George Braziller, 1972.

Felix, G. "Die nächsten Umgebungen von Regensburg." *Monatsblatt für die Verbesserung des Landbauwesens und für zweckmäßige Verschönerung des baierischen Landes* 1, no. 4 (1826): 13–15.

Finney, G. *The Counterfeit Idyll: The Garden Ideal and Social Reality in Nineteenth-Century Fiction*. Tübingen: M. Niemeyer, 1984.

Fish, D. T. "Trentham, the Seat of the Duke of Sutherland." *Gardeners' Chronicle,* April 20, 1872, 539–40.

Fishman, R. *Bourgeois Utopias: The Rise and Fall of Suburbia*. New York: Basic Books, 1987.

Flaubert, G. *Bouvard et Pécuchet*. Paris: Garnier Flammarion, 1966.

Flenley, R. "The Avenue Gardens, Regent's Park." In *William Andrews Nesfield: Victorian Landscape Architect*, ed. C. Ridgway. York: Institute of Advanced Architectural Studies, 1996.

Floyd, J. *The Book of Cottage & Villa Gardening*. London: Aldine Publishing, 1900.

Foerster, K. *Vom Blütengarten der Zukunft*. Berlin: Furche-Verlag, 1917.

Foerster, K. *Vom Blütengarten der Zukunft*. 2nd ed. Berlin: Verlag der Gartenschönheit, 1922.

Foerster, K. *Von Landschaft, Garten, Mensch*. Berlin: Heinrich Beenken, 1941.

Foglesong, R. E. *Planning the Capitalist City: The Colonial Era to the 1920s*. Princeton, NJ: Princeton University Press, 1986.

Forestier, J.C.N. *Grandes Villes et Systèmes de Parcs*. Paris: Hachette et Cie., 1906.

Fraser, N. "Rethinking the Public Sphere: A Contribution to the Critique of Actually Existing Democracy." In *Habermas and the Public Sphere*, ed. C. Calhoun. Cambridge, MA: MIT Press, 1994.

Freestone, R. "Greenbelts in City and Regional Planning." In *From Garden City to Green City*, ed. K. C. Parsons and D. Schuyler. Baltimore: Johns Hopkins University Press, 2002.

Freytag, A. "When the Railway Conquered the Garden: Velocity in Parisian and Viennese Parks." In *Landscape Design and the Experience of Motion*, ed. M. Conan, 119–34. Washington, D.C.: Dumbarton Oaks Trustees for Harvard University, 2003.

Friedmann, F. *Zipfel auf! Alles über Gartenzwerge: ein rein wissenschaftliches Lehr- und Lesebuch*. Schaffhausen: Meier Verlag, 1994.

Fuhrmeister, C. "Klatschmohn und Ochsenblut. Zur Ikonographie der Kriegsgräberstätten des Volksbundes Deutsche Kriegsgräberfürsorge." In *Gartenkultur und nationale Identität*, ed. G. Gröning and U. Schneider, 119–34. Worms: Wernersche Verlagsgesellschaft, 2001.

The Gardeners' Chronicle and Agricultural Gazette. August 15, 1863, 771.

The Gardeners' Chronicle and Agricultural Gazette. September 17, 1864, 889.

The Gardeners' Chronicle and Agricultural Gazette. September 30, 1865, 915.

Garfield, S. *Mauve: How One Man Invented a Color That Changed the World*. New York: W. W. Norton, 2001.

Gatchell, C. "Movie Pilferers in Parks." *The Park International* 1 (1920): 149–52.

Gautier, T. *Voyage en Espagne*. Paris: G. Charpentier & Cie., 1890.

Georgel, P. *Monet: Le cycle des Nymphéas; Catalogue sommaire*. Paris: Edition de la Réunion des musées nationaux, 1999.

Gerndt, S. *Idealisierte Natur: die literarische Kontroverse um den Landschaftsgarten des 18. und frühen 19. Jahrhunderts in Deutschland*. Stuttgart: J.B. Metzlersche Verlagsbuchhandlung, 1981.

Gilpin, W. *Remarks on Forest Scenery*. London: Printed for R. Blamire, 1791.

Girouard, M. *Cities and People: A Social and Architectural History*. New Haven, CT: Yale University Press, 1985.

Goethe, J. W., von. *Aus meinem Leben. Dichtung und Wahrheit*. [Halle: Otto Hendel]. English translation by J. Oxenford, *The Autobiography of Goethe: Truth and Poetry; From My Own Life*. London: H. G. Bohn, [1833] 1848.

Goethe, J. W., von. *Die Wahlverwandtschaften*. [Tübingen: s.n.] English translation by R. J. Hollingdale, *Elective Affinities*. Harmondsworth: Penguin, [1809] 1971.

Goethe, J. W., von. *Wilhelm Meister's Apprenticeship*, vol. 14. Harvard Classics Shelf of Fiction. New York: P. F. Collier & Son, 1917. Available online: http://www.bartleby.com/314/.

Goethe, J. W., von. "Wilhelm Meister's Journeyman Years," trans. K. Winston. In *Goethe: The Collected Works*, Vol. 10, ed. J. K. Brown. New York: Princeton University Press, [1809] 1971.

Gorer, R. *The Growth of Gardens*. London: Faber and Faber, 1978.

Gould, E.R.L. "Park Areas and Open Spaces in Cities." *American Statistical Association* 2–3 (1888): 49–61.

Goury, J., and O. Jones. *Plans, Elevations, Sections, and Details of the Alhambra, from Drawings taken on the Spot … in 1834 and 1837*. London: Owen Jones, 1842–1845.

Granet, F.M. "Memoirs of the Painter Granet," trans. and anno. J. Focarino. In *François-Marius Granet: Watercolors from the Musée Granet at Aix-en-Provence*, ed. E. Munhall. New York: The Frick Collection, [1802] 1988.

Green, D. *Gardener to Queen Anne: Henry Wise (1653–1738) and the Formal Garden*. London: Oxford University Press, 1956.

Green, N. *The Spectacle of Nature: Landscape and Bourgeois Culture in Nineteenth Century France*. Manchester: Manchester University Press; New York: St. Martin's Press, 1990.

Greenhalgh, P. *Ephemeral Vistas: The Expositions Universelles, Great Exhibitions, and World's Fairs, 1851–1939*. Manchester: Manchester University Press; New York: St. Martin's Press, 1988.

Grese, R. E. "The Prairie Gardens of O. C. Simonds and Jens Jensen." In *Regional Garden Design in the United States*, ed. T. O'Malley and M. Treib. Dumbarton Oaks Colloquium on the History of Landscape Architecture, vol. 15. Washington, D.C.: Dumbarton Oaks, 1995.

Grignan, G. T. "Le Congrès International des Jardins Ouvriers." *Revue Horticole* (1903): 531–32.

Groenewegen, P. D. *The French Connection: Some Case Studies of French Influence on British Economics in the Eighteenth Century*, report no. 202. Sydney: Department of Economics, University of Sydney, 1994.

Groenewegen, P. D. "La 'French Connection': Influences Françaises sur l'Economie Politique Britannique." *Dix-Huitième Siècle* 26 (1994): 15–36.

Groeningen, I., van. "Hidcote Manor Garden: Hidcote Bartrim, Gloucerstershire, England." In *Chicago Botanic Garden Encyclopedia of Gardening: History and Design*, vol. 1, ed. C. A. Shoemaker. Chicago: Fitzroy Dearborn Publishers, 2001.

Gröning, G. "Anmerkungen zu Gustav Vorherrs Idee der Landesverschönerung." In *Umweltgeschichte. Methoden, Themen, Potentiale*, ed. G. Bayerl, N. Fuchsloch, and T. Meyer. Cottbuser Studien zur Geschichte von Technik, Arbeit und Umwelt, vol. 1. Münster: Waxmann, 1996.

Gröning, G. "Barth, Erwin 1880–1933: German Landscape Architect." In *Chicago Botanic Garden Encyclopedia of Gardening: History and Design*, vol. 1, ed. C. A. Shoemaker. Chicago: Fitzroy Dearborn Publishers, 2001.

Gröning, G. "Das Gut Reichenbach (Radaczewo), Pommern—eine musterhaft verschönerte Feldflur?" In *Die "Ornamental Farm," Gartenkunst und Landwirtschaft*, ed. Stiftung Fürst-Pückler-Park Bad Muskau. Zittau: Graphische Werkstätten, 2010.

Gröning, G. "Die goldene Axt. Wachstum und Kontrolle in Pücklers Schriften - autopoietische Kräfte in der Konzeption des Landschaftsgartens." In *Von selbst, Autopoietische Verfahren in der Ästhetik des 19. Jahrhunderts*, ed. F. Weltzien. Berlin: Reimer, 2006.

Gröning, G. "Ideological Aspects of Nature Garden Concepts in Late Twentieth-Century Germany." In *Nature and Ideology: Natural Garden Design in the Twentieth Century*, ed. J. Wolschke-Bulmahn. Dumbarton Oaks Colloquium on the History of Landscape Architecture, vol. 18. Washington, D.C.: Dumbarton Oaks, 1997.

Gröning, G. "The Idea of Land Embellishment." *Journal of Garden History* 12 (1992): 164–82.

Gröning, G., and U. Schneider. "Gut Reichenbach (Radaczewo), Pommern—Modellhafte landwirtschaftliche Einflüsse bei einer Gutsanlage der ersten Hälfte des 19. Jahrhunderts." In *Landgüter in den Regionen des gemeinsamen Kulturerbes von*

Deutschen und Polen—Entstehung, Verfall und Bewahrung, Maj tki ziemskie na obszarze wspólnego dziedzictwa polsko-niemieckiego—problemy rozwoju, degradacji i konserwacji, Das Gemeinsame Kulturerbe—Wspólne Dziedzictwo, Vol. 4/ Tom IV, Instytut Sztuki PAN, ed. B. Pusback and J. Skuratowicz. Warszawa: Instytut Sztuki PAN, 2007.

Gröning, G., and J. Wolschke-Bulmahn. *1887–1987, DGGL Deutsche Gesellschaft für Gartenkunst und Landschaftspflege e.V. Ein Rückblick auf 100 Jahre DGGL.* Schriftenreihe der Deutschen Gesellschaft für Gartenkunst und Landschaftspflege, vol. 10, ed. Deutsche Gesellschaft für Gartenkunst und Landschaftspflege. Berlin: Boskett Verlag, 1987.

Gröning, G., and J. Wolschke-Bulmahn. *Die Liebe zur Landschaft. Teil III. Der Drang nach Osten, Zur Entwicklung der Landespflege im Nationalsozialismus und während des Zweiten Weltkrieges in den "eingegliederten Ostgebieten."* Arbeiten zur sozialwissenschaftlich orientierten Freiraumplanung, vol. 9, ed. U. Herlyn and G. Gröning. München: Minerva Publikation, 1987.

Guratzsch, H., and H. J. Neyer. *Wilhelm Busch. Die Bildergeschichten. Historisch-kritische Gesamtausgabe in drei Bänden.* Hannover: Schlütersche, 2002.

Gutowski, R. R., ed. *Victorian Landscape in America: The Garden as Artifact.* Proceedings from the Centennial Symposium, Morris Arboretum of the University of Pennsylvania, June 16, 1988.

Habermann, S. *Bayreuther Gartenkunst, Die Gärten der Markgrafen von Brandenburg-Culmbach im 17. und 18. Jahrhundert.* Grüne Reihe, Quellen und Forschungen zur Gartenkunst. Vol. 6. Worms: Wernersche Verlagsgesellschaft, 1982.

Haddad, H. *Le jardin des peintres.* Paris: Hazan, 2000.

Hall, S., and P. Du Gay, eds. *Questions of Cultural Identity.* Thousand Oaks, CA: Sage, 1996.

Harding, J., and A. Taigel. "An Air of Detachment: Town Gardens in the Eighteenth and Nineteenth Centuries." *Garden History* 24, no. 2 (1996): 237–54.

Hardy, S., and A. G. Ingham. "Games, Structures, and Agency: Historians on the American Play Movement." *Journal of Social Science* 17 (1983): 285–301.

Harris, D. "Women as Gardeners." In *Chicago Botanic Garden Encyclopedia of Gardening: History and Design*, vol. 1, ed. C. A. Shoemaker. Chicago: Fitzroy Dearborn Publishers, 2001.

Hartlaub, G. F. *Der Gartenzwerg und seine Ahnen.* Heidelberg: Heinz Moos Verlag, 1962.

Hartley, B. "Sites of Knowledge and Instruction: Arboretums and the Arboretum et Fruticetum Britannicum." *Garden History* 35, suppl. 2 (2007): 28–52.

Haskell, T. L. *The Emergence of Professional Social Science: The American Social Science Association and the Nineteenth-Century Crisis of Authority.* Baltimore: Johns Hopkins University Press, 2000.

Hawkins, K. "The Therapeutic Landscape: Nature, Architecture, and Mind in Nineteenth-Century America." Ph.D. diss., University of Rochester, 1991.

Hawthorne, N. *Mosses From an Old Manse.* [New York: Wiley and Putnam] New York: Modern Library, [1846] 2003.

Hayden, D. *Building Suburbia: Green Fields and Urban Growth, 1820–2000.* New York: Pantheon Books, 2003.

Heick, G. "Der Naturschutzpark in den Parkanlagen." *Die Gartenkunst* 13, no. 12 (1911): 223–27.

Helmreich, A. *The English Garden and National Identity: The Competing Styles of Garden Design, 1870–1914*. Cambridge: Cambridge University Press, 2000.

Helphand, K. I. *Defiant Gardens: Making Gardens in Wartime*. San Antonio, TX: Trinity University Press, 2006.

Henkel, K., and C. Bohlmann. *Garten des Lebens: ein Wandschirm von Pierre Bonnard*. Köln: DuMont, 2002.

Hennebo, D., and A. Hoffmann. *Geschichte der deutschen Gartenkunst*. Vol. 3. *Der Landschaftsgarten*. Koenigstein: Otto Koeltz Science Publishers, [1965] 1981.

Herbert, E. W. *Flora's Empire: British Gardens in India*. Philadelphia: University of Pennsylvania Press, 2011.

Herbert, E. W. "The Taj and the Raj: Garden Imperialism in India." *Studies in the History of Gardens & Designed Landscapes* 25, no. 4 (2005): 250–72.

Herbert, R. L., ed. *The Art Criticism of John Ruskin*. New York: Da Capo Press, 1987.

Heriz-Smith, S. *The House of Veitch*. Privately published, 2000.

Hermand, J. "Rousseau, Goethe, Humboldt: Their Influence on Later Advocates of the Nature Garden." In *Nature and Ideology: Natural Garden Design in the Twentieth Century*, ed. J. Wolschke-Bulmahn. Washington, D.C.: Dumbarton Oaks, 1997.

Herrington, S. "Kindergartens: Shaping Childhood from Bad Blankenburg to Boston." *Die Gartenkunst* 18, no. 1 (2006): 81–95.

Hesse, H. *Siddhartha*. Berlin: S. Fischer, 1922.

Hickman, C. "The Picturesque at Brislington House, Bristol: The Role of Landscape in Relation to the Treatment of Mental Illness in the Early Nineteenth-Century Asylum." *Garden History* 33, no. 1 (2005): 47–60.

Hinz, G. *Peter Josef Lenné*. Berlin: Deutscher Kunstverlag, 1937.

Hinze, V. "The Re-Creation of John Nash's Regency Gardens at the Royal Pavilion, Brighton." *Garden History* 24, no. 1 (1996): 45–53.

Hirsch, E. *Dessau-Wörlitz, Zierde und Inbegriff des 18. Jahrhunderts*. München: Verlag C.H. Beck, 1988.

Hobsbawm, E. "Introduction: Inventing Traditions." In *The Invention of Tradition*, ed. E. Hobsbawm and T. Ranger. Cambridge: Cambridge University Press, 1983.

Hockaday, J. *Greenscapes: Olmsted's Pacific Northwest*. Pullman, WA: Washington State University Press, 2009.

Hoffman, A., von. "'Of Greater Lasting Consequence'? Frederick Law Olmsted and the Fate of Franklin Park, Boston." *Journal of the Society of Architectural Historians* 47 (1988): 339–50.

Hoffmann, N. E., and J. C. Van Horne, eds. *America's Curious Botanist: A Tercentennial Reappraisal of John Bartram*. Philadelphia, PA: American Philosophical Society, 2004.

Hoschedé, E. "Les Femmes artistes," *L'Art de la mode* (April 1881). Reprinted in *The New Painting: Impressionism 1874–1886; Documentation*, 2 vols., ed. R. Berson. San Francisco, CA: Fine Arts Museums of San Francisco, 1996.

Howard, E. *To-morrow: A Peaceful Path to Real Reform*. London: Routledge, [1898] 2003.

Howoldt, J. E., and U. M. Schneede. *Im Garten von Max Liebermann*. Berlin: Nicolai, 2004.

Humboldt, A., von. *Ideen zu einer Physiognomik der Gewächse*. Tübingen: Cotta, 1806.

Hunt, J. D. *Gardens and the Picturesque*. Cambridge, MA: MIT Press, 1997.

Hunt, J. D. *Greater Perfections: The Practice of Garden Theory*. Philadelphia: University of Pennsylvania Press, 2000.

Hunt, J. D. *The Afterlife of Gardens*. Philadelphia: University of Pennsylvania Press, 2004.

Hunt, J. D., and P. Willis, eds. *The Genius of the Place: The English Landscape Garden 1620–1820*. Cambridge, MA: MIT Press, 1988.

Hunt, T. *Building Jerusalem: The Rise and Fall of the Victorian City*. New York: Henry Holt, 2005.

Husslein-Arco, A., ed. *Gartenlust. Der Garten in der Kunst*. Vienna: Brandstätter, 2007.

Huth, G., ed. *Allgemeines Magazin für die bürgerliche Baukunst* [special issue] 1, no. 2 (1790).

Hyson, J. "Jungles of Eden: The Design of American Zoos." In *Environmentalism in Landscape Architecture*, ed. M. Conan. Washington, D.C. Dumbarton Oaks, 2000.

Illingworth, J. "Ruskin and Gardening." *Garden History* 22, no. 2 (1994): 218–23.

Imbert, D. *The Modernist Garden in France*. New Haven, CT: Yale University Press, 1993.

Ireland, K. *Cythera Regained? The Rococo Revival in European Literature and the Arts, 1830–1910*. Cranbury, NJ: Fairleigh Dickinson University Press, 2006.

Irving, R. G. *Indian Summer: Lutyens, Baker, and Imperial Delhi*. New Haven, CT: Yale University Press, 1981.

Irving, W. *The Alhambra; or, The New Sketch Book (Tales of the Alhambra)*. Paris: A. & W. Galignani, 1832.

Jacques, D. *Georgian Gardens: The Reign of Nature*. London: B. T. Batsford, 1983.

Jäger, H. *Die Verwendung der Pflanzen in der Gartenkunst, oder Gehölz, Blumen und Rasen*. Gotha: Scheube; Darmstadt: Leske, 1858.

James, H. *The Aspern Papers: The Novels and Tales of Henry James*, vol. 12. New York: C. Scribner's Sons.

James, N.D.G. *A History of English Forestry*. Oxford: Basil Blackwell, 1990.

Janson, F. *Pomona's Harvest*. Portland, OR: Timber Press, 1996.

Jauss, H. R. *Toward an Aesthetic of Reception*. Translated by Timothy Bahti. Minneapolis: University of Minnesota Press, 1982.

Jekyll, G. *Gardens for Small Country Houses*. London: Country Life; New York: C. Scribner's Sons, 1913.

Jennings, A. *Victorian Gardens*. London: English Heritage and the Museum of Garden History, 2005.

Johnson, N. C. "Names, Labels and Planting Regimes: Regulating Trees at Glasnevin Botanic Gardens, Dublin, 1795–1850." *Garden History* 35, suppl. 2 (2007): 56.

Jones, D. "Designing the Adelaide Parklands in the 1880s: The Proposals of John Ednie Brown." *Studies in the History of Gardens & Designed Landscapes* 18, no. 4 (1998): 287–99.

Jones, H. S. "Recreation Tendencies in America." *Annals of the American Academy of Political and Social Science* 105 (1923): 243–50.

Jordan, H. "Public Parks, 1885–1914." *Garden History* 22, no. 1 (1994): 85–113.

Jühlke, F. *Die Königliche Landesbaumschule und Gärtnerlehranstalt zu Potsdam*. Berlin: Weigandt & Hempel, 1872.

Kames, H. H. *Elements of Criticism*, vol. 3. Edinburgh: A. Millar, 1762.

Kent, N. *Hints to Gentlemen of Landed Property*. London: J. Dodsley, 1775.

Kidd, A., and D. Nicholls, eds. *The Making of the British Middle Class*. Stroud, Gloucestershire: Sutton Publishing, 1998.

King, A. *Colonial Urban Development: Culture, Social Power and Environment*. London: Routledge & Kegan Paul, 1976.

King, G. *The Mad King: The Life and Times of Ludwig II of Bavaria*. Secaucus: Birch Lane Press, 1996.

Kirchner, F. *Der Central Park in New York und der Einfluss der deutschen Gartentheorie und –praxis auf seine Gestaltung*. Worms: Wernersche Verlagsgesellschaft, 2002.

Klein, B. *Die physiokratische Verlandschaftung der Stadt um 1800: Städtebau und Stadtauflösung in der Realität von Freiburg im Breisgau sowie in der Utopie des französischen Revolutionsarchitekten Ledoux*. Beiträge zur Kunstwissenschaft. Vol. 46. Munich: Scaneg, 1993.

Knaut, A. *Zurück zur Natur! die Wurzeln der Ökologiebewegung*. Greven: Kilda-Verlag, 1993.

Koch, H. *Gartenkunst im Städtebau*. Berlin: E. Wasmuth, 1914.

Kohlstedt, S. G. "'A Better Crop of Boys and Girls': The School Gardening Movement, 1890–1920." *History of Education Quarterly* 48, no. 1 (2008): 58–93.

Komara, A. "Concrete and the Engineered Picturesque: The Parc des Buttes Chaumont (Paris, 1867)." *Journal of Architectural Education* 58, no. 1 (2004): 5–12.

Koppelkamp, S. *Glasshouses and Wintergardens of the Nineteenth Century*. New York: Rizzoli, 1981.

Laborde, comte de, A. *Description des nouveaux jardins de la France et de ses anciens châteaux: mêlée d'observations sur la vie de la campagne et la composition des jardins = Description of the modern gardens and ancient castles in France: with local observations on rural life and gardening = Beschreibung der neuen Gärten und alten Schlösser in Frankreich: mit Bemerkungen über Landleben und Gartenanlagen*. Paris: Connaissance et Mémoires, [1808] 2004.

Ladd, F. J. *Architects at Corsham Court*. Bradford-on-Avon: Moonraker Press, 1978.

Laird, M. "American Gardens." In *Chicago Botanic Garden Encyclopedia of Gardening: History and Design*, vol. 1, ed. C. A. Shoemaker. Chicago: Fitzroy Dearborn Publishers, 2001.

Laird, M. "Approaches to Planting in the Late Eighteenth Century: Some Imperfect Ideas on the Origins of the American Garden." *Journal of Garden History* 11, no. 3 (1991): 154–72.

Laird, M. "'A Cloth of Tissue of Divers Colours': The English Flower Border, 1660–1735." *Garden History* 21, no. 2 (1993): 158–205.

Laird, M. "*Corbeille, Parterre* and *Treillage*: The Case of Humphry Repton's Penchant for the French Style of Planting." *Journal of Garden History* 16, no. 3 (1996): 153–69.

Laird, M. "The Culture of Horticulture: Class, Consumption, and Gender in the English Landscape Garden." In *Bourgeois and Aristocratic Cultural Encounters in Garden Art, 1550–1850*, ed. M. Conan. Washington, D.C.: Dumbarton Oaks, 2002.

Laird, M. *The Flowering of the Landscape Garden: English Pleasure Grounds, 1720–1800*. Philadelphia: University of Pennsylvania Press, 1999.

Laird, M. "From Bouquets to Baskets." *The Magazine Antiques, "England"* (June 2000): 932–39.

Laird, M. "From Callicarpa to Catalpa: The Impact of Mark Catesby's Plant Introductions on English Gardens of the Eighteenth Century." In *Empire's Nature: Mark Catesby's New World Vision*, ed. A.R.W. Meyers and M. B. Pritchard. Chapel Hill: University of North Carolina Press, 1998.

Laird, M. "Ornamental Planting and Horticulture in English Pleasure Grounds, 1700–1830." In *Garden History: Issues, Approaches, Methods*, ed. J. D. Hunt. Washington, D.C.: Dumbarton Oaks, 1992.

Laird, M. "Rekonstruktion des Herrengartens entsprechend der Pücklerschen Grundkonzeption." Unpublished report for the Stiftung "Fürst-Pückler-Park Bad Muskau" (November), 2001.

Lamb, H. H. *Climate, History and the Modern World*. 2nd ed. New York: Routledge, 1995.

Lambert, D. "Rituals of Transgression in Public Parks in Britain, 1846 to the Present." In *Performance and Appropriation: Profane Rituals in Gardens and Landscapes*, ed. M. Conan. Washington, D.C.: Dumbarton Oaks Research Library and Collection, 2007.

Land, D., and J. Wenzel. *Heimat, Natur und Weltstadt. Leben und Werk des Gartenarchitekten Erwin Barth*. Leipzig: Koehler und Amelang, 2005.

Lange, W. "Bilder aus der Gebirgslandschaft." *Die Gartenwelt* 5, no. 7 (1900): 74.

Lange, W. *Der Garten und seine Bepflanzung*. Stuttgart: Kosmos, Gesellschaft der Naturfreunde, 1913.

Lange, W. "Die Pflanzung im Garten nach physiognomischen Grundsätzen." *Die Gartenkunst* 6, no. 9 (1904): 169.

Lange, W. "Gartengedanken." *Die Gartenkunst*, 5 (1903): 100–102.

Lange, W. *Gartengestaltung der Neuzeit*. Leipzig: J. J. Weber, 1907.

Lange, W. "In welcher Weise kann der modernen Kunstrichtung in der Gartenkunst praktisch Rechnung getragen werden?" *Die Gartenkunst* 6, no. 5 (1904): 98.

Lange, W. "Meine Anschauungen über die Gartengestaltung unserer Zeit." *Die Gartenkunst* 7, no. 7 (1905): 114.

Lanman, S. W. "Colour in the Garden: 'Malignant Magenta.'" *Garden History* 28, no. 2 (2000): 209–21.

La Padula, A. *Roma, 1809–1814: contributo alla storia dell'urbanistica*. Rome: Fratelli Palombi, 1958.

Lasch, C., ed. *The Social Thought of Jane Addams*. New York: Bobbs-Merrill, 1965.

Lasdun, S. *The English Park: Royal, Private and Public*. New York: Vendome Press, 1992.

Laurie, K. "Humphry Repton 1752–1818: New Discoveries." *The Garden (Journal of the Royal Horticultural Society)* 108 (1983): 361–66.

Lauterbach, I. "Introduction." In *Georges-Louis Le Rouge, Détail des nouveaux jardins à la mode*. Reprint, Nördlingen: Dr. Alfons Uhl, 2009.

Lawrence, H. W. *City Trees: A Historical Geography from the Renaissance through the Nineteenth Century*. Charlottesville: University of Virginia Press, 2006.

Lawson, L. J. *City Bountiful: A Century of Community Gardening in America*. Berkeley: University of California Press, 2005.

Le Bon, L., and D. Lavergne. *Des nains, des sculptures*. Catalog of the exhibition "2000 nains à Bagatelle." Paris: Publications Artistiques Françaises, 2000.

Le Dantec, D., and J.-P. Le Dantec. *Reading the French Garden: Story and History*. Translated by Jessica Levine. Cambridge, MA: MIT Press, 1990.

Leighton, A. *American Gardens of the Nineteenth Century*. Amherst: University of Massachusetts Press, 1987.

Lekan, T. M. *Imagining the Nation in Nature: Landscape Preservation and German Identity, 1885–1945*. Cambridge, MA: Harvard University Press, 2004.

Le Rouge, G.-L. *Jardins anglo-chinois, ou, Détails de nouveaux jardins à la mode*. Paris: Connaissance et mémoires, [1774–91] 2000–2004.

Levee, A. "The Olmsted Brothers' Residential Communities: A Preview of a Career Legacy." In *The Landscape Universe: Historic Designed Landscapes in Context*, ed. C. Birnbaum. Wave Hill, NY: National Park Service and Catalog of Landscape Records in the United States, 1993.

Lewis, R. "Frontier and Civilization in the Thought of Frederick Law Olmsted." *American Quarterly* 29 (1977): 385–403.

Lieberman, L. "Romanticism and the Culture of Suicide in Nineteenth-Century France." *Comparative Studies in Society and History* 33, no. 3 (1991): 611–29.

Limido, L. *L'art des jardins sous le second empire: Jean-Pierre Barillet-Deschamps*. Seyssel: Éditions Champ Vallon, 2002.

Limido, L. "Un paysagiste français d'envergure internationale: Jean-Pierre Barillet-Deschamps, maître d'Édouard André." In *Édouard André (1840–1911) un paysagiste botaniste sur les chemins du monde*, ed. F. André and S. de Courtois. Besançon: Éditions de l'Imprimeur, 2001.

Linden, B.M.G. *Silent City on a Hill: Picturesque Landscapes of Memory and Boston's Mount Auburn Cemetery*. Amherst: University of Massachusetts Press in association with Library of American Landscape History, 2007.

Lindley, J. "On the Arrangement of Gardens and Pleasure-Grounds in the Elizabethan Age." *Journal of the Horticultural Society* 3 (1848): 1–15.

Longfellow, H. W. *The Song of Hiawatha*. Rutland, VT: Charles E. Tuttle, 1975.

Longstaffe-Gowan, T. *The London Town Garden 1740–1840*. New Haven, CT: Yale University Press, 2001.

Loti, P. *Le roman d'un enfant*. Paris: Calmann-lévy. English translation by Caroline F. Smith, *The Story of a Child*. Boston: C. C. Birchard, 1901.

Loudon, J. C. *An Encyclopaedia of Gardening*. London: Longman, Brown, Green, and Longmans, 1850.

Loudon, J. C. *The Landscape Gardening and Landscape Architecture of the Late Humphry Repton*. London: Privately published, 1840.

Loudon, J. C. *A Manual of Cottage Gardening*. Privately published, 1830.

Loudon, J. C. *Observations on the Formation and Management of Useful and Ornamental Plantations*. Edinburgh: Constable; London: Longman Hurst Rees & Orme, 1804.

Loudon, J. C. *On the Laying Out, Planting, and Managing of Cemeteries*. London: Longman, 1843.

Loudon, J. C. "The Principles of Landscape-Gardening and of Landscape-Architecture applied to the Laying Out of Public Cemeteries and the Improvement of Churchyards [...]." *Gardener's Magazine* 19 (March 1843): 104–5.

Loudon, J. C. *Remarks on the Construction of Hothouses*. London: Richard and Arthur Taylor, 1817.

Loudon, J. C. *The Suburban Gardener and Villa Companion*. London: Longman, Orme, Brown, Breen, and Longmans; Edinburgh: W. Black, 1838.

Loudon, J. W. *The Ladies' Companion to the Flower Garden*. London: W. Smith, 1841.

Loudon, J. W. *The Lady's Country Companion; or, How to Enjoy a Country Life Rationally*. London: Longman, Brown, Green, and Longmans, 1845.

Lowen, J. W. *Lies across America: What Our Historic Sites Get Wrong*. New York: The New York Press, 1999.

Mabil, L. *Teoria dell'arte dei giardini*. Bassano, 1801.

MacDonald, J. "Statistics of the Bloomingdale Asylum for the Insane." *New York Journal of Medicine and Surgery* 1 (1839): 307–43.

MacDougall, E. B., ed. *John Claudius Loudon and the Early Nineteenth Century in Great Britain*. Washington, D.C.: Dumbarton Oak, 1980.

Machor, J. L. *Pastoral Cities: Urban Ideals and the Symbolic Landscape of America*. Madison: University of Wisconsin Press, 1987.

MacKenzie, J. M. *Orientalism: History, Theory and the Arts*. Manchester: Manchester University Press, 1995.

Major, J. *To Live in the New World: A.J. Downing and American Landscape Gardening*. Cambridge, MA: MIT Press, 1997.

Mans, O. "Les Vingtistes parisiens." *L'Art modern* (June 27, 1886). Reprinted in *The New Painting: Impressionism 1874–1886; Documentation*, 2 vols., ed. R. Berson. San Francisco, CA: Fine Arts Museums of San Francisco.

Marcus, S. T. "Town Gardens of London 1820–1914: A Study of Domestic Horticulture." Thesis, Architectural Association, London, 1990.

Marcuse, H. *Legacies of Dachau: The Use and Abuse of a Concentration Camp, 1933–2001*. Cambridge: Cambridge University Press, 2001.

Marsh, G. P. *Man and Nature*. Cambridge, MA: The Belknap Press of Harvard University Press, [1864] 1965.

Marulli, V. *L'arte di ordinare i giardini*. Napoli: Stamperia Simoniana, 1804.

Marx, L. 1964. *The Machine in the Garden: Technology and the Pastoral Ideal in America*. New York: Oxford University Press, 1964.

Mayor, J. *To Live in the New World: A.J. Downing and American Gardening*. Cambridge, MA: MIT Press, 1997.

McClelland, L. F. *Building the National Parks*. Baltimore: Johns Hopkins University Press, 1998.

McCracken, D. P. *Gardens of Empire: Botanical Institutions of the Victorian British Empire*. London: Leicester University Press, 1997.

McKay, C. D. *The French Garden in England*. London: Daily Mail, 1909.

McKeever, W. A. "A Better Crop of Boys and Girls." *Nature-Study Review* 7 (1911): 266–68.

Metcalf, T. R. *An Imperial Vision: Indian Architecture and Britain's Raj.* Berkeley: University of California Press, 1989.

Migge, L. *Die Gartenkultur des 20. Jahrhunderts.* Jena: E. Diederichs, 1913.

Miller, W. *The Prairie Spirit in Landscape Gardening.* Urbana: University of Illinois Agricultural Experiment Station, 1915.

Miller, W. *What England Can Teach Us about Gardening.* Garden City, NY: Doubleday, Page, 1911.

Milton, J. *Paradise Lost.* London: John Bumpus, 1821.

Moran, D. M. *The Allotment Movement in Britain.* New York: Peter Lang, 1990.

Morgan, J., and A. Richards. *A Paradise Out of a Common Field.* London: Century, 1990.

Morgan, K. *Shaping an American Landscape: The Art and Architecture of Charles A. Platt.* Hanover, NH: Hood Museum of Art, University Press of New England, 1995.

Morris, M. S. "'Tha'lt Be Like a Blush-Rose When Tha' Grows Up, My Little Lass': English Cultural and Gendered Identity in *The Secret Garden*." *Environment and Planning D: Society and Space* 14 (1996): 59–78.

Morris, W. *Art and Beauty of the Earth.* Lecture delivered at Burslem Town Hall on October 13, 1881. London: Longmans, 1898.

Mosser, M., and G. Teyssot. *The History of Garden Design: The Western Tradition from the Renaissance to the Present Day.* London: Thames and Hudson, 1991.

Mosser, M., M. Duchêne, C. Frange, M. Baridon, J. Frange, and J. Moulin. *Le style Duchêne: Henri & Achille Duchêne: architectes paysagistes 1841–1947.* Neuilly: Editions du Labyrinthe, 1998.

Müller, D. "Ackerbau und Gärtnerei." *Hamburger Garten- und Blumenzeitung* (1855): 433–41.

Nadenicek, D. J. "Commemoration in the Landscape of Minnehaha: 'A Halo of Poetic Association.'" In *Places of Commemoration: Search of Identity and Landscape Design*, ed. J. Wolschke-Bulmahn. Washington, D.C.: Dumbarton Oaks, 2001.

Nadenicek, D. J. "Emerson's Aesthetic and Natural Design: A Theoretical Foundation for the Work of Horace William Shaler Cleveland." In *Nature and Ideology: Natural Garden Design in the Twentieth Century*, ed. J. Wolschke-Bulmahn. Washington, D.C.: Dumbarton Oaks, 1997.

Nadenicek, D. J. "Frederick Billings: The Intellectual and Practical Influences on Forest Planting, 1823–1899." Unpublished Report to Marsh-Billings-Rockefeller National Historical Park, 2003.

Nadenicek, D. J. "Nature in the City: Horace Cleveland's Aesthetic." *Landscape and Urban Planning* 26 (1993): 5–15.

Nash, R. F. *Wilderness & the American Mind.* New Haven, CT: Yale University Press, [1967] 2001.

Neale, A. "The Garden Designs of E. L. Bateman." *Garden History* 33, no. 2 (2006): 225–55.

Nicolson, M. "Alexander von Humboldt, Humboldtian Science and the Origins of the Study of Vegetation." *History of Science* 25 (1987): 167–94.

Noehles-Doerk, G., ed. *Kunst in Spanien im Blick des Fremden. Reiseerfahrungen vom Mittelalter bis in die Gegenwart*. Frankfurt am Main: Vervuert, 1996.

Nolen, J. "Parks and Recreational Facilities in the United States." *Annals of the American Academy of Political and Social Science* 35 (1910): 1–12.

Nolin, C. "Public Parks in Gothenburg and Jönköping: Secluded Idylls for Swedish Townfolk." *Garden History* 32, no. 2 (2004): 197–212.

Nolin, C. *Till stadsbornas nytta och förlustande: den offentliga parken i Sverige under 1800-talet*. Stockholm: Byggförlaget, 1999.

Nouvel-Kammerer, O., ed. *Papiers peints panoramiques*. Paris: Flammarion, 1990.

Olmsted, F. L. "Park." In *American Cyclopedia*. Reprinted in *The Papers of Frederick Law Olmsted*. Supplementary Series, vol. 1. *Writings on Public Parks, Parkways, and Park Systems*, ed. C. E. Beveridge, C. F. Hoffman, and K. Hawkins. Baltimore: Johns Hopkins University Press, [1875] 1997.

Olmsted, F. L. "Public Parks and the Enlargement of Towns." *Journal of Social Science* 3 (1871): 1–36.

Olmsted, F. L. *Writings on Public Parks, Parkways and Park Systems*, ed. C. E. Beveridge and C. F. Hoffman. Baltimore: Johns Hopkins University Press, 1997.

Olmsted, F. L., Jr., and T. Kimball, eds. *Forty Years of Landscape Architecture, Central Park*. Cambridge, MA: MIT Press, 1973.

Olmsted, Vaux, and Company. *The Preliminary Report upon the Proposed Suburban Village at Riverside, near Chicago*. New York: Sutton, Bowne, 1868.

O'Malley, T. "Art and Science in the Design of Botanic Gardens, 1730–1830." In *Garden History: Issues, Approaches, Methods*, ed. J. D. Hunt. Washington, D.C.: Dumbarton Oaks, 1992.

O'Malley, T. *Glasshouses: The Architecture of Light and Air*. New York: The New York Botanical Garden, 2005.

O'Malley, T. "'A Public Museum of Trees': Mid-Nineteenth Century Plans for the Mall." In *The Mall in Washington, 1791–1848*, ed. R. Longstreth. National Gallery of Art, Studies in the History of Art 30. Washington, D.C.: Trustees of the National Gallery of Art, 1991.

O'Malley, T. "'Your Garden Must Be a Museum to You': Early American Botanic Gardens." In *Art and Science in America: Issues of Representation*, ed. A.R.W. Meyers. San Marino, CA: Huntington Library, 1998.

O'Malley, T., E. Kryder-Reid, and A. L. Helmreich. *Keywords in Americam Landscape Design*. Washington, D.C.: CASVA; New Haven, CT: Yale University Press, 2010.

O'Malley, T., and M. Treib, eds. *Regional Garden Design in the United States*. Dumbarton Oaks Colloquium on the History of Landscape Architecture, vol. 15. Washington, D.C.: Dumbarton Oaks, 1995.

Oman, C. C., and J. Hamilton. *Wallpapers: A History and Illustrated Catalogue of the Collection of the Victoria and Albert Museum*. London: Sotheby Publ., 1982.

Pack, C. L. *The War Garden Victorious*. Philadelphia: J. B. Lippincott, 1919.

Paolini, C. *Il sistema del verde. Il viale dei colli e la Firenze di Giuseppe Poggi nell'Europa dell'Ottocento*. Florence: Edizione Polistampa, 2004.

Parshall, L. "C. C. L. Hirschfeld's Concept of the Garden in the German Enlightenment." *Journal of Garden History* 13, no. 13 (1993): 125–71.

Parshall, L. "Hirschfeld, Pückler, Poe—The Literary Modeling of Nature." In *Pückler and America*, ed. S. Duempelmann. Bulletin of the German Historical Institute, Washington, D.C., Supplement 4, 2007.

Parshall, L., ed. *Theory of Garden Art by C.C.L.Hirschfeld*. Philadelphia: University of Pennsylvania Press, 2001.

Pastiaux-Thiriat, G., and J. Pastiaux. *Un créateur de papiers peints, Joseph Dufour 1754–1827*. Tramayes: Syndicat d'initiative de Tramayes, 2000.

Peckham, M. *The Birth of Romanticism*. Greenwood, FL: Penkevill Publishing, 1986.

Percier, C., and P.-F.-L. Fontaine. *Choix des plus célèbres maisons de plaisance de Rome et de ses environs*. Paris: P. Didot l'aîné: Discours préliminaire, 1809.

Perry, F. *Water Gardening*. London: Country Life, 1938.

Pescott, R.T.M. *The Royal Botanic Gardens Melbourne: A History from 1845 to 1970*. Melbourne: Oxford University Press, 1982.

Pettigrew, W. W. "The Influence of Air Pollution on Vegetation." *Gardeners' Chronicle* 2 (1928): 292, 308–9, 335.

Pevsner, N. *A History of Building Types*. London: Thames and Hudson, 1976.

Pevsner, N. *Some Architectural Writers of the Nineteenth Century*. Oxford: Clarendon Press, 1972.

Pfeiffer, I. *Impressionistinnen—Berthe Morisot, Mary Cassatt, Eva Gonzalès, Marie Bracquemond*. Ostfildern: Hatje Cantz, 2008.

Philipp, K. J. *Karl Friedrich Schinkel: Späte Projekte/Karl Friedrich Schinkel: Late Projects*. Stuttgart: Menges, 2000.

Poe, E. A. *The Complete Tales and Poems of Edgar Allen Poe*. New York: Vintage Books, 1975.

Prangey, G., de. *Souvenirs de Grenade et de l'Alhambra*. Paris: Veith et Hauser, 1837.

Proust, M. *Jean Santeuil*. [Paris: Gallimard]. English translation by G. Hopkins. New York: Simon and Schuster, [1952] 1956.

Proust, M. *Remembrance of Things Past*. Translated by C. K. Scott Moncrieff. New York: Random House, [1913–27] 1970.

Proust, M. *Sodom and Gomorrah*, vol. 4. Translated and with an introduction by John Sturrock. London: Penguin, 2002.

Pückler-Muskau, H. F., von. *Andeutungen über Landschaftsgärtnerei*. Stuttgart: Hellberger'sche Verlagshandlung, 1834. English translation by B. Sickert and edited by S. Parsons, *Hints on Landscape Gardening*. Boston: Houghton Mifflin, 1917.

Pückler-Muskau, H. F., von. *Briefe eines Verstorbenen*, Edited by H. Ohff. Berlin: Kupfergraben, 1986. English translation by S. Austin. *Tour in England, Ireland, and France in the Years 1826, 1827, 1828 & 1829: With Remarks on the Manners and Customs of the Inhabitants, and Anecdotes of Distinguished Public Characters; In a series of letters*. London: Effinham Wilson, 1832; Philadelphia: Carey, Lea & Blanchard, 1833.

Quest-Ritson, C. *The English Garden Abroad*. London: Viking, 1992.

Racheli, A. M. "Ville e giardini nei primi piani urbanistici di Roma capitale: i progetti e le trasformazioni." In *La memoria, il tempo, la storia nel giardino italiano fra '800 e '900*, ed. V. Cazzato. Rome: Istituto poligrafico e Zecca dello Stato, 1999.

Rauch, J. H. *Public Parks: Their Effects Upon the Moral Physical and Sanitary Condition of the Inhabitants of Large Cities*. Chicago: Griggs, 1869.

Rees, R. *Interior Landscapes: Gardens and the Domestic Environment*. Baltimore: Johns Hopkins University Press, 1993.

Reps, J. "The Green Belt Concept." *Town and Country Planning* 28, no. 7 (1960): 246–50.

Repton, H. *Designs for the Pavillon at Brighton*. London: J. C. Stadler, 1808.

Repton, H. *An Enquiry into the Changes of Taste in Landscape Gardening*. London: J. Taylor, 1806.

Repton, H. *Fragments on the Theory and Practice of Landscape Gardening*. London: T. Bensley and Son, 1816.

Richards, J. "The Role of the Railways." In *Ruskin and Environment*, ed. M. Wheeler. Manchester: Manchester University Press, 1995.

Ridgway, C. "William Andrews Nesfield: Between Uvedale Price and Isambard Kingdom Brunel." *Journal of Garden History* 13 (1993): 69–89.

Riis, J. A. *How the Other Half Lives*. Mineola, NY: Dover Publications, [1901] 1971.

Ritvo, H. "At the Edge of the Garden: Nature and Domestication in Eighteenth- and Nineteenth-Century Britain." In *An English Arcadia: Landscape and Architecture in Britain and America*, ed. H. Ritvo et al. Papers delivered at a Huntington symposium. San Marino, CA: Huntington Library, 1992.

Rivière, G. "Les Intransigeants et les impressionnistes: Souvenirs du salon libre de 1877." In *L'Artiste* (1877). Reprinted in *The New Painting: Impressionism 1874–1886; Documentation*, 2 vols., ed. R. Berson. San Francisco, CA: Fine Arts Museums of San Francisco, 1996.

Robbins, M. C. "Park-Making as a National Art." *The Atlantic Monthly* 79, no. 471 (January 1897): 86–98.

Roberson, S. A. "Thomas Jefferson and the Eighteenth-Century Landscape Garden Movement in England." Ph.D. diss., Yale University, 1974.

Roberts, J. "English Gardens in India." *Garden History* 26, no. 2 (1998): 115–35.

Robinson, C. M. "A Railroad Beautiful." *House & Garden* 2 (1902): 564–70.

Robinson, W. *Garden Design and Architects' Gardens*. London: John Murray, 1892.

Robinson, W. *Gleanings from French Gardens*. London: F. Warne; New York: Scribner, Welford, 1868.

Robinson, W. *The English Flower Garden and Home Grounds*. London: John Murray, 1900.

Robinson, W. *The Parks, Promenades, and Gardens of Paris*. London: John Murray, 1869.

Robinson, W. *The Subtropical Garden*. London: John Murray, 1871.

Robinson, W. *The Wild Garden*. London: John Murray, 1870.

Rogger, A. *Landscapes of Taste: The Art of Humphry Repton's Red Books*. London: Routledge, 2007.

Roggero Bardelli, C. "Modelli per una capitale europea." In *Torino citta di loisir. Viali, parchi e giardini tra Otto e Novecento*, ed. V. C. Mandracci and R. Roccia. Turin: Archivio storico della città di Torino, 1996.

Roper, L. W. "Frederick Law Olmsted and the Port Royal Experiment." *Journal of Southern History* 31 (1965): 279.

Roscoe, T. *The Tourist in Spain: Granada*. London: Jennings, 1835.

Rosenzweig, R., and E. Blackmar. *The Park and the People: A History of Central Park*. Ithaca, NY: Cornell University Press, 1992.

Rotenberg, R. *Landscape and Power in Vienna*. Baltimore: Johns Hopkins University Press, 1995.

Rothfels, N. *Savages and Beasts: The Birth of the Modern Zoo*. Baltimore: Johns Hopkins University Press, 2002.

Royet, V. *Georges Louis Le Rouge: jardins anglo-chinois, Inventaire du fonds français: graveurs du XVIII siècle*. Paris : Bibliothèque Nationale de France, 2004.

Ruskin, J. *Sesame and Lilies*. New York: Charles E. Merrill, 1891.

Ruskin, J. *Sesame and Lilies*. In *The Works of John Ruskin*, ed. E. T. Cook and A. Wedderburn. London: George Allen; New York: Longmans, Green, [1865] 1905.

Russell, J., et al. *Rothamsted 1843–1943*. Harpenden: Rothamsted, 1943.

Rutherford, S. "Landscapers for the Mind: English Asylum Designers, 1845–1914." *Garden History* 33, no. 1 (2005): 61–86.

Saftenberg, Fr. "Ein Vorschlag." *Die Gartenwelt* 16, no. 5 (1912): 61–63.

Sales, J. "Garden Restoration Past and Present." *Garden History* 23, no. 1 (1995): 1–9.

Sanecki, K. N., and M. Thompson. *Ashridge*. Norwich: Jarrold, 1998.

Schenker, H. "Central Park and the Melodramatic Imagination." *Journal of Urban History* 29, no. 4 (2003): 375–93.

Schenker, H. *Melodramatic Landscapes: Urban Parks in the Nineteenth Century*. Charlottesville: University of Virginia Press, 2009.

Schenker, H. "Women, Gardens and the English Middle Class, 1790–1850." In *Bourgeois and Aristocratic Cultural Encounters in Garden Art, 1550–1850*, ed. M. Conan. Washington, D.C.: Dumbarton Oaks, 2002.

Schinkel, K. F. *Entwurf zu dem kaiserlichen Palast Orianda in der Krimm*. 4th ed. Berlin: Ernst & Korn, 1873.

Schlereth, T. J. "Early North American Arboreta." *Garden History* 35, suppl. 2 (2007): 196–216.

Schneider, U. *Hermann Muthesius und die Reformdiskussion in der Gartenarchitektur des frühen 20. Jahrhunderts*. Worms: Wernersche Verlagsgesellschaft, 2000.

Schnitter, J. *Anguis in herba, Gartenpädagogik und Weltveredlung im Lebenswerk des schwedischen Agitators Olof Eneroth*. Hamburg: disserta Verlag, 2011.

Schubert, D. *Die Gartenstadtidee zwischen reaktionärer Ideologie und pragmatischer Umsetzung:Theodor Fritschs völkische Version der Gartenstadt*. Dortmund: Institut für Raumplanung, Universität Dortmund, Fakultät Raumplanung, 2004.

Schulz, S. "Gartenkunst, Landwirtschaft und Dichtung bei William Shenstone und seine Ferme Ornée 'The Leasowes' im Spiegel seines literarischen Zirkels." Dr. phil. diss., Freie Universität Berlin, 2005.

Schulze, S., ed. *Gärten: Ordnung Inspiration Glück*. Ostfildern: Hatje Cantz, 2006.

Schuyler, D. *Apostle of Taste: Andrew Jackson Downing, 1815–1852*. Baltimore: Johns Hopkins University Press, 1996.

Schuyler, D. "The Mid-Hudson Valley as Iconic Landscape: Tourism, Economic Development, and the Beginnings of a Preservationist Impulse." In *Within the Landscape*, ed. P. Earenfight and N. Siegel. University Park: The Pennsylvania State University Press, 2005.

Schuyler, D. *The New Urban Landscape: The Redefinition of City Form in Nineteenth-Century America*. Baltimore: Johns Hopkins University Press, 1986.

Sckell, F. L., von. *Beiträge zur bildenden Gartenkunst*. 2nd ed. München: Lindauer, 1825.

Scott, F. J. *Victorian Gardens: The Art of Beautifying Suburban Home Grounds*. New York: D. Appleton, American Life Foundation, [1870] 1982.

Scott-James, A. *The Cottage Garden*. London: Allen Lane, 1981.

Scull, A. T. *The Most Solitary of Afflictions: Madness and Society in Britain, 1700–1900*. New Haven, CT: Yale University Press, 1993.

Sedding, J. D. *Garden-Craft Old and New*. London: Kegan Paul, Trench, Trübner, 1891.

Seiler, M. *Das Palmenhaus auf der Pfaueninsel: Geschichte seiner baulichen und gärtnerischen Gestaltung*. Berlin: Haude & Spencer, 1989.

Sharma, J. "British Science, Chinese Skill and Assam Tea: Making Empire's Garden." *The India Economic and Social History Review* 43, no. 4 (2006): 429–55.

Shaw, C. W. *The London Market Gardens*. 2nd ed. London: The Garden, 1880.

Shoemaker, C. A., and P. Miles. "Alpine Garden." In *Chicago Botanic Garden Encyclopedia of Gardening: History and Design*, vol. 1, ed. C. A. Shoemaker. Chicago: Fitzroy Dearborn Publishers, 2001.

Shteir, A. B. *Cultivating Women, Cultivating Science: Flora's Daughters and Botany in England, 1760 to 1860*. Baltimore: Johns Hopkins University Press, 1996.

Sidblad, S. "Swedish Perspectives of Allotment and Community Gardening." *Acta Horticulturae* 523 (2000): 151–60.

Silva, E. *Dell'Arte dei Giardini Inglesi*. Milano: Stamparia e Fonderia al Genio Tipografico; Sala Bolognese: Arnaldo Forni Editore S.p.A, [1801] 1985.

Silva Tarouca, E. E., and C. Schneider, *Unsere Freiland-Stauden*. Wien: Tempsky, 1913.

Sim, J. "Fernery." In *Chicago Botanic Garden Encyclopedia of Gardening: History and Design*, vol. 1, ed. by C. A. Shoemaker. Chicago: Fitzroy Dearborn Publishers, 2001.

Simo, M. L. *Forest & Garden: Traces of Wildness in a Modernizing Land, 1897–1949*. Charlottesville: University of Virginia Press, 2003.

Simo, M. L. *Loudon and the Landscape: From Country Seat to Metropolis*. New Haven, CT: Yale University Press, 1988.

Simo, M. L. *100 Years of Landscape Architecture: Some Patterns of a Century*. Washington, D.C.: ASLA Press, 1999.

Sloane, D. C. *The Last Great Necessity: Cemeteries in American History*. Baltimore: Johns Hopkins University Press, 1991.

Smith, L. D. *Cure, Comfort, and Safe Custody: Public Lunatic Asylums in Early Nineteenth-Century England London*. New York: Leicester University Press, 1999.

Solman, D. *Loddiges of Hackney*. London: Hackney Society, 1995.

Sonne, W. *Representing the State: Capital City Planning in the Early Twentieth Century*. Munich: Prestel, 2003.

Sox, D. *Quaker Plant Hunters*. York: Sessions Book Trust, 2004.

Sperlich, M. "Das neue Arkadien. Der Garten als utopische Landschaft." *Neue Heimat Monatshefte*, 26, no. 6 (1979): 22.

Steele, F. *Design in the Little Garden*. Boston: The Atlantic Monthly Press, 1924.

Steeley, J. W. *Parks for Texas: Enduring Landscapes of the New Deal*. Austin: The University of Texas Press, 1999.

Stiftung Fürst-Pückler-Park Bad Muskau, ed. *Englandsouvenirs. Fürst Pücklers Reise 1826–1829*. Zittau: Graphische Werkstätten, 2005.

Stiftung Preussische Schlösser und Gärten Berlin-Brandenburg, ed. *Preußisch Grün. Hofgärtner in Brandenburg-Preußen*. Berlin: Henschel, 2004.

Stilgoe, J. R. *Borderland: Origins of the American Suburb, 1820–1939*. New Haven, CT: Yale University Press, 1988

Stilgoe, J. R. "The Railroad Beautiful: Landscape Architecture and the Railroad Gardening Movement, 1867–1930." *Landscape Journal* 1, no. 2 (1982): 57–65.

Stovall, T. *The Rise of the Paris Red Belt*. Berkeley: University of California Press, 1990.

Strassburg, G., von. *Tristan*. Translated by A. T. Hatto. Harmondsworth: Penguin Books, 1967.

Strehlow, H. "Zoos and Aquariums of Berlin." In *New Worlds, New Animals: From Menagerie to Zoological Park in the Nineteenth Century*, ed. R. J. Hoage and W. A. Deiss. Baltimore: Johns Hopkins University Press, 1996.

Strohmeyer, U. "Urban Design and Civic Spaces: Nature at the Parc des Buttes-Chaumont in Paris." *Cultural Geographies* 13 (2006): 557–76.

Stroud, D. *Capability Brown*. London: Faber, 1975.

Stuart, D. *The Garden Triumphant: A Victorian Legacy*. London: Viking, 1988.

Sumner, C., and S. Marcus. "The History, Design and Planting of London Squares." In *London Squares: The Proceedings of the London Squares Conference*. London: London Historic Parks and Gardens Trust, 1995.

Sutherill, M. *The Gardens of Audley End*. London: English Heritage, 1995.

Sutton, S. B. *The Arnold Arboretum: The First Century*. Jamaica Plain, MA: Arnold Arboretum, 1971.

Sutton, S. B. *Civilizing American Cities: A Selection from Frederick Law Olmsted's Writings on City Landscapes*. Cambridge, MA: MIT Press, 1971.

Swinburne, H. *Travels through Spain, in the Years 1775 and 1776*. 2nd ed. London: printed by J. Davis for P. Elmsly, in the Strand, 1787.

Szczygiel, B, and R. Hewitt. "Nineteenth-Century Medical Landscapes: John H. Rauch, Frederick Law Olmsted, and the Search for Salubrity." *Bulletin of the History of Medicine* 74 (2000): 708–34.

Tagliolini, A. *I giardini di Roma*. Rome: Newton Compton, 1992.

Tagliolini, A., ed. *Il giardino italiano dell'ottocento: nelle immagini, nelle letteratura, nelle memorie*. Milano: Guerini e Associati, 1990.

Tankard, J. B. "Jekyll, Gertrude 1843–1932: English Horticulturist and Garden Designer." In *Chicago Botanic Garden Encyclopedia of Gardening: History and Design*, vol. 1, ed. C. A. Shoemaker. Chicago: Fitzroy Dearborn Publishers, 2001.

Tankard, J. B. "Munstead Wood: Heath Lane, Busbridge, Surrey, England." In *Chicago Botanic Garden Encyclopedia of Gardening: History and Design*, vol. 1, ed. C. A. Shoemaker. Chicago: Fitzroy Dearborn Publishers, 2001.

Tankard, J. B., and M. A. Wood. *Gertrude Jekyll at Munstead Wood*. Gloucestershire: Sutton; Sagaponack, NY: Sagapress, 1996.

Tausch, H. "Vom Bild der Natur zum imaginären Bilderbogen der Vergangenheit. Hermann von Pückler-Muskaus *Andeutungen über Landschaftsgärtnerei* und die Literarisierung des englischen Landschaftsgartens." *Archiv für das Studium der neueren Sprachen und Literaturen* 233 (1996): 1–19.

Taylor, D. E. "Central Park as a Model for Social Control: Urban Parks, Social Class and Leisure Behavior in Nineteenth-Century America." *Journal of Leisure Research* 31, no. 4 (1999): 420–77.

Taylor, G. *Some Nineteenth-Century Gardeners*. London: Skeffington, 1951.

Taylor, G. *The Victorian Flower Garden*, London: Skeffington, 1952.

Taylor, G. R. "Recreation Developments in Chicago." *Annals of the American Academy of Political and Social Science* 35 (1910): 88–105.

Taylor, H. "Urban Public Parks 1840–1900: Design and Meaning." *Garden History* 23, no. 2 (1995): 201–21.

Thomas, G. S. *The Rock Garden and Its Plants*. London: J. M. Dent, 1989.

Thomas, M. P. "Reception Theory and the Interpretation of Historical Meaning." *History and Theory* 32 (1993): 248–72.

Thompson, F.M.L. *English Landed Society in the Nineteenth Century*. London: Routledge and Kegan Paul, 1963.

Thouin, A. *Cours de culture et de naturalisation des végétaux*, vol. 3. Paris: Huzard, 1827.

Thouin, G. *Plans raisonnés de toutes les espèces de jardins*. Paris: De Lebégue, 1819.

Thümmler, S. *Geschichte der Tapete*. Eurasburg: Edition Minerva, 1998.

Tongiorgi Tomasi, L. *An Oak Spring Flora: Flower Illustration from the Fifteenth Century to the Present Time*. Upperville, VA: Oak Spring Garden Library and Yale University Press, 1997.

Topp, L. "The Modern Mental Hospital in Late Nineteenth-Century Germany and Austria." In *Madness, Architecture and the Built Environment*, ed. L. Topp, J. E. Moran, and J. Andrews. New York: Routledge, 2007.

Trévise, E., Duc de. "Le Pèlerinage de Giverny." *Revue de l'art* 51 (1927): 42–50, 121–34.

Tunnard, C. *Gardens in the Modern Landscape*. London: The Architectural Press, 1938.

Twain, M. *The Complete Short Stories of Mark Twain*, ed. C. Neider. New York: Bantam Books, 1981.

Twain, M. *The Diaries of Adam and Eve*, ed. S. Fisher Fishkin. New York: Oxford University Press, 1996.

Van Rensselaer, Mrs. S. *Art Out-of-Doors*. New York: Scribner's Sons, 1893.

Van Valkenburgh, M. R., and C. D. Van Valkenburgh. "A Contemporary View of Gertrude Jekyll's Herbaceous Border." In *Getrude Jekyll: A Vision of Garden and Wood*, ed. J. B. Tankard and M. R. Van Valkenburgh. New York: H. N. Abrams, 1989.

Veblen, T. *The Theory of the Leisure Class*. New York: Dover, 1899.

Vernon, C. "Wilhelm Miller and *The Prairie Spirit in Landscape Gardening.*" In *Regional Garden Design in the United States*, ed. T. O'Malley and M. Treib. Dumbarton Oaks Colloquium on the History of Landscape Architecture 15. Washington, D.C.: Dumbarton Oaks, 1995.

Villiers-Stuart, C. M. *Gardens of the Great Mughals.* London: A. & C. Black, 1913.

Volkmann, H. *Unterwegs nach Eden. Von Gärtnern und Gärten in der Literatur.* Göttingen: Vandenhoeck & Ruprecht, 2000.

Vorherr, G. "Anmerkung zum Beitrag Nachricht von der königl. Baugewerkschule zu München." *Monatsblatt für die Verbesserung des Landbauwesens und für zweckmäßige Verschönerung des baierischen Landes* 4, no. 8 (1824): 41–49.

Vorherr, G. "Baupolizei." *Monatsblatt für die Verbesserung des Landbauwesens und für zweckmäßige Verschönerung des baierischen Landes* 5, no. 7 (1825): 33–36.

Vorherr, G. "Sparcassen zur Beförderung der Landesverschönerung in Europa." *Monatsblatt für die Verbesserung des Landbauwesens und für zweckmäßige Verschönerung des baierischen Landes* 6, no. 9 (1826): 45–46.

Vorherr, G. "Ueber Entstehung und Zweck der Deputation für Verbesserung des Landbauwesens und für zweckmäßige Verschönerung des baierischen Landes, dann Nachricht über die Herausgabe dieses Blattes." *Monatsblatt für die Verbesserung des Landbauwesens und für zweckmäßige Verschönerung des baierischen Landes* 1, no. 1 (1821): 1–3.

Wagner, M. *Das sanitäre Grün der Städte. Ein Beitrag zur Freiflächentheorie.* Berlin: C. Heymann, 1915.

Wallach, A. "Some Further Thoughts on the Panoramic Mode." In *Within the Landscape*, ed. P. Earenfight and N. Siegel. University Park: The Pennsylvania State University Press, 2005.

Wallach, A. "Thomas Cole: Landscape and Course of American Empire." In *Thomas Cole: Landscape into History*, ed. W. H. Truttner and A. Wallach. New Haven, CT: Yale University Press; Washington, D.C.: National Museum of American Art, Smithsonian Institution, 1994.

Walpole, H. *The History of the Modern Taste in Gardening.* New York: Ursus Press, [1780] 1995.

Walton, J. K. "The National Trust: Preservation or Provision?" In *Ruskin and Environment*, ed. M. Wheeler. Manchester: Manchester University Press, 1995.

Ward, J. W. *G. Ferrand: "The Working Man's Friend" 1809–1889.* East Linton: Tuckwell Press, 2002.

Ward, S. V. "Ebenezer Howard: His Life and Times." In *From Garden City to Green City*, ed. D. Schuyler. Baltimore: Johns Hopkins University Press, 2002.

Warnecke, P. *Laube Liebe Hoffnung. Kleingartengeschichte.* Berlin: Verlag W. Wächter GmbH, 2001.

Watkin, D. "The Architectural Context of The Grand Tour: The British as Honorary Italians." In *The Impact of Italy: The Grand Tour and Beyond*, ed. C. Hornsby. London: The British School at Rome, 2000.

Waugh, F. A. "German Landscape Gardening." *The Country Gentleman*, August 25, 1910, 790.

Waugh, F. A. "A Horticultural School." *The Country Gentleman*, June 23, 1910, 604.

Waugh, F. A. *Rural Improvement: The Principles of Civic Art Applied to Rural Conditions, including Village Improvement and the Betterment of the Open Country.* New York: Orange Judd, 1914.

Webber, R. *Covent Garden: Mud-Salad Market.* London: J. M. Dent, 1969.

Webber, R. *Market Gardening.* Newton Abbot: David & Charles, 1972.

Webster, A. D. *London Trees.* London: Swarthmore Press, 1920.

Weidenmann, J. *Beautifying Country Homes.* New York: Orange Judd, [1870] 1978.

Wells, H. G. *The Door in the Wall, and Other Stories.* New York: Mitchell Kennerley, 1911.

Wescoat, J. L., Jr. "Mughal Gardens: The Re-emergence of Comparative Possibilities and the Wavering of Practical Concern." In *Perspectives on Garden Histories,* ed. M. Conan. Washington, D.C.: Dumbarton Oaks Research Library and Collection, 1999.

Wescoat, J. L., Jr., and J. Wolschke-Bulmahn. "Sources, Places, Representations, and Prospects: A Perspective of Mughal Gardens." In *Mughal Gardens: Sources, Places, Representations, and Prospects,* ed. J. L. Wescoat Jr. and J. Wolschke-Bulmahn. Washington, D.C.: Dumbarton Oaks, 1996.

Wharton, E. *Italian Villas and Their Gardens.* New York: Century, 1904.

Whitehead, G. *Civilizing the City: A History of Melbourne's Public Gardens.* Melbourne: State Library of Victoria and the City of Melbourne, 1997.

Wilkinson, A. *The Victorian Gardener: The Growth of Gardening and the Floral World.* Stroud, Gloucestershire: Sutton Publishing, 2006.

Williams, R. *The Country and the City.* New York: Oxford University Press, 1973.

Williams, R. "Edwardian Gardens, Old and New." *Journal of Garden History* 13, nos. 1 and 2 (1993): 90–103.

Willsdon, C.A.P. *In the Gardens of Impressionism.* London: Thames and Hudson, 2004.

Willson, E. J. *West London Nursery Gardens.* Fulham & Hammersmith Historical Society, 1982.

Wimmer, C. A. *Bäume und Sträucher in historischen Gärten: Gehölzverwendung in Geschichte und Denkmalpflege.* Dresden: Verlag der Kunst Dresden, 2001.

Wimmer, C. A. "Bed and Bedding System." In *Chicago Botanic Garden Encyclopedia of Gardening: History and Design,* vol. 1, ed. C. A. Shoemaker. Chicago: Fitzroy Dearborn Publishers, 2001.

Wimmer, C. A. "Der vergessene Gartenkünstler George Isham Parkyns." *Zandera* 22, no. 1 (2007): 27–36.

Wimmer, C. A. *Die Preußischen Hofgärtner,* ed. Stiftung Preussische Schlösser und Gärten Berlin-Brandenburg. Berlin: Druckhaus Hentrich, 1996.

Wimmer, C. A. "Victoria, the Empress Gardener, or the Anglo-Prussian Garden War, 1858–88." *Garden History* 26, no. 2 (1997): 192–207.

Wirth, C. L. *Parks, Politics, and the People.* Norman: The University of Oklahoma Press, 1980.

Wittmer, P. *Caillebotte au jardin: la période d'Yerres (1860–1879).* Saint-Rémy-en-l' Eau: Hayot, 1990.

Wolschke-Bulmahn, J. "The 'Wild Garden' and the 'Nature Garden': Aspects of the Garden Ideology of William Robinson and Willy Lange." *Journal of Garden History* 12, no. 3 (1992): 183–206.

Wolschke-Bulmahn, J. "Zwischen Hudson-River und Neiße. Fürst Pückler, die Muskauer Wasserfälle und das Hudson-River-Portfolio." *Die Gartenkunst* 10, no. 2 (1998): 300–309.

Wolschke-Bulmahn, J., and G. Gröning. "Lange, Willy 1864–1941: German Garden Writer, Garden Theorist, and Landscape Architect." In *Chicago Botanic Garden Encyclopedia of Gardening: History and Design*, vol. 1, ed. C. A. Shoemaker. Chicago: Fitzroy Dearborn Publishers, 2001.

Wolschke-Bulmahn, J., and G. Gröning. "The National Socialist Garden and Landscape Ideal: *Bodenständigkeit* (Rootedness in the Soil)." In *Art, Culture, and Media under the Third Reich*, ed. R. Etlin. Chicago: The University of Chicago Press, 2002.

Woodbridge, K. *Princely Gardens*. London: Thames and Hudson, 1986.

Wordsworth, D. *The Grasmere and Alfoxden Journals*. Oxford: Oxford University Press, 2002.

Woudstra, J. "The Changing Nature of Ecology: A History of Ecological Planting (1800–1980)." In *The Dynamic Landscape: Design, Ecology and Management of Naturalistic Urban Planting*, ed. N. Dunnett and J. Hitchmough. London: Spon, 2004.

Woudstra, J. "The Sckell Family in England (1770–1830)." *Die Gartenkunst* 14, no. 2 (2002): 211–20.

Wright, J. "Heckfield Place." *Journal of Horticulture* 5 (1882): 430–32.

Wroth, W. *The London Pleasure Gardens of the Eighteenth Century*. London: Macmillan, 1896.

Yanni, C. *The Architecture of Madness: Insane Asylums in the United States*. Minneapolis: University of Minnesota Press, 2007.

Young, T. *Building San Francisco's Parks, 1850–1930*. Baltimore: Johns Hopkins University Press, 2004.

Zaitzevski, C. "André Parmentier: A Bridge between Europe and America." In *The Landscape Universe: Historic Designed Landscapes in Context*, ed. C. Birnbaum. Papers from a national symposium, Armor Hall at Wave Hill, New York, 1993.

Zaitzevsky, C. *Frederick Law Olmsted and the Boston Park System*. Cambridge, MA: Harvard University Press, 1982.

Zijlistra, B. *Nederlandse tuinarchitectuur 1850–1940*. Zutphen: Walburg Pers., 1991.

Zola, É. *La Faute de l'Abbé Mouret*. Paris: Charpentier et Cie. English translation by E. A. Vizetelly, *Abbé Mouret's Transgression*. London: Mondial, [1875] 2005.

CONTRIBUTORS

Sonja Dümpelmann is associate professor of landscape architecture at the Harvard Graduate School of Design. Her published work includes essays on landscape architecture in fascist Italy, the transatlantic transfer of design ideas, public urban park planning, and pioneering female landscape architects. She is the author of a book on the twentieth-century Italian landscape architect Maria Teresa Parpagliolo Shephard (VDG, 2004).

Brent Elliott was formerly the librarian and archivist, and is now the historian, of the Royal Horticultural Society. He is the author of *Victorian Gardens* (B. T. Batsford, 1986), *The Royal Horticultural Society: A History 1804–2004* (Phillimore, 2004), and other works. He was formerly editor of *Garden History* (1984–88), and is now editor of *Occasional Papers from the RHS Lindley Library*.

Gert Gröning is professor emeritus of garden culture and open-space development at the Institute for History and Theory of Design, Berlin University of the Arts. He chairs the Commission for Landscape and Urban Horticulture of the International Society for Horticultural Science, and is a senior fellow for Garden and Landscape Studies at Dumbarton Oaks in Washington, DC. His list of publications is available at http://www.udk-berlin.de/sites/igtg.

Mark Laird is adjunct professor in the history of landscape architecture at the Graduate School of Design, Harvard University. He teaches early modern landscape history and offers a seminar on "Plants and Animals in Landscape Design,

Antiquity to Present". Supported by a Senior Fellowship from the Paul Mellon Centre in London, he has recently completed the manuscript of *A Natural History of English Gardening: 1650–1800*. His publications include *The Flowering of the Landscape Garden* (University of Pennsylvania Press, 1999) and *Mrs. Delany and her Circle* (Yale Center for British Art, 2009).

Iris Lauterbach is an art historian and research fellow at the Zentralinstitut für Kunstgeschichte, Munich, and a professor of garden history at the Munich Technical University. Her publications include subjects ranging from European garden history of the early modern period to the cultural policy of the postwar period.

Heath Massey (Schenker) is professor of landscape architecture at the University of California, Davis. She is the editor of *Picturing California's Other Landscape: The Great Central Valley* (Heyday Books, 1999) and author of *Melodramatic Landscapes: Urban Parks in the Nineteenth Century* (University of Virginia Press, 2009).

Daniel Nadenicek is dean of the College of Environment and Design and also holds the Draper Chair in Landscape Architecture at the University of Georgia. He is widely published on the general topic of landscape history. He serves on the editorial boards of *Landscape Journal* and the University of Georgia Press, and is on the board of directors of the Library of American Landscape History.

Linda Parshall, professor emerita of German, specializes in eighteenth- and nineteenth-century German literature and garden history. Her publications include: C.C.L. Hirschfeld, Theory of Garden Art, trans. & introduction (University of Pennsylvania Press, 2001); her translation of Prince Pückler-Muskau's Letters of a Dead Man is scheduled to appear in 2015.

Joachim Wolschke-Bulmahn is professor of the history of open-space planning and landscape architecture at the Institute of Landscape Architecture of Leibniz University, Hannover (since 1996). He was Director of Studies in Landscape Architecture at Dumbarton Oaks, Harvard University, from 1991 until 1996, and is a founding member of the Center of Garden Art and Landscape Architecture at Leibniz University Hannover, and has been its executive director since 2003.

INDEX